A TREATISE ON MIND

VOLUME 6

Meditation

and the Initiation Process

Other Titles in the Series

The I Concept

Volume 1: The 'Self' or 'Non-Self' in Buddhism

Volume 2: Considerations of Mind - A Buddhist Enquiry

Volume 3: The Buddha-Womb and the Way to Liberation

Cellular Consciousness

Volume 4: Maṇḍalas - Their Nature and Development

Volume 5: An Esoteric Exposition of the Bardo Thödol (Part A)

Volume 5: An Esoteric Exposition of the Bardo Thödol (Part B)

The Way to Shambhala

Volume 7: The Constitution of Shambhala

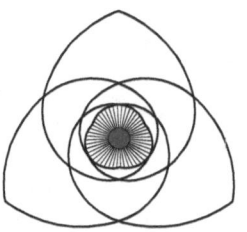

VOLUME SIX

Meditation

and the Initiation Process

BODO BALSYS

UNIVERSAL DHARMA
PUBLICATIONS
SYDNEY, AUSTRALIA

ISBN 978-0-9923568-5-9

First Published 2014
Fourth Edition 2025

Āḥ!

Homage to the Lord of Shambhala.
Inconceivable, inconceivable, beyond thought
Is the bejewelled crown of this most excelled Jina.
He whose Eye has taught many Buddhas.
And who will anoint the myriad,
that in the future lives will come.
As I bow to His Feet my Heart's afire.
Oh, this Bliss, this Love for my Lord
can barely be borne on my part.
It takes flight as the might of the Dove.
The flight of serene *nirvāṇic* embrace.
The flight of Light so bright.
The flight of Love so active tonight.
The flight of enlightenment for all to come to
their mind's Heart's attire.

Obeisance to the Gurus!
To the Buddhas of the three times.
To the Council of Bodhisattvas, *mahāsattvas*.
To them I pledge allegiance.

Oṁ Hūṁ! Hūṁ! Hūṁ!

Dedication

Thanks to my students, past, present and future, and in particular to those that have helped in the production of this Treatise.

Oṁ

Acknowledgments

Special thanks to Angie O'Sullivan, Anne Kocek,
Kylie Smith, Eliane Clarke
and Ruth Fitzpatrick
for their efforts in making this
series possible.

Oṁ

Contents

Preface xi

1. General Considerations 1
   Introduction 1
   The search for truth via mind 5
   Seven attributes of consciousness 10
   Levels of meditative attainment 13
   The ***chakras*** 15
   Psychic powers 23
   The esotericism in the Bible 28
   The wisdom tradition, astralism and magic 37
   Psychic powers versus the Heart centre's wisdom 43

2. Healing, the Elect and Group Evolution 52
   Healing oneself 52
   The role of ***devas*** in healing 59
   The main points to consider in meditative healing 61
   Meditation and the Sambhogakāya Flower 66
   The elect and the shortening of days 74
   The Rays and an introduction to group evolution 89
   The battle with evil 96
   The Great Invocation 103

3. The Practice of Meditation 104
   Meditation and lifestyle changes 104
   Breathing exercises, mantras and ***kuṇḍalinī*** 109
   The awakening of ***chakras*** 115
   Preliminary considerations for meditation 118
   Suggested meditation technique 125
   The power to visualise 129
   A note on silence 132
   Quotations 135

4. Meditation Teachers 142
   The Bodhisattva path 142
   The three ***lokas*** 144
   Meditation instructors—Part A General concepts & Rinpoches 150
   Meditation instructors—Part B Guruparamparā 156
   Meditation instructors—Part C The concept of a Tulku 168
   Meditation instructors—Part D The Hindu guru 181

5. The first two Initiations 187
Introductory statements 187
The Biblical account 189
The Initiations defined 194
The first Initiation 197
The way of compassion 201
The first Initiation continued 206
The second Initiation 213
General considerations of Initiation 223

6. The Third, Fourth and Fifth Initiations 233
The third Initiation 233
Jesus' temptations in the desert 242
The fourth Initiation: the Crucifixion/Renunciation 257
The Divine Will 262
The cross of Life 267
The fifth Initiation: the Ascension/Revelation 275
The way of the Initiate 288
The rising of Lazarus 293
Those whom Jesus loved 296
The advent of the new epoch 301

7. The Beatitudes: The way of evolution of Prime Causative Agents 307
Definition of Causative Agents 307
The Beatitudes 314

8. The Laws of Group Evolution 337
The zodiac and the laws of group evolution 337
1. The law of Sacrifice 341
2. The law of Magnetic Impulse 345
3. The law of Service 350
4. The law of Repulse 352
5. The law of Group Progress 356
6. The law of Expansive Response 361
7. The law of the Lower Four 364
The laws of the cosmic mental plane 367
The major cosmic laws and the appearance of phenomena 373
The major cosmic laws 378
Conclusion 395

Bibliography 398

Index 401

Figures

Figure 1. The seven major *chakras* 17
Figure 2. The space-time continuum 85
Figure 3. The three Outpourings 280
Figure 4. The group laws 339
Figure 5. The cosmic mental plane laws 397

Tabulations

Table 1. The five Initiations 190
Table 2. The five *vayūs* 324

Preface

This treatise investigates Buddhist ideas concerning what mind is and how it relates to a concept of a 'self'. It is principally a study of the complex interrelationship between mind and phenomena, from the gross to the subtle—the physical, psychic, supersensory and supernal. This entails an explanation of how mind incorporates all phenomena in its *modus operandi,* and how eventually that mind is liberated from it, thereby becoming awakened. Thus the treatise explores the manner in which the corporeally orientated, concretised, intellectual mind eventually becomes transformed into the Clear Light of the abstracted Mind; a super-mind, a Buddha-Mind.

A Treatise on Mind is arranged in seven volumes, divided into three subsections. These are as follows:

The I Concept
Volume 1. *The 'Self' or 'Non-self' in Buddhism.*
Volume 2. *Considerations of Mind–A Buddhist Enquiry.*
Volume 3. *The Buddha-Womb and the Way to Liberation.*

Cellular Consciousness
Volume 4. *Maṇḍalas - Their Nature and Development.*
Volume 5. *An Esoteric Exposition of the Bardo Thödol.*
(This volume is published in two parts)

The Way to Shambhala
Volume 6. *Meditation and the Initiation Process.*
Volume 7. *The Constitution of Shambhala. (In two parts)*

The I Concept represents a necessary extensive revision[1] of a large work formerly published in one volume. Together the three volumes investigate the question of what a 'self' is and is not. This involves an analysis of the nature of consciousness, and the consciousness-stream of a human unit developing as a continuum through time. It will illustrate exactly what directs such a stream and how its *karma* is arranged so that enlightenment is the eventual outcome.

Volume 1 analyses Prāsaṅgika lines of reasoning, such as the 'Refutation of Partless Particles', and 'The Sevenfold Reasoning' in order to derive a clear deduction as to whether a 'self' exists, and if so what its limitations are, and if not, then what the alternative may be. The analysis resolves the historically vexing question of how—if there is no 'self'—can there be a continuity of mind that is coherently connected in an evolutionary manner through multiple rebirths.[2] In order to arrive at this explanation, many of the basic assumptions of Mahāyāna Buddhism, such as Dependent Origination and the Two Truths, are critically analysed.

Volume 2 provides an in-depth analysis of what mind is, how it relates to the concept of the Void *(śūnyatā),* and the evolution of consciousness. The analysis utilises Yogācāra-Vijñānavādin philosophy in order to comprehend the major attributes of mind, the *saṃskāras* that condition it, and the laws by means of which it operates.

The enquiry into the nature of what an 'I' is requires comprehension of the properties of the dual nature of mind, which consists of an empirical and abstract, enlightened part. As a means of doing this, the *ālayavijñāna* (the store of consciousness-attributes) is explored, alongside the entire philosophy of the 'eight consciousnesses' of this School.

Volume 3 focuses on the I-Consciousness and the subtle body, by first utilising a minor Tantra, *The Great Gates of Diamond Liberation,* to investigate the nature of the Heart centre and its functions, then the

---

1 The book was inadequately edited hence contains many errors and grammatical mistakes that have been corrected in this treatise.

2 My earlier work *Karma and the Rebirth of Consciousness* (Munshiram Manoharlal, Delhi, 2006) lays the background for this basic question.

chakras below the diaphragm. This is necessary to lay the foundation for the topics that will be the subject of the later volumes of this treatise concerning the nature of meditation, the construction of *maṇḍalas,* and the yoga of the *Bardo Thödol.*

The focus then shifts to investigate where the idea of a self-sustaining I-concept or 'Soul-form' may be found in Buddhist philosophy, given the denial of substantial self-existence prioritised in the philosophy of Emptiness. Following this, the pertinent chapters of the *Ratnagotravibhāga Śastra* are examined in detail so that a proper conclusion to the investigation can be obtained via the *buddhadharma.* This concerns an analysis of how the *ālayavijñāna* is organised, such that the rebirth process is possible for each human consciousness-stream, taking into account the *karma* that will eventually make each human unit a Buddha. In relation to this the ontological nature of the *tathāgatagarbha* (the Buddha-Womb) must be carefully analysed, as well as the organising principle of consciousness represented by the *chakras.* I thus establish that there is a form that appears upon the domain of the abstract Mind. I call this the Sambhogakāya Flower. The final two chapters of this volume principally define its characteristics.

The second subsection, *Cellular Consciousness,* is divided into two parts. Volume 4 deals with the question of what exactly constitutes a 'cell', metaphysically. The cell is viewed as a unit of consciousness that interrelates with other cells to form *maṇḍalas* of expression. Each such cell can be considered a form of 'self' that has a limited, though valid, body of expression. It is born, sustains a form of activity, and consequently dies when it outlives its usefulness. This mode of analysis is extended to include the myriad forms manifest in the world of phenomena known as *saṃsāra,* including the existence and functioning of *chakras.*

Volume 5 deals with the formative forces and evolutionary processes governing the prime cells (that is, *maṇḍalas* of expression), and the phenomenon that governs an entire world-sphere of evolutionary attainment. This is explored via an in-depth exposition of the *Bardo Thödol* and its 42 Peaceful and 58 Wrathful Deities. The text also incorporates a detailed exposition concerning the transformation of *saṃskāras* (consciousness-attributes developed through all past forms of activity) into enlightenment. The entire path of liberation enacted by a *yogin* via the principles of meditation, forms of concentration, and related techniques *(tapas, dhāraṇīs)* is explained. In doing so, the soteriological purpose of the various wrathful and theriomorphic deities is revealed. This volume is published in two parts. Part A explores chapter 5 of the Bardo Thödol concerning the transformation of *saṃskāras* via meditating upon the Peaceful and Wrathful Deities. This necessitates sound knowledge of the force centres (*chakras*) and the way their powers (*siddhis*) awaken. Part B deals with the gain of such transformations and the consequence of conversion of the attributes of the empirical mind into the liberated abstract Mind.

The third subsection, *The Way to Shambhala*, is also in two parts. They present an eclectic revelation of esoteric information integrating the main Eastern and Western religions. Volume 6 is a treatise on meditation and the Initiation process.[3] The meditation practice is directed towards the needs of individuals living within the context of our modern societies.

Volume 6 also includes a discussion of the path of Initiation as the means of gaining liberation from *saṃsāra*. The teaching in Volume 5 concerning the conversion of *saṃskāras* is supplementary to this path. The path of Initiation *is* the way to Shambhala. As many will choose to consciously undergo the precepts needed to undertake Initiation in the future, this invokes the necessity of providing much more revelatory information concerning this Kingdom than has been provided hitherto.

How Shambhala is organised is the subject of volume seven, which details the constitution of the Hierarchy of enlightened being[4] (the Council of Bodhisattvas). It illustrates how the presiding Lords who govern planetary evolution manifest. This detailed philosophy rests on the foundation of the information provided in all of the previous volumes, and necessitates a proper comprehension of the nature of the five Dhyāni Buddhas. To do so the awakening of the meditation-Mind, which is the objective of *A Treatise on Mind*, is essential.

---

3 The word Initiation is capitalised throughout the series of books to add emphasis to the fact that it is the process that makes one divine, liberated. It is the expression of divinity manifesting upon the planetary and cosmic landscape.

4 The word 'being' here is not pluralised because though this Hierarchy is constituted of a multiplicity of beings, together they represent one 'Being', one integral awakened Entity.

How to engage with this text

In this investigation many new ways of viewing conventional Buddhist arguments and rhetoric shall be pursued to develop the pure logic of the reader's mind, and to awaken revelations from their abstract Mind. New insights into the far-reaching light of the *dharma* will be revealed, which will form a basis for the illustration of an esoteric view that supersedes the bounds of conventionally accepted views. Readers should therefore analyse all arguments for themselves to discern the validity of what is presented. Such enquiry allows one to ascertain for oneself, what is logical and truthful, thus overcoming the blind acceptance of a certain dogma or line of reasoning that is otherwise universally accepted as correct. Only that which is discovered within each inquiring mind should be accepted. The remainder should, however, not be automatically discarded, but rather kept aside for later analysis when more data is available—unless the logic is obviously flawed, in which case it should be abandoned. There is no claim to infallibility in the information and arguments presented in this treatise, however, they are designed to offer scope for further meditation and enquiry by the earnest reader. If errors are found through impeccable logic, then the dialectical process may proceed. We can then accept or reject the new thesis and move forward, such that the evolution of human thought progresses, until we all stand enlightened.

This treatise hopes to assist that dialectical evolution by analysing major aspects of the *buddhadharma* as it exists and is taught today, to try to examine where errors may lie, or where the present modes of interpretation fall short of the true intended meaning. The aim is also to elaborate aspects of the *dharma* that could only be hinted at or cursorily explained by the wise ones of the past, because the basis for proper elaboration had not then been established. This analysis of *buddhadharma* will try to rectify some of the past inadequacies in order to explore and extend the *dharma* into arenas rarely investigated.

There will always be obstinate and dogmatic ones that staunchly cling to established views. This produces a reactive malaise in current Buddhist ontological and metaphysical thought. However, amongst the many practitioners of the *dharma* there are also those who have clarified their minds sufficiently to verify truth in whatever form it is presented, and will follow it at all costs to enlightenment. The Council of Bodhisattvas heartily seek such worthy ones. The signposts or guides upon the way to enlightenment have changed through the centuries, and contemporary practitioners of the *dharma* have yet to learn to clearly interpret the new directions. The guide books are now being written and many must come forth to understand and practice correctly.

If full comprehension of such guide books is achieved, those *dharma* practitioners yearning to become Bodhisattvas would rapidly become spiritually enlightened. Here is a rhyme and reason *for* Buddhism. The actual present dearth of enlightened beings informs us that little that is read is properly understood. The esoteric view presented in this treatise hopes to rectify this problem, so as to create better thinkers along the Bodhisattva way.

The numbers of Buddhists are growing in the world, thus Buddhism needs a true restorative flowering to rival that of the renaissance of debate and innovative thinkers of the early post-Nāgārjunian era. In order to achieve this it must synthesise the present wealth of scientific knowledge, alongside the best of the Western world's philosophical output.

Currently the *buddhadharma* is presented as an external body of knowledge held by the Buddha, Rinpoches, monks and lay teachers. This encourages practitioners to hero worship these figures and to heed many unenlightened utterances from such teachers, based on a belief system that encourages people to *uncritically* listen to them and adopt their views. When enlightened teachers *do appear* and find consolidated reasons for firing spiritual bullets for the cause of the enlightenment of humanity, then all truth can and will be known. The present lack of inwardly perceived knowledge from the fount of the *dharmakāya* on the part of many teachers blocks the production of an arsenal of weapons for solving the problems of suffering in the world. Few see little beyond the scope of vision in what they have been indoctrinated to believe, allowing for only rudimentary truths to be understood. While for the great majority this suffices, it is woefully inadequate for those genuinely seeking Bodhisattvahood and enlightenment. The cost to humanity in not being given an enlightened answer as to the nature of awakening, is profound.

We must go to the awakening of the Head lotus to find the most established reasoning powers. Without the 1,000 petals of the *sahasrāra padma* ablaze then there is little substance for proper understanding, little ability to hold the mind steady in the dynamic field of revelation that the *dharmakāya* represents. How can the unenlightened properly understand Buddhist scriptures, when there is little (revelation) coming from the Head centres of such beings? Much still needs to be taught concerning the way of awakening this lotus, and to help fill the lack is a major purpose of *A Treatise on Mind.*

Those who intend to reach enlightenment must go beyond the narrow sectarian allegiances promoted by many strands of contemporary Buddhism. Buddhism itself unfolded in a dialectical context with other heterodox Indian (and Chinese, etc.) traditions, and prospered on account of those engagements. When one sees the unfolding of enlightened wisdom in such a fashion, the particular information from specific schools of thought may be synthesised into a greater whole. Each school has various qualities and types of argument to resolve weaknesses in the opposing stream of thought. This highlights that there are particular aspects in each that may be right or wrong, or neither wholly right or wrong. Through this process we can find better answers, or if need be, create a new lineage or religion which is expressive of a synthesis of the various schools of thought.

The Buddha did not categorically reject the orthodox Indian religio-philosophical ideas of his time, nor did he simply accept them—he reformed them. He preserved the elements that he found to be true, and rejected those 'wrong views' which lead to moral and spiritual impairment. If the existing system needs reformation it becomes part of a Bodhisattva's meditation. The way a reforming Buddha incarnates is dependent on how he must fit into such a system. Thus he is essentially an outsider incarnating into it to demonstrate the new type of ideas he chooses to elaborate. If there is a lot of dogmatic resistance to the presented doctrine of truth, then a new religion is founded. If there is some acceptance then we see reformation. There is always room for improvement, to march forward closer to enlightenment's goal, be it for an individual or for a wisdom-religion as a whole. There is a need for reform throughout the religious world today.

By way of a hermeneutical strategy fit for this task, we ought look no further than the Buddha himself. The Buddha proposed that all students of the *dharma* should make their investigations through the *Four Points of Refuge*. These are:

1. The doctrine is one's point of refuge, not a person.
2. The meaning is one's point of refuge, not the letter.
3. The sacred texts whose meaning is defined are one's point of refuge, to those whose meaning needs definition.
4. Direct awareness is one's point of refuge, not discursive awareness.[5]

These four points can be summarised or rephrased as: the doctrine (*dharma*), true or esoteric meaning, right definition, and direct awareness are one's point of refuge, not adherence to sectarian bias, semantics, the dialectics of non-fully enlightened commentaries, or to illogical assertions. What may be long held to be truthful, but is not, upon proper analytical dissection, needs rectifying. Also, in other cases, a doctrine or teaching may indeed be correct, but the current interpretation leaves much to be desired, and hence should be reinterpreted from the position of a more embracive or esoteric view.

Hopefully this presentation finds welcoming minds that will carefully analyse it in line with their own understandings of the issues, and as a consequence build up a better understanding of the nature of what constitutes the path to enlightenment. Their way of walking as Bodhisattvas should be enriched as a consequence.

For a guide to understanding the pronunciation of Sanskrit words, please visit our website.
http://universaldharma.com/resources/pronounce-sanskrit/

Our online esoteric glossary also provides definitions for most of the terms used in this treatise.
http://universaldharma.com/resources/esoteric-glossary/

---

5 Griffith, P.J., *On Being Buddha, The Classical Doctrine of Buddhahood*, (Sri Satguru Publications, New Delhi, 1995), 52.

My eyes do weep as I stare into this troubled world,
For I dare not place my Heart in my brother's keep.
He would grapple that Heart with hands so rough
So as to destroy the fabric of its delicate stuff.
Oh to give, to give, my Heart does yearn,
But humanity must its embracive,
Humbling, pervasive scene yet to learn.
To destroy and tear with avarice they know,
But little care to sensitive rapture they show.
How to give its Blood is my constant fare,
For that Love to bestow upon their Hearts I bemoan.
But they hide their Hearts behind mental-emotional walls.
No matter how one prods these walls won't fall,
So much belittling emotional self-concern prop their bastions.
Oh, how my eyes do weep as I stare.
I stare at their fearsome malls and halls.
That lock Love out from all their abodes
And do keep them trapped in realms of woe.

Oṁ Maṇi Padme Hūṁ

1

General Considerations

Introduction

The practice of meditation is increasing in popularity, and it has become commonplace for people to consider it as a practical means of relaxation and to enhance productivity in their chosen fields of work. This allows beginners to find some guidance concerning this art from teachers in their neighbourhood. Though meditation practice is a way of life for many upon this planet, very few actually realise the true import of this most sacred art. Many seek emotional solace, or to calm their minds so that they are better equipped to handle the vicissitudes of everyday life and its various stressful situations. However, it is fair to say that the majority seek what they consider to be enlightenment or liberation. All meditation practices are useful, but such usefulness depends upon the motive, spiritual age, and strength of enquiry of the seeker. Seekers will find that to which they are karmically attracted. They will apply themselves according to the extent of their own sense of goal-fittedness. Beginners there are aplenty, but others require more ambitious motives to be satisfied, related to gaining enlightenment. They will seek out advanced teachers, but here problems arise as to who is best equipped to teach them. While certain yoga-meditation lineages have maintained their unique methods for centuries, other forms of meditation teachings, drawn from various religious traditions, have produced many new visualisation techniques and practices.

This present book caters to seasoned veterans of the art that have reincarnated in a new cultural situation, and who must find the appearing *maṇḍala* of Initiates to which they esoterically belong. They need the most efficacious teachings that waste not a lot of their time in mentalistic meanderings or erroneous doctrines. The blind *cul-de-sacs* of yogic and Tantric practices are legion, and some Tantras are outright dangerous.

With the foundation of Buddhist esotericism built in the previous books of this series, this book incorporates an exegesis stemming from the sister religion to Buddhism—Christianity. Quotes from the Bible shall be specifically used to illustrate the nature of the path of Initiation, followed by an explanation of the group laws. Such integration should act as a beacon for those wishing to delve deep into comprehending the mysteries of Life. The Eastern and Western modes of travelling to enlightenment must be incorporated into one grand vehicle of liberation. The higher wisdom can then be gained to enrich one's meditative experiences. All that read this text will have incarnated many times into both religions for good reason, and the time has come to reveal the hidden Mysteries of both Schools of thought.

My books aim to show that more exists in the content of an enlightened Mind than what is generally understood as the Void *(śūnyatā),* the Clear Mind, *mokṣa*[1]. Such terms have been used to indicate a sense of finality of the meditation process, but the fact is that they only veil the nature of an enlightened Mind. The terms actually signify the beginning of a meditative path that will lead one inevitably far from being 'human', and this earth zone of residence. Much more must be achieved to travel the vast reaches of *dharmakāya,* which I often abbreviate to 'cosmos', referring to the sum of multidimensional Space. The term *dharmakāya* refers to the vehicle *(kāya)* of the *dharma,* which by extension is the *buddhadharma*, and is inclusive of the moral law governing the expression of the past, present and future of that Space. An objective of meditation then, is to awaken to the Mysteries of *dharmakāya.*

A great *yogin* therefore does not spend decades in a cave or monastery achieving the ultimate goal of 'no mind', where nothing at all is contained in the mind. Instead, great wisdom is attained and

---

1 *Mokṣa* (Tib. tharpa): liberation, release, enlightenment, literally the state of awareness at the 'other shore' of manifest being.

expressed in terms of the foundation of all truth, the Love-Wisdom (*Bodhicitta*, the compassionate force of the liberating mind).

Certainly if the concept of the Bodhisattva (one who has vowed to never cease striving for the liberation of all sentient beings) has any meaning, then the quest for enlightenment is woven around the content of such a one's Mind. If one is a meditator and a Bodhisattva (or aspiring to become one), then we have more to explain than just *śūnyatā*. One must look to the organisation of the Council of Bodhisattvas, the Hierarchy of Light and Love, the mysteries of which the Bodhisattva is Initiated into. This happens by way of the meditation-Mind, and constitutes much of what Bodhisattvas (which are inclusive of all great *mahasiddhas, yogins,* and saints of the various religions) receive in meditation. The mysteries of the Initiation process and the way of group evolution are intricately linked with the subject of gaining enlightenment through meditation and are explicated in the later chapters of this book. Such information is also inclusive of the sum of what is received from the domain of the Kingdom of Shambhala, to which the Bodhisattva of the higher degrees has access. The revelation of such content constitutes the information presented in the final volume of this series, for which this teaching concerning the way of meditation lays the foundation. Such information has always been veiled, being part of the context of the 'ear whispered truths' given to the student in meditation by his/her religious preceptor.

Now, however, in this modern epoch much of what was formerly hidden can and must also be revealed. So be it. Let the earnest student of meditation no longer flounder in darkness because of teachers who have never been initiated into the mysteries of the Bodhisattva path and its consequent revelations. Let the student now learn what constitutes the path to liberation and firmly acknowledge their true placing upon this path, of where they esoterically fit in the scheme of things. (Their affiliation within the Ashrams of the Hierarchy of Light.) They can also begin to ascertain the nature of their true inner teacher on the way to enlightenment.

The way of meditation is the key, as it reveals everything that was achieved in past lives and shines a beacon of light into the future. The way of meditation reveals the hidden domains of Light. In that Light stand the sum total of the membership of the Council of Bodhisattvas. They work as a completely integrated, enlightened unity for the benefit of all who herald their ways and aspire to gain enlightenment and liberation for the all. The Council works with telepathic methodology to assist their students wherever they might have incarnated, according to a unified plan for the education of all humanity. They unfailingly direct and guide the feet of all their students, even if those students acknowledge not yet their existence. They open the doors to the meditation and intuitive experiences whereby they will come to know that which was formerly hidden. The teachings presented here will assist greatly the lines of communication both ways, once the earnest student of meditation comprehends the possibilities of the existence of this Hierarchy and begins to work meditatively with foreknowledge that internal contact with the enlightened ones is indeed possible. In fact, they will find it essential if they are to follow the path to liberation. The liberated Master will however *not be found* by incessant internal demand, through calling their names or visualisation of images. Only a life dedicated to selfless service and elimination of ego-posturing will enable such contact to be possible. Right karmic timing also holds the key, as service-orientated meditation work from past lives will flower at the reciprocal cycle in the present life.

Let us then open the floodgates of all esoteric possibilities for those that earnestly follow the instructions in this meditation manual. Let us eliminate the blindness of our lives, and if necessary, change those views that we've held for so long, to produce certainty of the way that things actually are. Let us thereby assist others to overcome the facades of ignorance by revealing the nature of the Lords of Light and Love to them, by becoming one ourselves. Let us assist all to work with the plan for the enlightening of people everywhere upon the planet. Let us together work to make this planet truly sacred, and the humanity upon it to fully manifest the potential of the divinity they are capable of expressing. Let the way of Love be the all of what one sees and does, to enact the self-same methods of liberation that the great Ones achieved in the past, though now upon a higher spiral of achievement. Let that Love shine through for all to see, and so stand as an integrated member of that Hierarchy of Love we also call the Council of Bodhisattvas. Let planetary Initiation into the Mysteries of being/non-being be the way we all follow.

The search for truth via mind

The start of one's search for truth should begin by an endeavour to understand exactly what the mind is. Buddhist philosophers have endeavoured to do this for millennia, and the best results of their efforts is seen in the Yogācāra-Vijñānavādin philosophy, and supplemented by the Mādhyamika revelations. The need now is to elaborate this subject from a new refreshing viewpoint, and to supplement what was provided by such astute philosophers as Asaṅga and Vasubandhu, the founders of this school. The mind freed from gross and subtle emotions is the basic framework required for comprehension.

The answers to life's major quest—liberation from the vicissitudes of *saṃsāra,*[2] will thus be achieved through understanding and analysing the mind/Mind. Indeed, *saṃsāra* is sustained by mind and through an application of the appropriate wisdom in meditation it can be dissolved into Mind's true essence to establish its natural radiance.

There are many forms and intentions in meditation techniques geared to controlling the attributes of mind. The simplest are teachings aimed purely to quieten the mind, to produce various forms of mental and emotional relaxation, allowing one to better cope with everyday stress and travail without emphasis on the *chakras.* Such teachings are generally quite valuable to participants. The instructors generally do not boast possession of great psychic power, and genuinely assist the meditative well-being of their students. From such simple beginnings one can progress through a well graded sequence of yoga disciplines to reach the highest yoga Tantras *(uttarayogatantra),* or the rDzogs-Chen of the Nyingma School. Many dedicate their lives to follow such techniques, with varying degrees of success. However, much simpler fare is advocated in this book as it is not easy to sort out the knots in the Tantras (as my rendering of the *Bardo Thödol* in Volume 5 has demonstrated). One wonders if competent teachers exist that can actually

2 *Saṃsāra:* cyclic existence, life-death cycle, the empirical realm. The ocean of causality, the perpetual turning of the wheel of births and deaths. Anything associated with the material world, to that which is ephemeral and ever-changing, and hence phenomenal, having no true substantiality of its own. It refers thus to the realms of illusion (corporeality) into which the personality incarnates and begins to identify with by means of the concrete mind.

untie these knots so that the full fruit of the Tantra practice is gained.

The focus of most instructions is upon the individual, who generally has strong emotional characteristics. When the emphasis is upon building intricate visualisations of deities and other constructs that require much mental activity to produce, meditators will not be successful unless they have developed sufficient emotional quietude. Through quiet, contemplative focus, building an image based upon what is conceived of as a reality can act as a template to allow the Real to manifest. Such visualisation practices can include building the complex imagery of a Buddhist *maṇḍala* step by step in the mind and holding the image steady so that the import of each deity can be revealed. One builds in faith as if the construct is genuine. If the paradigm of the *maṇḍala* is based upon the true living vital expression existing upon the domains of Causation, then the Real can replace the veil built by the meditator. Like attracts like, and the lower energy qualification acts as a conduit for the dynamics to manifest as a much more intense valid cognition. The theory is correct as far as its generalisation goes, and certainly there were many enlightened ones that in the past carried the visualisation through to victory. However, the practice of visualisation will not be successful when individuals with strong emotions are required to produce detailed imagery that requires refined mental activity beyond their ability.

The sheaths of the personality vehicle, wherein the average meditator is focussed, are integrally interwoven with what is considered mind. All meditators must work to comprehend their nature because they reside in a body of mind-substance. Paraphrased below is some of the useful information on the nature of the sheaths that was earlier provided in Volume 2 of this treatise from the chapter entitled 'An Enquiry into the Nature of the Self'. First we must analyse the nature of the personality vehicle, or mechanism of response to external stimuli, through which all humans function and gauge their place in the physical and subjective universes. The *saṃskāras* constituting mind are a composite of:

1. *The dense physical domain*, which most people identify with and take to be the 'real'. It is the fleeting phenomenal world all around us, which the senses contact and register as impressions by the concrete mind. In collating these impressions the mind registers them to be things. The world becomes the realm of the sense-perceptions with

which people assert their identities, around which their entire thought life revolves. It is the focus of the investigations of the scientific community, where modern Physics has a certain comprehension of the true nature of its ephemera. This is seen in terms of atoms and compounds, as well as energy and energy fields underlying the things that we actually perceive by means of the senses. The nature of the *karma* that conditions all outer seeming has however not yet been investigated.

2. *The etheric,* the body of energy, the vitality *(prāṇa)* that the physical body receives from its environment and from the food eaten. It allows the exchange of energies between the human unit and all other entities in our biosphere. *Prāṇa* is conveyed in many fine subjective channels in the body *(nāḍīs).* They roughly underlie our nerves and blood vessels. The etheric body is the reason why acupuncture works as a healing technique, especially in relation to anaesthetic effects, as the needles either block or reroute the subjective energies to specified targets, producing the results experienced by the patients. The meridians of acupuncture therapy are minor *nāḍīs* near the surface of the body. All psychic powers (*siddhis*) are expressions of the *chakras.* They are the wheels of energies manifesting as flowers as a result of the intersections of various *nāḍīs.* The evocation of one or other of the inherent energies of the seven major *chakras* is an objective of yoga and the higher Tantras, as explained in the earlier volumes of this treatise.

The intensity of the energies conveyed by the *prāṇas* determines the force of the *saṃskāras*[3] that any meditator must overcome, before the natural state of Mind is possible. The potency of the Peaceful and Wrathful Deities is conveyed in this manner, and becomes a conscious process in the higher stages of yogic austerities. Some of

3 *Saṃskāra*: from the Sanskrit roots, *sam* and *kri*, meaning the action (*kri*) that will improve, refine or make an impression in consciousness. *Saṃskāras* are the impressions from actions done in former incarnations and which are carried through to this one, thereby becoming the basis for one's present *karma*. They also refer to the effects of present actions that will bear fruit in later lives. *Saṃskaras* are actions that tend to bind one to the wheel of rebirth; to repetitious pain and/or pleasing dispositions, mental conformations, the inception of imagery, and all emotions. They can also be the tendencies to enlightenment.

the mental-emotional energies are therefore easily won over, and others become a battleground for the individual.

3. *The emotional body* incorporates all of the desires and emotions, fears, phobias, incessant moods and feelings, as well as the sum of our imaginative lives. It produces the various colourings of the *aura,* and is probably the most important consideration to take into account in all aspects of our lives. The aura instantly reflects the colourings of our fears, desires, thoughts and feeling perceptions.

   The emotions may produce sensations of exhilaration, peace, or happiness. Unfortunately, the emotions often immediately distort the very pliable thought-forms (which often come in a flash, and are mere impressions) obtained in meditative states, or other cognitive processes, into what the person thinks or desires to see or visualise, or what is surmised to be the reality.

   The meditator must therefore carefully pacify the emotions, because a myriad of distortions and images can occur through emotional perturbations influencing the images that form in the mind. Even the slightest emotional tremor can cause distortions in what is perceived as true. This 'reality' that people know or imagine to be real on the physical plane is not so in the realms that one contacts in meditation. Therein the transience of everything is correctly perceived, as well as how all experiences form a basis pertaining to the evocation of wisdom.

   Most people are very impressionable, receiving emotional energies from their friends, or others close to them in any environment, especially when involved in social or group activity, which conditions their thinking and consequent action. The impressions produce a type of excitable euphoria that acts as a soporific to higher reason. A reality based upon subjective desires is created. Such effects are easily seen at religious, political, and sports gatherings. Heightened and often more subtle forms of emotional euphoria can also accompany the meditation experience, which must also be controlled, otherwise distortions in perceptions will occur. Calm, 'cool', clear reasoning is what produces valid meditative insights. Once the emotions are stilled there is no turbulence or warmth generated, or fusion with *manasic* substance. This allows the mind to attune to the rarefied, elevated strata of Mind. Clarity of mind therefore ensues, allowing unperturbed images and accompanying logic to manifest.

As explained in Volume 5, wrathful forces arise that are feminine *(iḍā)* in nature[4] that assist in the conversion of mental-emotional *saṃskāras* into their respective attributes of Mind. All *saṃskāras* must be transformed by such means if one is to reside at the *saṃsāra-śūnyatā* nexus[5]. This produces a clarity of vision akin to a stainless mirror that makes the affirmations of the Heart's Mind immediately impelling.

4. *The concrete mind (the intellect)* cognises and organises sense perceptions. These isolated bits of perceived information are stored, classified, and correlated with the mind's information bank. It consists of people's everyday thoughts, gleaned in the material world from the results of their contact with dense objects, the environment as a whole, what they have read in books, from their schooling, and conversations with others. It is styled the 'sixth sense' in Buddhism. There is also an imaginative input of created picture images by the intellect, or from the desire-mind. Such thought life is rarely impartial and is often conditioned by people's subjective desires. This form of mind reifies, makes thoughts more concrete, rendering one unable to think deeply and abstractly upon things of consequence. To prevent this, the meditation process aims to still all the modifications of mind (*citta-vṛtti*) that come from this source, or else utilises the associated images to produce instant deep-seated analysis.

   When wedded to *kleśas* (affliction, dissident emotions, the three poisons: delusion, attachment, hatred), the intellect can be divided into seven attributes: the will of mind, loving mind, the critical mind, pride of mind, concrete mind, desire mind and wrongly faceted mind. They are expressions of the desire or the emotions integrated with mind *(kāma-manas)* and are explained in Volume 2 of this series,

---

4 In the *Bardo Thödol* they are viewed as female theriomorphic deities.

5 The *saṃsāra-śūnyatā* nexus was explained in detail in Volume 4, chapter 3 of this treatise.

hence need not be discussed here. These aspects, and the associated more animal-like emotional attributes of mind, govern all aspects of the personality, causing much misery, because of the inherent nature of the mind to segregate, critically dissect, to attach to and assert itself upon all manifest Life. These seven qualities should therefore be well understood by all aspirants for enlightenment.

To one fluent in the symbols of Tibetan Buddhist iconography, the Wrathful Deities can be evoked to help in the transformation of these aspects of mind. In particular, the masculine Wrathful Deities appear from out of the Void and assist the practitioner to convert attributes of mind into the Void Elements via Mind. They represent the pure attributes of the Fires of Mind, whereby all *manasic* propensities of *citta-vṛtti* transform into the unbounded, universally expressed, instantaneous revelatory Mind of Truth. All Wrathful Deities are therefore transformative fires taking the line of least resistance to manifest in the form that they do because the communality of the Buddhist mind-set has created them to be so. All things are attributes of mind and are created by mind/Mind. Similar images appear within the common mindsets of other religious dispensations, which assist serious practitioners to overcome major *saṃskāras*. However, the highly refined system of iconography developed in Buddhism, based on a sophisticated understanding of metaphysics, mind and the art of meditation is the world's most developed tool to assist meditative prowess. This system has been instigated by the greatest of all sages, the Buddha, and further developed by a large number of succeeding enlightened *mahāsiddhas* who are very high degree Bodhisattvas.

Seven attributes of consciousness

The mind is the bridge between the sub-human and para-human states of awareness. It can be a combination or product of any of seven characteristics described below. All their interrelations contribute to demonstrate the consciousness in a person. These are:

1. *Instinct,* developed by all levels of sentient evolution. There are five of these: the instinct of self-preservation, of self assertion, of sex, of group or herd activity, and towards knowledge. For humans they are

instincts because they are below the threshold of consciousness, but subtly impel all of our actions in one way or another. Their effects in the development of human consciousness are seminal, and they have a relationship to the attributes of the five-sense consciousnesses.

2. *Feeling,* nascently evolved in the plant kingdom. This expression makes us respond to external stimuli in some way. In the plant kingdom we have the demonstration of the magnificent varieties of their floral displays. When expressed in terms of the emotions of humans it can produce many colourful auric displays of affection, anger, even hatred, all of the emotional permutations people are afflicted by. When wedded with desire and elements of *manas,* then we have the basis for the comprehension of the nature of the *saṃskāras* associated with the theriomorphic deities. It represents the major energies that vitalise the minor *chakras* in the body.
3. *Desire,* developed by the animal kingdom. It causes one to attach to objects of perception, and when integrated with the emotions or the intellect, produces the ups and downs of pleasure and pain. Unhappiness or misery comes about because the objects of attachment are impermanent and illusional. The Buddha's Four Noble Truths stem from this observation.
4. *Intellect,* an expression of the human kingdom. Here we have pure *manas* (mind), of which much has been written in this *Treatise on Mind.* Mind is divided into two parts; the concrete and the abstract Mind. The concrete mind is a term signifying the reifying attributes of *manas* when expressed in terms of any combination of the qualities so far discussed. The abstract Mind is refined *manas* that incorporates elements of any of the three attributes of consciousness discussed above.
5. *Imagination,* a combination of intellect and desire. It can be creative, euphoric or destructive, depending upon the intensity of the desire incorporated into one's thought-form making propensity. In its higher aspect, when integrated with the Will, it is the basis to all *maṇḍala* construction.
6. *Pure Reason, intuition.* The intuition implies the power of vision, and is not to be confused with what the imagination construes

or constructs. The seer visions and must translate the visual picture-images by means of the intellect into words that people can understand. They can then interpret those words according to what they imagine them to mean, and this is governed by their emotional-mental conditionings and reactions. The vision of the seer is not so conditioned, as there is no emotion or desire involved. He/she has become a vehicle through which the enlightened consciousness of the Sambhogakāya Flower can manifest because of the ability to broadcast the energy of Love-Wisdom. A purified, receptive, coordinated and consecrated personality is what enables this to occur. The vision, if genuine, always benefits the whole, a group or mass of beings, or society in general, and only incidentally the personality involved. Imagination is always focussed upon or emanates from the personality and related conditionings, even if idealistic or inspirational. Intuition is the 'voiceless voice' that inspires all the men and women of destiny who change aspects of civilisation in some beneficent way.

The intuition is the expression of the Clear Light of Mind manifesting pure Reason as instantaneous revelation of Truth. The meditating one resides here after having successfully battled the *kleśas*. The peaceful emanations of Buddhas and Bodhisattvas then arise as they represent the attributes of the enlightened Mind that come as a consequence of pacifying the *citta-vṛtti* of lower mind states.

7. *The Ineffable or universal Mind (*the *dharmakāya*). This Mind transcends consciousness as we understand it. The *dharmakāya* is effectively an expression of a Buddha-Mind that had gained *parinirvāṇa* in a long past aeon, within which all things are contained, for everything can be considered an aspect of the thought processes of such a Mind. This is but a description of the appearance of a Buddha-field via which a 'thus gone' Buddha manifests. The key to the revelation of the nature of the evolutionary process and the appearance of a universe is found in this idea when thought out clearly. The fleeting, phenomenal appearance of things, the entire physical world that we as personalities live in and are involved with, can be likened to the images produced by the Imaginative Mind of such a One. The cells in the brain of that Being are embodied

by great angelic beings (*ḍākinīs, devas)* that fashion the images from out of the substance of their own forms. Lesser units of consciousness evolving within the bodies of such beings embody the various diversified aspects of the material world. All of Nature thus comes into existence.

Levels of meditative attainment

Most humans possess a soul-form, the Sambhogakāya Flower, the *tathāgatagarbha,* that resides in the domain of Mind (the *ālayavijñāna).* There is also an ultimate human expression residing in the *dharmakāya,* an eventuating Buddha-Mind (or Monadic form, meaning 'One', ultimate unity) that is the cause of and incorporates the entire human psyche on all levels of experience throughout the three times (past, present and future) and beyond. It can be considered a unit of the Ineffable cosmic universal Mind.[6] It is that which maintains a form of Individuation for all liberated Ones, that for instance distinguishes one Buddha from another.

We saw in *The I Concept* that there are three levels of enlightenment. The first level pertains to one who is capable of consciously being absorbed in the *ālayavijñāna* environment, the second level transcends consciousness, giving the meditator the ability to naturally reside in *śūnyatā* (emptiness, void of mind). The third level presents the Initiate with the ability to be absorbed in the bliss of *dharmakāya.* With respect to the world of meditation, one must astutely discern as to which of these three levels one's capabilities innately lie, in accordance to the highest achievements attained in previous lives. Most meditators are still aspirants vying to attain the mysteries of the first level of expression. It is not easy to reside consciously in the *ālayavijñāna* environment manifesting as the higher abstract levels of Mind. Here the gain of one's past life experiences are stored, as well as the results of humanity's aeonic quest to obtain Mind. Much harder is the striving to die to all *manasic* experiences whatsoever, including that associated with the Sambhogakāya Flower, to experience *śūnyatā.*

---

6 See also the chapter entitled 'The Soul Concept and the Tathāgatagarbha Doctrine' in Volume 2 of this series.

Many lives of striving and practical accomplishment produce meditators that have sufficiently refined *saṃskāras* that will allow them to quickly attain and be stabilised in high meditative states. Those whose experiential zone can be stabilised in *śūnyatā* are very few indeed, whilst the awakened, incarnate Masters of Wisdom that make the *dharmakāya* their natural home are rarely little more during any period of time than what can be counted upon the fingers of one hand. Their lives are generally veiled in our societies, as they naturally shun the world of fame and prefer (in relative obscurity) to train the disciples with whom they have karmic affiliations. The glamoured affection of devotees is particularly a hindrance to their meditative service work. They train disciples to develop the yogic disciplines that will help them positively transform all unruly *saṃskāras* and to overcome the challenges that group service work, with view of passing Initiation tests, presents.

Relatively few seeking meditative experiences have the *karma* to successfully meet the challenges to obtain the fruits of enlightenment's quest in any particular life. However all sincere seekers will be offered the opportunity to do so by the Masters of Wisdom once they have passed the preliminary testings upon the path before them. All such training is veiled in the vicissitudes of *karma* and the types of service work to be developed at any time. The Bodhisattva ethos of unceasingly striving to wisely liberate all sentient beings from the throes of their suffering always governs this path and training. Those whose prime objective is their own liberation from suffering consequently cannot travel very far upon this path of liberation. The Masters of Wisdom embody the various Ray lines, and consequently are engrossed in service arenas of the fields of human livingness. They train their disciples according to these Ray lines of service, rather than just upon a narrowly defined religious agenda.

In this teaching concerning the nature of meditation it is taken for granted that one believes in rebirth of consciousness, and that rebirth happens exclusively into human forms that can carry such a consciousness. Transmigration into animal bodies simply does not occur, contrary to popularly held beliefs found in exoteric Buddhism and Hinduism.[7] Those aspiring to become enlightened must therefore awaken

7 Detail can be obtained from my book, *Karma and the Rebirth of Consciousness* (Munshiram Manoharlal, New Delhi, 2006). Concerning the popularly held belief

to a complete understanding as to the way *karma* works via rebirth. Proof of one's past life experiences comes inevitably through meditation. Without an understanding of the process of rebirth (of consciousness and needed psycho-spiritual aggregates from previous lives) much concerning the meditative lifestyle, subjective realisations, the process of evolution itself and the law of *karma* would be meaningless.

Despite the generally accepted erroneous view of transmigration, the Buddhist doctrine greatly facilitates the ability of one to achieve the sublime heights of meditative bliss, providing one has a capable instructor who can properly unravel some of the tangled knots of core (pith) teachings present in the fundamental texts. It is in the presentation of the doctrine of *śūnyatā*, the yogic precepts concerning the nature of mind/Mind, the higher Tantric teachings, plus the background philosophy wherein Buddhism excels. The Buddhist religion has been an effective vehicle of training high Bodhisattvas by revealing the highest meditation teachings possible, but now must adapt appropriately to meet all the challenges of our modern era. Following a meditative life there is however generally an incarnation in other religious or scientific dispensations to present doctrines that amalgamate with or are adjuncts to the Buddhist dispensation. The earlier insights gained are then melded into the socio-religious thoughts of that new incarnation. Everything consequently comes to be included as part of one great interlocking system of the process of enlightenment unfolding for humanity as a unit.

The *chakras*

The topic of meditation is vast, and only the most useful and necessary teachings shall be provided in a simplified though coherent form, so that anyone wishing to practise can gain realisations relatively quickly and safely. A general overview of the nature of the *chakras* (psychic centres) and psychic development is also necessary to help the novice

---

of transmigration or rebirth into animal forms in Hinduism and Buddhism, W.Y. Evans-Wentz states in *The Tibetan Book of the Dead* (Munshiram Manoharlal, New Delhi, 2000), that this is a purely exoteric account, and then passionately argues the 'esoteric interpretation' (41-61) that transmigration is irrational, 'on the authority of the various philosophers, both Hindu and Buddhist, from which the author has received instruction', that only rebirth into another human form is possible. My book delves into many arguments as to why such metempsychosis is impossible.

correctly wade through some of the murky waters stirred up by the extant literature. For expediency, some basic information already provided in the earlier books shall be repeated.

The existence of seven major *chakras* are promulgated in all important meditation texts.[8] *Chakras* govern the sum of manifest Life via the *nāḍī* system from which they stem. The conditionings of cosmos, the earth and Nature are all governed by *chakras*. All that we see around us and come to know can be viewed in terms of energy. These multidimensional flowers are energy receptors, accumulators, and emanators on all levels of expression of Life. The *chakras* have various colourings and numbers of petals possessing differing properties according to the nature of the energy *(prāṇa)* in the *chakra* channels. Sometimes they are also described as wheels or saucer like depressions, with a number of spokes of radial energies.[9] They are multidimensional because they channel *prāṇas*, and their related psycho-spiritual experiences, to and from the various sheaths of an individual and thus from the dimensions of perception of which these sheaths are an integral part.

Chakras are the means to transcend our sense-oriented perceptions in the mundane world, allowing us to experience states of great subtlety and beauty and the supernal realms of Divinity that are equated with the heavens of our religious traditions. They are also the means to experience hell states. They are the open doors (gates) to the mysteries concerning all states of consciousness, past life experiences, that relating to the Council of Bodhisattvas,[10] *śūnyatā,* and the *dharmakāya*. These gates represent the means to liberation from earthly woes, or else 'the broad way to destruction',[11] depending upon how these centres are utilised and awakened.

---

8 See 140-159 of *Foundations of Tibetan Mysticism* by Lama Anagarika Govinda, (Century Hutchinson, London, 1987), whilst *The Serpent Power* by Arthur Avalon (Ganesh & Co., Madras, 2004), suffices for a Hindu perspective of this subject. *The Chakras* by C. W. Leadbeater (Theosophical Publishing House, Madras, 1987) is a useful Western account. The best extant account today, however, exists in the works of A.A. Bailey, specifically *Esoteric Healing*. (Lucis Publishing Company, New York.)

9 See, for instance, Lama Anagarika Govinda, *Foundations of Tibetan Mysticism,* 140-146, 193.

10 The community of the saints, or the Holy Ghost of the Christians.

11 *Matt. 7:13-14.* 'Enter ye in at the straight gate; for wide *is* the gate, and broad *is* the

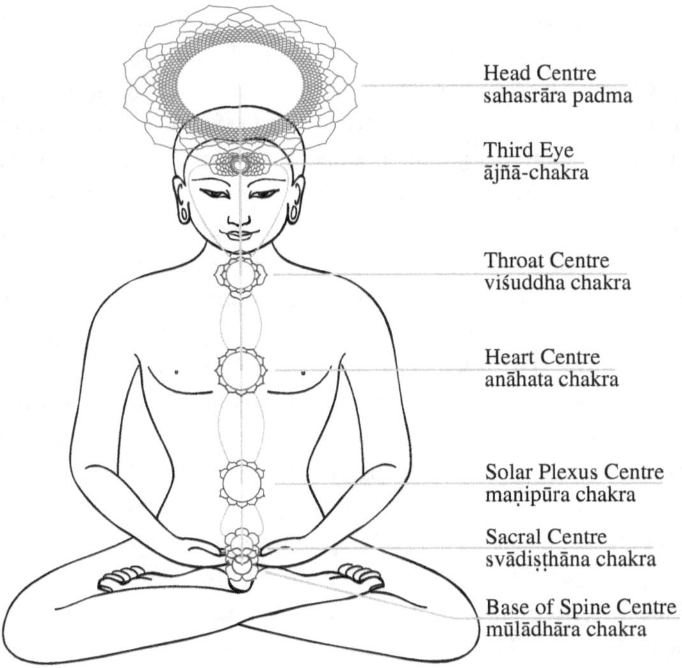

Figure 1. The seven major *chakras*

The Head Centre (*sahasrāra padma*)

The thousand petal lotus, centred at the top of the head, unfolds completely in an adept of meditation (Master of Wisdom) expressing the spiritual Will of the enlightened person. Its major colouring is white and gold. The Element *Aether* is under full control of the one whose Head centre is awakened. *Aether* is the most rarefied of the five *prāṇas,* the Element governing the fifth plane of perception *(ātma)* and is therefore that from which they stem, as well as every type of force or form constituting the material universe. This fifth plane is

way, that leadeth to destruction, and many there be which go in thereat. Because straight *is* the gate, and narrow *is* the way, which leadeth unto life, and few there be that find it'. *(King James version* of the Christian Bible, which all future Biblical quotes come from.)

that wielding the *dharmakāya*. The *prāṇas* are the five types of vital energy bearing the *saṃskāras* that underlie and consolidate all manifest space. We thus have the five-fold structure of a human being, of the sense-consciousnesses, and the Wisdoms of the five Dhyāni Buddhas.

The Head centre reflects the attributes of the Sambhogakāya Flower, and is organised into a group of twelve major petals that are directly related to the twelve petals of the Heart centre. In the local cosmos these twelve petals are represented by the twelve constellations of the zodiac. This allows a direct relation between the Sambhogakāya Flower and the dense incarnation of the human unit. In its simplest definition, meditation is a process that can bring about an alignment (in consciousness) between this trinity; the Sambhogakāya Flower, the Head lotus and the Heart centre. Strand after strand of transformed *saṃskāras* are projected by the personality to demonstrate the abstracted consciousness of Mind (wherein this Flower resides). Each strand is met by a reciprocal approach or energy and revelation from the Sambhogakāya Flower. This pathway (the *antaḥkaraṇa*) is called the 'rainbow bridge', a term taken from Nordic mythology.

This bridge-building is concurrent with the awakening of the tiers of the Head centre. The ability to fully awaken these petals constitutes the treading of the higher way of the mysteries of being/non-being. At first the Head lotus is infused with the Element *Fire,* and later with the *prāṇas* of the higher Elements.

Antaḥkaraṇas are conceived of as lines of lighted energy, of elevated thought, linking the empirical mind to its abstract counterpart. There is a gap in consciousness between the two attributes of mind, which needs to be bridged by means of fiery aspiration, coupled with appropriate image building.

The Fiery strands are built by means of the creative imagination. Images can be created based upon the paradigm of the Real, to build a construct that approaches the divine. This can then be utilised by manifesting divinity whereby the image etherealises into what actually is. The building process can be accomplished through the visualisation of *maṇḍalas* of deities and their qualities. There can also be a more direct appropriation of imagery, such as visualising the petals of the Sambhogakāya Flower. (We saw earlier in this treatise that they take the attributes of the downward looking Lord, Avalokiteśvara.[12])

Whatever imagery is utilised, the process must be accompanied with the transformation and transmutation of base *saṃskāras* to generate the Clear Light of Mind. Once this path is trod then the Initiation process also proceeds. It elevates one from lower dimensions of perception to the higher ones. Once the links have been formerly established and abstract reasoning becomes the norm then there is no more need for such visualisations. Receiving and processing the resultant downpour of energies and impressions becomes automatic for the Initiate, and is part of the process accompanying an enlightened one.

A higher bridge between the abstract Mind and the *dharmakāya* is built upon the path of Initiation. This is the *śūnyatā-saṃsāra* nexus, explained in the earlier volumes of this *Treatise on Mind.* All of the petals of the Head centre then come to be fully active and capable of conveying the sum of the qualities of being/non-being. When fully developed, the Head centre bears the full potency of the *dharmakāya.*

The Third Eye *(ājñā chakra)*

This *chakra* has 96 petals, divided into two parts of 48 petals each, and is said to be situated between the eyebrows. The left side is coloured predominantly purple-blue and the right predominantly rose-yellow. It unfolds in spiritual aspirants, mystics and occultists, and coordinates the integration between the energies of the personality and the Sambhogakāya Flower, via the developed Head lotus. It relates the various Elements together, thus it provides the ability to vision on any of the dimensions of perception when awakened. The right and left *nāḍīs* (psychic channels conveying *prāṇa*) integrate here. The left *(iḍā) nāḍī* stream conveys the energies of materialistic activity associated with the development of intelligence. These qualities sustain the activities of the personality, which allows the Eye to awaken the powers of the *chakras*, and the *manasic* pathways between their petals. As the Eye directs so energy is projected, and what the Eye perceives there consciousness is focussed.

The right hand *(piṅgalā) nāḍī* conveys the energies of consciousness,

---

12 See Volume 4, page 312, where Avalokiteśvara's mantra Oṁ Maṇi Padme Hūṁ is explained in terms of the qualities of this Flower.

of Love-Wisdom, equated with the development of the Son aspect in Nature, of the triplicities: Father, Son, Mother; Monad, Soul, form; Life, quality, appearance; *sattva, rajas, tamas,* etc. This *nāḍī,* therefore, at first conveys primarily Watery *prāṇas* (as controlled by the Solar Plexus centre), which later are transformed into the Airy quality that awakens the Heart centre.

The central channel is called the *suṣumṇā.* It conveys the Will (Father) aspect and is the channel for the central Fires that sustain all that is. It finds its outlet in the jewel in the heart of the lotus of each of the centres.

The Head and Ājñā centres are an integral unit, as they overlap each other. The presiding Dhyāni Buddha[13] is Vairocana.

The Throat Centre *(viśuddha chakra)*

This *chakra* has sixteen silvery-blue petals, and is situated in the neck. It unfolds in all intelligent, creative, and artistic people. It expresses the full potential of the creativity of the mind, thus the creative or liberating Word, the potency of the mantra-making capacity of the *yogin,* as well as the entire articulation of the intelligentsia. It gives us control of the Element Fire (mental energies) when fully unfolded, therefore it is the prime centre that controls the evocation of the *iḍā nāḍī.* The *prāṇas* generated in the Sacral centre concerning the lower creative (generative) Fires come eventually to be transmuted into the higher creativity and are absorbed in the Throat centre. Through it then the mind/Mind can come to be understood. The presiding Jina is Amitābha.

The Heart Centre *(anāhata chakra)*

This is a golden twelve-petalled lotus situated between the shoulder blades. It unfolds in all dynamically active, compassionate people who are associated with groups, or concerned with integrating the many into unity, as do all Bodhisattvas. The Life-energy (*jīva*) is anchored here, thus it is the centre wherein the force of enlightenment (*bodhicitta*) emanates. From the silent recesses of the Heart speaks the 'Voice of Silence' (the intuition) that is one's guide to enlightenment. The Heart centre controls the Element Air, the substance of space, and the energy of *śūnyatā* that

13 The Dhyāni Buddhas are Buddhas of meditation. The alternate term for them is Jina.

transforms the attributes of all *saṃskāras* into the Void Elements. The *piṅgalā nāḍī* is directed by the awakening Heart centre, and its *prāṇas* are eventually absorbed therein. The self-focussed *saṃskāras* from the Solar Plexus centre must eventually be converted into the group conscious qualities of the Heart centre. Eventually the Heart centre will control the *prāṇas* of the Solar Plexus centre (therefore of all the minor *chakras*), as explained in the earlier volumes of this series. The presiding Jina is Akṣobhya.

The Solar Plexus Centre *(maṇipūra chakra)*

This centre has ten petals that are green in colour, admixed with rosy-red, and is situated in the naval area. It expresses the qualities associated with the Watery emotional body: our feelings, selfishness, hatreds, irritations, moodiness, cupidity, imaginative faculty, devotion and aspiration. When coupled to *manas* it produces the ubiquitous desire-mind. This combination makes it the most powerful *chakra* activated in the average person. The touch sense-perceptor best conveys its qualities. It embodies the mechanism that allows the personality to focus its will upon any object desired, or any aspiration. It generates the concept of an 'I', the separative ego who discriminates between itself and others. The full potency of the personal will is developed and controlled by this centre, causing the many attachments to things desired, all in relation to the potency of the image created of a separated 'self'. The Solar Plexus centre is the domain of normal human intelligence. It is the 'abdominal brain' and is therefore the organ of clairvoyance, opening the entire psychic, astral world, to the seer. The Solar Plexus gains control of the Watery Element when fully unfolded. The watery astral realm constitutes the sum total of the massed glamours, idealism, and emotionality of humanity and is constituted from the substance of this Element.

The effect upon this centre of the energy derived from *śūnyatā* at its central point at first intensifies the personal will; all of the characteristics of the self-seeking ego are consolidated by its grip upon the *māyā* of *saṃsāra*. Generally, this will is used in its negative aspect to destroy and make war for separative selfish purposes. Later it manifests as a constructive force, to sustain a momentum against all odds to build the new. The will is then used to destroy the archaic and obsolete, so that forms can be built that can better sustain a more vibrant aesthetic energy input from the higher domains. Later, upon the path of enlightenment, when the energy of the Heart centre is evoked, then the Will-to-Love is utilised to destroy the attachments to *saṃsāra,* so that the Real can be revealed and liberation gained.

The entire meditation path is built upon this use of the Will. It becomes the sustaining force transforming basic *saṃskāras,* and used for the development of the *dhāraṇīs*[14] and yogic discipline *(tapas)* that transform consciousness, allowing one to reside in the Clear Light of the Mind. This teaching on the Will was developed in Volume 4 of this series, hence need not be repeated. The mind is involved with appropriate *maṇḍala* building upon the path of meditation, thus the importance for earnest students to study the material provided earlier. The presiding Jina is Ratnasambhava.

The Sacral Centre *(svādiṣṭhāna chakra)*

This centre has six petals, coloured differently, according to the type of *prāṇa* each petal expresses, giving an overall sun-like appearance. It conveys the forces of the base animal instincts, the sexuality, vitality, and plant-like qualities in us. It is very strongly developed in most, especially the sensual, physically focussed types, thus all forms of physical plane interrelationships stem from its potency. It is the stimulus for the magnetic lure of such concepts as 'the body beautiful', physical prowess, and the health and vitality of the form. When fully unfolded it produces control of the vital energy (*prāṇa*) throughout the body, attunement to the energy body governing the earth, and thus control of bio-magnetic fields and healing currents. The *iḍā* and *piṅgalā nāḍīs* stem from its petals, and it forms a functioning unity with the Base of Spine Centre. The presiding Jina for this union is Amoghasiddhi.

---

14 *Dhāraṇī*: that which is borne, a means for fixing the mind to an idea, a vision or an experience gained in meditation. They may represent the quintessence of a teaching as well as the experience of a certain state of consciousness, which thereby can be recalled or recreated deliberately at any time. Therefore they are called supporters, receptacles or bearers of wisdom (*vidyādhara*). They are not different from mantras in their function but may attain a considerable length. They sometimes represent a combination of many mantras or seed syllables (*bījas*), or the quintessence of a sacred text. They are a product as well as a means of meditation: 'Through deep absorption (*samādhi*) one gains truth, through a *dhāraṇī* one fixes and retains it'. (From Govinda, *Foundations of Tibetan Mysticism*, 31-2.)

The Base of Spine Centre *(mūlādhāra chakra)*

This centre, situated at the base of the spine, has four petals, coloured orange-red. It is the primal centre, expressing the feminine (*kuṇḍalinī*) forces that give a viability to the material world (thus our dense physical body), and is directly related to the awakening of the Head centre. Each of its petals is responsible for channelling the *prāṇas* of one or another of the four kingdoms of Nature. Its Element is the Earth, over which it gives complete control for those in whom *kuṇḍalinī* has 'risen'. (This is the Fiery serpentine energy that is the internal heat sustaining Life, and gives all lives a coherent form and maintains evolutionary purpose.)

There are also twenty-one minor centres. Of these, only the barest outline of a few have ever been given in publications on the *chakras*. They can be listed: one for each foot, knee, and hand. One situated at the stomach, another at the liver, two for the gonads and we also have the dual Splenic centre. One is situated at the diaphragm, one at each breast, one centred between the shoulder blades, one for each ear and eye, and another centred at the back of the head. Detailed understanding of their qualities, areas of influence, and inter-relationships is necessary to the instructor if the dangers of meditation are to be avoided.

Psychic powers

Detailed information has been a veiled secret for millenia because of the wilful ones seeking psychic powers, for whatever reason they may offer. The karmic consequences of psychic wrongdoing are quite grave.[15] Instructors who give out such details without proper consideration are esoterically blind and do not understand the law of *karma*, or the subtleties of the way of travelling associated with *the left hand path.* (Other than those that wilfully follow such a path.) This way is that of the self-focussed intellect; wherein concrete knowledge, materialistic domination of all forces (psychic or material), resources

15 These consequences will be explained later. It is evident that the majority of present meditation instructors do not have such knowledge. This series of works will however reveal much more than has been previously deemed safe because the general advancement of knowledge of humanity now allows further detail to be published. Much of what can be presently revealed was provided in Volumes 4 and 5 of this series.

and people around, becomes the objective of the seeker. Here the powers of the mind are exemplified and used to serve the individual above all other considerations.

The path of self-centredness and selfishness, exemplified by the black magician and his followers, when coupled with psychic development, leads *backwards* in evolutionary time. Such people consciously awaken forms of psychicism that were prevalent in the far distant past in Atlantean times, and should no longer be a focus of human evolution. The massed misuse of psychic powers and evil doing caused the 'God' of that time to destroy the then Atlantean civilisation by means of the great flood. This civilisation and flood is a myth to the present day materialists, who think in terms of intellectual development only, but is an esoteric reality to those that have developed the ability to revisit their past lives, meditatively or by means of trances, as for instance, did the well known psychic seer Edgar Cayce. It concerns part of the esoteric history of the earth, the evidence of which has been ruthlessly suppressed or ignored by modern materialistic science. However the detail is found recorded in the archives of the spiritual Hierarchy (the White Brotherhood) of our planet. These Bodhisattvas have gained the fruits of the meditative way and achieved enlightenment in past lives, and are an organised *maṇḍala* within the greater space of which the sum of human consciousness plays its part. From another perspective this *maṇḍala* represents the Heart centre of the planet. The process of meditation is the key that allows access to these archives when properly instructed by a senior member of the Hierarchy.

Such information is obtained in a distorted fashion through mediumistic, lower psychic powers, through the use of drugs, dreams, or by forcefully awakening the lower *chakras* through ego-centred visualisation techniques and ritualised magic (when divorced from correct moral and ethical development). The focus of correct development necessitates the control and purification of the sheaths of substance through which one incarnates and through correct service work to all humanity. It incorporates the Bodhisattva vow, which esoterically refers to bringing any class of people or species of Life that the Bodhisattva primarily wishes to help to the next evolutionary step for them.

Considerable information has been presented in Volumes 4 and 5 of this series concerning the technicalities of awakening perceptions safely, with respect to the activities of the Peaceful and Wrathful Deities, and the nature of the meditation upon Mind. All who wish to proceed on the course of awakening higher perceptions and the corresponding *siddhis* should carefully study these volumes and this present one. People should be warned, however, that too much focus upon one or other of the *chakras* and the psychic powers derived from them can produce an overemphasis upon the personality vehicle via a self-centred dramatic 'I'. If lower psychic powers are unduly awakened via self-will then there is a danger of obsession, or of possession by dark forces. Here we see an effect of grievous error on the part of the unsuspecting or ill-informed instructor, producing much attendant *karma*. The emotions produce vortices of energies between the personality and any object of desire, and this process can be intensified by some meditation practices. Problematic emotional intensifications or accompanying devitalisation can be ignored, or even misunderstood by the teacher.

For the great majority of aspirants, however, the lure of lower base psychicism is a glamour that overrides all other spiritual considerations. (It is often the subjective motive, even when verbalised otherwise.) As the dangers of premature psychic development are great, some space should be given to the explanation of these dangers, emphasising that the energy of Love-Wisdom (*bodhicitta*) is the key to avoiding them. Love breaks down all barriers to divine reasoning and the necessary spiritual perceptions. In all things, however, *wisdom* must be first developed if that Love is not to be blind.

The fundamental difference between the Hindu and Buddhist system should also be noted here. Hindu Tantrism (Śaktism) involves an endeavour to unite with the psychic power that can be evoked from awakening the *chakras*. These powers are given feminine characteristics, as the reflex of the psychic power (*śakti)* of their deities. With respect to meditation, the focus is specifically upon Shiva, the god of the *yogins,* and his consort Parvati. The feminine principle is the power behind the creative urge, or world formation, and therefore is material in its nature, related to the *iḍā nāḍī,* and often generates the left hand path. For Buddhist Tantrism, however, what is desired is not psychic power but wisdom *(prajñā)* and that which is the way of the right hand path. The specific development therefore is that of the *piṇgalā nāḍī*. As Govinda states:

> To the Buddhist *śakti* is *māyā*, the very power that creates illusion, from which only *prajñā* can liberate us. It is therefore not the aim of the Buddhist to acquire power, or to join himself to the powers of the universe, either to become their instrument or to become their master, but, on the contrary, he tries to free himself from those powers, which since aeons kept him a prisoner of *saṃsāra*. He strives to perceive those powers which have kept him going in the rounds of life and death, in order to liberate himself from their dominion. However, he does not try to negate them or to destroy them, but to transform them in the fire of knowledge, so that they may become forces of Enlightenment which, instead of creating further differentiation, flow in the opposite direction: towards union, towards wholeness, towards completeness.[16]

Each of the major *chakras* are doorways of various energies conveyed by the physical body and affecting consciousness. They therefore control the entire psyche of the individual. The endocrine glands, for instance, are the externalisations of the major *chakras*, therefore if any of these *chakras* are prematurely awakened then one can expect a corresponding increase of secretions from the associated gland, with inevitable physiological effects.

As well as *karma,* we must also look to the fact that there are hosts of psychic entities, disincarnate beings, mischievous nature spirits, psychic vampires, demons, and abominations of mind created by the dark side of human nature and by the forces of evil. There exist all types of maleficent thought and desire forms created by humanity throughout aeons of evolutionary time who seek access into physical embodiment (incarnation). People who foolishly tinker with psychicism before they have the means to control such manifestations open the doorways to these forms. The resulting experiences are fearful visitations, entities trying to possess them, vampirism, and a host of other unwelcomed psychic

16 Govinda, *Foundations of Tibetan Mysticism,* 97. On page 139 he further states that 'in place of the *śakti* we find in Buddhism the *ḍākinī*, i.e., in place of the power principle the knowledge-principle in its intuitive spontaneous form; in place of the force nature, the unifying force of inspiration'.

effects. There are also the predatory emanations of the sorcerer who is always on the lookout for potential victims in the foolish who dabble thus with psychic powers, for accomplices or victims in his black arts.

Having 'eyes and ears opened', the enlightened being thus comprehends esoteric truth, and will not reveal potentially destructive information to anyone until the person has proved himself. This is achieved through strict adherence to moral observations and disciplines that purify *saṃskāras*, thus awakening compassionate understanding through the evocation of the powers of the Heart. The means is the application of concepts of selfless service. The only safe *chakra* to aim at awakening is the Heart centre because of its association with the energy of Love, though problems can arise here too, if too much emotional energy is directed to the chest area.

Many teachers give meditation techniques that are said to awaken the Heart *chakra*, but this is rarely the case. It should be emphasised that the Heart centre has nothing to do with the emotions, such as those producing elated feelings, rapture, euphoria, and loving aspiration. (That is a function of the Solar Plexus centre.) Ecstatic forms of loving emotions and associated visualisations may be seeded from the Heart but are Solar Plexus based. Such effects are focussed upon a central 'I' that is experiencing the form of rapture in relation to a perceived 'something beyond'. Whenever the focus is via an 'I' concept then the Solar Plexus centre is involved, though it is true that the energies from the Heart centre may have been drawn to it, to produce the more ecstatic, compassionate aspects of the experience.

Therefore, when teachings promote the experience of exhilarating feelings or joyous emanations, the Solar Plexus centre is actually the focus. When a person experiences a lot of merriment or elation of spirits as a result of a believed 'heart awakening', then one can rest assured that the Heart centre has *not* been awakened. Minor *chakras* are also often unduly stimulated, as all minor centres are aspects of the Solar Plexus centre.

The Solar Plexus centre produces the many vibrant images that most people visualise in their meditation experiences. Through lack of knowledge, such people often mistake these for the real. Such experiences are, however, valuable if correctly interpreted. They are a necessary stage in the process of becoming enlightened. It should be noted that when a practitioner of meditation still has a predominantly emotional disposition in the way they respond to friends and family, and in their everyday situations and experiences, so the focus of their life experience is the Solar Plexus centre. It takes considerable effort of emotional control (but not suppression) for people to rise out of that centre to experience and visualise upon a higher plane of perception, or higher centre, to obtain realisations closer to truth.

The path of Love means sacrificial service based upon the expression of a divine Reason that takes one away from *saṃsāric* affiliations. Pure logic is evoked to help liberate the all in the wisest possible way. The awakening of the Heart centre produces direct dispassionate perceptive understanding (absorption or identification with the object of the meditation), and manifests a clear *cold* reason. It is embodied light that is direct illumined revelation. The Heart's awakening necessitates the demonstration of *bodhicitta* to be genuine. It thus generates the Bodhisattva path. The Heart centre knows only group consciousness, that which is decentralised and stripped of a 'self' concept. Selflessness is its leitmotiv, and when pursued produces experience of the Void *(śūnyatā)*.

It should also be noted that a major effect of contact with the higher realms of perception is that one gets energised with increasingly more intense forms of energy. The effects of such contacts (visualised in terms of light of varying degrees of intensity) causes the major problems associated with meditation, and the meditation instructor must therefore understand the effects of such energisations in the body and psyche of the individual concerned. Intensification of the emotions is perhaps the first of the effects, and this should serve as a warning. Emotions can swing quite dramatically from a state of elation, to depression, to produce fears of various types, with such energies externalising themselves in the corporeal body. It is clear from every perspective that right emotional control should be at the forefront of all meditation teachings, unfortunately, the necessary techniques are rarely given in the West, except in relation to the gross, obvious emotions.

The esotericism in the Bible

The principles related to gaining enlightenment are not unique to Eastern religions. Much esotericism is incorporated in the Bible that is not understood at all. It is an important spiritual text, which requires a refined and subtle meditative disposition to interpret, and contains many Mystery teachings that compliment the *buddhadharma*. The veiled mysteries in the Bible now aught to be revealed, as it contains part of the wisdom teachings of the ages (albeit in a veiled, symbolic, and metaphorical form) enunciated by some of the best teachers of the Council of Bodhisattvas. The teachings shall be utilised to supplement what has already been presented, and also to remind Buddhists that enlightened ones can be found in all religious dispensations. The results of their labours of Love are easily perceptible to those with eyes opened to see. The teachings of the Buddha and Jesus represent two views relating to gaining enlightenment, both of which are valid. Where one religious stream is weak, the other fills in the gaps, when the texts are properly interpreted. A syncretic religious dialogue thus needs to be instigated between East and West, and an integration of these two religious dispensations can now begin to be accomplished.[17]

Orthodox Christianity has never understood such Wisdom teachings, as those that eventually usurped the religion founded by Jesus and his immediate followers (early on in the Christian epoch) never followed his teachings of Love, or the way of being initiated into the Mysteries that he instigated. (This is evident in their methodology of vying for *temporal* supremacy over the Roman Empire and the Pagan religion of the time.)

My aim is to present some of the keys found in the New Testament[18] needed for successful meditation, for understanding the related psychic phenomena, as well as the path of Initiation. Many that follow the path of meditation have an avowed disdain for the Bible, and it is important that such erroneous attitudes be rectified. Also, it will be seen that these teachings are complementary, rather than contravening the invaluable meditative lore found in Buddhist Tantric sources.

Jesus was an exemplary Bodhisattva who was overshadowed (i.e.,

---

17 This theme is explored in Volume 1 of this series.

18 The text used is from the *King James authorised version,* as the translation of this version was overseen by an enlightened being. In contradistinction, modern versions have later theological dogma woven in, in the name of simplification and correctness, thus over-riding with doctrinal views the meaning of many passages that were problematic to modern theologians.

incarnated into) during his baptism experience 2,000 years ago by the cosmic Christ (a Bodhisattva of vast duration who embodies the cosmic principle of Love) that descended in the form of a dove,[19] hence the term Christ-Jesus given in the gospels. In the East he would have been termed an Avatar[20] (a descent from Divinity into a human vehicle). The early formulators of present Christian dogma, misunderstanding the process of Divine Embodiment, made this Bodhisattva to be the unique 'son of God', and then to 'be God', by speculating upon such phrases in the Bible as 'He that overcometh shall inherit all things: and I will be his God, and he shall be my son'.[21] The implication here is that everyone that 'overcomes' shall be a 'son of God' (which was then equated with Jesus). The phrase 'I will be his God' is, however, but a version of *guruparamparā* explained in the fourth chapter of this book. Note that the 'inheriting' of 'all things' happens once one earnestly follows the teachings of the *guru* (the spiritual preceptor) and has passed the required Initiation testings. Such inheritance is but the effect of a successful meditative lifestyle, after all of the allurements associated with the transient material world and associated *saṃskāras* have been overcome.

The doctrine of 'Divine Incarnation' is also presented in the concept of the *Tulku* in Tibetan Buddhism:

> Something, or someone that has no 'individuality' or *ego* in the ordinary sense decides to work on the earth for the sake of all beings. He (or 'it') therefore takes birth over a certain period of time, in a series of human individuals, and it is these who are named '*Tulkus*'.[22]

---

19 *Matt. 3:16:* 'And Jesus, when he was baptized, went up straightway out of the water; and lo; the heavens were opened unto him, and he saw the Spirit of God descending like a dove, and lighting upon him'. Also *Luke 3:22* states: 'And the Holy Ghost descended in a bodily shape like a dove upon him, and a *voice* came from heaven, which said, "Thou art my beloved Son; in thee I am well pleased"'. Here we see that this process of overshadowing Jesus was quite complex in that not one, but two divine principles incarnated into him then, that symbolised by the 'Spirit of God' and that denoted by the phrase 'the Holy Ghost'. They are similar but not the same.

20 *Avatar*: from the root *Av,* meaning 'above', and *atara,* which means 'to descend'.

21 *Rev. 21:7.*

22 Chögyam Trungpa, *Born in Tibet,* (Shambhala Publications, Boston, 1995), 270.

Indeed, one of the important aspects of the meditation process is that of the development of *quiescence,* the relaxation of mind and of the emotions, to such an extent that an aspect of Divinity (or the Sambhogakāya Flower) can overshadow the mind, and take over all normal functions of the personality. To all extents and purposes the personality becomes the aspect of Divinity/Buddha/Bodhisattva/Christ that has incarnated into it, and accordingly manifests works in the formed realms. Far 'greater works' can be accomplished by this means than what would have been possible before such an embodiment.

The process of Divine Embodiment or overshadowing is actually the higher correspondence of *obsession.* In obsession, the obsessing entity enters via a minor awakened *chakra* in the person, causing mediumistic utterances and similar troublesome occurrences. In Divine Embodiment the meditator *consciously* steps out of his/her vehicle and allows the Divinity, the overshadowing enlightened Being, to utilise it for a purpose. He/she becomes a conscious co-operator in the act of serving humanity by this means. In the Bible there are two types of Divine Embodiment indicated:

a. By means of the 'Spirit of God'—relating to the Monadic aspect, the *dharmakāya.*

b. By means of 'The Comforter, *which is* the Holy Ghost',[23] relating to the soul aspect, the Sambhogakāya Flower. The 'Holy Ghost' can also refer to the Hierarchy of enlightened being.

Central to understanding the problem of premature awakening of psychic perceptions, and thus obtaining the Mysteries of 'the kingdom of God', is a key passage in the New Testament:

> And he said unto them, Unto you it is given to know the mystery of the kingdom of God: but unto them that are without, all *these* things

23 *John 14:26.* 'But the Comforter, *which is* the Holy Ghost, whom the Father will send in my name, he shall teach you all things, and bring all things to your remembrance, whatsoever I have said unto you'. This is but another way of describing the descent or unfoldment of the meditation-Mind, which when established will allow one to remember (past life happenings), to see 'all things' (pertaining to the inner realms) in the mind's eye. The concept of the 'Holy Ghost' is that which descends like a cloud or which envelops all with that which is 'holy'. This can also be conceived of as the breath of revelation conveyed by the Hierarchy of enlightened beings when the person is receptive to such impression.

> are done in parables; That seeing they may see, and not perceive; and hearing they may hear and not understand; lest at any time they should be converted and *their* sins be forgiven them.[24]

After this passage Jesus gives the parable of the sower, which directly relates to this statement. Before delving into this passage it is important that the meaning of the term 'God' is further clarified, by summarising a little of the information given earlier in Volume 2 of this treatise, as Buddhism purports to be non-theistic, and therefore there will be some trouble amongst some Buddhist readers in reconciling this word into their belief system.[25]

Whether one wishes to equate Mind with 'Perfect Buddhahood', or 'God', or abstract it in terms of 'Space' is a matter of personal predilection, for it is all of these things, as they are all symbols of the inexplicable. The concept of 'God' used here refers to the statement 'God is (universal) Mind', for it has a validity in relation to the knowable universe. It is the only facet of Deity that can be comprehended by our minds, being reflections of That Mind, moulded according to the patterning of Divine Mentation.

The process of liberation develops the faculty to identify with That which is the expression of the Buddha-Mind that had aeons ago gained its release from identification with even the most subtle types of substance that constitute the dimensions of perception associated with human evolution. The Buddha-Mind incorporates the substance of such space in a similar manner as the Sambhogakāya Flower incorporates the personality for each succeeding incarnation, but is not bound by it.

It should also be noted that the 'God' (One who attained Buddhahood in a past evolutionary aeon) spoken of in this text is considered a Planetary Logos. Such a Logos incorporates the lives of a planetary Scheme and the related kingdoms as their Logoic Body of Manifestation.[26] It is inclusive of these kingdoms because the Logos

---

24 *Mark 4:11-12.*

25 See the chapter titled 'On the Evolution of Consciousness', in Volume 2 of this series.

26 Such a Scheme represents the sheaths through which a Logos manifests. The Scheme incorporates seven globes of evolutionary space, each of increasing density until the fourth (densest) globe is reached. The sequence is followed by three globes of increasing subtlety. The present earth is the fourth globe of such a Scheme. Rounds of

has completely evolved through and transcended the stages of evolution that the various entities constituting those kingdoms must yet unfold. Consequently, the Logos can compassionately direct the evolutionary development of the associated lives. The compassionate Identification is so complete that the Logos appropriates the qualities needed for the enlightenment of the residents of the planetary sphere. This is accomplished by utilising the substance and lives of those kingdoms as the subjective and objective sheaths into which the Logos incarnates. An entire world-sphere is thus effectively the *nirmāṇakāya*[27] of this Buddha, which can be termed an Ādi (primordial) Buddha. It is possible therefore, for one that possesses a similar degree of enlightenment as Jesus, to attain a specific communication, or 'covenant', in a seeming 'personal' manner with such an entity. The chapters on the Initiation process show how such enlightenment is possible. Without undertaking the needed Initiations such a 'covenant' with 'God' is not possible.

Mark 4:11-12 has confounded the orthodox theologian for millennia, for they would ask, 'surely the objective of Jesus' teachings would be to convert the listener to them, to make them see and perceive, hear and understand in such a way that *their sins* should be forgiven them?' They question thus, for such conversion is the *entire emphasis* of the Christian religion, with its rites of Baptism, zealous proselytism, and the avowed ability of Catholic priests to 'forgive the sins' of those who approach them at the confessional.[28] This vexing verse should not be avoided, as it, like all similar statements, holds the clue to comprehension of many esoteric mysteries. As orthodox commentators have no foundation for understanding the esoteric teachings of Jesus, or any other high Initiate,

---

evolution proceed through each such globe, and upon the earth they have produced the marvellous diversity of Nature we know so well. The globes of a Scheme are similar to the subtle sheaths of a human unit into which a Sambhogakāya Flower incarnates.

27 *Nirmāṇakāya* (Tib. sprul pa'i sku): 'transformation body', the emanation (form) body of a Buddha. One of the three bodies or vestures of a Buddha (*trikaya*). It is the outer or phenomenal appearance, the tangible something that can be contacted on the realms of illusion, the incarnation body. The other two vestures are *dharmakāya*, and *sambhogakāya*.

28 How 'sins', i.e., one's *karma*, can be forgiven via confessionals could only have been conceived in the minds of unscrupulous clergy vying for temporal power over the masses, because 'sins' can really only be redeemed through one's rectifying 'works', for 'as you sow that you shall also reap' *(Gal. 6:7)*.

so we get the belief system of today.[29]

One's 'sins' *(karma)* are only forgiven through working them off by suffering the exact reciprocal of what was engendered. For as Paul says:

> Be not deceived; God is not mocked: for whatsoever a man soweth, that he shall also reap. For he that soweth to his flesh shall of the flesh reap corruption; but he that soweth of the Spirit shall of the Spirit reap life everlasting.[30]

The phrase 'soweth to his flesh' is but another way of describing the generation of desire based mental-emotional *saṃskāras.* The sowing 'of the Spirit' can be rephrased to 'generating the acts that produce enlightenment'.

The information in *Mark 4:11-12* is so important that it appears four more times in the Bible. First in the original passage of *Isaiah 6:8-12,* where an injunction is given directly to Isaiah from God, then also in *Matthew 13:15, John 12:40* and *Acts 28:27.* The statement in *Matthew 13:15* that refers to those who need to be spoken to in parables states:

> For this people's heart is waxed gross, and *their* ears are dull of hearing, and *their* eyes they have closed; lest at any time they should see with their eyes, and hear with their ears, and should understand with *their* heart, and should be converted, and I should heal them.

This ability to 'see with their eyes, and hear with their ears', refers to the internal 'eyes and ears', which are the *chakras.* When opened they allow one to experience aspects of the inner realms. People's hearts have been 'waxed gross' by the expression of the desire-mind via excessive Solar Plexus centre activity. It prevents the Heart's true purpose from manifesting. With the understanding that would come if their Heart *chakra* had been prematurely awakened, aspects of the 'mysteries of the kingdom of heaven' *(Matt. 13:11)* would be perceived long before people are ready to receive them. Their grossness of heart

29 This is probably the best they can do, as they have eliminated from their eschatology whole categories of phenomena relating to the subjective planes of perception, the psyche of the human unit, and its relation to the universe, because of narrow-minded, materialistic dogma formulated from the third Century after Jesus' death onwards.

30 *Gal. 4:7-8.*

(lack of compassion, basic materialistic attitudes) and dullness of mind structure, would fight right interpretation. It refers also to the lack of adequate vibrancy of the cellular and etheric substance of the brain, preventing such perceptions from being obtained. Such people have not undergone the training and preparation that Jesus' twelve apostles had, who were given to know of the Mysteries. A training that is partly revealed exoterically, but is mostly veiled by the proverbs that Jesus gives, and the general phraseology of the gospels.

> And the disciples came, and said unto him. Why speakest thou unto them in parables? He answered and said unto them, Because it is given unto you to know the mysteries of the kingdom of heaven, but unto them it is not given. For whosoever hath, to him shall be given, and he shall hath more abundance: but whosoever hath not, from him shall be taken away even that he hath. Therefore I speak to them in parables: because they seeing see not; and hearing they hear not, neither do they understand.[31]

This refers to people who are converted to aspects of these esoteric teachings for which they have no true capacity to understand and lack wise guidance. Their tendency then will be to desire psychic powers for selfish purposes, and so commit mistakes such as abusive psychic control of others, aggrandisement of material resources for themselves, and sex-magic that are associated with the glamours of wrongly awakened psychic perception. This will necessitate the demonstration of future healing work upon them alluded to in statements like 'and I should heal them' by the teacher, who's *karma* it is to rectify mistakes made by their students. The teacher is *always* karmically responsible for the results of his teachings if the student earnestly follows them. Thus if those teachings produce psychic disaster then the teacher is doubly culpable, for the effect of erroneous or short-sighted teachings upon the mind and emotions of the student, and for the disastrous manner in which they manifest. To such students, the little that they have will have to be taken from them.

Jesus was well aware of the law of *karma* and of the dangers associated with giving out real esoteric knowledge (the Mysteries) to the unready. They are those who are selfishly or pridefully motivated,

---

31 *Matt. 13:10-13.*

and who would 'kill and stone the prophets and those sent to them'.[32] This is done by means of critical thought-forms and various types of desire-mind reactions, concretising the teachings into unyielding 'stone', as well as by the unthinking narrow-mindedness of the orthodoxy, who will only think in terms of rigorous, prescribed ideas and thought-streams peculiar to their specific religious tradition. It should be noted that the esoteric doctrines of the Mysteries are always fluid, mutable, and are capable of interpretations from many levels of perception at once. They are universal in application and incorporate the essential teachings of all major myths and religious traditions.

Parables and other veiled teachings constitute the sum of the information given in the Old and New Testaments, which is also the case for other religious texts. Indeed, the more ancient the text, the more veiled, and it is from such information that orthodox Christians derive their belief system. The true esoteric import can only be understood by those that have been trained, or are in the process of being trained, in the Mysteries. They receive these 'ear-whispered truths' from the enlightened Teacher whilst seated for meditation, and within the meditation substance that emanates from the all-expansive embrace of the awakening lotus of the Heart.[33]

Such information is not simply empirical knowledge well reasoned out by means of the intellect. It lies outside the bounds of empiricism

---

32 *Matt. 23:37.*

33 In *The Tibetan Book of the Dead,* 3-5, W.Y. Evans-Wentz states that:
'Some of the more learned lāmas, including the late Lāma Kazi Dawa-Samdup, have believed that since very early times there has been a secret international symbol-code in common use among the initiates, which affords a key to the meaning of such occult doctrines as are still jealously guarded by religious fraternities in India, as in Tibet, and in China, Mongolia, and Japan.

In like manner, Occidental occultists have contended that the hieroglyphical writings of ancient Egypt and of Mexico seem to have been, in some degree, a popularized or exoteric outgrowth of a secret language. They argue, too, that a symbol-code was sometimes used by Plato and other Greek philosophers, in relation to Pythagorean and Orphic lore; that throughout the Celtic world the Druids conveyed all their esoteric teachings symbolically... the Pitakas lack much of the Buddha's yogīc teachings, and that it is chiefly these teachings which, in many instances, have been handed down esoterically to the present day.

"Esoteric Buddhism", as it has come to be called—rightly or wrongly—seems to depend in large measure upon "ear-whispered" doctrines of this character, conveyed according to long-established and inviolable rule, from guru to shiṣhya, by word of mouth alone.'

and argumentative reasoning. Indeed, it is the effect of Divine Reason, where such Reason is the result of internal revelation-vision projected to the 'mind's-eye' by the Sambhogakāya Flower, or the inner Teacher. It is not an expression of the mental images concocted by the imaginative mind utilising the conditionings formed from this life alone. Rather, it is the gain of many past lives of achievement in the gross world, and in domains yet undreamt by our empiricists. Indeed it is still little understood, except in generalised terms, by many meditation teachers.

The wisdom tradition, astralism and magic

The Mysteries of the Kingdom of 'God' have always existed, since before 'the foundation of the world'.[34] True esoteric schools that assist people to rightly awaken their Divinity have always appeared throughout history. Such, for instance, are the ones started in ancient Greece by Orpheus, and then Pythagoras of Crotona, with related temples of Initiation externalising at such places as Ephesus and Delphi in Greece, Heliopolis and Alexandria in Egypt. Later, Tibet became the locus for the containment of the ancient Mystery tradition, with its adept *yogins* (Initiates of the meditation path) utilising the veiled terminology of the Tantras, and that which is 'ear-whispered' to convey their more esoteric doctrines.

Jesus was taken to Egypt by his parents when he was a child, which implies that he was taken to an esoteric School for proper education.[35] Egypt was the home of the ancient Mystery Schools, then centred around Alexandria, and its vast library that housed the sum of ancient knowledge. There were, for instance, communities of Buddhist monks living there (from whom he could have gained teachings) as a consequence of Alexander the Great having earlier conquered Kashmir and Afghanistan, then a major base for Buddhism. For Jesus to appear suddenly on the world stage at the river Jordan he needed prior spiritual training and preparation for his mission. All ancient civilisations founded centres for such learning, and up until the time of the invasion of Tibet by the Chinese, certain localities in Tibet (e.g. Shigatse) served as the focus for such Schools.

---

34 *Matt. 13:35:* 'I will utter things which have been kept secret from the foundation of the world'.

35 *Matt. 2:13.*

In the West there was the Masonic and Alchemical traditions, early Rosicrucianism (for which there are now modern imitators) with its story of Christian Rosencreutz, and Jewish mysticism centred upon the Kabbalah. There are also examples of groups centred around certain enlightened individuals, such as Francis Bacon, Jacob Boehme, and Comte de Saint-Germain, as custodians of these Mysteries. The student must, however, take care not to speculate too much on the personages of the past. In fact, those who claim to demonstrate great occult knowledge are rarely (if ever) enlightened adepts on the white path. Many speculative and sensationalised claims are made by glamoured occultists and mystics concerning such personages. These stories sound reasonable but are often distortions of the truth.

Some undoubted emissaries of the White Brotherhood, however, were H. P. Blavatsky[36] and her esoteric successor, Alice A. Bailey. Up to the present decade much of what was to be revealed to humanity by the White Brotherhood was found in their books, but even in such books as Blavatsky's *The Secret Doctrine* some of the information is veiled. (These were then promptly distorted by later Theosophists and others who grasped only the more exoteric and elementary aspects of the teachings.[37]) We also have Helena Roerich, who gave out many very beautiful stanzas of coded information in her books on *Agni Yoga*.

The teachings on the *chakras* presented in the books by A. Bailey are of great value, but much is also omitted because of the problems of the 'hard of heart'. My books have revealed considerably more,[38] to lay the basis of a future science that will eventually supplant the dogmatic materialism of the present epoch. With regards to claims made in the past concerning how to awaken the powers of the *chakras* in various occult and yoga texts, the student needs to consider the next two possibilities.

---

36 For instance, Evans-Wentz states in *The Tibetan Book of the Dead,* 7 footnote 1, that 'The late Lāma Kazi Dawa-Samdup was of the opinion that, despite the adverse criticism directed against H. P. Blavatsky's works, there is adequate internal evidence in them of their author's intimate acquaintance with the higher lāmaistic teachings, into which she claimed to have been initiated'.

37 Despite this, Blavatsky's Teachings have laid a firm foundation for all subsequent presentations of the nature of the Council of Bodhisattvas.

38 For reasons explained in the earlier volumes of this *Treatise on Mind.*

a. The teacher is ignorant of the true nature of the law of *karma* and the mysteries of the enlightened being. He is one of the converted but 'hard of heart', pridefully walking in the vale of illusion and glamoured perceptions, ensnared by the lure of the lower psyche, and is esoterically 'blind and deaf'. The blind leading the blind is a quick road to disaster. Why follow them? Being indirectly responsible for the effects of the teachings upon the pupil, the teacher must be constantly meticulous in reviewing the motives, methods and teachings, to ensure that everything coming in thought, word, or deed is harmless, serving only to develop that which expresses the greatest good in the student. The earnest aspirant must therefore seek out such a one instead of the spiritual charlatan. The *karma* from following unwise instructors may also lead one to develop psychic, psychological, or physical sicknesses.

b. He is on *the left hand path*, consciously or unconsciously walking the way of the black magician. This is the wide gate and broad way 'that leadeth to destruction' *(Matthew 7:13)*. This way represents the road to darkness and unmitigated evil. The exponents of this path follow the 'father of all lies', as explained in *John 8:40-46*. Beginners are at first generally quite unaware of this process, because the wish-fulfilling gem of their desire natures is fed all the way. They hear only what they want to hear, and take only aspects of teachings that suit their ambitions, distorting them as they will, and disregard the inevitable warnings from 'above' (from Hierarchy or the Sambhogakāya Flower). The dark ones work upon them with telepathic suggestion and subtle forms of psychic coercion, thus they become increasingly enmeshed in the mire of separative, self-willed, selfish activity. They develop much apparent power on the material and psychic levels, but the consequence is imprisonment in the hell realms of karmic retribution. (The lower astral, mental and dense physical planes.)

The activity of the Wrathful Deities helps to overcome the *saṃskāras* in a later life when conversion back to the white *dharma* is happening. Many Initiates have a mixture of both types of *karma,* whereupon generally in the earlier part of their life they must deal with the effects of nefarious psychic activity from past lives, and later they tread the pure white path under the enlightened guidance of a Master of Wisdom. Milarepa was a prime example.[39] In Milarepa's case this necessitated seven years of near back breaking 'healing' at the hands of his *guru* Marpa. Marpa was not directly responsible for the instructions given to Milarepa by a black magician, but once he accepted Milarepa as a disciple he took on the responsibility of helping him to gain enlightenment in the most propitious way. In doing so, as much as possible of Milarepa's *karma* had to be cleansed.

Points a and b above, as well as the taking of hallucinogens, are often perceived as the quick way to developing psychic powers. This may be so, because they feed the line of least resistance associated with the practitioner's desires. Little needs to be mastered except the appropriate projection of the Will and certain lines of occult knowledge. However, they are in fact the long, arduous, tortuous path in the 'outer darkness' where there shall be much 'weeping and gnashing of teeth'.[40] This is the road of perpetual karmic involvement with the arenas of sickness, death, transience, sensual allurements, and the dull, though sometimes alluring colourings in the murky depths of the astral sea, or its Fiery abode, because of the nature of the *manasic saṃskāras* accrued.[41] *Matthew 25:29-36* states:

> For unto every one that hath shall be given, and he shall have abundance: but from him that hath not shall be taken away even that which he hath. And cast ye the unprofitable servant into outer darkness: there shall be weeping and gnashing of teeth. When the Son of man shall come in his glory, and all the holy angels with him, then shall he sit upon the throne of his glory: And before him shall be gathered all nations: and he shall separate them one from another, as a shepherd divideth *his* sheep from the goats: And he shall set the sheep on his right hand, but the goats on the left. Then shall the King say unto them on his right hand, Come, ye blessed of my Father, inherit the kingdom prepared for you from the foundation of the world: For I was an hungred, and ye gave me meat: I was thirsty, and ye gave me

39 See W.Y. Evans-Wentz, *Tibet's Great Yogī Milarepa,* (Oxford University Press, London, 1951).

40 *Matt 25:30.*

41 Note that the word astral means 'starry'.

> drink: I was a stranger, and ye took me in...Then shall he say also unto them on the left hand, Depart from me, ye cursed, into everlasting fire, prepared for the devil and his angels: For I was an hungred, and ye gave me no meat: I was thirsty, and ye gave me no drink: I was a stranger, and ye took me not in: naked, and ye clothed me not: sick, and in prison, and ye visited me not.

This passage relates to the difference between the right hand path (the forces of Love and Light) and that of the left hand path (of materialism, the dark brotherhood). The term 'sheep' here refers to the way of the white brotherhood because they follow the group laws to liberation, and symbolically offer the fleece off their backs to benefit others. They are led by 'the good shepherd' (the Christ, the head of the Hierarchy of Light). The 'goats' in this metaphor refer to the dark brotherhood because they are more individualistic in nature and are often found in craggy terrain, which symbolises the sharp nature of the separative concretion of mind. The left hand path is the *iḍā* way of intelligent development and materialistic thinking brought to an extreme. The right hand path is the *piṇgala* way of development of Love-Wisdom.

Both the 'sheep' and the 'goats' follow the Initiation path, but there is a sharp divide at the stage of the third Initiation, which is implied by the phrase 'When the Son of man shall come in his glory, and all the holy angels with him'. This alludes to some of the visions provided at that Initiation, which happens at Shambhala ('the kingdom prepared for you from the foundation of the world'). Those following the left hand path cannot enter that domain, hence there is a parting of the ways.

The word 'everlasting' of the phrase 'everlasting fire, prepared for the devil and his angels' implies lasting forever, or for a very long time. Christian theologians however have emphasised 'forever'. Be that as it may, what is implied here is that the Fiery *saṃskāras* developed by dark brotherhood activity follows the perpetuator forever. They must one day be converted into those of Love-Wisdom, and this may take more than one solar incarnation, literally 'forever'. Until then there is a perpetual cycle of generation of evil *karma,* which inevitably must be paid back. There is a special zone, the 'eighth sphere', reserved for such recalcitrants wherein they experience the *karma* of much of their *manasic* misdeeds.

This then is the 'everlasting fire' mentioned above, and indeed is a hell zone for the residents therein until they are released at an appropriate cycle—for all must be given a chance for redemption and evolutionary progress, but the *saṃskāras* linger on. Such a compassionate course of action is the only way possible for a 'God' that 'is love'.[42]

One must note that there is no such thing as time upon the astral plane, wherein the heaven and hell states that normal humans experience exist. Time only relates to our three-dimensional world of experience, where a linear sequence is seen from the past to the far distant future. The term 'forever' in this astral zone therefore refers to a continuum in consciousness that appears virtually endless.

In the *Tibetan Book of the Dead,* the astral body is styled the 'pure (or shining) illusory body'[43] (Skt. *māyāvirūpa*), upon which one's *karma* will descend (or upon the 'thought body') as 'the fearful ambush of the *Bardo*'.[44] This astralism (ceaseless glamour-filled selfish activity, as well as the anger, lust and ignorance that lies at the heart of the Buddhist wheel of Life and rebirth) becomes a hell-like entombment for the consciousness after the death of the physical vehicle.[45] One must then reap the karmic consequences of the emotional abuse of other's as well as one's own psyche. The hell states mentioned in all religious scriptures exist as a product of collective beliefs on a worldwide scale over a large time period.

It is consciousness that reincarnates, not the former personality structure, so once the body dies, then all these allurements and activities descend upon the person producing the Bardo experiences. This then is the true meaning of the passage in *Heb. 9:27* 'And as it is appointed unto men once to die, but after this the judgment'. Theologians have interpreted this to refer to only one birth for an individual. This is true for the bodily nature, which dies but once, but not the consciousness,

---

42 *1John 4:7-8,* which states: 'Beloved, let us love one another: for love is of God; and every one that loveth is born of God, and knoweth God. He that loveth not knoweth not God; for God is love.'

43 Evans-Wentz, *The Tibetan Book of the Dead,* fn 1, 100.

44 Ibid., 107. On Page 160 ff. Evans-Wentz gives the exoteric description of such *karma* from the Buddhist perspective.

45 Which can also be viewed as the 'everlasting fire, prepared for the devil and his angels' in *Matt. 25:41.*

which perpetually reincarnates. After each death there certainly is a 'judgement' based upon the *saṃskāras* generated and consequent *karma*, which determines where one goes in the Bardo state. Perpetual rebirth of consciousness until it is perfected is the only thing that will make one perfect 'unto the measure of the stature of the fulness of Christ'.[46]

Psychic powers versus the Heart centre's wisdom

The path of meditation and the transformation of *saṃskāras* is that which helps make one 'perfect'. Meditation awakens knowledge of the inner worlds, and offers an important field of service therein. When it comes to the astral plane, such ability concerns the development of the minor *siddhis*. Before such psychic powers can be granted, the personality's self-sustaining ego must first die, and this is the major battle on the way to enlightenment, the meditator's personal Armageddon. Our societies have many who claim to have psychic powers through this or that system of knowledge and who are willing to teach others the development of such powers for a fee. Psychics they may indeed be, though generally of the lower psyche, involving mediumship, or aberrant clairvoyant and clairaudient perceptions that are often clouded by emotions and misleading ignorance. Charging a fee for spiritual teachings generally violates the law of Love that guides all enlightened beings. The spiritual lore is freely given to the teacher from 'above' and must be freely disseminated to all worthy recipients. As in all things, wisdom must, however, be applied. *Karma* is involved in all transactions, and the teacher must understand this law well. The teacher is obliged to give teachings freely because of the law of Love (compassion), nevertheless, various material circumstances of the teacher generally necessitates monetary assistance so that the service can best be promulgated.

Psychic powers certainly are not an object in themselves, and wisdom on the path to enlightenment is a vastly more valuable attainment. The development of psychic powers in themselves produces many karmic consequences, and liberation from *saṃsāra* is rarely one of them, unless the ego is extinguished.

---

46 *Eph. 4:13*, 'Till we all come in the unity of the faith, and of the knowledge of the Son of God, unto a perfect man'.

The higher spiritual perceptions develop via the centres above the diaphragm to awaken the complete capacities of enlightenment. This incorporates past life recall when needed, and telepathic communication with any member of the Council of Bodhisattvas, the great sages of past ages one has *karma* with. We then have the ability to vision and perceive all things in the phenomenal and psychic realms (the cosmos as a multi-dimensional whole), and to envision the trend of *karma* into the future. All manifests according to the degree that the Initiates have developed true Love for all kingdoms of Nature, including the *devas*[47] with whom they share service work. Initiation testings must therefore be passed on the way to full enlightenment. The Initiation path conditioned all past sages, such as Krishna, Buddha, and Christ-Jesus, in a similar manner that it does candidates for eventual Buddhahood today.

The Initiate works from the realms of reality, the domains of light supernal, cosmic Might, via the all-embracive oneness of the Heart in the Head and the Heart centre, the fount of *bodhicitta*. The Heart centre helps seed enlightening visions and counters the sometimes murky impressions, and often sensationalised images coming from below the diaphragm via the Solar Plexus centre. The Solar Plexus centre is the Achilles' heel of those who have not yet mastered their emotions. Generally, they confuse Solar Plexus phenomena with something far higher and subtler, because clairvoyant abilities are an effect of this centre, plus the awakened Inner Round set of minor *chakras*. (They are governed by the Solar Plexus centre.) Clairvoyant images, however, are valid and do reveal images pertaining to truth when the Solar Plexus centre is properly stilled, and thus acts as a mirror reflecting the reality from above the diaphragm. This reality concerns impressions from the Sambhogakāya Flower, the Hierarchy of Light, and for Initiates of the higher degrees, Shambhala and some happenings in cosmos. Any petal or combination of petals of the Heart centre (reflecting the Heart in the Head) may be fully awakened to channel such images. The petals of the Heart are responsive to the potencies of the twelve signs of the zodiac, which are the higher correspondence of these petals in cosmos.

Most meditators, however, receive the subtle images and vibrant revelations that come from the Heart centre via a receptive Solar Plexus

---

47 The angels of Christianity.

centre, often producing a certain intensity of feeling. The images often then come to be veiled in the symbolic representations and colourations possible for the Solar Plexus. Such feeling-perceptions then manifest as high revelations for the meditator.

Ecstatic visualisations have been the mainstay of the infancy of the religious development of humanity, producing the mythologies and stories of Gods and their exploits, of the ancient religions. The symbolism pertaining to such myths veil much esoteric truth. The past focus was upon the development of the *chakras* below the diaphragm. Nowadays the focus of spiritual development should be upon the centres above the diaphragm. Full enlightenment and liberation is the objective, and not mere visualisations, adoration of, and communications with any aspect of the trinity represented as 'God' (Father, Son, Mother), His emissaries, the Holy Angels, or various deities. The complete integration of the powers of the Heart and Mind (of the Heart and Throat centres) is needed for the development of the necessary Love-Wisdom, with the power of the force of Love (*bodhicitta*) being the expression of all resultant activity. Then the Ājñā centre and the full potency of the Head lotus can be awakened. Eventually the meditator will live entirely in the Head centre, which absorbs and synthesises all of the *prāṇas* from the *chakras* below it. The Head, Heart, Throat, and Ājñā centres then function as a unity in the awakened One.

The awakening of the Head lotus happens at the attainment of the third Initiation. Centralisation of the Initiate's focus upon the Heart centre happens at the second Initiation, and is mastered at the fourth. The Throat centre is empowered at the first Initiation. So powerful is the pull of the emotions in human life that the battle to overcome the vicissitudes of the Watery *saṃskāras* of the Solar Plexus centre takes the entire time from the path of aspiration to the third Initiation to accomplish.[48]

Psychics extract thought-forms from the whirling oceans of thoughts in the astral realm that come from the massed image-producing activity of people's Solar Plexus and Inner Round *chakras*. Any of these can be mistaken as communications from Deity by the unenlightened. Apparitions from deceased entities, or projections from the forces of evil

48 As the path of Initiation is the subject of the later chapters little more needs to be said concerning them here.

(the dark brotherhood), are also often seen as visitations from enlightened beings or space travellers (e.g., abductions) and the like. Many psychic phenomenon is mistaken for what it is not. (The dark brothers are also masters of forms of meditation techniques necessary to their path, and manifest very potent types of phenomena to fool the unwary.) Myriad are the forms of delusion associated with the partial awakening of the psychic centres below the diaphragm, and myriad are the deluded.

Awakening psychic powers without developing the necessary virtues, such as egolessness, desirelessness, overriding compassion, and the disciplining of the body, speech, and mind needed for psychic purity, is the path of the black magician. Great karmic consequences are accrued upon this path, no matter what the claim making of the exponent concerned may be. The mentalistic use of the personal will to force the (lower) *chakras* to awaken is a major problem with many meditation teachings, because it is the basis of Solar Plexus magic practiced by the sorcerer. The resultant strongly ingrained *saṃskāras* will later have to be cleansed, often taking millennia to be accomplished, through much karmic woe, the right use of the will and the agency of the Wrathful Deities.

Note the wording in *Matthew 7:15-16* with respect to this: 'Beware of false prophets, which come to you in sheep's clothing, but inwardly they are ravening wolves. Ye shall know them by their fruits. Do men gather grapes of thorns, or figs of thistles?' The qualities of *the wolf,* or pack of wolves, out to ravish the flock of 'the good shepherd'[49] is one of the major character traits of our brothers of dark countenance. A sheep symbolises the characteristics of a disciple (here symbolically of the Christ, the head of the Council of Bodhisattvas), at an early stage of their spiritual journey. The disciple is at first meek, gentle hearted, ignorant of most facets of the spiritual life, thus easily led astray by those of forceful or deceitful demeanour. The good shepherd is a Bodhisattva, a practitioner of the white *dharma*, who engenders qualities of peace and tranquillity in all that is done, and is ready at any time to give 'the wool' off his/her back to help the needy and dispossessed of the spiritual warmth they desire.

The law of Love is such that a highly Initiated member of the

---

49 *John 10:14,* 'I am the good shepherd, and know my sheep, and am known of mine'.

Hierarchy, the symbolic good shepherd, always incarnates during any cycle and situation of need in the world to help them safely travel the green pastured way to the realm of enlightenment. Karmic law is at all times woven to produce the most beneficent results, taking what is often the most maleficent *karma* generated by the disciple into account. All such *karma* must be cleansed upon the upward way of liberation from *saṃsāra's* woes.

The Initiate knows the way, through painful past experiences, of how to avoid the wolves, the brambled paths, and craggy meandering ways that prevent the onset of enlightenment. The sheep-like novices must listen to spiritual leadership. Teaching them rightly is always the major task of a 'good shepherd', and the method concerned involves testings undertaken on the path of Initiation for those who are part of the Initiate's *maṇḍala*.

The quality of the teaching and related distortions of spiritual teachers are self-evident for those possessing wisdom, but well-nigh impossible to discern by most aspirants and beginners upon the path. However, at whatever level one is at spiritually, so one will find an appropriate teaching or teacher that is the rightfully ordained one. Any teaching is right that will lead a person from one stage or level of understanding to the next higher one, which advances him or her deeper into the path of Love. The distortions and errors in many teachings do not matter much at first. All forms of understanding and experiences are useful (and indeed, often are needed) for the novice.

One should be warned that the apparently miraculous healing of some of the symptoms of one or other of the diseases that afflict people is the surest way to lure the gullible to part with their valuables. These valuables can be of an emotional, psychic, mental, or monetary kind. Being a healer is consequently one of the best disguises for the wolves to take, especially when coupled with the facade of being a spiritual teacher, or being divinely inspired.[50] Jesus stated:

---

50 Black magicians possess much capability to heal the physical body, as our gross form is concrete substance, and therefore is a direct expression of the material domain they rule (and are conditioned by). Psychic manipulation of material substance is their forte, the base of their power, and in doing so many are converted to their circles. But their method of healing reveals their true colours. Their methodology is that of the lower psychicism, thus they are not able to utilise bright vibrant colours and the related

> Wherefore by their fruits ye shall know them. Not every one that saith unto me, Lord, Lord, shall enter into the kingdom of heaven; but he that doeth the will of my Father which is in heaven. Many will say to me in that day, Lord, Lord, have we not prophesied in thy name? and in thy name have cast out devils? and in thy name done many wonderful works? And then will I profess unto them, I never knew you: depart from me, ye that work iniquity.[51]

Those that 'prophesied in thy name', that 'in thy name have cast out devils' and accomplished 'many wonderful works' are those that manifested as spiritual teachers, demonstrating psychic powers, or apparently philanthropic enterprises with egoistical motives. They have not 'the will of my Father which is in heaven', which refers to passing the Initiation testings that will allow them to overcome the allurements of the lower psyche. This path necessitates developing the Will-to-Love, and later the Will-of-Love on the way of demonstrating the Divine Will, which is the above mentioned 'the will of my Father'.[52] They must follow the same path internally that Jesus had done exoterically, that will allow them a direct covenant with his 'Father', the One Initiator.[53] The demonstration of the lower psychic powers will not do, but the mastery of the Watery emotions of the Solar Plexus centre and awakening the Heart centre will. The way of Initiation holds the key.

We then see that such 'workers of iniquity' principally masquerade as spiritual teachers, healers, and philanthropists, seemingly doing their 'good works' in the name of the Lord, oft with great outer pretentiousness, but inwardly their motives are rarely truly loving. The outward good works are often the facade of those who have amassed fortunes in ethically unsound ways (though legally allowable); by lies, deceit, selfish financial manipulation and legalised thievery. They have cloaked their activities (and teachings) in righteousness by giving

---

prāṇic radiance in their works. Dull colours, gross energies, or those tinged with the grey or black are what they wield, easily discernible by the meditation-Mind, and by clairvoyance. Correct healing concerns more than healing just the symptoms on the physical body, and this they cannot do.

51 *Matt. 7:20-23.*

52 The Divine Will manifests in the form of the Will-of-Love *(bodhicitta)* in Bodhisattvas.

53 Sanat Kumāra: the planetary Logos, who will be explained in Volume 7 of this series, *The Constitution of Shambhala.*

a portion of their wealth for charitable works, or giving simple truths easily found elsewhere to mask self-serving fabrications. They thus endear large sections of the unthinking public to them. The bulk of their fortunes or teachings, however, serve not the common good, but their own power and pleasure-seeking enterprises.

The Bible warns, 'God is not mocked',[54] especially since we see that 'it is easier for a camel to go through the eye of a needle, than for a rich man to enter into the Kingdom of God'.[55] Those whose *karma* it is to possess large financial, psychic, or teaching resources, are tested in their ability to rightly handle such responsibility, for they must learn to dispense it wisely in such a manner that the greatest number are served thereby. The karmic rewards for not doing so, for selfish activity, have been hinted at above. This is especially so in our world which is overwhelmingly ruled by avarice. Here also we see the necessity for learning the art of meditation, to at all times discern what is right or wrong to do, through the development of a clear, calm, meditative mind when lucid, truthful perceptions can manifest with certainty.

When the conscious awakening of psychic perceptions are involved, students should take much care to ascertain that they have the best teacher available and not the masquerading wolf. The right and left hand paths, leading to 'heaven and hell' respectively, are discernible by those that take the trouble to do so. Beware those who promise quick (psychic) rewards, or great personal power; or who amass financial reserves for themselves; or those that demand strict obedience to every whim that comes from their mouths. In all of these forms of activity you have the disguises for the charlatan.

If a person had little meditation training in previous lives, then it is obvious that he/she would find meditation teachings and techniques difficult to understand and master. A great deal of encouragement, explanation, and time needs to be applied. The beginner tends to be glamoured by some of the elementary effects of the meditation process, mistaking lower psychic states to be of the highest order. He/she would tend to have little or no understanding of the differing grades of subtlety, or distortions of truth associated with the various teachings

---

54 *Gal 6:7.*

55 *Matt. 19:24.*

or experiences. The strong desire for psychic power is revelled in by the mind of the seeker. This often causes the neophytes to move from teacher to teacher, or to be very devoted to the first teacher that deftly feeds their glamours.

Once aspects of psychic phenomena have been obtained, then the tendency will be to boast great psychic capabilities, and to capitalise upon them in one way or another. Such people become psychically deluded, basking in clouds of desire-mind substance, in astralism. They little realise that all such phenomena are aspects of the great illusion (*saṃsāra*) and have no inherent reality, other than the outer seeming. Seers and clairvoyants prophesise the future with little genuine understanding of the source of their visions. Distortions of the truth everywhere sprout forth sickly wings, and phantasmagorical beasts of mind-substance devour the unwary. Huge beasts are everywhere on the prowl, and multitudes, even the educated elite, are devoured by such false utterances, broadcast far and wide by the mass media. Proper development of the meditation-Mind is what will allow a person to see his/her way clear of such monsters.

This is the basis of what Jesus referred to in *Matt. 24:4-24:*

> And Jesus answered and said unto them, Take heed that no man deceive you. For many shall come in my name, saying I am Christ; and shall deceive many... And because iniquity shall abound, the love of many shall wax cold... For there shall arise false Christs, and false prophets, and shall shew great signs and wonders; insomuch that, if *it were* possible, they shall deceive the very *elect.*

Those that boast of psychic powers, and related intellectual prowess, are viewed by the enlightened as being naïve, similar to playing with matches in a highly inflammable area. Here 'the elect' are the Initiates that follow the ways of developing wisdom and Love in all things.

The Book of Golden Precepts, a Buddhist text about the attainment of the enlightened state, starts off, with good reason, with the phrase:

> These instructions are for those ignorant of the dangers of the lower Iddhi. (The word *Iddhi* is the Pali equivalent of the Sanskrit term *siddhi*, meaning psychic power.)[56]

56 Translated by H. P. Blavatsky under the title *The Voice of the Silence.* (Theosophical Publishing House, Wheaton, Illinois,1998).

The lower psychic states (and planes of perception from which they derive) are of the same nature as a drug induced experience, and can certainly become the realms of *hell*, as the obsessing state can be carried after the death of the personality.

The average Westerner lives at a fast pace, and usually in an emotionally charged atmosphere. His/her mind seems always to be preoccupied with things to do, whilst the affluence of the consumer society offers myriads of indulgences, from TV, computer games, to continuous rounds of partying. There is an incessant bombardment of visual images, audible barrage, and alluring sensations, whilst there are a host of printed material, sensationalised images, and movies to attract attention. All forms of sensual pursuit are at one's disposal, including a panoply of legal and illegal drugs that numb the mind and senses, providing transitory euphoria, dulling perception, or else producing irascible, nervous excitement and emotional-mental exhaustion.

In the light of the above, it seems a minor miracle that any can find the energy to overcome these allurements and regularly sit to quieten the mind and emotions so that the higher perceptions and corresponding sensitivities can be obtained. This then is the task of the modern meditator. He/she must live the dual life of being the *yogin,* abstracted via meditative pursuit into the inner world of creative livingness, and yet also be outwardly focussed amidst the hustle and bustle that our civilisation inflicts upon us.

2

Healing, the Elect and Group Evolution

Healing oneself

The question often asked by the beginner is: 'what has healing got to do with true meditation practices?' The answer will always be the same by the enlightened one, *'everything!'* Right meditation and healing are virtually synonymous terms, in that one produces the other.

The application of any meditative technique must always be healing in its effect, if it is to produce enlightenment, thus being true white magic. Healing produces the elimination of everything within the consciousness and threefold personality structure that is associated with, or causative of, disease, disharmony and premature death. This is a natural consequence of techniques associated with the meditative path that cleanse and transform gross *saṃskāras* and associated base mental-emotions. This cleansing takes much time, for many lifetimes of creating such attributes are not easily or quickly eliminated.

In successful meditation practice a quiescent, awakening personality is acquired, and it contacts the subtle domain of the abstract Mind, from which divine Fiery energy pours down. This Fiery energy automatically throws out the grosser substance (of disease) that offers resistance to it. The person must consequently deal with its effects in a conscious way. There are many overlapping cycles of such activity. Progress is made from cleansing the coarsest aspects of the body, speech, and mind (physical, astral, and mental substance) to the subtlest, until eventually the person stands transformed, transfigured, and consubstantial with that which is his/her fundamental integral Being. This is an objective of the incarnation process. When the Clear Light of Mind, or the Void, is a natural expression of one's awareness then disease or sickness (as normally understood) is no longer possible.

The detail of this transfiguration process that occurs as a consequence of practical meditation is described in Volumes 4 and 5 of this treatise. The key lies in the attitude of impersonality achieved by the student. The nature of the student's mind-patterns must change. One must decentralise one's entire thinking process away from the concept of 'I' or 'me'. This necessitates embracing concepts of the whole, of one's essential unity with the interrelated multi-dimensional universe, without making oneself the centre of attention therein. *Saṃsāra* and *śūnyatā* must come to be an integrated whole in the Mind's Clear Light. We therefore have the engendering of the *saṃsāra-śūnyatā* nexus. To reside at this nexus is a major objective of meditation.[1]

We begin with the 'turning about in the deepest seat of consciousness',[2] away from the 'lower four' (the major *chakras*, centres of consciousness below the diaphragm, associated with the field of desire, sensual sensations and images), to the 'higher three' above the diaphragm (the Heart, Throat and Head centres) wherein the enlightenment-consciousness will be found. The student will later discover that such terms as 'higher three' and 'the lower four' have many levels of interpretation and application; for the application of meditation will lead to various fields of experience, states of awareness and learning procedures through contact and identification with beings previously undreamt of.

Meditation helps one to heal oneself, and ultimately, the surrounding environment, which is the extension of one's life in all directions of space. Meditation is the expression of the law of *karma* when properly unfolded,

---

1 As the philosophy concerning this nexus was explained throughout the previous volumes of this treatise I shall not delve into it here.

2 See Govinda, *Foundations of Tibetan Mysticism*, 75, where he states: 'It is the re-orientation, the new attitude, the turning away from the outside world of objects to the inner world of oneness, of completeness - the all-embracing universality of the mind. It is a new vista, 'a direction of the heart' (as Rilke calls it), an entering into the stream of liberation. It is the only miracle which the Buddha recognized as such and besides which all other *siddhis* are mere play things.'

and is based on the paradigm of the laws of evolution, when properly taught. This means that the stages of development of the meditation progress in a similar manner as that undertaken by the unitary expansion of the greater evolutionary space. Indeed, 'God' (an evolved Buddha from a long past world-cycle of evolution) is in a state of meditation as the entire 'creation', the spatial universe, unfolds. The meditation-Mind of Deity works in, through, and envelopes all that is, and that which must come to be. If the individual on the path to enlightenment is to be freed from the bonds of space-time and the transience of the personality nature, then he/she must learn to emulate the greater meditation-Mind unfolding. Meditation is thus the key to eventual absorption into the spaciousness of the greater Mind. For this we have no adequate terminology in any language, and of which the comparable Sanskrit terms, *parinirvāṇa, parinispanna*[3], *prajñāpāramitā*[4] and *dharmakāya* inadequately convey the intended meaning.

Regarding healing, the true healer does not really 'heal' as such, but rather assists the patient to effect his/her own recovery, and will take pains to ensure that the mistakes that caused the illness in the first place are not committed again. Neither will the true spiritual healer ask for money, or any other fee for his healing service. He/she knows that a healer cannot profit from another's distress, but will work on a donation basis through this example of giving, and generating goodwill from the patients to meet future physical plane needs. Ideally, the karmic interrelationships between the healer and the healed is known, that one must work with the laws of Love, colour and sound, and (at a later stage) consciously with the *devas* that embody all manifest Life to effect the healing.

Right education is *always* the true healing practice, and takes much wisdom and skill in action to apply. It should be understood that healing the physical body of its various aches and illnesses is *not* the most important thing, but rather the elimination of the deep-seated karmic causes and related inherited psychological and physiological tendencies (*saṃskāras*) from past lives. The healer must begin to truly treat the entire personality and not just the symptoms. The emotional-mental

3 That which comes from the 'absolute', thoroughly established absolute reality.

4 The perfection of Wisdom, the result of perfected discriminative awareness of a Buddha.

causes of illnesses, specifically of how the emotions produce ailments such as influenza, cancer, and all inflammatory sickness, should be analysed and treated. A quick fix, whether pills or herbs, is not the answer, for then similar or worse ailments will crop up later.

Everything must be viewed in terms of *energy,* as all things are constituted thus; but specifically so with all organisms that are alive, and that have their own specific inherent vitality (*jīva*). There can either be an excessive amount of *jīva* or a dearth. One category of entity (e.g., vitamins) has vitality to give (of varying colourings) and another vampirises. If the energy to be given is of the type needed by the body, then we have a vital, healthy physical body. If energy is strong but adverse to the well being of the body, then we have inflammatory types of disease (such as influenza). If the agent (such as some poisons and bacteria) devitalises, then we have diseases of congestion (e.g., tuberculosis) as substance builds up, but the vital life is drained away.

Much error has crept into orthodox healing practices in the desire of the healer to keep the body (the form nature) alive at all costs, despite the clear indications of the indwelling consciousness to vacate it. Healers must learn to work with the factor of death as a healing potency, and not against it, and this necessitates much meditative insight on the part of the practitioner. Once healers begin to understand and accept the laws of reincarnation and *karma*, they will then see the absurdity of many of the quandaries created by such things as euthanasia and treatment of chronically ill, or totally (mentally) incapacitated patients. There is really no such thing as death, except possibly, the 'death' of the human psyche, as a consequence of left hand practices. *(See Matt. 10:26-8.)*

The true healer will recognise the healing factor in the death of all aspects of the personality, and the teaching value of all illnesses, for they *teach what not to do.* They are caused by the transgressions of the laws of Love and Life, and the patient must be educated to recognise this. The *karma* always manifests in such a way that it rightly educates the individual, and if the lessons are not learnt, then they will be repeated in another way, until eventually the person learns to do what is right.

It is similar to a child learning how to walk. He must fall over many times, sometimes with painful results, before the skill is learnt. Similarly, the child must first touch the heat of a flame in order to understand, that although pretty, it is hot and can burn. Millennia-long cycles of karmic education concerning sickness, disease and suffering teaches the spiritual child how to walk in the realms of enlightened being/non-being, freed from all such ailments. He/she has fallen into *saṃsāric* involvement and allurement many times, and has learnt to detach from such activity, to rise up from the realms of darkness and to enter those of light. He/she has been burnt by premature tampering with psychic fires often enough to know what not to do. Consequently, we have the development of wisdom and compassion, the recognition of the activities in others that cause sicknesses and the like, that the wise one had formerly manifested and has now mastered. The right cures can then be offered to those that will listen and are willing also to undergo the disciplines that will produce mastery.

Such an enlightened understanding is well-nigh impossible to the materialist and orthodox 'healer', who will not consider the factor of reincarnation. Such a one generally manifests contempt and disdain at any suggestion of a subtle energy body, *saṃskāras, karma*, *chakra*s, and *devas*, as factors to be taken into account in the healing of diseases. The role that meditation plays in ascertaining the causes of ailments, as well as in assisting the patient to overcome physical, psychic, and psychological problems, will also need to be acknowledged.

The blindness of those trained in Western materialistic ethics and values is a major factor in propagating many aspects of sickness and disease in our societies. This is because true causes are not analysed, only the symptoms, and secondary disease-bearing factors, as are the microbes and viruses, upon which the diseases are blamed. When 'causes' are found, then only the most material, concrete ones are examined, such as direct poisons, germs, carcinogenic chemicals and the like. Other than direct poisons, such things only produce effects *after* the subtle causes have been operating for quite a while, and bodily warnings have gone unheeded. After all, if one produces a cesspool of base energy fields in one's body, then the inevitable effect is the massive breeding of primitive forms of life that are vitalised by the energy levels of this cesspool. They are the germs (etc.) responsible for disintegration and death when the body has not the vitality to fight off the mass invader.

People have thus been conditioned to look at the wrong factors as the causes of their distress. Centuries of mass socio-political, materialistic indoctrination have kept them in ignorance, thus laying the fertile ground work for the later concrete factors of disease-bearing organisms that concentrate symptoms at focal points within the body. This forces them to go to medical specialists who utilise an increasingly sophisticated array of elaborate and costly appliances and technological contrivances to analyse the symptoms, dissect the body, transplant organs, apply chemicals, and the like, to effect their 'cures'. For this the patient must pay the increasingly costly fees demanded.

True healing is far simpler,[5] as ordained by the same laws of Life, Light and Love embodied by the Logos, from whose Mind the amazingly ingenious and wondrous human form emanated in the first place. These laws have been in operation and incorporated into the perfectly integrated universe at large, long before the advent of modern science. Certainly, the many divinely inspired healers, such as Jesus, knew and utilised them.

Taking pills may alleviate the symptoms, but will do naught to challenge the true causes; it only postpones the inevitable. There are no miracle cures, except those associated with the disciplined self-cleansing activity and purity of lifestyle. In fact, it should be noted that the true healer knows that the healing potency comes not from oneself; one is only the *conscious* channel for divine energies, having developed the needed understanding and capacity to do so. As stated by Jesus: 'Verily, verily, I say unto you, The Son can do nothing by himself'.[6] The healer adds this incoming energy to the patient who is in the process of healing, and thus effects the cleansing of the diseased areas, or else

---

5 See, for instance, the life story of Dr. Edward Bach, originator of the Bach Flower healing system, who started out a Harley St. specialist, and progressively found simpler methods of healing, until he eventually could practise distant healings, even over the phone. The story is given in his biography: Nora Weeks, *The Medical Discoveries of Edward Bach, Physician.* (C. W. Daniel Company, Essex, 1973).

6 See *John 5:19-21.* 'Then answered Jesus and said unto them, Verily, verily, I say unto you, The Son can do nothing of himself, but what he seeth the Father do: for what things soever he doeth, these also doeth the Son likewise. For the Father loveth the Son, and sheweth him all things that himself doeth: and he will shew him greater works than these, that ye may marvel. For as the Father raiseth up the dead, and quickeneth *them*; even so the Son quickeneth whom he will'.

takes the diseased *prāṇas* into his/her own body, cleansing them with the radiance of the aura possessed. There are other healing techniques utilised by the true healer that space prevents delving into here.[7]

Beware of highly processed factory produced drugs, especially those derived from mineral substances. They are but corpses and skeletons of what was once vital and alive. They produce effects in the now, but postpone the inevitable. The *karma* of the postponed sickness will simply come out in another more virulent form in another part of the body at a later time, or in a later life.

The Western trained doctor, however, does have an excellent knowledge in anatomy and physiology and in surgical methods of healing, especially in trauma cases. Allopathic medicine therefore has its rightful place, but someday will work side by side with the more esoterically trained healer. The most effective cure for the patient can then manifest, with the emphasis being upon preventative techniques, where the patient is taught to heal him/herself. The role for the huge pharmaceutical industries that prey upon the sick and diseased for maximal profits will be severely limited. Doctors will no longer serve as agents for the egregious cupidity of the multinational corporations.

It should be noted that, esoterically, one views physical plane incarnation as death, for then the indwelling vital Life dies to the bountiful spiritual realms it is accustomed to, and incarnates into an illusional, corruptible form. One should therefore not deem the physical form to be all important. Important it is, because without it no enlightenment is possible, but it is not all there is to life. The subtle etheric form, the *chakras* and *nāḍīs,* are far more important, as this body represents the true principle or sheath into which the human unit has incarnated. The dense form is but the automaton. It automatically responds to the energies passing through the *nāḍīs.* This energy body therefore should be far more the focus of the healer and the patient than the objective form. The healer needs to be trained in techniques related to rightly dealing with the *prāṇas* associated with the form. Acupuncture is one such method, but it only deals with the smallest and most limited of the *chakras.*

---

7 See most texts on alternate healing methods, and for a more esoteric account: A.A. Bailey, *Esoteric Healing* (Lucis Publishing Company, New York).

The role of *devas* in healing

The true healers are the greater *devas* (solar *devas)* working via the doctors who use their 'corpses'–the agency of the prescribed drugs–as the foci for their work. The *devas* are the angels of Christianity, and are noted for their healing propensities, as in *John 5:4:*

> For an angel went down at a certain season into the pool, and troubled the water: whosoever then first after troubling the water stepped in was made whole of whatever disease he had.

One need not go to such a pool for healing, as the *devas* are omnipresent, and can be contacted consciously via right meditation techniques.

The psychic emanations from introducing 'corpses' into the body are effective in producing their own types of symptoms of disease, and in time *must* be eliminated from the living vital tissue. When done so, they will tend to affect further sicknesses. The patient goes to doctors for further chemotherapy, artificial organs and the like, and so the cycle continues. True meditation techniques will give one conscious contact with these angelic forces, as the *devas* are always predisposed to work with the compassionate ones that care, for they embody the realms of form, and their work is greatly facilitated by conscious cooperators. Such cooperative endeavour is the way for the medical profession of the future.

Govinda states that:

> the Tibetan word *'lha'*, which generally corresponds to the Indian word *'deva'*, i.e., an inhabitant of higher planes of existence (comparable to the Christian hierarchies of angels) is used also for *Dhyāni-Buddhas* and *-Bodhisattvas*...The meaning of the term *'lha'* depends on the context in which it is used and can have accordingly the following definitions:
>
> 1. Inhabitants of higher planes of existence *(deva)* who, though superior to man in certain ways, yet are subject to the laws of the world;
> 2. Earth-bound spirits, demons and genii of certain places or elements;
> 3. Mind-created forms or forces, like *Dhyāni-Buddhas, etc.*[8]

8 See Govinda, *Foundations of Tibetan Mysticism*, 111.

The lesser *devas* are the fairies, pixies, nature spirits and so forth. However, the greater *devas* specifically concerned with this healing work are self-conscious, of equal or greater intelligence than humans and could be better equated with the *gandharvas, apsaras*, and *ḍākinīs* of Tibetan Buddhism. Govinda explains that *ḍākinīs* are 'female embodiments of knowledge and magic power who—either in human or super-human form—played an important role in the lives of the *Siddhas*'.[9] He further states 'Thus *Dākinīs* become the genii of meditation, spiritual helpers, who inspired the *Sādhaka* and roused him from the illusion of worldly contentment. They were forces that awakened the dormant qualities of mind and soul'.[10]

The cycle is rapidly approaching when the *devas* (specifically those ruled by the violet Ray, 'the *devas* of the shadows'[11]) will make an approach to come closer to humanity's vision, so that cooperative work can be facilitated between the two kingdoms. Hence much information now needs to be promulgated to make people aware of their existence in such a way that they can envision a close rapprochement. The rules and mechanism associated with *deva* contact therefore need to be made known. The foundation is the development of Love by those who desire to cooperate, and a great deal of wisdom needs to accompany them. A new era of (magical) healing of human ails and of the planetary woe can then ensue.

The *devas* of the shadows are those that embody the etheric substance of all lives. Hence the *chakra* and *nāḍī* system of a human unit are constituted out of *deva* substance. As the *prāṇas* from *chakras* are utilised to effect healing, and all else concerning the corporeal manifestation of the human psyche, so we can see the importance of this grouping of intelligent lives. It will take time for humanity to comprehend that the forms into which they have incarnated are appropriated from the substance embodied by the *devas*. Such revelation will obviously drastically alter human perception as to how they perceive themselves, and how healing is best effected. The golden new age will manifest when there is active cooperation between the two kingdoms.

9 Ibid., 190.

10 Ibid., 192.

11 A.A. Bailey, *A Treatise on Cosmic Fire*, (Lucis Publishing, New York, 1977), 643 ff.

They are parallel streams of evolution, where the feminine *devas* embody the substance from which all we see in nature is constructed, and the masculine human kingdom represents the developing consciousness-bearing directive wills. Eventually there will be a marriage and fusion between the two kingdoms, which the Initiation process will reveal.[12]

The main points to consider in meditative healing

There are various factors involved in the appearance of disease, such as *karma* (individual, group, and national) and environmental factors. The mental-emotional conditioning of people is most important. One must also consider the quality of the auric substance that can be absorbed into one's psyche from those one lives with or has a close working relationship to. The substance can facilitate forms of sickness, especially if there is auric vampirisation draining one's vitality because of another's weak psychic constitution. Proper allowances and psychic protections need to be made when relating to such people. The devitalised, psychically weak ones, need to be taught how to strengthen their auras. (Generally the cause is the result of emotional distress, drugs, and/or unhealthy lifestyles.) Many aspects of city life (i.e., the environment) are not conducive to a healthy lifestyle, with many causes of distress, noisy atmosphere, and forms of group contact, that facilitate the development of forms of sickness. The widespread contagion of influenza and epidemics are symptomatic of such conditioning. Nevertheless, the simple logical rules outlined below, if followed, should minimise the need to visit the medical profession.

- Beware of the critical mind, irritability, fears and all forms of emotional extremism, as they are major factors in devitalising the body (as energy is expended and dissipated in the emotional and vital bodies) causing the production of illnesses.
- Beware of the ingestion of chemicalised, devitalised, and highly processed foods, all forms of drugs, narcotics and stimulants. These

12 The subject of the interrelation between the two kingdoms is too vast to provide further detail here. More detailed information can be found in Bailey's *A Treatise on Cosmic Fire* (specifically pages 633-679). Geoffrey Hodson provides a clairvoyant description in his book *The Kingdom of the Gods,* (Theosophical Publishing House, Adyar, 1987).

either devitalise or poison the body, causing areas therein for the breeding of disease bearing factors.

- Beware of the ingestion of animal products, too much fat, white sugar, white flour, white rice, (they are pure carbohydrates from which nutritional value has been totally removed[13]), and all forms of fast foods, fad foods, and high-priced gimmicks, artificial vitamins, etc., with which many overload their digestive and eliminatory systems. Devitalisation happens when the body cannot properly digest the type of foodstuff ingested. They either deprive it of essential nutrients, or it must utilise much energy to convert and store (such as fat).
- Eat simply and wisely, consume products that have ripened in the sun, and enjoy what you eat.
- Listen well to the body, it will tell you when sicknesses are approaching. Also learn to fast, abstaining from all solid foods and especially to bouts of emotionality, when sickness approaches. Then you will learn to quickly heal yourself with a minimum of cost and maximum effectiveness. The fasting allows the body to put the sum of its vital forces to rectify the imbalances and disease in the areas of need, as this is what the healing factors in the body have been designed to do.
- Work with the body's natural defences as much as possible, developing peace of mind, and a meditative lifestyle, knowing

---

13 The widespread indoctrination in the early twentieth century and acceptance of things 'white' as best for you is one of the great crimes of our present civilisation against the well-being of people everywhere. It is especially grave in the case of the medical profession, who do not warn their patients of the adverse effects of making the mainstay of every meal, foods that have little or no nutritional value. This practice is particularly acute in the Third World where proper nutrition is often a question of life and death for the impoverished. One must overcome one's addiction to such foods. One must seek that which contains full whole grain or whole meal, to avoid overly processed foods where the essential nutrients (as in white sugar) have been removed, similarly with the removal of the skins of potatoes, because of an inbred prejudice for food to look 'nice'. 'Pure white and deadly' is a phrase that all should have in their minds. Those who wish to develop Bodhisattva attributes should carefully reflect upon this subject, as what food to eat concerns more than just the health of the physical body.

well that most sicknesses are but the effects of wrong actions in thought, word or deed, and will pass, once the true causes have been ascertained and eliminated. Look specifically to the emotional body, for most diseases (especially cancers, inflammations, and fevers) stem from constant emotional activity. This concerns the continuous agitation of auric substance (centred upon the Solar Plexus centre), the endocrine glands, and the areas of influence in the body that they control. Specialised attention may however be needed in cases where long periods of bad eating habits, toxin intake and 'riotous' lifestyle, have caused major abnormalities to manifest in the bodily organism.[14]

- Live as much as possible in harmony with all of the laws of Life, which naturally govern all biological processes. The central factor of which is the sun, with its life-giving waves of light. Light is the factor underlying all that we can come to know. Plants exist specifically to capture sunlight and convert it to the starch, proteins, etc., that animals need to sustain their lives. This is part of the reason for the need of a vegetarian or vegan diet if one wishes to generally avoid diseases. Plants offer a direct source of sun-like vitality needed for good health, whilst animals offer a debased secondary source, adulterated with its own often diseased emanatory *prāṇas*, fears and associated toxins.
- The law of *karma* is an emanation of the rectifying influence of the greater Sun at the Heart of all life, ruling over all of the imbalances of the energy equation in the environment, of the bodily nature of the universe as a whole. No evolving form is perfect, consequently forms of sickness can be found on all levels of expression in our universe, and all such expressions of disharmony must eventually come to be harmonised. The human form but reflects the Life of the greater whole. In the last resort, sicknesses and diseases are the karmic effects of wrong emotional-mental thought processes that impact upon the physical body via the *nāḍī* system. The energy imbalances which cause the production of pathogens must then come

14 Many books by members of the alternative medical profession are also helpful, especially those espousing a vegetarian or vegan lifestyle.

to be rectified. Not all sickness is the result of this life's actions. The sowing of the corruptions that were not rectified in the overall energy equation for the unit in a former life consequently come due in the present life. Sometimes many lives of coarse actions sow the seeds for a most virulent sickness in a later life. The karmic due must be paid back and cannot be avoided. Meditation then is the key to analysing such causes and how best to proceed with alleviating the symptoms to effect cure.

To be able to truly heal oneself one must learn (via a meditative lifestyle) to:

a. Be *serene* enough to listen to the silent voice of the conscience, which is but a touch of revelation from the Heart of Life. When listened to it allows one to avoid bad decisions that would produce *karma* that has to be cleansed later.
b. To be *alert* to the rectifying waves of the manifesting *karma*, and offer no hindering action to their outcome (seemingly either good or bad as far as our personality desires are concerned). Karmic factors that cause sickness and disease need to be carefully factored in all of one's considerations.
c. To be sensitively *alive* to the streams of vital health-giving light and revelations from higher sources that are healing in their effect.
d. To *watch* carefully the effects of all of one's actions in the material world that would sow the seeds (*saṃskāras*) of disease and disharmony that would sprout sickly weeds in the future.

One of the major outcomes of the practice of meditation is to be serene, alert, alive, and to constantly watch the effects of one's actions in the ephemeral world. By its very nature a healthy mind produces emanatory good health far and wide, to the sum total of all that the mind contacts and influences. This is more than just the physical body of the person concerned. It affects every modulation in the fabric of life wherein manifest the energies and karmic streams associated with that mind. These streams come from the past and are modulated in the ever-present bath of energy that impacts the eternal Now. The organising consciousness (that is the meditating Mind) projects the streams in such a way that future events mould the pathways that the embodied form must follow.

The embodied form is our personality structure, and if it follows without hindrance or resistance the pathway of the projected energy streams from contact with higher meditative sources, then perfect health will inevitably ensue. Such a person will become enlightened, a divine healer. If there is resistance to these modulations, then we have friction, heat, consequent pain; the grinding inertia producing dis-ease, strife, the lack of conscious understanding of the way of manifesting ephemera all around that is the normal way of those bound to the personality world. They are moulded by the past and resist that which the future ordains for them. Ignorance is thus fostered, and from ignorance comes the hosts of diseases in the world of suffering that people know well.

What has been described here is the background to the Buddhist concept of the twelvefold formula of Dependent Origination, which is claimed to be the basis of the perpetual cycle of births and deaths. It has its basis in ignorance *(avidya),* a non-recognition of reality, which is responsible for our present state of consciousness. The Buddha started, as Govinda points out, with the simple question:

> 'What is it that makes old age and death possible?' And the answer was: 'On account of being born, we suffer old-age and death!' Similarly, birth is dependent on the process of becoming, and this process would not have been set in motion, if there had not been a will to live and a clinging to the corresponding forms of life. This clinging is due to craving, due to unquenchable 'thirst' after the objects of sense-enjoyment, and this again is conditioned by feeling (by discerning agreeable and disagreeable sensations). Feeling, on the other hand, is only possible by the contact of the senses with their corresponding objects. The senses are based on a psycho-physical organism, and the latter can only arise if there is consciousness! Consciousness, however, in the individually limited form of ours, is conditioned by individual, egocentric activity (during countless previous forms of existence), and such activity is only possible as long as we are caught in the illusion of our separate egohood.[15]

15 Govinda, *Foundations of Tibetan Mysticism,* 245.

The production of perfect health reflects the way that one can escape this wheel of Dependent Origination. It is a means whereby that which is not the 'self' can be identified and then merged with. Eliminate egocentric activity and you eliminate the causes for disease, and thus the need for rebirth into cycles of suffering.

When seeking for those who purport to heal human woes, look always to the true motives of the healer concerned; what is gained personally, what is done unselfishly and truly for the good of others. True humbleness and right motive zealously applied on the path of Love (i.e., the liberation that *bodhicitta* confers) guarantees success, for humbleness leads one eventually to the highest teachings, and right motives to truthful revelations. However, the success attained is not necessarily what the aspiring one imagined it might be at the beginning of the quest.

Meditation and the Sambhogakāya Flower

Meditation techniques must now meet the needs of the modern aspirant. It is no longer necessary to isolate oneself in a monastery, or place of abstraction, as did the *yogins* of the past ages. Nor would such forms of abstraction allow one to rightly manifest the necessary service work that the awakening, compassionate insight would demand (except for the relative few).

The bulk of the world's spiritual aspirants must be able to bring the zone of quietude down into their living rooms and working environment. The new temples of solitude wherein the Mysteries of enlightened being/non-being can be revealed must thus be built right in the heart of our cities, to the outer environs, and be accessible to all.

Many people have developed meditative states of mind without having formerly sat for meditation. This happens specifically when they are engaged in purely creative activity, such as painting a picture, or work in a contemplative arena, such as gardening. The person is so absorbed in the thought-stream that all sense of time, or even of his/her whereabouts is lost. Our creative geniuses get most of their highest inspirations in this manner. A businessman, for instance, who is one-pointed in making money is also unfolding aspects of the meditation-mind.

We see, therefore, that in its simplest connotation meditation is but a method that assists one to focus the forces of the mind upon a task at hand. That task can be the attaining of any goal in either the temporal or spiritual worlds. Usually this concentrating and focussing activity is directed at the improvement of the psychological states of the mind of the individual, the relieving of bodily aches and pains, and increases the capacity to handle all the perturbations of the person's environmental and social life. It helps to produce physical and emotional control, and increases sensitivity to subtle impressions and sensory stimuli through the refinement of the thinking process. This can lead to the development of psychic perceptions.

To the serious student these are not prime objectives, but side effects. The stilling of the mind and all forms of sensory activities brings into consciousness the qualities and forces from the indwelling Sambhogakāya Flower (the unit of spiritual consciousness that has caused the personality to come to be in the first place), *śūnyatā,* and finally the *dharmakāya.*

In its own domain (the abstract realms of the mind), the Sambhogakāya Flower[16] is group conscious, ensconced in Love and wisdom, which demonstrate as active service in the realms of form. It is the repository of all the experiences gained through millennia of incarnations of the successive personalities that were its vehicle of evolutionary growth. It is completely impersonal and knows not the vicissitudes of the sexual and sensual experiences evolved by the personality, except in terms of unfolding consciousness. It is a sphere of consciousness living in a sea of consciousness, and obeys all of the laws of Life associated with consciousness evolving in the realms of Light (which is its domain). Group life, group activity, the one-ness, interrelatedness and interdependence of all that is, is its mode of activity, as a part of a continuing chain or Hierarchy of enlightened being. It is that which the meditating person aspires to attune to. The person must bring into conscious interplay on the physical plane the laws and

---

16 This is also equated with the *tathāgatagarbha* in my other books, and can be considered a 'Soul', but not as the Christians and Hindus think of this term. For full explanation see Volume 3 of this treatise.

rhythms of Life, which are expressed by the Sambhogakāya Flower on its own level, in conjunction with the vast storehouse of revelatory awareness that it contains within its form.[17]

There is however more to the mystery of what constitutes a human than just the indwelling Soul-form (Sambhogakāya Flower). Within its own sphere this Soul-form undergoes phases of transition or awakening, and matures with each consecutive incarnation. In due course it will be 'extinguished' by the meditating one able to pass the tests that will allow passing on to the 'other shore'[18] of consciousness.

The Sambhogakāya Flower, with its intense light-bearing (consciousness-engendering) qualities, is the radiant sun of our being, the 'Christ within us', but veils an infinitely vaster entity or principle, the *dharmakāya* of a Buddha. (This is Monadic, the *Spirit* within, being a major interpretation of the term 'Father' constantly referred to by Jesus.) It has no discernible attributes directly realisable by mind, but can be known by means of the use of symbols that veil the potency of the real (for example, the wisdoms of the five Tathāgatas), or by identification with it through meditative bridge-building in conjunction with active, enlightening service work. It is the Real when related to the ephemeral illusionality around us, and is all-knowing, omnipotent in its Livingness, with respect to the human unit.

---

17 Evans-Wentz states that the use of the term soul in Buddhism is 'objectionable, since Buddhism, as a whole, denies the existence of a permanent, unchanging personal-consciousness entity such as the Semitic Faiths and animistic creeds in general understand thereby...wherever any similar or equivalent term occurs herein it should be taken to imply something akin to "consciousness-principle" or "compound of consciousness" as implied by the Tibetan *Hpyo,* or else as synonymous with the term "life-flux" as used chiefly by Southern Buddhists'. (*The Tibetan Book of the Dead,* 85-86, *fn* 7.) This description of 'consciousness-principle' or 'compound of consciousness', which is by nature impermanent (in that it evolves), tarries well with my depiction of the Sambhogakāya Flower in Volume 3. Such a concept is not necessarily negated by the descriptions of a Soul in Christianity, as it is just a matter of how Biblical phrases are interpreted.

18 The phrase 'the other shore' relates to the *Heart Sūtra's* (*prajñāpāramitāhṛdaya-sūtra*) famous statement concerning the final achievement of the enlightened being, *'gate, gate, pāragate, pārasamgate, bodhi! svāhā!'* (Gone, gone, gone to the other shore, altogether gone, enlightened mind, hail that one.) This refers to the final extinction of consciousness as we know it, when one travels beyond the shore of the births and deaths of *saṃsāra.*

The objective of the higher forms of meditation techniques, therefore, is to build the bridges *(antaḥkaraṇas)* to the Sambhogakāya Flower, or else to *śūnyatā* by the more advanced meditators, and later to that which can be equated with cosmic-consciousness (*dharmakāya*). As one begins the process of *dharmakāyic* Identification, one enters into vast cosmic domains to interrelate with enlightened Beings that inhabit all stellar spaces. When manifesting a creative function related to the genesis and evolutionary sustenance of a world sphere the qualities of those inhabiting this space are symbolised by the personages in ancient myths. The symbolism must therefore be unveiled in terms of transmuted correspondences, where things pertaining to the mundane world are to be viewed in terms of the expressions of enlightenment (similar to the treatment of the Peaceful and Wrathful Deities provided in Volume 5), remembering all the time that we are observing reified depictions of 'thus gone' Buddhas.

Almost unimaginable domains are entered into at the advanced levels of meditation unfolded by the highest of Bodhisattvas. In fact, Bodhisattvas know that these domains are their true spiritual home, from which emanate all phenomena and the laws governing manifest space. Here we have the birthright of the process of repeated Incarnations; of the making of a Buddha, allowing all ties to the dense plane to be eliminated, freeing such a one to travel far into the All that is cosmos.

Śūnyatā produces the liberation of consciousness, the death of the mind-structure that would in any way try to perceive it, yet the perspicacity of Life persists. The experience associated with *dharmakāyic* Identification is beyond the awareness obtained from births and deaths of the personality in the three worlds of human evolution (mental, emotional, and physical). It produces revelation of the order and magnitude of cosmos and the interrelatedness of the liberated Buddhas that reside therein.

Before the 'death' that the experience of the Void signifies is produced, the student must be safely guided through the many arenas of danger that may occur, to master all *saṃskāras* preventing the onset of liberation. Tests must be passed so that consciousness can be sensitively expanded to attune to the inner universe. Heightened energisations from transmutative, transfiguring, radiating light must be accommodated, as well as the raising of the Fiery nuclear energy from the dynamic generator of all that is sustained by the One Heart. (This *kuṇḍalinī* energy flows up the central, *suṣumṇā nāḍī*, at the appropriate time.) The making of a God-man, a Christ incarnate, a Buddha in expression proceeds in this fashion.

The process of stilling the mind allows one to listen closely to the *Voice of Silence,* heard in the innermost recesses of the Heart. This manifests first as one's conscience, prompting one to act in a certain way that will benefit others, as well as oneself. It is the 'inner voice' that directs the person to do right, urging that which will produce the highest realisations if carefully listened to. It is the internal urging that causes a person to do what he or she knows must be done, to act in a certain way, or to be at a specific place at the right time, despite the chattering of the desire-mind trying to override the impression.

It concerns the process of the awakening *intuition*, which develops through the meditation process to become lucid, clarified vision in the mind's Eye. The person sees what must be done in accordance with his/her part of the Plan in the scheme of things, and does it. The intuition is thus not just a vague internal prompting or urge that makes people think they must do things in a certain way, but rather is the result of consciously having built the bridges to the Sambhogakāya Flower in any particular life. It is the effect of inner attunement with the subtly impelling thought-forms from this Soul-form, projecting the purpose for this and all succeeding incarnations.

The intuition manifests throughout life at the various stages of one's creative development. It pushes this activity to its inevitable conclusion as far as *karma* permits. This is because the intuition is the messenger of the plan for that life. It manifests as points of contact during various stages of life as the person aspires upwards in meditative awareness, high aspiration, or contemplation upon service work, the creativity at hand. When enlightenment ensues, the intuition *(satori,* 'awakening') becomes the normal state of consciousness. The intellect then falls below the threshold of consciousness, it becomes an instinct, an automaton.[19]

---

19 Daisetz Teitaro Suzuki, states: 'Satori may be defined as an intuitive looking into the nature of things in contradistinction to the analytical or logical understanding of it. Practically, it means the unfolding of a new world hitherto unperceived in the confusion

The clue to the entire concept of *prevision,* of being able to see the future, lies in the intuition. The person must however be wary not to confuse the intuition with glimmerings obtained from the vortices of thought-forms existing on astral realms, from which the majority of the so-called prophetic and mystical visions stem. The intuition reveals the Real, a vision from the *dharmakāyic* realms. The astral thought-forms on the other hand are often based upon seeds of truth, but are coloured by the desire-minds of those that have created them.

Nevertheless, prescient revelations are possible on the higher levels of the astral plane, as it does act as a mirror for impressions from the abstract realms. It is the Bardo realm to which people go after they have died. There are libraries and halls of records to be found therein, as learning does not cease because one has died to the physical body. The true esoteric history of the world, for instance, can be found freed from the bias, omissions, and fabrications generated by the victors of the various wars on earth. Neither is there any loss due to fire, water damage or wanton destruction. Therefore, records exist for the entire history of humanity, including that of the Lemurian and Atlantean epochs. Some seers get impressions from these inner libraries when they prophesy, as a consequence of contacting what is called the Akashic records. (Such people also see through their own auric colourings, which often distort the subtle impressions obtained. Much depends upon how controlled their emotions are, and proficiency in meditation.)

Prophetic visions are possible because, before the personality incarnates, the Sambhogakāya Flower must formulate a carefully delineated plan for the purpose of that incarnation in the realms of the abstract Mind wherein it resides. The Sambhogakāya Flower must weave the tapestry of *karma* in conjunction with cyclic law, and as it is completely group-conscious, its formulations become an integral part

---

of a dualistically-trained-mind. Or we may say that with satori our surroundings are viewed from quite an unexpected angle of perception. Whatever this is, the world for those that have gained satori is no longer the old world that used to be; even with all its flowing streams and burning fires, it is never the same again. Logically stated, all its opposites and contradictions are united and harmonised into a consistent organic whole. This is a mystery and a miracle, but according to Zen masters such is being performed every day. Satori can thus be had only through our personality experiencing it.'
Essays in Zen Buddhism, (Munshiram Manoharlal, Delhi, 2000), Vol. 1, 230.

of the thought process of the group which it is part of. Thus groups of individuals are rayed down to live out roles in the material world, as planned on the inner realms.

The group laws that are the subject of the last chapter of this book manifest via the abstract Mind wherein the Sambhogakāya Flower resides. The aspiring individual comes into contact with these laws through building the links *(antaḥkaraṇas)* to this domain. The laws are an expression of the Heart of Life which directly conditions these Flowers, and accordingly they are organised according to a twelve-petalled Heart centre, as well as by Ray lines. The process leading to enlightenment then consists significantly of bringing these laws into play in the outer world of seeming *(saṃsāra).*

The path of Initiation is concerned with this process, and an Initiate is one that comprehends the mysteries concerning the way of working with group laws, according to the level of expression that one is Initiated into. The laws of group evolution also significantly condition life upon the astral plane, as this domain reflects the conditions from the higher domains, albeit in a reified fashion.

On its own level the Sambhogakāya Flower mimics the creative process undertaken by a Logos, with regard to the manifest world we see all around us. This world is but the *nirmāṇakāya,* the body of manifestation of the Logos/Ādi Buddha. By extension, the entire universe is but the expression of the meditation-Minds of 'thus gone' Buddhas, who have become so countless aeons ago. They manifest the semblance of Deities evolving via each time-space continuum they establish. Comprehension of such an evolutionary process is well established in all who have attained enlightenment through meditation. The process is clearly seen in their mind's Eye. For those that rely on concrete knowledge, however, such revelation is viewed in terms of theories and hypothesis.

Meditation gives one a direct realisation of the true nature of being/non-being, of all the factors involved with the process of evolution. This is specifically so in relation to what is perceived of as a 'self', and thus of one's past lives and related experiences, both in and out of incarnate existence. Also, as all lives are integrated into a unity, so every aspect of the total past of human evolution can be gleaned, including that which existed 'before the foundation of the world'.[20] Here theories no longer exist, because direct realisations show the Truth beyond words and ideas. In the more advanced meditative stages, such realisations come from realms of experience beyond the rational mind, from that which *śūnyatā* veils (the *dharmakāya).*

When envisioned on the scale of national and planetary *karma*, then we see that the progress of entire civilisations have been planned ahead, the paradigm of the process existing in the archetypal realms of the Mind. The 'individual' Sambhogakāya Flower therein is, however, fully aware of its part within the group context, but not necessarily within the greater whole of cosmos. The advanced Bodhisattvas that work upon the realm of the archetypal Mind, or higher, are responsible for the interrelated blending of the visionary impetus of the sum of the soul groupings. These Bodhisattvas are *'the elect'*, liberated ones, Adepts, Masters of Wisdom, and Chohans of the Ray lines of endeavour. They have completely evolved out of the sphere of activity associated with *saṃsāra,* and even from the realm of the Sambhogakāya Flower.

The upper echelons of the Hierarchy of enlightened being are thus responsible for, amongst other things, the wise direction of the course of evolution of the human kingdom. They work continuously with the streams of thought-forms that project *future* events, moulding the *past actions* of humanity, through the work of their disciples and representatives upon the earth, in such a way that *the present* is continuously formed. This manifests in conjunction with the law of *karma*, and the factor of human free will, so the course of the originating Plan is followed as much as possible. This is the 'blueprint' for the sum of the streams of evolution, of which the human stream is but one. The present that is thus created is called the *eternal Now,* and is timeless—as time is but a concept viewed in terms of cycles of events effected upon the physical plane, where human consciousness is presently focussed upon.

The individual meditator can contact this universal stream of lighted, organised meditation substance to get glimpses of what the future beckons on many different levels of expression. The glimpses then become energy vortices that must be utilised and adapted for one's

---

20 *John 17:24, Matt. 25:34.*

service work, so that the ideal becomes the present reality for humanity. It must be remembered here that one who can work in such a fashion is at all times guided by the law of Love, having passed the many testings upon the way along this line that will allow identification with the meditation-Mind of a Logos, the universal source of Love. The Logoic Mind is continuously meditating upon its Plan, and a meditating unit comes to cognize that Plan so as to appropriately play his/her role in it.

Such is the nature of an enlightened Mind. All enlightened Minds are thus preoccupied, and from this perspective one can view the process of meditation as that which causes one to first identify, then merge consciously with the collective Minds of the Hierarchy of enlightened being. The laws of Group Progress and Expansive Response (explained in chapter 8) come into play here. All that can be known is but an aspect of the community of Minds that cause all that exists. Through right meditation the individual begins the process of merging with the meditation-Minds of those that have undergone this process in the past, from the highest, most exalted cosmic Entity (or Creative Deity), to those that are undergoing 'the fellowship of the Christ's sufferings'[21] upon the earth. This 'fellowship' is but a version of the Bodhisattva vow, wherein the enlightened one that has well developed the way of *bodhicitta* realises he/she cannot enter the final gate of liberation from this planet until all beings have been released from suffering.[22] The Bodhisattva suffers pain in seeing all those that are distressed and who suffer injustice in some way, and so has vowed to try to rectify the causes of all suffering. All minds become One Mind, and the vastness of the riches of revelatory awareness become apparent to the meditating one.

The elect and the shortening of days

The Hierarchy of meditative Minds (or of Light) seed all earnest aspirants with *images* pertaining to their enlightened domain, giving aspirants the

---

21 *Phil. 3:10.*

22 See the book by Marion L. Matics: *Entering the Path of Enlightenment* for detail concerning the orthodox presentation of the nature of this path. The way of the Bodhisattva is also found in the saying of Christ-Jesus in *John 12:32,* 'And I, if I be lifted up from the earth, will draw all men unto me', and *Matt. 28:20,* 'Lo. I am with you alway, *even* unto the end of the world. Amen'.

visualisations and telepathic suggestions they need to travel along this path when they pass the necessary testings on the way. Out of necessity one must therefore become *telepathic* as one progresses. Telepathy is the card of access to the bank of universal Mind. Telepathy necessitates the development of serene calm whereby the subtle voice of the inner teacher can be listened to, and images that form in the mind can be quietly and instantaneously analysed for what they are or veil. Any emotional input will instantly distort the impressions into what is desired, thus into what they are not. The student must learn how to avoid the various forms of subtle emotional input if the meditation-Mind is to be truly developed. To do so *saṃskāras* must be transformed. This is the main task of meditators, if they are to progress along the path to enlightenment.

In the Buddhist Tantric system the mind's unique place as a creative and 'transformative agent' is also exemplified. This is described by Roger Jackson *et al:*

> The mind is the supreme transformative agent in the universe, for as it is conditioned, so, ultimately, is the world conditioned. Inasmuch as "all we are is a result of what we have thought", then conditioning the mind to divine pride is a form of imagination that ultimately can effect a transformation of the ordinary into the divinity that is imagined. For example, the five aggregates (or five defilements) can be transformed into the five types of wisdom of the five tathagatas, or "dhyani buddhas," who head the different tantric lineages.[23]

People must be helped to find their own inherent way to light, making all related decisions regarding energy impacts without undue or forceful coercion. They must develop the needed capabilities from within-without, and thus gain mastery through proper awakening of the Christ-Light. The awakening of the powers of Love cannot be forced upon them, as the making of spiritual robots serves not evolutionary purpose, which is to make all of us perfected beings—to 'let this mind be in you, which was also in Christ Jesus: Who, being in the form of God, thought it not robbery to be equal with God'.[24] There is a slow and gradual course of

---

23 Geshe Lhundup Sopa, Roger Jackson, John Newman, *The Wheel of Time. The Kalachakra in Context*, (Snow Lion, Ithaca, New York, 1991), 21.

24 *Phil. 2:5-6.*

evolution, allowing for the mistakes of the myriads upon the way, and the karmic process associated with the rectification of those mistakes. Inevitably, the path to liberation is found and ardently followed, then the evolutionary process accelerates considerably. The awakening of *bodhicitta,* the mind-substance *(citta)* of liberating compassion *(bodhi),* which is the 'mind...that was also in Christ Jesus', is a major objective of the path of enlightenment. *Bodhicitta* is a compassionate force that works to liberate all from suffering.

The implications of the quote from *Philippians 2:5-6* is completely ignored by the Christian community, as their present ontology has no way to account for such a development. Literally, it is asking for the adherents of the faith to develop a similar Mind that a planetary Logos or greater possesses. The esoteric philosophy relating to gaining enlightenment by transforming *saṃskāras* and passing the tests of Initiation into the Mysteries of being/non-being easily provides the answer.

The term 'Christ Jesus' implies an Avataric descent from the Christ principle (the 'Son') to the receptive vehicle—Jesus. Also implied in the quote is the Father ('God', the Will or Causative principle), Son (Christ, or the embodiment of divine compassion), and form (Jesus, the receptive vehicle).[25] A similar descent happens to all meditators that aspire upwards in consciousness after having done the necessary work of producing a quiescent mind. In their case the Christ can be literally experienced, as he is the head of the Council of Bodhisattvas, the Hierarchy of Light. Any advanced member of the Council can project telepathic impressions to a meditator. The Sambhogakāya Flower can also stand as the Christ in the case of younger Initiates. In this simile the 'Father' or 'God' is considered to be either the Monad (or Spirit within) or the Lord of Shambhala (the planetary Head centre).

All humans are 'in the form of God' as we are built in the 'image of God',[26] though Christ-Jesus is, however, closer to being 'equal to God' than the rest of humanity because he is the most advanced Initiate (Bodhisattva) amongst us. He has transmuted all possible *saṃskāras*

---

25 As shall be later explained, Jesus undertook those same steps exoterically as the Initiate must undergo internally on the way to the higher Initiations. The way is that of awakening the mind of compassion *(bodhicitta).* Described here is a version of the three bodies of a Buddha: *dharmakāya, sambhogakāya* and the *nirmāṇakāya.*

26 See *Genesis 1:26-27.*

associated with human livingness, and has attained a level of cosmic consciousness *(dharmakāya)* that the rest of us must yet attain. Hence he can guide us along the path he has travelled to the Kingdom of 'God' (Shambhala) wherein he resides.

Matt. 24:22-31 presents a symbolic description of some more esoteric qualities and attainments of *'the elect'*, those that have passed their Initiation testings.

> And except those days should be shortened, there should no flesh be saved: but for the elect's sake those days shall be shortened.
>
> Then if any man should say unto you. Lo, here *is* Christ, or there; believe *it* not.
>
> For there shall arise false Christs, and false prophets, and shall shew great signs and wonders; insomuch that, if *it were* possible, they shall deceive the very elect.
>
> Behold, I have told you before.
>
> Wherefore if they shall say unto you, Behold, he is in the desert; go not forth: behold, *he is* in the secret chambers; believe *it* not.
>
> For as the lightning cometh out of the east, and shineth even unto the west; so shall also the coming of the Son of man be.
>
> For wheresoever the carcass is, there will the eagles be gathered together.
>
> Immediately after the tribulation of those days shall the sun be darkened, and the moon shall not give her light, and the stars shall fall from heaven, and the powers of the heavens shall be shaken.
>
> And then shall appear the sign of the Son of man in heaven: and then shall all the tribes of the earth mourn, and they shall see the Son of man coming in the clouds of heaven with power and great glory.
>
> And he shall send his angels with the sound of a trumpet, and they shall gather together his elect from the four winds, from one end of heaven to the other.

As well as referring to the then future, the verses of this chapter can be interpreted in terms of the meditation process, with the related symbolism to be interpreted in a similar manner as a Buddhist Tantric text to one well versed in this process. To give this extract proper justice the reader should refer to the background information presented in my previous books and incorporate it with the treatment of the important symbolism here. These verses have been explained somewhat in relation to the process of evolution and the happenings associated with the dawning New Age in my revised book *The Revelation*.[27] However, here the focus shall be upon the aspects of the symbolism that relates to the way of meditation.

The process of the *shortening of days* concerns the awakening of Initiate consciousness, because the Initiate ('the elect') lives increasingly in future time, and can accomplish day-to-day things faster than ever before. This means that *saṃskāras* pertaining to the future are continually meditated upon and worked with via the efficiency of an enlightened Mind to bring about their fruits, effectively producing a shortening of the days. Because of the information explosion and labour saving devices provided by modern technology, what previously necessitated an onerous amount of time to produce now happens much quicker, and consciousness perceives time to fly by. This has also produced many challenges for the Initiate, and in overcoming them, so a quickening pace of action has occurred. The Initiate increasingly resides in a meditative state, in abstracted spaciousness. The consequent lucidity fostered upon the consciousness that registers the revelation in terms of explainable vision, or imagery, is considered 'day light', the darkness of ignorance therefore is 'night time'.

I stated in my earlier book that the nations of the earth are quickening their pace of living. More is done each day than ever before and people are in a great hurry to make, explore, and manipulate things. The slow, leisurely pace of the past, when every moment of the day simply flowed along virtually unnoticed, is long gone for most. Humanity is enslaved to the concept of time, and yet, because of the multiplicity of activities constantly engendered by people, time races by, and rarely is there time to accomplish what needs to be done. This effectively makes the days 'shorter', which is of benefit to 'the elect' because much can be given to, and quickly developed by humanity, in the fervent pace of life. Those embodied in the 'flesh' (who are the objective of 'the elect' to 'save') can learn more in a mere lifetime, or even in a few years, than what it may have taken in many past lifetimes, with regard to developing the attainment of the enlightenment-consciousness and that associated with the new era.[28]

---

27 Balsys, *The Revelation*, revised edition 2, 2024.

28 Ibid., 306-307.

The awakening of the spontaneous awareness of intuition has always been equated with a flash of lightening in meditation texts. The direction *east* then concerns the place of the awakening light of enlightenment within the Heart centre, the spiritual Sun in our beings. The *west* symbolises the arena of service work the Initiate provides for humanity. It is the direction to which the illumined one looks when gazing outwards from an awakened eastern position.

The *carcass* symbolises the effect of dying to the personality vehicle, the unregenerate *saṃskāras* which come as a consequence of the awakening of spiritual perceptions, and which must be transformed. *Eagles* represent the forces of the intuition that must oversee the process of transforming *saṃskāras.* The term also refers to the Hierarchy of enlightened beings. They have come to help the one who is going through the process of dying to his/her material self as the meditation process proceeds. They have mastered the material domain and can look upon the ephemeral realms ('the carcass') from great spiritual heights, with lucid 'eagle-eyed vision' (utilising the awakened third Eye).

The way that *'the elect'* could be deceived is presented above by the symbolism of the desert and secret chambers. The *secret chambers* refer to the *chakras* and their related powers. The desire is strong to awaken these *chakras* before the individual has been properly prepared for their potency and related qualities. The excuses given refer to the search for the Christ presence, but in reality, strong desire to dominate others or to demonstrate the powers of accomplishment is the motive. One must beware the 'false prophets' that would use the psychicism derived from having awakened the lower *siddhis* to deceive all into believing that they are great spiritual beings. It thus refers to those that follow the ways of the 'left hand path'.

The *chakras* are chambers of transcendence, doorways to higher perceptions, flowers of purposeful resolve. Each one of them conveys a different category of *saṃskāra* that the mind must transform and elevate with the help of their agency. The entire process works similarly to a distillation apparatus. They are *secret* in that they are hidden in the subjective sheaths and veiled by the form, known only to those whose developing aspirations and meditative resolve have awakened these 'eyes' that see. There are effectively five levels of *chakras,* each level dealing with the refinement of one or other of the Elements. Thus there are five different main units of transformation. The *saṃskāras* are constituted of the five Elements and eventually their qualities must be transformed into the Wisdoms of the five Dhyāni Buddhas.

The *desert* refers not only to the way of hermits and anchorites, but also to the experiences of the disciple in the corporeal realms, who endeavours to overcome attachment to allurements. One must master and overcome the deserts of materialism (as symbolised by the esoteric qualities of the sign Scorpio the scorpion); of the need for material comforts, the power and prestige of the things that money can buy. The disciple must also grapple with the tendency towards fanaticism of all types, as related to fanatical interpretation of religious Scriptures, or in relation to one's personal visions, and mistaking these things as the highest revelations from 'God'.

In the desert we have war, death, strife, desire for possessions, cruelty, greed, deception, and all of the endless debacle that keeps a person tied down to the wheel of birth and death. All of the sexual mores and problems in our societies, the turmoil and conflict associated with the battle of the sexes, the question of imposed celibacy as opposed to widespread promiscuity must here be solved. Note the ability of the desert to cause mirages of all types of phantasmagorical (astral) images. Increased involvement with *saṃsāra* is not what one seeks for enlightenment (the 'Son of man'). Certainly here will be found many 'false Christs' manifesting enticing teachings that will actually increase attachment to forms of transience rather than liberation from them. The principle of liberation (the Christ) will not be found by engendering materialistic activities, but gained by working to overcome them.

Another symbol of the *desert* is the serpent or viper, which has the ability to poison, and is also related to the premature awakening of lower psychic powers. The desert is a place of dehydration and death, through the inability to fully master the use of the Watery Element—the sum total of our emotions and aspirations. It is a place of desire-mind unfolding, and symbolises the stage of evolutionary development that humanity is now at. It represents the entire material domain that the mind must learn to master and to transform into an oasis of revelatory light. Meditation is a means that allows a person to control all aspects of human livingness so that they act as factors assisting the enlightenment process, or can be used to compassionately serve others.

The word *behold* in the Bible always means to look, or vision, with the inner Eye (Ājñā centre) functioning. It concerns the ability to view things in terms of their esoteric, subjective sense, and implies awakening to lofty spiritual vision. Note that Jesus reminds his disciples, once they awakened to such vision, that they have been *'told all this before'*. This prod to memory is significant, as it relates to some of their major testings or temptations, as representatives of 'the elect' upon the earth. In the vision they are given they are shown when they received similar instructions in past lives, or in this one. They see clearly the Initiation path that has led them to where they are at, the mistakes made in the past, and their means of rectification.

The 'coming of the Son of man' concerns the awakening within of the Christ principle and therefore enlightenment (*bodhicitta*). The 'son' refers to the evocation of the qualities of the *piṇgalā nāḍī*, of compassionate consciousness (when referring to the principle that the Christ bears), to that aspect of a human unit that gives birth to a higher form of consciousness along the *piṇgalā* line. The 'clouds of heaven' can symbolise that which veils the inner domains. In a modern day context, seeing 'the Son of man coming in the clouds of heaven' may also be literally interpreted as him coming through the clouds in an airplane. The 'power and great glory' that accompanies 'the Son of man' refers to the energies of spiritual Will and Love-Wisdom that accompanies the enlightened One, and which demonstrates as a radiant aura. It describes the auric sheaths, such as those represented around Buddhas and Bodhisattvas depicted in Buddhist art ('great glory'), and psycho-spiritual abilities (power) of such fully enlightened beings. This aura includes the entire *maṇḍala* of enlightened Being, and of the externalisation process of the Hierarchy that will accompany the actual appearance of the Christ as a Buddha. The members of Hierarchy are close to the Christ in spiritual stature, and must come with him to fulfil his task in the new era.

We now come to the direct yogic section of the passages, following the statement 'wherever the carcass is, there will be the eagles gathered together', which is also a description of the testings for Initiation undertaken in the sign Scorpio the scorpion. The eagle is the triumphant disciple that has mastered the battlefield of life ('the carcass') and is soaring high in spiritual accomplishment.

The *'tribulation in those days'* refers to the entire period of testings for Initiation, when the major mental-emotional *saṃskāras* of an individual have to be converted into Love-Wisdom and spiritual Will. The process of mastery causes the consequent tribulation period. This subject is explained in chapter 5, which deals with the first and second Initiations. The lures of *saṃsāra* are a most ancient addiction and must be overcome, producing considerable trouble and suffering in the disciple's life (or for the world disciple) when this feat is to be accomplished. There are times in human history when many human units will be simultaneously undergoing the process, causing such tribulation for the many. The present epoch is one such period, where many are vying (generally unknowingly) to pass first Initiation testings. Though all eras have their own periods of wars and massed tribulation, this present era differs because of the intellect developed by the mass of people. This, plus the development of compassionate activities by many, is what makes this era unique, raising the spectre of large scale Initiation. The background of the present world situation in all fields relating to this Initiation can certainly be understood as 'those days' of the above quote. The ruling entities of the entire three-fold body of expression (mental, astral, and physical) of a human unit (or of our current civilisation) must come to be understood and mastered to pass the tests.

The description of the *'Sun and Moon'* symbolise the properties of the *piṇgalā* (Sun) and *iḍā* (Moon) *nāḍīs* at the time of the arousal of *suṣumṇā* energies. These are well known symbols in yoga-meditation philosophy, and are applicable at the time of the awakening or enlightenment of 'the elect' as a consequence of mastering the vicissitudes of the threefold personality. This must be done if the powers of Love-Wisdom are to be fully evoked. Here the terms 'Sun and Moon' refer specifically to the *chakras* that embody the qualities of these *nāḍīs*. The Heart centre (governing the right hand *piṇgalā nāḍī*) has become a radiant fiery sun by the ability of the person to overcome all forms of tribulation, and the Solar Plexus centre (governing the left hand *iḍā nāḍī*), through which the energies of the personality are expressed, reflects this luminescence. It thereby shines with a vitality similar to the reflected light of the moon.

The *'darkening of the sun'* refers to the opening of the central iris, or 'jewel in the heart of the lotus' (of the Heart centre). This appears as an expanding, electrical, indigo-blue disc to the inner vision of the seer, and is the aperture or door of entry into space, through which consciousness must travel if the person is to be liberated from the form. The energies of liberation are most intense. For the prepared individual such a darkening produces liberation, for others it can spell disaster when the effects of the associated strong energisations produce death and destruction because of the inability of the form to safely contain the energies. The other effect can be to strengthen unruly *saṃskāras,* intensify passions, emotions and fanaticisms, because energy follows the line of least resistance. Such lines of development are what the average masses of people experience.

Similarly, all releases of energy from Shambhala (the planetary Head centre) must be carefully metered by its governing Lords because of the possible effects of this energy amongst humanity. When carefully metered, an energy stimulus along a Ray line can be very advantageous for humanity, and streams of troublesome *karma* that need to be expunged from the human psyche can also be brought to the fore.

The light of the personality nature that is expressed by the Solar Plexus centre dims and becomes obscured as the person becomes liberated. The delusive egotistic consciousness that would normally dominate the integral personality no longer rules, thus the moon (the energies of the personality) 'shall not give her light'. The person no longer lives below the diaphragm, but in the centres above it, causing the lunar light governing the ephemeral personal life to be dimmed considerably. It is superseded by the light from the Heart of life. Because such a one comes to be confronted with the domain of Mind in its entirety, unobstructed by the points of light that represent the sentience of innumerable beings (that relate to the material world), so 'the stars' (signifying luminous liberated beings) fall from 'heaven' (the higher mental domains). They are no longer exalted images, but become fully known. At the attainment of the fourth Initiation, in the inexplicable experience of non-being, the mental domain falls below the level of awareness. This attainment signifies the experience of the Void *(śūnyatā),* as was undertaken by Jesus upon the cross, when he shouted out 'My God, my God, why hast thou forsaken me?'[29] The Initiate has become master of all the forces and powers of heaven (the domains of the mind), and thus they are 'shaken', for they no longer dominate the Initiate's activities.

For the average individual the stars are abstractions, points of light in the night sky, but for the Initiate they signify the source of the zodiacal and planetary energies that condition the evolution of our planet. As one undertakes Initiation and awakens to the perception of the inner realms (heaven), so these forces 'fall' into consciousness, they become part of the living experiences of such a one, who must utilise their energies in a similar manner that the average person deals with physical plane objects. All is a sea of energies, and in the highest Initiations the cosmic paths open up by extending *antaḥkaraṇas* to the Logoic domains representing the solar systems to which they must travel. The stars therefore are no longer abstractions, immensely far away entities, but are part of the living experience of the Initiate, hence they symbolically 'fall', as one ascends to the domain of the cosmic ethers to meet them.

The *'sign of the son of man'* then becomes the symbol of one's own enlightened consciousness, whilst *'the tribes of the earth'* that shall mourn become the various elements and forces constituting one's own body nature. When the enlightened one's Mind returns to waking consciousness, it effectively appears 'in the clouds of heaven' which represent the substance of the various thought-forms pertaining to the mundane world. Such a Mind appears amongst the domain of average thinkers as demonstrating 'power and great glory'. When the purpose is to produce the liberation of all the forces associated with the corporeal form (e.g., of the mind-set of humanity), we then have a resultant 'mourning' for these forces by those that are sentimentally attached to them. The gross form and forces must, however, inevitably be gradually transformed into a body of light.

---

29 *Matt. 27:46.*

When the phrase *'the tribes of the earth'* is taken to represent the nations and the various races of people, then the concept of them 'mourning' refers to their reaction to the truth of what they must do to be released from the cycles of activity that cause so much suffering. They are addicted to this activity, and thus 'mourn' their inability or unwillingness to change their actions, or for those that take up the challenge, the sense of the loss of what they are attached to.

The 'sign of the son of man in heaven' is also a rendering of the astrological sign *Aquarius the water bearer,* the sign that our sun is now moving into, and which will herald the Christ's reappearance.

The meaning of the *trumpet* in the last line of the quote is explained in relation to the figure of the time-space continuum.

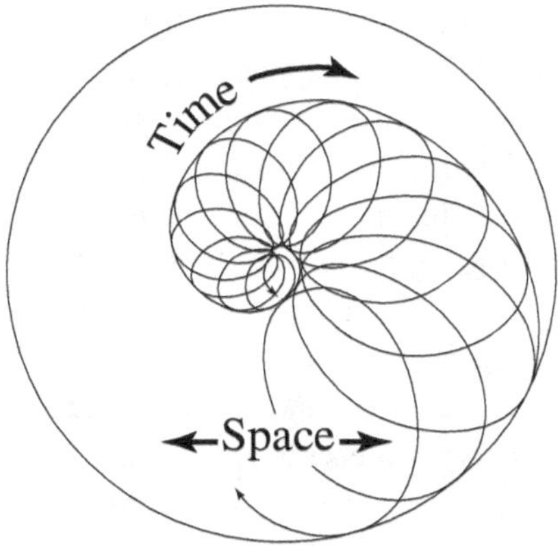

Figure 2. The time-space continuum

When this continuum is clothed in materiality it forms a symbolic seashell, one of the major religious symbols in Eastern philosophies, often depicted in the hands of *yogins* and the major Hindu and Buddhist Deities. It can also be pictured as a *trumpet* that conveys *sound,* as also does the shell. In part, it produces the esoteric interpretation of such phrases as that given in *Rev. 4:1:* 'and the first voice which I heard was as it were of a trumpet talking to me'. This means that *kuṇḍalinī* energy was effectively flowing, allowing John to listen to the 'inner Voice' produced by the resultant enlightenment.

This continuum also graphically depicts the way of awakening the meditation-Mind as it builds its path in consciousness from the infinitesimal point in time and space that represents the self-conscious individual focussed upon the object of perception, the central dot *(bindu),* the seed or the focal point of meditation, to the outer limits of possible cognition or revelation, represented by the circumference. The path is a spiral, as consciousness travels this way, through repeated cycles of activity, onwards and outwards in space through time, becoming increasingly expansive as it evolves.

This is but an elaboration of the spiral ꩜ depicted in the centre of the *vajra* (Tib: Dorje*),*[30] the 'diamond sceptre'[31] that symbolises immutable power in Buddhism. The *vajra* organises consciousness in terms of the five Rays of Mind as it travels out to encompass space. The movement outward is according to the process of expansion of the petals of the *chakras*, and happens in consciousness in the most developed forms of meditative absorption. Its power is the objective of the process of gaining enlightenment.

The Rays organise the movement of the petals of the flowers and their expansion according to the nature of the flow of *prāṇa* within the *nāḍīs*. Further expansion happens as the meditative consciousness progresses through cleansing the sheaths of substance (body, emotions, and mind) by means of the disciplines *(āsanas)* that allow an increasing flow of more intense forms of energy within consciousness. Eventually, all that binds one to the phenomena of three-dimensional space is broken and liberation from it ensues. The person then enters into conscious identification with the multidimensional universe.

Another way of viewing the flow of the *prāṇas* is that each *prāṇic* stream is but the flow of a specific *saṃskāra*. We see that the *saṃskāra* starts at a point of generation and expands over time in the form of consciousness-space as increasingly more factors are built into it. The *saṃskāra* becomes truly expansive as it becomes increasingly refined by converting base substance into the refined attributes of the Fiery and Airy Element. Such transformation becomes the major challenge

---

30 See Govinda, *Foundations of Tibetan Mysticism,* 63, where the stages of unfoldment of a *vajra* are depicted.

31 Ibid., 62.

and work of all meditators seeking enlightenment.

The spiral motion depicts the movement of a wind, the *prāṇas* moving through the *nāḍīs*, in the form of the principle of Life *(jīva),* the inherent vitality keeping the body alive. It was the meditative awareness of this that allowed Paul to state in *1Cor. 15:52:*

> In a moment, in the twinkling of an eye, at the last trump: for the trumpet shall sound, and the dead shall be raised incorruptible, and we shall be changed.

Here the trumpet Sound is that of the *prāṇas* being conveyed through the *chakras* of the person just before the ('incorruptible') astral form leaves at the moment of death. 'The last trump' is the mantric Sound that calls forth the consciousness of the deceased, complete with its inherent vitality, on to the new field of experience that the death of the physical vehicle affords. The process of dying, and that of meditation, are essentially synonymous processes. The *Tibetan Book of the Dead,* for instance, clearly links the two, as it serves a dual role as a guide for meditation to effect complete liberation from the formed realms, as well as being a liturgy for the deceased.[32]

Spiral-cyclic motion is observed in the flow of *prāṇas* from the central point in Figure 2 of the time-space continuum to the circumference, and then returns to its source in cleansed or modified form, before it is consequently recycled again. The above-down motion of the spiral is symbolised by the yin-yang (a term derived from Taoist sources). Here the general outline of the spirals of the horns of a ram is also depicted, and when the symbolism is extended metaphorically to the signs of the zodiac we get an esoteric reason why the Ram heads the twelve signs and impels their motion cyclically through the time-space continuum.

When the spiral is projected in the four directions in time and space, then we get the *four winds*, symbolised by the swastika 卍. These winds represent the four Elements (or *prāṇas*, synthesised by the fifth one, Aether), as well as the four kingdoms in Nature, and the 'four Guardians' of a typical *maṇḍala,* from which the varying levels of 'the elect' are

32 See Evans-Wentz, *The Tibetan Book of the Dead*, lix.

derived. They are 'winds' *(vayus)* because our concern is enlightenment and the associated states of qualified energy of differing degrees that the winds represent. Each wind has a different colour and symbolic permutation in the fabric of Life. We thus have the awakening of the full potency of the meditation-Mind (as explained by the symbolism of the qualities of the *maṇḍala* of the five Dhyāni Buddhas[33]) with the central Buddha synthesising the qualities of the other four.

When we view this process from above-down, and from within without, we see the powers of Divinity descending and causing effects in the material realms. This is what is implied in such statements as in *Rev. 8:13:*

> Woe, Woe, Woe, to the inhabitors of the earth by reason of the other voices of the trumpet of the three angels, which are yet to sound.

Angels represent high members of the *deva* kingdom that are responsible for the evolution of the kingdoms of Nature and for the dissemination of *karma* throughout space. Therefore, when they Sound out their trumpets, then this means major planetary or terrestrial changes, or of the effects of the law of *karma* upon us, such as through famines or drought. The Sounding of such trumpets convey Logoic *saṃskāras* possessing a specific force and qualities (embodied Entities) that will effect terrestrial changes via the agency of the *devas.* The entire philosophy of the purification of the sheaths of substance by a meditator through transforming *saṃskāras* is here implied, but on a vast scale, where one needs to visualise in terms of the meditator being a Logos.

The attainment of the meditation-Mind, and the resultant internal experiences of one type or another, is concomitant with the number of previous lives spent in pursuit of the Mysteries of the divine. If for instance, a person has spent a life in the past learning directly from the Buddha, and later from Jesus, and as the millennia progressed, under a number of other enlightened sages, then this acquired experience will greatly assist him/her to quickly master the entire life process and obtain the enlightened Mind. This person would tend to quickly catch up to where he/she left off in the past, though within the context of the new cultural and environmental situation.

---

33 Cf. Govinda, *Foundations of Tibetan Mysticism*, 121.

Such a one would already have been initiated into the associated Mysteries in past lives. The former attainment must be recapitulated, and then the testings passed in the present life will allow surpassing of the high point of the past. The person is then an Initiate, one of 'the elect', 'the first born among many brethren, *predestined* thus by God, to be conformed in the image of his Son'.[34] What exactly is this *'predestination'?* It is the *karma* of the 'works' of the Sambhogakāya Flower projecting its impetus (of what the future is to be) into the (present) space of the personal-I, to cause the activity of the personality in the outer seeming that is the phenomenal world in which we reside.

The Rays and an introduction to group evolution

The major Ray lines and the basic qualities of the signs of the zodiac are hidden in the key terms of the following passage. They shall be outlined in the order presented by the text. Their explication should help future Biblical scholars to delve deeper into other lists presented in the New Testament, and gain much more from them than they currently do.

Collossians 3:12-17 should be read here for a description of some of the characteristics needed to be developed by 'the elect':

> Put on therefore, as the elect of God, holy and beloved, bowels of mercies, kindness, humbleness of mind, meekness, long suffering.
>
> Forbearing one another, and forgiving one another, if any man have a quarrel against any: even as Christ forgave you, so also *do* ye.
>
> And above all these things *put on* charity, which is the bond of perfectness.
>
> And let the peace of God rule your hearts, to which also ye are called in one body; and be ye thankful.
>
> Let the Word of Christ dwell in you richly in all wisdom; teaching and admonishing one another in psalms and hymns and spiritual songs, singing with grace in your hearts to the Lord.

These qualities are equally applicable, or necessary, for those developing the meditation-Mind, and which will allow 'the peace of God' to 'rule in your hearts'. This is the effect of the energy of Love that must be evoked as the prime healing potency, and which was the mainstay of Jesus' ministry as he worked his miracles amongst the

34 See *Romans 8:29-33.*

sick and diseased, and also of the seventy he specially trained to do likewise.[35] What was possible then can now be manifoldly repeated on this higher evolutionary arc.

Nowadays, 'psalms and hymns' become prayers and invocations to divinity, whilst 'spiritual songs' are another term for *mantras,* evoked 'with grace in your hearts to the Lord'. The science of *invocation* (the descent of the energies of divinity from above down), and *evocation* (of the energies of the *chakras*, from within to influence the phenomenal world without) is in fact the basis to successful meditation and healing outcomes. Invocation and evocation must be coupled with the virtues outlined above, if one wishes to travel the white path, as care must be taken not to manifest any of the attributes of the metaphorical ravening wolf.

First we see that *'the elect of God'* relate to the first Ray of Will or Power because this energy has to be developed by 'the elect' to overcome attachment to *saṃsāra* and thereby gain the necessary Initiations that will lead them to the Kingdom of 'God' (Shambhala).

The second Ray of Love-Wisdom is implicated by the phrase *'holy and beloved'* because the demonstration of the Love of 'God' (the divine in all things), of humanity and of Nature, makes one 'holy', saintlike, spiritually righteous. The accompanying wisdom makes one 'beloved' because it expresses the way of the Bodhisattva that widely gives to all in need.

The phrase *'bowels of mercies'* refers to the qualities of the third Ray of Mathematically Exact Activity, whereby the principle of Love is wisely and actively demonstrated by producing merciful and charitable acts for humanity. The mercy is for those that commit selfish and often cruel acts upon others, specifically upon those that attack proponents of the pure white *dharma* in some way. Such actions are not held against them, rather wisdom is utilised to help them see the errors of their actions, the type of *karma* that results, and how to best rectify the effects of their actions. The energy of the Heart is drawn to the lower *chakras* that become the 'bowels' of receptivity of the emotionally based *saṃskāras* for which the 'mercy' is applied to help convert.

'Kindness' is an expression of the fourth Ray of Beautifying Harmony overcoming Strife, as it concerns being considerate to those

35 *Luke 10:1-24.*

in difficulty or having emotional or financial problems. The effect of kindness therefore is to produce harmony, joyousness, and prosperity in the midst of what otherwise would be stressful or harmful.

'Humbleness of mind' is what must be developed by all upon the meditation path to overcome ego-posturing and the pride that often accompanies those who are mentally focused, as all meditators must be if enlightenment is the goal. We therefore have the fifth Ray of Scientific Reason implicated here.

'Meekness' refers to the quiet, submissive, emotionally calm attitude that must accompany those that are ruled by the sixth Ray of Devotion, if they are to receive exalted impressions from the zone of the Divine.

The term *'long suffering'* refers to life in the material domain, wherein one continually suffers the blows from the *karma* engendered in past cycles of activity. This is ruled by the seventh Ray of Cyclic Activity and Ceremonial Ritual.

After this, one can discern twelve statements relating to the twelve signs of the zodiac. They shall be cursorily analysed in the context of group evolution, for which the meditative lifestyle prepares one. A group is but the embodiment of a *maṇḍala* that is properly structured and which has a purpose for its existence. All beings upon the path to enlightenment innately, and later consciously, work as part of a group for the purpose of liberating the all from the thrall of *māyā*. It is the Bodhisattva way. For this reason Jesus had his twelve apostles and Buddha established his *saṅgha* (spiritual community). *Collossians 3:12-17* is accordingly written in terms of group evolution, and thus provides a basic guide to the information that will be detailed in the last chapter. The group laws are the law of Sacrifice, of Magnetic Impulse, of Service, of Repulse, of Group Progress, Expansive Response, and of the Lower Four. These laws govern the way of expression for all members of the Ray Ashrams of the Masters of Wisdom.

1. First we have the phrase *'forbearing one another'*, where the word 'forbearing' refers to manifesting great patience. This refers to the first sign of the zodiac, Aries the ram, that instigates the turning of the wheel of the zodiac. Great patience must be evidenced to see the course of action associated with the remaining signs through to the end of their forms of activity. Another cycle can then occur upon a

higher turn of the wheel. To effectively help others one must see the task through to its end, even if it takes years. For Initiates such tasks, for which they sacrifice their time and effort, may take lifetimes.

All upon the path to enlightenment, who consequently follow the laws of group evolution, must practice great forbearance in all of their activities. They must work to help their group brothers and sisters through all of their trials and difficult periods, even if it takes many years. All must work together, utilising skilful means and much wisdom to help the group pass through their Initiation testings. Through forbearance sacrifices are made by all group members to produce a unity or synthesis of purpose.

2. The next phrase is *'forgiving one another'*, which refers to the wisdom and compassion developed in the second sign of the zodiac, Taurus the bull, who clothes the initial impulse engendered by the Ram. Taurus feeds the principle of desire, and thus the activities that happen as a consequence, where people manifest many wrong attachments and emotions impulsed by this energy. With respect to the group context, forgiveness does not just mean overcoming resentment for wrong actions or misdeeds manifested against the group harmony or an individual, but also in assisting the individual to not manifest a similar action again. Specifically, in group evolution, irritability concerning other's quirks, actions and what may have been said, as well as the critical mind, must be specially guarded against. There is always much to forgive if the group is to move forward along the Initiation path. This is a general principle affecting all of the laws, and without it there would be no sense of spiritual camaraderie within a group that bonds them in service together.
3. The phrase for Gemini the twins is *'above all these things put on charity'*. One of the twins is mortal and the other immortal. At first they are reprobating and fighting each other, but must learn to hold hands in service and to be charitable to each other in every way. Compassionate giving lies at the heart of a group's activity. It is the key to residing in the sacred precincts (adytum) of the temple presided over by Gemini. The charitable actions amongst all group members bonds them into one strong vehicle of service and directs their sense of group progress.

4. '*The bond of perfectness*' refers to the sign Cancer the crab, which is concerned with the process of incarnation, and establishing the bond between the higher self and the incarnate individual. The group members must work to meditatively align themselves with this bond *(sūtrātmā)* and thereby to channel energies and impressions from their Sambhogakāya Flowers via it. As this is accomplished, so inevitably perfectness of expression comes into manifestation, as the individual increasingly takes on the attributes of divinity. The Sambhogakāya Flower is group conscious, it knows no other way, thus the collective vertical alignment must manifest horizontally to inspire all of the group members to incorporate a manifesting divinity that magnetically coheres the individuals into one group structure ('shell'). The magnetic impulse of Love between them integrates them in the *maṇḍala* of service in a similar way that a hermit crab carries its shell wherever it goes.
5. Leo the lion governs the attributes of the phrase '*the Peace of God rule your hearts'*. The governing sign ruling Leo on all levels of expression is the sun. The sun stands for the Heart of Life, be this Heart the Heart centre, the Soul, or the Hierarchy of Light (the planetary Heart centre). To the Heart centre, therefore, the disciples must go in their meditations if they are to be awakened and to overcome the natural element of pride associated with this sign. The entire group structure must come to emulate the qualities of a Heart centre, to provide life-giving spiritual nourishment to all around. At first the major energy emanating from the Heart is peace, to smooth over any form of emotional turbulence or agitation. Next there is the expression of serenity, and finally the quiescence of *śūnyatā*. The way of the Heart when directed to serve humanity, produces the expansive response of the group as it attracts to it an increasing number of serving disciples.
6. The qualities of the next sign, Virgo the virgin, govern the succeeding phrase *'to which also ye are called in one body'*. Virgo is the universal Mother that governs the entire body of manifestation of any form, which she helps build. Within the *maṇḍala* of the group structure, the quality of peace from Leo must resonate to overcome strife or discord. The entire group can therefore produce

the establishment of one form of service work, vertically extended to the Heart of Life, and horizontally projected to succour the many with the nourishing 'milk' from the Mother.[36] The mother sacrifices her time and life to help her child grow to maturity. It is a persistent effort carried through decades of service. Similarly, the way of the law of Sacrifice resonates through 'the one body' of the group as being the keynote of their service to each other and to humanity.

7. The beneficence of the 'gift waves' from the guru within (the Christ presence) and the increasing vigour whereby the accompanying service to the many manifest, is always a cause of being *'thankful'*. The corresponding sign is Libra the balances, which governs the cyclic outpouring of the forces of life stemming from the interlude between breaths in meditation, as well as the manifestation of the law of *karma*. We have the in and out-breathings of the meditative process; of the pulsations of a heart-felt thanks for the gifts of the manifesting divinity and the opportunity to serve by means of the group. Each member of the group is also thankful for the opportunity to overcome the *māyā* of their material selves (the 'lower four'), with the kindly assistance of those who will see things about them that they are blind to. Thus, together they joyously eliminate hindrances *(saṃskāras)* upon their journey to liberating light, while the *karma* between group members is also satisfactorily resolved.
8. The next sign, Scorpio the scorpion, refers to all of the battles and tests that the path of discipleship imposes, in order to become perfected and to stand upon the mountaintop of revelation and of Initiation into the Mysteries of being/non-being. Once having passed all of these testings, the *'Word of Christ'* can then dwell *'richly in all wisdom'* in the disciple and the group as a whole. Then can the words of wisdom be promulgated upon the mountainside to the aspirants that gather to hear, in a similar manner that Jesus did when he gave out the Beatitudes. Without such testings, no true forging of group bonds can be made. Having successfully overcome obstacles together they can reap the fruits of their accomplishment upon the mountaintop of revelation.

36 We therefore have a fusion between the signs Leo and Virgo, which is seen astrologically in the qualities of the sphinx, which has a lion's body and a woman's head.

9. The word *'teaching'* refers to the qualities of the ninth sign of the zodiac, Sagittarius the archer, who fires the arrows of the loving dispensation of the group to all possible targets with sure-sighted accuracy. Vast is the arena whereby this gospel of glory, the 'Word of Christ', is broadcast. The objective of the spiritual 'ambition' (one of the keynotes of the Sagittarian) of the group is then to spread the doctrines of their *dharma* to as great an audience as possible.
10. The quality of *'admonishing one another'* refers to the attributes of Capricorn the goat, who embodies the mountain of mind/Mind which the goat dutifully climbs and eventually comes to master. To admonish is to warn or reprimand someone concerning some grievous error, fault or of something that may prove harmful. Here, therefore, the group mind is wisely utilised to work out the imperfections within the group structure, so that it can function more effectively, efficiently and wisely. It becomes ever more productive and can then grow into its next stage of spiritual development. This is not done with the critical mind, but lovingly, and proverbially in the form of 'psalms and hymns'. (Songs of praise of one for the other, and for the glory of the divinity manifesting through the group, which incorporates the qualities of the next sign of the zodiac.) Once the imperfections have been removed, then the highest possible summit of attainment can be reached.
11. Aquarius the water bearer is represented by a person bearing a pitcher of the Waters of Life and Love, which is poured freely to all around. In terms of the group's activity, these Waters manifest in the form of *'psalms and hymns and spiritual songs'.* They are devotional and aspirational techniques of praise and reverence to divinity, and are an educational service to others. Rephrasing the concept in the eastern terminology we then have mantras, invocations, hymns of obeisance to deities, and the *dhāraṇīs* of liberation. Whatever the terminology or method, the effect is similar, producing a well-being of group harmony, and the down flow of spiritual force pertaining to enlightenment. The energy waves generated can then flood the general auric space of the planet, to help cleanse the murky astral spheres, and to produce a sense of joy in the often bleak lives of people, thus spiritually uplifting all around. The mantric Sound

attracts to the group many spiritual forces that can help in the service, both upon the inner realms, and upon the outer field of service. All are nourished by the joyous emanation of the group Sound.

12. Finally we have the sign Pisces the fishes, which terminates one major cycle of activity. The accompanying phrase is *'singing with grace in your hearts to the Lord'*. In Pisces, the fishes are joined by a bond, where one is swimming in the waters of *saṃsāra* and the other represents liberated Life. One must learn to sever the bond in order to swim free in the 'other shore' of liberated Life. Here the group 'singing with grace' represents the fish swimming in *saṃsāra,* and 'the Lord', or Logos, the liberated One. Singing 'with grace in your hearts' is a mechanism of travelling along the lighted Path towards liberation. The term 'grace' refers to the bestowal of blessings from the Lord at Shambhala. The process of such bestowal can only happen as the tests of Initiation have been passed and the group moves up to the Kingdom of 'God' via the law of Attraction, and by rectifying *karma,* to produce a grand synthesis of liberated life.

The battle with evil

The various stages of attainment of enlightened perception that an individual passes through must also transpire for humanity, when they similarly undertake the process *en masse* in the future. As they are the world disciple, the 'Son of man', or Christ-child, travelling on the road to enlightenment, so the symbolism found in chapter three of *Collosians* will manifest externally for them. Outer plane happenings and internal revelations are both veiled by the same imagery, and whenever humanity is to tread the next step onwards on their path to Light, so a great One incarnates to exoterically embody the process that they must internally travel. Such was the case, for instance, at the time of Krishna and the establishment of the *bhakti* (devotional) schools in India, the Wisdom tradition of the Buddha, or with the appearance of Christ-Jesus and his doctrine of Love 2,000 years ago. The next imminent step in that salubrious revelatory process has been prophesied with respect to the appearance of Maitreya, who will fuse all previous lines of expression, plus add the new doctrine of the Will.

That which opposes the Hierarchy of Light, the tireless workers for the common good, are their brothers of evil,[37] who work to manipulate the effects of the factor of human free will. These forces utilise great cunning and intelligence with an intensely one-pointed wilful, selfish, separative, avaricious, and predatory motive, to build their arenas of power in the world. They care naught for free will, other than the way it serves their ambitions, and do whatever they can to project and uphold the conditionings of the past from where humanity has evolved. These conditionings are directly related to the material domain, and do not serve the present or future good of the whole. We have, for instance, the rigid, entrenched conceptualisations and assertions of the minds of our intelligentsia; the selfish pleasure-seeking and bigoted attitudes of the masses, the worst conditionings associated with scientific materialism, unabated rampant capitalism (the power and pleasure that money can buy), totalitarian attitudes, and dogmatic religious tendencies.

Such conditionings are prevalent because the dark brotherhood find great scope for activity and the projection of their separative purpose from their bases of power amongst the easily manipulated desire-minds of humanity. They are rulers of the world of materialistic incentive, based on the lowest common denominators of greed, fear, selfish and separative attitudes, coldness of mind, and the bigotry of the masses. They will fight to the utmost to prevent any changes or movements towards loving development by utilising the methods of outright lies, distorted propaganda, and the various forms of psychic and physical coercion to achieve their aims. They work with the innate fears, ignorance, selfishness, and apathetic attitudes of the majority. They also work from high places with occult methods and magical endeavour (e.g., telepathically). They will not abide in the truth, nor bear the embrace of Love. Absolute power and dominion over all in the lower psychic and material realms is their goal. Thus the battle line is drawn. A battle line to which the opening gates of the meditation-Mind definitely leads the aspirant, for he/she must be rightly trained to work consciously for the good of the whole, with the forces of Light, and not be a pawn in the hands of the hosts of evil.

---

37 A general discussion on this subject of what evil is and is not was provided in my revised book *The Revelation*, chapter 8, 'The Question of Evil'.

Information concerning this battle with evil is not presented here to produce fear of what might happen in the meditation process. It must be emphasised that no harm can come to one following the precepts of the Hierarchy of Light and Love (the Council of Bodhisattvas). They have infallible methods of right education for those in their care, taking *karma* always into account, if the student follows their instructions.

What needs to be emphasised is that such a battle must inevitably happen to all that seriously wish to travel the path of Love in action, once psychic perceptions begin to awaken, as the dark brotherhood (and the evil *saṃskāras* of the many) will always oppose such people. Most servers of humanity work exoterically, and thus are oblivious of the part that the Hierarchy of Light play in protecting them from *the Evil* so that they can do their work in relative security, as far as their own *karma* allows. However, to be most effective, such workers must begin to take their own protection in hand, and learn to directly counter those forces that oppose their fields of service. They must come to know of the methodology of the forces of evil and how to counter them in their own terms, and this teaching is given in meditation or in contemplation (and has always been part of the 'ear whispered' instructions of all spiritual lineages).[38] In this way they will release the members of the Hierarchy that have been protecting them, so they can concentrate upon higher forms of service work.

This is the way of evolution for all, and the 'strait gate'[39] of Initiation into the Mysteries of the kingdom of Shambhala is found in the aptitude to do this service work consciously. We should witness here the testimony of Jesus in the four Gospels, because the great bulk of his teachings, healing work, and exorcisms concerned his fight against evil. Like all Initiates, it is what he came upon the earth to do. The path of Love-Wisdom demands it.

---

38 Many disciples fighting the effects of evil in our societies are not esoterically inclined, nevertheless, methods of protection will avail themselves, according to the dictates of *karma*.

39 *Matt. 7:13-14*: 'Enter ye in at the strait gate: for wide *is* the gate, and broad *is* the way, that leadeth to destruction, and many there by which go thereat: Because strait *is* the gate, and narrow is the way, which leadeth unto life, and few there by that find it.' The 'ravening wolves' of the next verse: 'Beware of false prophets, which come to you in sheep's clothing, but inwardly they are ravening wolves' directly refer to the members of the dark brotherhood.

The true spiritual teacher must therefore be skilfully educated in the subtleties of the ways of the lords of dark face, if he/she is to lead the disciple into the good, the true, and the everlasting Life of the realms of the Hierarchy of Love. Much *karma* falls into the lap of those ignorant of such subtleties but who take on board the instructions of disciples for training, unless they teach that stream of revelation related to the evocation of *bodhicitta*.

This battle that Jesus continuously fought is one that the orthodox scriptural commentators have never understood. The subtleties of 'the devil' (etc.) have always eluded them, having contemptuously snubbed, suppressed, and sneered at teachings concerning magical endeavour (which Jesus so evidently demonstrated throughout his short life), as well as the Mystery teachings of the old Pagan and Near Eastern religions (into which it is evident that Jesus was versed in). They therefore have remained ignorant to everything associated with the ways of the black magician, as well as to that which is related to the work of all Bodhisattvas, and such ignorance invites disease, obsession, and *the Evil*. Indeed, such attitudes inform us of how outstandingly successful the forces of evil can be in the manipulation and taking over of an entire religious dispensation. The methods of the Inquisitional period in Europe is an example of the extreme effects of such fostered ignorance, and the resultant narrow-mindedness and bigotry stemming from it.

The mainstream Christian preacher, as well as the many sectarian and charismatic groups, have therefore mistaken evil to be what it is not, for example; other religious teachings and philosophies. They have spread the doctrine of fear, and totally over-emphasised the wrong things to be the 'pawn of Satan', such as various forms of sexuality. They have never understood the working of *karma*, nor the nature of the protective shield that the Hierarchy of Light ('the elect') have for aeons projected over infant humanity.

The coming epoch will be ruled by the Airy Element, when the awakening of the intuitive capabilities of humanity (symbolised by the air) will be greatly stimulated. The development and nurturing of the qualities of the intuition will lead one into the domain of the realms of Light, and the proper exemplification of the teachings of what *śūnyatā* veils for the entire world to ponder. The inner Eye awakens and begins to see All, the inner Ear awakens and begins to hear, and the Mind can then know the All, whilst the Heart awakens and embraces All. That Heart becomes an aspect of the One Heart beating out the rhythms and pulsations of cosmic Life, dynamically drawing All to it.

Here we have the major objective of the meditation process. Though one is eventually absorbed into the all-encompassing sphere of the One, 'individuality' is never lost, but rather refined, redefined and reconstructed, becoming a vehicle of service and sacrifice to enable all beings to relinquish the ties they have with the realms of suffering and death. This is accomplished according to the Ray equipment and positioning to which the person belongs within the Hierarchy of Light. It becomes a transcendent, transmogrified vehicle of Light, the appearance *(nirmāṇakāya)* through which the vestures of a Buddha (the Spirit within) can manifest outwardly.

Only one unending chain of Individuality exists, from the smallest to the greatest co-worker, beating out the pulsations from the Heart of Life to all forms in the body Logoic that need to be nourished by That Heart's Blood. (They are like many sparks constituting one flame, and many flames embody one blazing sun of spiritual endeavour.) Right meditation techniques allow one to ascend the way of the Christ, and as a Christ (the prototype Bodhisattva of the highest degree), into Light and Love supernal. Arenas of fluctuating happiness become the zone of joy as the related service work proceeds. Evil (all forms of corruption, sickness and disease) is overcome, and the person begins to die to the vicissitudes of the egocentric personality life, its attachments to things ephemeral, and its self-serving attitudes. Joy becomes bliss as the higher way of unbridled insight into Life Dynamic is trod.

To become a Christ you must 'work out your own salvation... Do all things without murmurings and disputings. That ye may be blameless and harmless, The Sons of God, without rebuke'.[40] To be 'Sons of God' means to definitely partake in the divinity of 'God'. This concept was directly in Paul's mind when he stated in *Philippians 2:5-6:* 'Let this mind be in you, which is also in Christ-Jesus: who, being in the form of God, thought it not robbery to be *equal with God'*. Elsewhere (in

---

40 *Phil. 2:12-16.*

Eph. 4:13) Paul asks us all to 'come in the unity of faith, and of the knowledge of the Son of God, unto a perfect man, unto the measure of the stature of the fullness of the Christ'. We also find the statement of Christ-Jesus at the end of the fifth chapter in *Matthew:* 'Be ye therefore perfect, even as your father which is in heaven is perfect'.

What does becoming as perfect as the Christ, or His 'father in heaven' mean, and how is it possible in merely one life to become 'equal with God', especially if one has to 'work out' one's own salvation, salvation thereby implying utter perfection? Only the reincarnation process, backed by the law of *karma*, will guarantee that perfection as evolution progresses. It will cause one to eventually work out one's own salvation through attained mastery of everything concerning the phenomenal material world and of the personality structure into which one incarnates, through the testings associated with gaining entry into the Mysteries of enlightened being.[41]

In the latter stages of evolution, the achievement of such utter perfection that is implied here necessitates the Bodhisattva path as outlined in the Buddhist doctrine. This has its basis in the path of right meditative involvement. Such mastery does not mean denial, or suppression of the allurements of the senses (as in celibacy, or a programme of severe austerities, as the Buddha discovered upon his path to enlightenment), but right control of all that is, to the degree that Christ-Jesus demonstrated such mastery. (The attainment of Christ has surpassed the tenth, or highest stage of the Bodhisattva *bhūmis*[42], which will be explained in the chapters on Initiation.) Think also on what it means to actually do 'greater works' than Jesus did 2,000 years ago, as He promised us we would in *John 14:12.*

True meditation practices focus on the path of developing compassion for the sufferings of all sentient beings, which in turn awakens the

---

41 Mysteries, therefore, which incorporate the law of *karma* and the factor of the rebirth of consciousness, which definitely exists in the New Testament, but which has been ignored by the orthodox Christian, as my book *The Revelation* aptly demonstrates.

42 These ten stages are explained in *The Jewel Ornament of Liberation* (by sGam.po.pa), trans. Khenpo Konchog Gyaltsen Rinpoche, (Snow Lion, Ithaca, New York, 1998).

potencies of the Heart. This produces the power to visualise and intuit the future that lies in the portals of worlds presently unseen. Awakening to group service work is then necessitated, because the process of such interrelationship allows compassionate insight in all of one's undertakings to be fine-tuned. This is symbolised by the twelve apostles that Jesus gathered around him, thereby embodying the potencies of the twelve petals of the Heart centre. The meditator will then *see,* beyond thought, that all sentient beings are an interrelated whole. The way up the ladder of being/non-being consists of a mergence or fusion with the whole through increasingly greater, successive arcs of reticulated meditative insight and combined service with all other meditators. The work ensues at a similar or greater level of attainment than for the apostles. The Lord of Compassion (the Christ/Maitreya Buddha) can then focus his gaze one's way, and direct one into the arenas of service associated with the Council of Bodhisattvas, who are his foremost disciples. In this way the great awakening proceeds and the salvation of the 'little ones' (the spiritual children) that constitute the bulk of humanity will unfold with certainty.

The Great Invocation

From the point of Light within
The Mind of the Primordial One,
Let Light stream forth into all minds.
Let Light descend on earth.

From the point of Love within
The Heart of the Lord of Love,
Let Love stream forth into all Hearts,
May Maitreya issue forth where people dwell.

From the centre where the Divine Will is known,
Let Purpose guide the little human wills,
The purpose which Bodhisattvas know and serve.

From the centre which we call humanity,
Let the Plan of Love and Light work out,
And may it seal the door where evil dwells.

Let Light and Love and Power restore the Plan on earth.
So let it be and help us do our part.

Oṁ Maṇi Padme Hūṁ

This is a modified version of 'The Great Invocation' found in the works of A.A.Bailey.

3

The Practice of Meditation

Meditation and lifestyle changes

There is no intention here to present a detailed explanation of the various techniques and processes involved with the many forms of meditation systems and teachings that are currently in existence. Much detail can only be learned whilst the student is practising meditation. A teaching is only of value as long as it is practical, serves the current need, and posits the basis that will allow future growth to occur. Each student of meditation has a different psyche to another, and different prominent *saṃskāras* to master, therefore meditation techniques must inevitably be fine tuned to serve their particular needs. Practical experiences are of the utmost importance, for only that which one has discovered for oneself can be of true and lasting value. Ultimately that is all that one can truly know. The technique outlined will serve as a basis for one to gain direct meditative experience of the knowledge detailed throughout the volumes of this treatise.

It is not important to possess a great deal of meditation theory beforehand. Succinct, correctly constructed information is however important, as much that is presented in current meditation teachings can be misleading. Too much concrete theory can complicate matters, making the awakening of the meditation-Mind more difficult if the mind fixates upon engendered images of what it thinks meditation *ought* to be. The mind should simply allow the impressions to come. An overly active mind is detrimental, for it is busily looking for this or that image or impression; it may be restless or impatient with the entire process, being critically analytical of whatever may be happening or not happening. (This is one of the greatest blocks to the flow of the meditation-Mind.) It will also conjure up images of past events, or to what it thinks the future may be; carry on a conversation with itself (chatter) as to what it wants to do, and so forth. The mind is in fact 'the great slayer of the Real', yet the mind must be used to 'slay the slayer'.[1] This is the major dilemma of most students at the onset of the process of becoming enlightened beings.

The major problem for most is how to control the chattering mind and direct it to the purpose of achieving the necessary 'mindful' state. Mindfulness in every action of thought, word, or deed, is often the answer, but one is to be mindful without the mind being focussed upon any particular thing, unless that 'thing' be the seed for meditation. This implies that at first there is a careful observation over the entire life process, to ensure that everything done produces the desired goal. The mind observes a panorama of that process, and this allows it to see the arenas of disharmony and need (factors of mind needing improvement or clarifying). Once that need is satisfied, and the disharmony rectified, this then frees the mind to concentrate upon the meditation process.

The mind must be controlled so that it can focus upon the task at hand and produce the seed for meditation, and after the seed has been sown the mind must humbly abdicate its kingdom. The development of the seed must proceed in a natural way without the mind influencing it, as any influence of the seed-thought by the self-focussed mind would distort the results according to the patterns projected by the mind, and not be productive of Truth.

Meditation is not something done at a certain time, and then forgotten about for the rest of the day. To be effective, the experiences and qualities must be carried through to every part of the working day. The entire environment one lives in should be conducive to the development of the meditation-Mind, or be transformed to suit the purpose of the ideal. (It concerns the production of salutary peace-engendering qualities, the evoking of elements of calmness all around.)

1 H.P. Blavatsky, *The Voice of the Silence: being chosen fragments from the Book of the Golden Precepts*, (Theosophical Publishing House, Wheaton, IL, 1998), 13.

This then becomes the individual's prime meditation and the basis to his/her service work.

The emphasis, however, is not so much upon the external environment, but the internal one, and the mode of controlling the modifications of the mind and emotions.[2] It cannot be overemphasised that all types of emotional states (the continuous agitation of the person's aura), be they subtle or more obvious (e.g., irritation, anger, frustrated ambitions, fears, anxieties, glamour, and their cousins—uncontrolled merriment and laughter), are the greatest hindrances to the meditation-Mind. Because of the real difficulty of exercising control over these emotions we can see why only a tiny fraction of the many thousand meditators upon the earth at any time actually achieve enlightenment in that life.

The activity of the entire lifestyle must be observed in all genuine meditation teachings, as a cause always produces an effect. Observing the interdependent chain of cause and effect is therefore part of the development of the meditation-Mind. Meditation and the meditative lifestyle produces *necessarily a healing* effect. Such healing is the essence of the enlightenment process. The process involves throwing off all toxins of body, speech and mind that would produce disease (meditative dis-ease) within the *environment* in which one lives. The word 'environment' must be analysed in the broadest possible context—within the human body, within a social context, or to the biosphere and greater cosmos of which the earth is but a part. The cleansing of one's karmic ties to everything associated with manifest space is thus implied. The effect is essentially what is called 'liberation' in many meditation texts. All we see around us is but part of one great interrelated whole, and the meditation process brings one's consciousness immediately into

2 See also *The Yoga Sutras of Patanjali*: I. K. Tiamni, *The Science of Yoga* (The Theosophical Publishing House, Wheaton, IL, 2001), 6. Verse two states: *Yogaś citta-vṛtti nirodaha*—yoga is the inhibition of the modifications of the mind. The rest of the yoga sutras essentially concern unfolding the detail of this particular verse. These teachings compliment Buddhist Yogācārya teachings on the same subject, the difference being the Hindu-Buddhist dispute concerning the nature of whether an *ātman* exists or not, and thus its ramifications into the theistic concerns of the Hindus. Nevertheless, both Buddhist and Hindu yoga systems produce valid results, whilst arenas of resolution of the doctrinal distinctions between the two viewpoints can be found via meditation.

a multidimensional identification with that unity. As one's consciousness becomes united with that All, then of necessity the rectification of the arenas of disharmony in one's consciousness proceeds apace. The means to such rectification is what is here called 'service work'.

If one is not willing to undergo self-discipline as far as one's lifestyle is concerned, then of what use is meditation to that person, or of any *true* cure for ailments of the human psyche?

The question is then asked by many, 'does this mean that I must forego all the good things in life in order to gain an enlightened mind?' The answer will always be: 'what people think are the "good things" are not necessarily so, and on close examination, definitely not so'. People's social and ethical values need to change; they must learn to closely examine the true causes for their sicknesses, worries, and fluctuations in fortune, the possibility of debilitating diseases, and even senility with the onset of old age. There is a price to pay for all forms of abuse and dissipation of the vital energy that people squander when they project the widely emotional forms of activity that constitutes their 'good time', and of the many forms of drugs and intoxicants they continually abuse their bodies with. They will suffer when these intoxicants work their way out of the body. People have not been taught to rightfully add cause to effect.

The basic teaching of control of the emotions is already developed by our major religious exponents, and is embodied in the *Four Noble Truths* and the *Eightfold Path* that is the basis to Buddhist philosophy. People must learn to follow the middle way between all extremes of emotional dissipation and perturbations of mind, with their related thought patterns and verbal expressions. 'Not that which goeth into the mouth defileth a man, but that which cometh out of the mouth'.[3] All verbalised emotional-mental exaggerations produce effects in the realms of form, such as bodily ailments, environmental aberrations, and unpleasant social interactions and relationships. This is because from a meditative viewpoint (mantric) Sound is causative of all that we see around us. Sound is the means of controlling and psychically precipitating energies, which then embody the substance from which everything is constituted. Proper comprehension of this process

3 *Matt. 15:11.*

necessitates true knowledge of the way that the *chakras*, Sound, the elementals (elementary Lives), and the Elements interrelate. Coupled with this comes the necessity of comprehending the way that the greater Lives, the *devas,* Wrathful and Peaceful Deities, govern the way whereby everything comes to be in manifestation.

The type of lifestyle of the average socially oriented person has its teaching value. Much can be learned concerning the problem of suffering, the impermanence of happiness, the transitory nature of all phenomenal life, the right use of money, the problem of the various forms of sexual gratification, the responsibilities of child care, the use and abuse of the various forms of power in the many departments of life, and social responsibilities. Even the virtue of manifesting altruistic activities, such as philanthropic or socially and environmentally bettering enterprises, must be properly learnt. However, the higher ethical questions, such as what it all means, what is the purpose to life, why so much suffering, pain, social and national iniquities, conflict, international strife, warfare, famines, etc., are never really answered in this way.

Contemporary empirical philosophers can look into the semantics, rationalisations, empiricism, conjectures, and arguments about this or that theory of life. They can call themselves Absolutists, Agnostics, Altruists, Atheists, Communists, Conceptualists, Idealists, Realists, Materialists, Existentialists, Humanists, Empiricists, Monists, Meliorists, Mystics, Pantheists, Theists, Phenomenalists, Pluralists, Pragmatists, Relativists, Transcendentalists, Utilitarianists, and the like; but in the end the only thing that can truly give the answers is meditation. This is because the meditative lifestyle will produce the inner experiences and awaken the all-seeing Eye (Ājñā centre) that will enable the person to See, and consequently know reality in all its multi-dimensional splendour and unfolding beauty. This is the 'eye' that Jesus referred to: 'The light of the body is the eye: if therefore thine eye be single, thy whole body shall be full of light. But if thine eye be evil, thy whole body shall be full of darkness'.[4]

---

4 *Matt. 6:22-3.* This phrase can also be interpreted in relation to one being singularly focussed upon liberation and the means of its acquisition, that a 'body of light' shall be the outcome. However, the mechanism of focussing this singular purpose is the eye.

Filling up the body with light and its consequent transformation into a body of pure conscious energy is one of the major functions of the meditative lifestyle, as it is light of varying degrees and intensities that must be channelled by the meditator to accomplish many forms of service. Such light is seen as the transfiguring halo depicted around the heads of Christian saints, and also radiating from the Bodies of the Buddhas and Bodhisattvas of Buddhism. It is the 'virtue'[5] of the enlightened being that heals those around. The eye must be single, because singleness of purpose, clear one-pointed aspiration and focus, is the keynote for the enlightened one. The forces of materialism that oppose his/her activities are to be overcome if that one is to undeviatingly project purposeful energies to the task at hand. Where the Eye is focussed, there energy is directed and the magical activity or task is accomplished.

Breathing exercises, mantras and *kuṇḍalinī*

Many seem to think that the strange and contorted bodily positions and exercises associated with Hatha yoga are necessary for the pursuit of meditation, but generally the opposite is the case. Hatha yoga had its apogee of usefulness many millennia ago. Such emphasis upon the agility of the body now serves only to imprison the mind in the stranglehold of the form. All that is necessary are those exercises that serve to keep the body healthy, vitalised with life-giving *prāṇa*, nothing more, nothing less. Whatever is done to that end can be considered Hatha yoga. This can include such things as gymnastics, aerobics, Tai Chi, martial arts, or military disciplines.

Of the orthodox yoga postures, the most useful are *padma āsana* (the lotus position depicted in the most popular versions of the seated Buddha) and *siddhi āsana*; for when mastered they serve to keep the spine comfortably erect and the mind poised for meditation. They can be found explained in any good book on Hatha yoga, but are definitely not necessary for Western practitioners. A chair that allows one to sit straight suffices, or one can sit with a cushion against a wall. One must simply sit without slouching for the necessary time (say half an

5 *Mark 5:30, Luke 6:19,* and *8:46.*

hour). The development of the meditation-Mind will take care of the rest. The time taken for the meditation experience is unimportant, and long meditation sessions are generally unnecessary for the student.

Strenuous breathing exercises are also not necessary, where so many seconds are counted on inhalation, so many in holding the breath, and then again for exhalation. This can be dangerous for many beginners. It necessitates an enlightened teacher as the guide, one who knows the specifics as to why the exercise was assigned, the minutiae of the psychic, physiological, and psychological stages of the student, and what the outcome is to be. Breathing exercises are a way of forcefully opening the door to the lower psychic states, and therein lies the danger. Often, however, lower psychic states are mistaken for the highest enlightenment, and in the related glamoured action lies much karmic woe. All that is necessary for successful meditation practice is simply to breathe naturally and rhythmically and then to forget about the breathing process. It will take care of itself, once the mind is rightfully focussed. The next thing is to have no anxieties or expectations. Simply allow the flow of the meditation-Mind to manifest as it should and must.

Many meditation instructors give out 'personal' *mantras* (words or phrases signifying or evoking spiritual power) to their students. These are usually in a foreign language, such as Sanskrit, and hence particularly useless to one not brought up to understand the idiosyncrasies of the intonation of the Sound and the meaning of the mantra. If the practitioner has little comprehension of the syllables utilised, an expletive or profanity might just as well be given to produce similar effects.

True mantric Sound emanates from the stillness of the Heart, and is the result of the successful meditation practice, not the cause. In any case, the mantra is useless without the power to rightly visualise its purpose, and to consciously project it upon its task. They can then be very efficacious. However, it should be noted how often those that use mantras (of varying lengths) by projecting Sound through their mouths, inadvertantly draw upon (emotional) Solar Plexus energies in their desire to achieve preconceived objectives. This may have the effect of producing an exhilarating feeling, and sometimes related psycho-spiritual experiences, because of the heightened qualities of the emotions that are expressed and the wish-fulfilling gem of the desire-mind that is evoked. The enlightened Mind cannot however be obtained in this way.

Who can observe the stillness of a pool of water, if one continuously throws rocks in to agitate its surface? How can the internal Sound, the Voice of Silence *(nāda)* be heard, if the mind and mouth keep on tumbling out clattering activity? Only the foolish, who, wishing to hear the gentle sounds of a breeze passing through leaves, would go about banging old tin cans.

True mantric Sound is never given, and indeed, cannot be given to the beginner by the wise. It is fortunate for humanity that the secret science concerning the power of mantra has never been revealed exoterically, except in highly veiled terms, or that which can be deemed safe, such as the oft repeated Tibetan mantra Oṁ Maṇi Padme Hūṁ, because its purpose is the evocation of compassion. In Atlantean times, aspects of this sacred science were common lore, but the resultant abuse of the related *siddhis* is the major reason why that civilisation was devastated and the continent had to suffer the catastrophic 'flood' that sank it. Since then, such esoteric knowledge has been wisely withdrawn from the scrutiny of selfish minds, the sensually demanding, callous and greedy attitudes of the many who would wish to wield psychic power.

One does not place dangerous weapons in the hands of babes, unless severe lessons of what not to do are to be learnt.

The effective use of mantra is a science a practitioner is Initiated into only once the proper living ethics of the Bodhisattva path are well ingrained, and the various *saṃskāras* related to the concept of 'self' have been transmuted. Many are the tests one must pass on the upward way to liberation before such tools evoking the magical effects of possessing *siddhis* can be mastered. Nevertheless, there are many useful mantric devices, prayers and invocations that can be given to noviciates to rightly focus their minds. They can thereby invoke the will to change obstructing *saṃskāras;* to produce inspiration and right aspiration to gain the attributes of enlightenment; and to evoke the energies and response from the inner realms of the liberating Ones. These devices are an essential part of every personal *sādhana* (devotional practices, rules of training), and for the generation of the *tapas* (yogic austerities) that over time will produce success.

The mantras that are taught should thus be carefully designed to produce the greatest good, by not focussing upon the individual at all, except in the arenas of what is needed to be done to become a fully compassionate enlightened being. Such mantras are thus essentially *prayers* that *evoke* the necessary qualities from the individual, and can *invoke* the energies from the highest centre of light on this earth. The purpose is to assist us in the task of serving the needy, salvaging the desolate, rectifying wayward forces, and sanctifying the aspiring ones on the path with the blessing from the most High.

Many mantras are also used as means to focus the mind. They eliminate the constant incursion of the chattering mind, unwanted images of all types, and help to hold the mind at a point of tension so that the seed idea can grow and unfold into the revelations and related symbols needed for one's journey to purposeful, awakened fulfilment.

It could help those who would evoke the power of mantras to read chapter 3 of the *Epistle of St. James*, as useful advice is presented concerning the use of the mouth and tongue.[6] In many ways the entire path to enlightenment revolves around how one uses the mouth, to produce the third of the Buddha's Eightfold Path, right or perfect speech. People say what they think, and they oft think as they desire. Others lie and distort information, use malicious gossip, slander, etc. Others try to speak truth at all times, and those upon the path to liberation must also wisely use the mouth to help liberate the ignorant and the distressed from their woes, to assist their path to enlightenment. Thus *James 3:2* states: 'If any man offend not in word, the same is a perfect man, *and* able also to bridle the whole body'. To be a perfected being one must be able to utilise mantras properly without disaster; therefore, one must be able to 'bridle the whole body', i.e., control all of the elements, passions, desires, and associated forces, specifically of the doorways to psychic powers that are the *chakras*.

In *James 3:6* we have: 'And the tongue is a fire, a world of iniquity: so is the tongue among our members, that it defileth the whole body, and setteth on fire the course of nature; and it is set on fire of hell'. This is

---

6 The presentation is of course from a Theistic viewpoint, nevertheless, the same basic considerations hold true between those seeking 'salvation' from without-within, as for those similarly striving from within-without.

the same psychic (or *prāṇic*) 'fire of hell' that is evoked through wrong mantra usage, which indicates the way of the black magician. At the end of the chapter[7] James gives us the way out of the dilemma of the wrong use of the tongue, and this is the ability to develop receptivity to the 'wisdom that is from above'. That is, awakening the 'inner ear' to listen to the silent voice that comes from one's guru or true spiritual preceptor. This is the source of all true mantric Sound. Thus we have the words 'let him show out of a good conversation his work with meekness of wisdom...but the wisdom that is from above is first pure, then peaceable, gentle, and easy to be intreated,[8] full of mercy and good fruits, without partiality, and without hypocrisy. And the fruit of righteousness is sown in peace of them that make peace'. Meekness, humbleness, compassion, truthfulness, and righteousness, are keywords to those that would use mantras effectively, without gross *karma*-producing consequences.

Another common meditation technique taught to beginners concerns focussing upon one or other of the *chakras*. As previously stated, this practice is highly dangerous and futile. It also stimulates the obsessive qualities of the Solar Plexus centre in combination with those of the Throat and Sacral centres. Generally, such stimulation is in conjunction with the inanity of trying to raise *kuṇḍalinī* before the individual has been properly prepared. Warnings concerning this frequently appear in all serious meditation texts, thus need not be detailed here.

What should be noted, however, is that what the average meditator imagines to be '*kuṇḍalinī* rising' is rarely so, but rather the most material aspects of that force fusing with Sacral centre energies, which greatly stimulate the fires of desire and of the vital body. Unless the substance of the body is sufficiently refined, and the *nāḍīs* have been prepared, *kuṇḍalinī* finds its outlet of expression through the lines of least resistance. Consequently, it can burn its way through the most commonly used pathways in the body. The Fire also pours into the centres that were the focus of expression in past eras of human development, hence they have become a hindrance to present spiritual evolution. Such outlets produce, for instance, various forms of mediumship, elementary psychic states, and later schizophrenic behaviour.

---

7 Verses 13-18.

8 Old English for entreat, to ask someone earnestly to do something.

The nature of the awakening of *kuṇḍalinī* is symbolised in *II Peter 3:10-15,* concerning the coming of 'the day of the Lord'.

> The day of the Lord will come as a thief in the night; in which the heavens shall pass away with a great noise, and the elements shall melt with fervent heat, the earth also and the works that are therein shall be burned up.
>
> Seeing then that these things shall be dissolved, what manner of persons ought ye to be in all holy conversation and godliness.
>
> Looking for and hasting unto the coming day of God, wherein the heavens being on fire shall be dissolved, and the elements shall melt with fervent heat.
>
> Nevertheless we, according to his promise, look for new heavens and a new earth, wherein dwelleth righteousness.
>
> Wherefore beloved, seeing that ye look for such things, be diligent that ye may be found of him in peace, without spot, and blameless.

This passage does not just refer to the ending of the world, but also to the attainment of enlightenment (the Christ-Presence) by the meditating one when *kuṇḍalinī* rises rightly, transforming consciousness (the heavens) and that which people regard as the form (the burning up of 'the earth', etc.). Enlightenment comes 'as a thief in the night', i.e., spontaneously, automatically, without the person wishing for, or thinking of it. It comes when one's consciousness is not focussed upon the self at all, when it is 'asleep' so to speak. A 'great noise' refers to the Sounds (trumpeting) of the many *chakras* that are awakened as this energy arises through them all. The fusion of all the five Elements with 'fervent heat' and the 'dissolving' of all aspects of consciousness, symbolised by the term 'the heavens', are virtually identical to the descriptions given in Buddhist Tantric texts concerning the attainment of the highest enlightened states. This happens when this Fire has reached the pinnacle of attainment in the human unit, the 1,000 petalled lotus, thus awakening the sum of all the related qualities. When the 'earthiness' of the pineal and pituitary glands are infused with living Fire, then the all-seeing Eye is awakened and the person will be able to manifest the types of miracles of healing, etc., attributed to all enlightened beings.

In the Tibetan Buddhist philosophy this fire is called *gTum-mo,* which Govinda states:

> It is the all-consuming incandescent power of that overwhelming Inner Fire which since Vedic times has pervaded that religious life of India: the power of *tapas*...Just as worlds are born from fire, 'through the power of inner heat' (as the hymn of creation in the *Ṛgveda* tells us) and are dissolved again through the same force of fire, in the same way *tapas* is as much creative as it is liberating.[9]

The 'new heavens' and the 'new earth' wherein 'dwelleth righteousness' is but a description of the realm(s) of enlightened being, and Shambhala. One is born into them as a consequence of the process of liberation from the trammels of the form once 'the elements' have melted with fervent heat and 'the earth also and the works that are therein' (*saṃsāra*) come to 'be burned up'. Literally, the way to such realms is to be 'without spot', i.e., being unblemished. This phrase means that the aura of a person can have no aberrant, dull, or greyish colouring whatsoever. There can not be the slightest trace of discordant energy about the aura, which thereby must be of the intensest hue attainable by the meditating one. If there was a 'spot' therein then this would become a force vortex, signifying the path of least resistance for the rising Fires, which would find an outlet there. They would then intensify it, with consequent disastrous results. The 'spot' thus represents an unwanted or negative psychological or emotional characteristic, generally manifesting as a greyish tone.

The development of peace, or tranquillity, is the only way that meditation can unfold and the Fires be safely liberated. The final term in this chapter—'blameless', refers to the fact that such a one cannot be guilty of wrongdoing, of manifesting the *karma* that would prevent the rising of the energies of liberation.

The awakening of *chakras*

All life and related processes are seen in the form of the petals of the various *chakras* unfolding, with the lines of interrelationships being the *nāḍīs* associated with the etheric body. Each *chakra* has a fundamental colour, with various numbers of petals arranged in geometric ordering

9 Govinda, *Foundations of Tibetan Mysticism*, 161.

according to the divine mathematics of the centre concerned. They become open gates, or force plexuses, for energies and impressions coming to and from the various levels of multidimensional space, and the hierarchies of entities, *deva*, human and supra-human, that embody that space.

The *chakras* are of immense importance, being a focus of attention for all *yogins* for the aeons that people have been developing the art of meditation. One must realise that even the Logos (the 'God' to our planetary or solar system) is but a Meditator, having evolved past the human stage many cycles of aeons ago via becoming a Buddha. Consequently, 'He' has gained the Powers and Mind to embody all the forces and entities within the solar form by means of the *chakra* and *nāḍī* system within 'His Body'. The hierarchies of entities represent, or become factors of this system, and as *all etheric bodies are interrelated,* so we have one unified, integral pulsating dynamo of energy, of energy fields. Everything we can know is thus integrated as a *maṇḍala,* a unified cosmos of Beings, and the sustaining energy is pumped by a dynamic central informing source, the Heart of Life and Love, to which all meditators on the white path consciously aspire.

When everything concerning the true nature of the spiritual/psychic evolution of the human kingdom is understood, then the qualities of the *chakras* and the right sequence or geometrical ordering of their awakening will be clearly discernible. A detailed divulgence of such abstruse and technical information can, however, only be revealed when humanity is sufficiently grounded in the Love principle, so that scientific investigators can utilise the gained revelations to benefit all.

It is important that any future gifts to humanity by the Hierarchy of Light concerning the direct control of elementary forces through the use of sound, colour and spiritual power, should not be controlled by a greedy and ruthless few, or even by powerful individual nations, who would capitalise (monetarily or otherwise) from such knowledge. Such gifts are those of miraculous revelatory *(manasic)* beneficence, of wings of healing, the mastery of the laws of light, gravity, the Airy Element, of sound, and the power associated with some of the lesser creative *(deva)* lives. This information has always existed amongst the enlightened, but through planned events concerning the externalisation of the Hierarchy of Light into outward objectivity, the world's intelligentsia will begin to seriously look at things esoteric that they were formerly ignorant of.

It should be emphasised that the *chakras* awaken of their own accord when a person manifests the right attitudes of mind and heart, and undergoes the necessary disciplines for psychic purification. The refinement of substance and increased receptivity to incoming energies of a more potent vibrancy does the job. The activity of the *chakras* increases to meet the need. Only at the final stages of their awakening are esoteric visualisation techniques needed. Beware any attempt at forcing them to awaken. Such will quickly lead into the arena of influence of the dark brotherhood, and physiological, psychic, or psychological trouble. One then effectively tries to force events that run counter to their Soul's plan for that incarnation. It may even lead to premature death—for early disincarnation may be preferable to risking the type of *karma* implicated.

The effect of uncontrolled, prematurely awakened lower psychic powers can be symbolised by a frenzied pack of sharks feeding upon carrion. Let those desirous of quick results beware. All too often warnings go unheeded by those wanting quick phenomenal results. For the misinformed curious person, the adolescent adventurer, or foolish speculator, much anguished journeying lurks in the murky depths of the astral sea of psychic phenomena.

Often meditation teachers give instructions along this line: 'if you visualise the form of this or that *chakra*, sound out the given mantra, and do the necessary mental exercise, then you will awaken *siddhis* and become an enlightened being'. However, how can one gain the compassionate insight of an enlightened one if the meditation technique, visualisation, breathing process, and verbalisation are all aimed at oneself? Even focussing upon awakening the powers of the Heart centre by such methods will not meet its aim.

The Heart centre is *only* awakened through group endeavour focussed upon truly compassionate undertakings, which decentralise from the dramatic personal 'I'. This is because it channels the energies of *buddhi* (or *bodhicitta),* of universality, oneness, far-sighted comprehensive and all-embracive vision. This necessitates a state of ego-lessness as its foundation. It is the open gate to the effects of the power of the vast ineffable cosmic magnet that is the Logoic Heart beating out its rhythms.

Self-focussed attention resists the pull of that magnet and deflects the embrace of the associated vision and energies.

Endeavouring to force this *chakra* to awaken by means of the power of the mind serves to stimulate veiled aspects of egotism, and forms of heightened emotional identification (generally mistaken as love) to other people. Subtle forms of egoism are all too common among meditators.

Preliminary considerations for meditation

The technique here outlined has as its foundation the information presented in the fourth and fifth volumes of this treatise. The objective concerns the cleansing, transformation, and sublimation of *saṃskāras* until they can be channelled into the precincts of the Heart lotus. The first three volumes also provide further background information related to what must be achieved in meditation, the nature of the Mind, the effects of contact with the Sambhogakāya Flower, the *śūnyatā-saṃsāra* nexus, and the higher experience associated with the *dharmakāya*.

Many of the processes concerning the transformation of *saṃskāras* happen automatically in the serious practitioner upon the path of developing *bodhicitta*. Therefore, much of the detail presented about the individual petals of the *chakras* and related *prāṇas* is more or less academic, but needed by the meditation instructor. In the more advanced practice, the activities of the Wrathful Deities will be noticeable and will have to be taken into account, especially with respect to strong *saṃskāras* that are to be converted. Other attributes of training, such as comprehending the nature of and response to the nefarious predations from the dark brotherhood, demands a competent instructor. This subject will thus be relegated as part of the 'ear whispered' tradition for some time yet.

It should be noted that the Wrathful Deities are Mind-born, and therefore are a heritage of the Buddhist Mind-set. They take different forms in other religious dispensations, as they embody the wrathful, transmutative forces of the Mind concerning the *saṃskāras* of desire-mind. Most Initiates that are on the path of yoga-meditation have had Buddhist incarnations wherein these Deities have been invoked, therefore they normally appear again at the corresponding level of development to a former life.

The purpose here, however, is to not reiterate the meditation teachings that would be provided by an instructor from one or other of the Buddhist sects espousing the Tantras of their lineage tradition. One such exposition was given in Volume 5 on the *Bardo Thödol,* which suffices to indicate the nature of such a meditation sequence, if so developed. The information is important, and shows the types of qualities visualised by those seeking enlightenment in that tradition. It is not necessary for those that meditate to visualise these Deities; however, a substitute process must happen in consciousness that affords the same transformations of *saṃskāras.* The stages of the path of meditation will consequently produce necessary imagery relating to these transformative forces. The imagery will differ for the various modern practitioners because of their Ray constitution, plus the differing qualities of the *saṃskāras* to be transformed. Sometimes internal recognition rather than imagery may manifest, denoting an individual's success over a specific characteristic. What some find easy to master, others will find difficult.

It is obvious therefore that much relating to the meditation process concerns gaining mastery of one's mind, and the forces passing through and controlling the output of that mind, called *saṃskāras.* Without such work there is no real progress towards enlightenment. The imagery realised will manifest in accordance with the quality of the *saṃskāras* that must be transformed and eventually transmuted into enlightenment-attributes. This entire process is intricately interwoven with the subject of Initiation, which determines one's progress to the higher domains. Considerations concerning the subject of Initiation must accompany any description of the meditation process if comprehension of the true purpose of meditation is to be achieved. Initiation is therefore explained in the later chapters of this book. All in all, the Initiation process is the way of walking the path to liberation, thus resulting with entry into the kingdom of Shambhala. The serious practitioner knocks upon that Door once gross *saṃskāras* have been refined to the extent that the attributes of the abstract Mind come into prominence, and the Clear Light of Mind is generated. The Lords of Shambhala then work to help assist the candidate to enter their Halls, by projecting the needed imagery into the Mind of the Initiate. They help awaken the Mind to many revelations concerning that august, supremely bounteous, centrally governing domain.

At any rate, at all stages of the path, the members of the Hierarchy of Light, the Council of Bodhisattvas, will have taken the worthy candidate under their wing. (Again according to the Ray type, and the laws and rules governing the various Ashrams of the Masters of Wisdom, which will be described in Volume 7 of this *Treatise on Mind*.)

The objective here is to simplify the presentation, by providing seed instructions on meditation, to start the process unfolding that awakens the meditation-Mind. Having said this we can now proceed with a suggested technique that is aimed at bringing the beginner to a position wherein revelations are possible. Comprehension of the related images will then lead the practitioner to seek out advanced teachings, and to access perceptions that can deliver awakening, according to the intrinsic level of what was attained in past lives.

This meditation procedure is a modernised version of the Vajrayāna. It should provide the student with visualisations that produce guidance upon the path, subtle understandings of many enigmatical things, and to link the practitioner with various teachers from the liberated domains. An appropriately developed hermeneutic for these visualisations takes time, and inevitably will require an experienced teacher to guide the way to Shambhala. A heuristic approach, where a sound ontology is obtained concerning the doctrine of liberation and the nature of enlightenment, also takes much time to develop. Practitioners must therefore understand the vastness of their undertaking, to be prepared to seriously devote their lives to meditative development, and all that it implies. Once firm contact has been made with this Hierarchy, and their instructions earnestly followed, then the Way to Shambhala is assured.

The visualisation technique relates to journeying to the spiritual Sun. Many now incarnated into the Western world have the ability to quickly journey thus, with little or no prior meditation practice, because the capacity has been developed in past lives through various contemplative and meditative regimes. It is an inherent memory that is recalled at the right moment. The Sun is the giver of Life and light to all upon our planet. It also represents the vitalising Heart centre, which is the source of Life to our beings. The Head centre is also sun-like, with its twelve main petals. The heart in the Head represents the gateway to the Sambhogakāya Flower, which is sun-like with respect to its instrument, the meditating personality. The sun visualisation is the way of approach to the domain of the Hierarchy of enlightened being, which is sun-like to its many adherents. The way of travel in the meditation-Mind offers many revelatory vistas to explore, as well as countering infernal, irksome perturbations from the past.

The purpose of the meditation is manifold.

a. To introduce practitioners to the Masters of Wisdom constituting the Council of Bodhisattvas.
b. To introduce the immeasurably beautiful universe of the inner realms.
c. To introduce the *deva* (angelic) kingdom, so as to manifest a working relationship with them.
d. To bring practitioners in touch with their own fundamental inner being, and thus learn somewhat about the purpose for their incarnation and the *karma* (specifically group *karma*) conditioning all lives.
e. To teach what the path of Love-Wisdom (developing *bodhicitta)* truly is. This also concerns awakening to inner plane weapons of defence to counter the dark Rays and machinations that our brothers of darkness (with whom the student may have much *karma*) will use to try to counter the aspirations of aspirants upon the path of loving service. It should be understood that all reference to defence against the dark brotherhood is literally synonymous with the teachings concerning the transmutation of *saṃskāras.* The forces of evil represent the past attributes one had developed that no longer serve a useful function in the disciple's psyche. They need to be comprehended, encountered and positively transformed. This work also incorporates understanding one's psychological attributes. In the latter stages of meditative development it can involve the ability to take the form of the Wrathful Deities, to transform the most nefarious attributes of the dark hosts by means of the *saṃskāras* of enlightenment. Through truly compassionate wrath much good can be accomplished. The dark brotherhood thus represent externalised (often mythologised) entities, sorcerers, and the like, as well as the

darkened attributes of one's own psyche that have a sympathetic affinity with these externalised forces.

All practitioners have varying degrees of *karma* with these dark entities. All have committed many mistakes in past lives. We have selfish magical invocations, and left hand practices in various religions, such as that of ancient Egypt to contend with. Practitioners had often abused positions of power as part of a ruling or military elite, amassed egregious financial wealth at the expense of the common good, or were actively involved in iniquitous religious practices, as in the Inquisitional period in Europe. In all such activities the participants did not only generate unfortunate *saṃskāras,* but also imbibed energies and impressions from active agents of evil, from both the inner realms and physical plane livingness. They have consequently created *karma* with them. Indeed such *karma* is well-nigh ubiquitous and generally of most ancient standing. Cleansing this *karma* then becomes the most important part of a practitioner's training. The process of transforming these psychic attributes concerns much of the teachings labelled 'ear whispered' in the Tantric texts and hagiographies of Buddhist *yogins.*

f. To introduce the student to the more esoteric aspects of the ancient Wisdom Religion, referred to in the Bible as the 'Mysteries of the Kingdom of God'.[10]

g. Hopefully the student following this path will consequently become enlightened, consciously finding their rightful place within the Hierarchy of Love, the Council of Bodhisattvas, thence into the precincts of Shambhala.

The student of meditation must be rightly focussed and prepared to live a life of compassionate service to help humanity and all sentient beings. Being rightly focussed is a lifestyle activity and not just something one does just prior to and whilst sitting for meditation. Everyday, all of the time, one must be meditatively focussed and working upon transforming incessantly aberrant *saṃskāras.* This necessitates constantly watching one's psyche for the appearance of undesirable character traits, emotions, wrong thought projections, and

---

10 *Luke 8:10.*

then transforming them whilst they are manifesting, turning them into peace-engendering compassionate qualities.

This battle with unruly emotions and thoughts is not easily won. The grosser attributes are generally easily recognised and thus dealt with, but there are many subtle and persistent maggots of deceit that the practitioner is often not aware of, and which generally necessitates his/her group brothers and sisters to lovingly point out. The teacher in their midst should be especially diligent, to wisely reveal these qualities in the student at the correct time. All *saṃskāras* cannot be dealt with at once. Many lives have often gone into their production and sometimes a decade or two is needed to transform their base effects in one's psyche. Often specific karmic incidents need to be waited for before they can be properly noticed by the practitioner as something needing attention.

The manifestation of *karma* is the best teacher, and produces many untoward situations to assist one to eliminate many forms of attachment to *saṃsāra*. Many are the relationship issues with others that need attention, especially concerning those one is emotionally close to. It is not easy for disciples to properly discern what is right to do, or say, in the face of demands and emotional exchanges with those they live with. Here lie many of the tests on the Initiation path. Wisdom must be evoked at all times, and of course, a continuous meditative discourse is needed. The presumption here is that this enlightenment-path is one of riding *saṃsāra* to Shambhala. Celibacy is not advocated, but one can be so. Total isolation from human affairs is also not needed, such as living in a secluded place, or hermitage cell.

The path necessitates the generation of compassion through the full face of the living experience and involvement with all that life offers. One, however, should not be so foolish as to purposely live in the most adverse conditionings for one's practice. It is best, therefore, to live in spiritual communities, so that all the members of a *saṅgha* can assist each other, as they are working towards the same goal. Also, the practitioner must be engaged with the attendant problems of the world, socially, politically, and religiously—to play his/her part in offering solutions. Only in the crucible of experience can true compassion *(bodhicitta)* be wrought. It cannot be an idealistic theme, the active livingness of life must make it so. Indeed, the awakening meditation-Mind will revolve around this theme of service, of what needs to be done in the world, according to the Ray line of application and karmic disposition.

There is no such thing as self-enlightenment, by which is meant that one gains enlightenment by tending only to one's own discipline and spiritual needs. Compassionately focussed meditation all the way to Shambhala is the only way one can get there, and needs to be so if one is to be assisted by the Lords of Life. Beginners in the art of meditation, however, can be too self-focussed, and this needs to change so that they turn their attention first to co-endeavours with their group brothers and sisters, and then to the world's needs in general. Only through this form of group sharing and meditation can the Heart centre be awakened, and through the Heart, the Heart in the Head centre as well. The transmutative magic that is the effect of contact with the energy of *śūnyatā* is then possible. The attributes of *saṃsāra* must be transformed into the reality of the *dharmakāya* by this means. One must always remember here the three jewels of Buddhism—the Buddha (the spiritual teacher at the heart of all), the *dharma* (the doctrine of liberation), and the *saṅgha* (the spiritual community). They are one, working as a unity, and all three are needed if one is to gain enlightenment.

In relation to this, therefore, it is important for the aspiring one to seek out and find the most awakened teacher possible. One must not be satisfied with mere reputation, but must truly test the teacher as to the quality of wisdom, prescience, and compassionate action such a one actually possesses. Great knowledge in terms of a lineage tradition or book learning must be supplemented by the above qualities if the teacher is worthy of being called a guru or Master. To this must be added the ability of the teacher to wisely direct the course of his/her students over a number of years in such a way that past-life perceptions come to the fore, so that they can be worked upon in a meaningful manner. The teacher must also be able to reveal the inner universe of the Presence of the guiding council of the Hierarchy of Light, and later the Lords of Shambhala. Other than this, there are no fast rules as to the right teacher for a student, because there are many karmic situations that play out which leads the student to those that he/she has interrelated with in past lives, and which must be played out anew in the new cycle.

Suggested meditation technique

The meditation technique can be best described as a sequence of steps:

1. Sit quietly in a relaxed position with a straight spine. Limbering-up exercises are useful because they help warm up the body and make it supple for meditation. Next, think of the day's past activities, realise the mistakes made during the day, especially the verbal ones, work out what needs to be done to rectify them in the future and evoke the courage to do so. Comprehend the nature of the *saṃskāras* you possess and look at the most obvious ones to transform.
2. After these thoughts have passed through the mind, endeavour to produce a tranquil state of mind, breathe slowly and rhythmically, but without thought focussed upon the breathing process.
3. Then silently say the following mantra, visualising clearly its intent:

Oṁ

May the will to enlightenment be evoked.

May my Heart awaken to compassionate purpose.[11]

May humbleness be the keynote of the path to serve the all.

Oṁ

The above is a third Ray mantra, and posits the engendering of the Bodhisattva path, which is the means par excellence of gaining liberation, where the awakening of the unit is seen as part of the completion of an entire *maṇḍala* of expression of which that unit is a part. Thus there can be no real progress for the unit unless the entire *maṇḍala* is uplifted with the practitioner.

A second Ray version of this mantra is derived from the books of A.A. Bailey, and is an Invocation, meeting the need. It can be used instead, if desired:

Oṁ

I know, oh Lord of Light and Love about the need.

Touch my Heart anew with Love, so that I too may Love and give.

Oṁ

---

11 One should use the plural 'our' when working in the context of a group.

A first Ray version would be seen as any short pithy mantra, such as that attributed to Guru Rinpoche:

Oṁ Āḥ Hūṃ

where the practitioner has proper comprehension of the nature and purpose of the mantra.

4. What the 'compassionate purpose' of the mantra is must then be visualised. Its meaning can be viewed from three angles of vision:
   a. That which is lacking in one's psyche, thus hindering the path to enlightenment.
   b. Community, social, and world need, in relation to the field of service one has developed, and the qualities, equipment and personnel needed to fulfil one's self-appointed task.
   c. Understanding of the plan to rectify strife and suffering in the world in both the long-range vision and short term application, and how it relates to the integrated work of one's spiritual brothers and sisters also working along these lines. In its higher attributes this plan concerns the part one plays in the establishment of a new world order, based on sound foundations and right motives: such as good-will to all people, peace, brotherhood, harmonious cooperation, interrelated inter-dependence and sharing of resources on all levels of Life. It also implies a cooperative endeavour with Lords of Love-Wisdom on the behest of humanity to help ameliorate all sickness and distress upon the planet.

All such activity incorporates environmentally sound global planning. It is an extension of the cooperative communal spirit that will allow the externalisation of the Hierarchy of enlightened beings (of which the reader is presumably a member), with the consequent objective appearance of the Heavenly City, the New Jerusalem, on the Earth.[12] Inevitably this will produce the 'etherealisation' of dense substance. Thus the consciousness-aspect of all kingdoms of Nature will be uplifted, producing the eventual transformation of our

12 *Rev. 21:1-6.*

forms into bodies of living radiant Light. Inevitably, a forthcoming Initiation of the myriads in our civilisation into the mysteries of being/non-being will result, demonstrating thereby the power of a Logos by the humanity of our planet. This power first emanates from the Head Centre (Shambhala) of the present planetary Logos, to empower the collective Minds of all groups of people.

Meditation upon the need is but another way of defining the nature of the generation of *bodhicitta*. Once this has been contemplated upon, then quietude, thus the elimination of thoughts, must be produced.

5. Next the will must be evoked to overcome all obstacles, allowing the silent exhalation of the import of the chosen mantra, and to generate the true humbleness that will pave the way to experience what the Heart offers. One's consciousness is then absorbed into the Heart centre, which generates a golden light that vitalises the Plan.

   The meditator may also use *The Great Invocation* as the preliminary mantra, clearly visualising its intent before proceeding to the next stage. Its import is then richer, and can produce a vibrant energisation and visions. The mantra is presented on page 103 of this volume. The Divine Will emanates from Shambhala, wherein resides 'the Primordial One', the Logos (or Lord of Life) of our planet. The meaning of the remainder of the mantra should be clear enough to the reader.

6. The inflow of the energy of Love (from inner plane sources) into one's Heart should be experienced by now, and that energy being directed to all arenas where 'the need' can be fulfilled. Note that the colouring of the energy of Love (the second Ray of Love-Wisdom) is indigo-blue, and the practitioner should be able to perceive this colour in meditation. Alternate colours that can be received instead are an intense white or golden light. One should not react if such energisation doesn't manifest, instead one should go with the flow, allowing the meditation to proceed without desire-mind interference. Nor should one be concerned if experiences do not happen at first. Successive practise over weeks or months should inevitably produce the results.

7. Now pacify all aspects and modifications of mind (*citta-vṛtti*), make it serene allowing whatever impressions that might come to simply be, without the mind interfering in any way. Therefore, become as calm as possible, and don't worry if such impressions do not arise at first. Sincerity of motive inevitably will produce results.

The meditation can finish here for the beginner who is still learning the art of holding the mind still, and who finds the process of visualisation difficult.

When the person has been consolidated in the meditative rhythm and feels at ease with the progress, then he/she may wish to extend the meditation with the *Journey to the Sun visualisation,* as outlined below:

> You are to imagine a deep indigo-blue ocean as far as the eye can see. It appears to be absolutely calm. On the surface of this ocean you see a boat with yourself in it. The boat can be of any shape, size, make, or from any epoch, e.g., from a rowing boat to a sailboat. There may also be other people on the boat, some of whom you may recognize. As you travel upon this boat you are aware that there is a horizon line in the distance and as you get closer to the horizon a golden sun begins to slowly appear above it. As you draw closer to the sun it gets progressively larger and begins to radiate its warmth to you.
>
> Finally, when you are close to it you see a door appear in the centre of the sun and you find yourself going through this door somehow. (There are a number of different means to do this.) Once inside the sun certain things may happen to you (e.g., it may be indicated that you go somewhere or do something); you may see certain symbols, images, or people may appear, who may speak a few words.

There is no set image or sequence of events that happen inside the Sun, as everyone has different needs and must be spiritually educated accordingly. The happenings inside the sun will therefore differ from person to person.

From this point on the meditator must be directly guided to undergo further training concerning the control of *saṃskāras* and associated *karma.* Certain forms of service work will also be found that can be associated with meditation, for which the practitioner must be prepared. Progress will proceed according to the qualities developed and the nature of the experiences and energies received.[13]

The meditator should try to carry the gain of the meditation and resultant quietude throughout the day, so that a quiet, contemplative rhythm becomes part of his/her entire way of life.

It is important that the person allow the meditation to unfold naturally and not try to force producing a set imagery. The indigo-blue ocean, for instance, may at first appear quite stormy (instead of calm), thus indicating that one is unable to properly calm the emotions, or else has recently experienced strong emotionality. Another person may find that the experience concerns being below the waves and not on top of them, and so forth. Continuous meditation application guarantees eventual success, but one must travel with an open heart, not the will of mind or subtly disguised desire-mind.

The best times for seated meditation are just before going to sleep, dawn, noontime, and at dusk. One should sit as often as one likes, but without any forceful attitudes of mind. It is not important to sit for long periods of time, but rather work with the inspiration of the meditation that unfolds before you.

Peace be unto you

Oṁ Svāhā!

The power to visualise

The quotations presented below have been derived from the writings of A.A. Bailey and Helena Roerich, as they have been telepathic 'amanuenses' of very high level Bodhisattvas. They demonstrate the high quality of teachings in their books aimed mainly for the Western

13 Once such experiences have happened, and the person has verified that it is not simply imagination, then *The School of Esoteric Sciences* can be contacted for further instructions and explanations of the meaning of the impressions obtained inside the Sun. The web page: www.universaldharma.com/contact/ will provide contact details and links to other information for serious students wishing further guidance in their meditation life.

audience, and will be used to supplement the Buddhist teachings so far presented. Hopefully the Buddhist student can thereby gain further insight from streams of revelation that are not directly phrased in the familiar terms with which they are accustomed. This then should produce a syncretism of valid teachings on meditation that are aimed to produce the same result of enlightenment and consequent liberation from *saṃsāra.*

Below is a quotation taken from *Discipleship in the New Age,* Vol. 1. It contains technical information concerning the visualisation process that may prove useful to the student.

> The secret of true meditation work in its earlier stages is the power to visualise. This is the first stage to be mastered. Disciples should lay the emphasis upon this process; in it lies eventually the ability to use the creative powers of the imagination, plus mental energy, as a measure to further the ends of the Hierarchy and to carry out the Divine Plan. All the new processes in meditation techniques (for which the New Age may be responsible) must and will embody visualisations as a primary step for the following reasons:
>
> 1. Visualisation is the initial step in the demonstration of occult law that "energy follows thought". This, of course, everyone interested in occult study recognizes theoretically. One of the tasks confronting disciples is to achieve factual knowledge of this. Pictorial visualisation (which is a definite feature of the work in many esoteric schools) is simply an exercise to bring about the power to visualise. In the work of those disciples who are being trained for initiation, this external aspect of visualisation must give place to an interior process which is the first step toward the *direction of energy.* The visualising of pictures is intended to focus the aspirant within the head at a point midway between the pituitary body and the pineal gland. In that area, he draws pictures and paints scenes and thus acquires the faculty to see—in large and in detail—that which he desires and for which he intends to work. The visualising of what might be called "directed process" goes on in a more focussed manner and in the area directly around the pineal gland. The pineal gland then becomes the centre of a magnetic field which is set in motion—in the first place—by the power of visualisation. At that point, energy is gathered by the disciple and then directed with intention to one or other of the

centres. This focussed thought produces inevitable effects within the etheric body and thus two aspects of the creative imagination are brought into play.

2. The power to visualise is the form-building aspect of the creative imagination. The process falls into three parts, corresponding somewhat to the creative process followed by Deity Itself:

   a) The gathering of qualified energy within a *ring-pass-not.*

   b) The focussing of this energy under the power of intention, i.e., at a point in the neighbourhood of the pineal gland. The energy is now focussed and not diffused.

   c) The despatch of this focussed energy by means of a pictorial process (not by an act of the Will at this time) in any direction—that is, to certain centres in a certain order.

   This process of energy direction can become a spiritual habit if disciples would begin to do it slowly and gradually. At first, the visualising process may seem to you to be laboured and profitless but, if you persevere, you will find eventually that it becomes effortless and effective. This is one of the most important ways in which a Master works; it is essential, therefore, that you begin to master the technique. The stages are:

   a) A process of energy gathering.

   b) A process of focalisation.

   c) A process of distribution or direction.

   The disciple learns to do this within himself and later to direct the energy (some chosen and particular kind, according to the demand of the occasion) to that which lies without himself. This constitutes, for example, one of the major healing techniques of the future. It is also used by the Master in awakening His disciple to certain states of consciousness, but with these you have naught to do.

3. The power to visualise correctly is one definite mode to ascertaining truth or falsity. This is a statement difficult for you to comprehend. Visualisation is literally the building of a bridge between the emotional or astral plane and the mental level and is, therefore, a personality correspondence to the building of the antahkarana. The astral plane, the second aspect of personality, is the correspondence to the form-building aspect of the Trinity,

> the second aspect. The creative imagination "pictures a form" through the ability to visualise and the thought energy of the mind gives life and direction to this form. It embodies purpose. Thereby a rapport or line of energy is constructed between the mind and the astral vehicle and it becomes a triple line of energy when the soul of the disciple is utilising its creative process in some planned and definitely constructive manner.
>
> This visualising process and this use of the imagination form the first two steps in the activity of thought form building. It is with these self-created forms - embodying spiritual ideas and divine purpose - that the Masters work and hierarchical purpose takes shape. Therefore, my disciples, it is essential that you begin with deliberation and slowly work in this manner and to use the above information constructively and creatively. The need of the times is increasingly great and the utmost of work and of purpose is desired.[14]

A note on silence

It is important that every person passing through any system of meditative training is aware from the outset as to the importance of silence, esoterically understood. It is the major tool to be developed if transcendence of consciousness and related powers are to be achieved. Silence necessitates the right control of speech. Speech is sacred and has power. It has a direct effect upon our subtle constitution, producing either constructive or destructive effects, depending upon the nature and quality of the uttered word, through speech or in thought. Progress on the path is thus not possible without right control of thought. Only in the silent reservoirs of the Heart can the Voiceless Voice be discovered. When consciously responded to it can lead to the portals of Light and Love.

The path of silence will allow the spiritual group to focus its intent in unison and together to vocalise the mantric Word or Words that will effectively produce the appropriate changes in the world, and the necessary magical effects in the realm of form. This form of activity is then the basis of the flowering of the new Aquarian dispensation.

14 A.A. Bailey. *Discipleship in the New Age,* Vol. 1, (Lucis Press, New York, 1976), 89-92.

Silence allows the manifestation of the invocative appeal of healing that produces the rectification of the diseases and imbalances of our societies, as well as in our personalities.

Imposed silence, however, in which there is a reticence to speak when clearly something should be said, cannot be condoned. Those who would dam back the flow of creative energy and of the ability to rightly Love and speak the truth when the truth matters, will but sow for themselves the seeds of future sicknesses, and add to their store of *karma*. To rightly use the power of speech effectively necessitates the development of wisdom, clear-headedness and straight-knowledge. Constant meditation upon the use of the spoken word and its application will produce this end.

One should reflect at the end of each day upon where one has erred in speech, offered abrasive comment, hasty critical judgement, or else frittered away one's store of *prāṇa* through idle gossip. Note how often what Master Morya in the *Agni Yoga* books calls 'imperil' (irritability) is reflected in one's speech, effectively causing psychic attacks to another person. Irritability is the main quality that imperils the existence of the ability of the serving disciple to walk the way of enlightenment. It opens the door for evil adversaries to influence, attack or work through the disciple. The power of the dark brotherhood is magnified by those that manifest such tendencies.

Reflect as to how many common ailments, such as colds, flu, and other inflammatory reactions have their true causes in such activity. Then try consciously not to manifest these habitual patterns of impulsive verbal diarrhoea in similar situations in the future. Note also the effects of such emotionality upon the auras of people, especially when vile emanations are projected, and the low grade *devas* ('elementals', the 'devils' of the Bible) that are attracted to them. If one could clearly see the effects of critical and coarse speech upon one's aura one would be horrified. A hell state is built, to be karmically experienced in a physical body or in the after-death state.

Silence implies emotional control, the strangling of glamour-forming tendencies right from the outset. It is the hallmark *per se* of the accomplished magician (*siddha*). Learn therefore when to speak and when not to speak. Only utter a word when it has a possibility of beneficent result in the world, keep silent in the face of adversity, control the tendency to idle chatter, gossip, innuendos, and abrasive remarks. Realise that the path to meditative development means the reception of intensified energies that will reinforce or empower such tendencies. If not properly controlled, they will produce self-destructive or harmful consequences, *saṃskāras* that will later need to be purged or transformed with the help of the activities of the various Wrathful Deities.[15]

Meditative development necessitates quietness and serenity in all pursuits within everyday life. Keep silent to hear the voice of the inner instructor and come to know the path to the mysteries of being/non-being. To come to master the evolutionary journeying, one must be able to control the evocation of sound and the potency of its effects. One will then master one's own creative amplitude. In silence one must work in the realms of meaning and express the power of enlightenment.

Be silent and the Voice of Silence will speak clearly to the inner ear. The pursuit of an attitude of silence cultivates the solid base or construct whereby the dynamic stillness, which we call serenity, can resonate. Serenity is the expression of the adamantine jewel in the Heart of All. It is power itself, be-ness, the primal potential of all actualisation in the realm of Meaning. It is Shambhalic substance, and thus one who is truly serene has taken a piece of Shambhala, to reside in Shambhalic Peace! This phrase means but little to the aspirant, but to the Initiate represents a consummating goal of the entire evolutionary process. Impregnable, immutable, ineffable meaning rests in this word serenity, and its realisation leads one into the infinitude.

Serenity differs from peace in that peace is a conditioning made by the aspirant that allows him/her to live in meditative calm. Peace has inherent within it a direct relation to conflict, in that it is that condition that ensues after conflict and turmoil has held sway. It thus connotes relative calm, an interlude between two fields of mutable activity. Serenity is absolute and knows not conflict, only that which is expressive of the All into the One—the field of abstraction, all-pervasive unity. Serenity is that which manifests or imposes itself upon one by the divinity within. From that divinity emanates the Sounds governing

---

15 This process is explained in Volume 5 of this *Treatise on Mind*.

all manifest being. It is an attribute of the enlightened Mind. Serenity grows in the Heart until it encompasses all that is and will come to be.

True serenity is very difficult to accomplish. The cultivation of a broad-minded compassionate silence is the key.

Oṁ Oṁ Oṁ

Thus the Heartbeat of the serene One metes out the vicissitudes of time and space. The night sky is but the symbol of that One's Mind.

Oṁ Oṁ Oṁ

Thus He Speaks, but your ears hear not that Sound.

Oṁ

Quotations

Below are some quotes from various sources of the Bailey and Roerich books regarding speech and silence:

> One of the greatest instruments for practical development lying in the hands of small and great, is the instrument of SPEECH. He who guards his words, and who only speaks with altruistic purpose, in order to carry the energy of Love through the medium of the tongue, is one who is mastering rapidly the initial steps to be taken in preparation for initiation. Speech is the most occult manifestation in existence; it is the means of creation and the vehicle for force. In the reservation of words, esoterically understood, lies the conservation of force; in the utilisation of words, justly chosen and spoken, lies the distribution of the love force of the solar system—that force which preserves, strengthens, and stimulates. Only he who knows somewhat of these two aspects of speech can be trusted to stand before the Initiator and to carry out from that Presence certain sounds and secrets imparted to him under the pledge of silence.
>
> The disciple must learn to be silent in the face of that which is evil. He must learn to be silent before the sufferings of the world, wasting no time in idle plaints and sorrowful demonstration, but lifting up

the burden of the world; working, and wasting no energy in talk. Yet withal he should speak where encouragement is needed, using the tongue for constructive ends; expressing the love force of the world, as it may flow through him, where it will serve best to ease a load or lift a burden, remembering that as the race progresses, the love element between the sexes and its expression will be translated on a higher plane. Then, through the spoken word, and not through the physical plane expression as now, will come the realisation of that true love which unites those who are one in service and in aspiration. Then love between the units of the human family will take the form of the utilisation of speech for the purpose of creating on all planes, and the energy which now, in the majority, finds its expression through the lower or generating centres will be translated to the throat centre.[16]

Beyond all demarcations, we inevitably reach the synthesis of the heart. We need not recall that silence issues from the intermingling of all sounds. Hence, let us learn to coordinate the heart with silence. But this silence will not be emptiness; it will suffuse space with the synthesis of thought. Just as the prayer of the heart has no need of words, so the silence that is pregnant needs no formulas. Intense silence demands many cumulations of thought and benign desires. Thus, the heart, intensified by silence, replete as a dynamo, beats out the rhythm of the Universe, and personal desires are transmuted into the guiding Universal Will. Thus is cooperation with the distant worlds evolved.[17]

Silence may be teeming with voices and darkness may be suffused with light. Hence, he who regards Space as empty will not apprehend the mighty life manifested in silence as the highest Word of Cosmos, nor the invisible as the manifest Eye of Cosmos. The law of Cosmos is inviolable, and even man has accepted the Voice of Silence. Where speech is meagre, the voice of the heart affirms silence. Cosmos in silence makes manifest the language of the heart, and the Cosmic Voice may become audible.

Sensitiveness and vigilance can aid us in giving ear to the Voice of Silence. The beauty of Cosmos is manifested in Silence. The beauty of silence is expressed in all the higher manifestations of life.

---

16 A.A. Bailey, *Initiation, Human and Solar,* (Lucis Press, New York, 1970), 74-75.

17 Helena Roerich, *Heart (*Agni Yoga Society, 1982), 45, quote number 68.

Let us learn to harken to silence! The infinitude of Cosmos creates the manifestation of the Silence.

The transmission of thought is also a manifestation of Silence. We often use it. Before the consummation of the thought manifestation, We send the ray of Silence. The rays of Silence call forth those sacred pains in the Chalice.

There are rays which are sent into the heart, invisibly and imperceptibly. They are most penetrative, and the organism must assimilate them. At first they evoke anguish, yet they are comparable to pure Fire. Thus one who sends experiences a manifestation of the highest joy, and one who receives will manifest the same joy after assimilation. In the most sacred Mysteries these rays were called "Agni Invisibilae." Thus, remember![18]

Let each of you gain that control of speech which has often been your goal but seldom your achievement, and remember that the most powerful factor in the control of speech is a loving heart. Wild and fearful talk, hateful gossip, cruel innuendo, suspicion, the ascribing of wrong and wicked motives to persons and peoples, and the divergences of attitude which have separated the many different nations in the world are rampant today and have brought the world to its present distressing situation. It is so easy to drift into the same habits of speech and thought which we find around us and to discover ourselves participating in attack and the spirit of hate. Guard yourselves strenuously against this and say nothing which could inflame hate and suspicion in connection with any race, any person, any group or any leaders of groups and nations. You will have to guard yourselves with care, so that even in defence of that which you may personally or nationally approve you do not find yourselves full of hate and breaking the law of love - the only law which can truly save the world. Perhaps the key to your success along this line will be *the silence of a loving heart.*[19]

The disciple who seeks to enter within the Portals of Initiation cannot do so until he has learnt the power of speech and the power of silence.

---

18 Helena Roerich, *Infinity,* (Agni Yoga Society), quote numbers 80-81.

19 A.A. Bailey, *The Externalisation of the Hierarchy*, (Lucis Publishing, New York 1982), 82.

This has a deeper and a wider significance than perhaps is apparent, for it holds, if rightly interpreted, the key to manifestation, the clue to the great cycles, and the revelation of the purpose underlying pralaya. Until a man comprehends the significance of the spoken word, and until he utilises the silence of the high places for the bringing about of desired effects on one plane or another, he cannot be admitted into those realms wherein every sound and every word spoken produces powerful results in matter of some kind.[20]

Through speech a thought is evoked and becomes present; it is brought out of abstraction and out of a nebulous condition and materialised upon the physical plane, producing (could we but see it) something very definite on etheric levels. Objective manifestation is produced, for "Things are that which the Word makes them in naming them." Speech is literally a great magical force, and the adepts or white magicians, through knowledge of the forces and power of silence and of speech, can produce effects upon the physical plane. As we well know, there is a branch of magical work which consists in the utilisation of this knowledge in the form of Words of Power and of those mantras and formulae which set in motion the hidden energies of nature and call the devas to their work.

Speech is one of the keys which open the doors of communication between men and subtler beings. It gives the clue to the discovery of those entities who are contacted on the other side of the veil. But only he who has learned to keep silent, and has arrived at the knowledge of the times to speak can pass this veil and make certain esoteric contacts. Magic consists, we are told in the *Secret Doctrine,* in addressing the Gods in Their own language; therefore, the speech of average man cannot reach Them.

Therefore, those who seek to learn the occult language, those who yearn to become aware of the words which will penetrate to the ears of those who stand on the other side, and those who seek to utilise the formulae and phrases which will give them power over the Builders, have to unlearn their previous use of words and to refrain from ordinary methods of talking. Then the new language will be theirs and the new expressions, words, mantras and formulas will be entrusted to their care.[21]

20 A.A. Bailey, *Initiation, Human and Solar,* 198.

21 A.A. Bailey, *A Treatise on Cosmic Fire*, (Lucis Publishing, New York, 1982), 981.

A second failing of disciples (and particularly of the working and accepted disciples in the world at this present time) is incorrect speech, conveying ambiguous meanings and motivated by criticism, or by an individual desire to shine. In olden days, the neophyte was forced into a prolonged silence. Speech was not permitted. This was inculcated as a check upon physical utterance of wrong words and ideas, based on inadequate knowledge. Today, the neophyte must learn the same lesson of attention to personal perfection and to personal work through the means of that inner silence which broods over the disciple and forces him to attend to his own work and business, leaving others free to do the same, and so learn the lesson of experience. A great deal of present right activity is hindered by the speech interplay between disciples, and much time is lost through wordy discussion of the work and activities of other disciples. Humanity as a whole, needs silence at this time as never before; it needs time in which to reflect, and the opportunity to sense the universal rhythm. Modern disciples, if they are to do their work as desired and to cooperate with the Plan correctly, need that inner reflective quiet which in no way negates intense outer activity but which does release them from wordy criticisms, feverish discussions, and constant preoccupation with the dharma, the motives and methods of their fellow disciples.[22]

The third characteristic of the new server is *joyfulness.*
This takes the place of criticism (that dire creator of misery)
and is *the silence that sounds.*

It would be well to ponder on these last words, for their true meaning cannot be conveyed in words, but only through a life dedicated to the newer rhythms and to service of the whole. Then that "sounding joy" and that "joyful sounding" can make its true meaning felt.[23]

Still another important factor in the group preparation for initiation is the cultivation of silence. How, we ask ourselves at times when the functioning of the Ashram is under discussion, can we train our disciples to realise that, essentially, silence is *not* refraining from

22 A.A. Bailey, *Esoteric Psychology* Vol. II, (Lucis Publishing, New York, 1981), 44.

23 Ibid., 132-133.

speech. So many disciples seem to think that it is, and that they have to learn not to talk if they hope to take initiation. Some would do a great deal better if they talked more than they do - along right lines. The silence imposed in an Ashram is refraining from certain lines of thought, the elimination of reverie and the unwholesome use of the creative imagination. Speech is consequently controlled at its source, because speech is the result of certain inner sources of ideas, of thought and of imagination; it is the precipitation (at a certain point of saturation, if I might so express it) of inner reservoirs which overflow on to the physical plane. The retention of speech and the suppression of words, if they are the result of a realisation that what is to be said is wrong, or undesirable, or unwise, or wasteful of energy, will simply increase the inner banking up and will lead eventually to a still more violent display of words at a later date; it may also bring about serious and disastrous conditions within the astral body of the disciple. The silence of thought is to be cultivated and, my brothers, I do not mean silent thinking. I mean that certain lines of thought are refused admission; certain habits of thinking are eradicated and certain approaches to ideas are not developed. This is done by a process of substitution, and not by a violent process of suppression. The initiate learns to keep his thought apparatus in a certain effective condition. His thoughts do not intermingle the one with other, but are contained (if I may thus pictorially word it) in separate compartments or carefully filed for reference and later use. There are certain layers of thought (again speaking symbolically) which are held within the Ashram itself and are never permitted to enter the mind of the disciple or the initiate when not consciously working in the Ashram; others are related to the group and its work and are given free play within the group ring-pass-not; still others are of a more mundane nature and govern the daily life and relationships of the disciple with personalities and with the affairs of civilised living and physical plane events. These are only indications of what I mean, but will suffice to show (if you duly meditate) a little of what is meant by the silence of the initiate. Within the permitted levels of contact, speech is free and unimpeded; outside those levels, no indication is given that the other spheres of thought activity, with their conditioning speech, even exist. Such is the silence of the initiated disciple.[24]

---

24 A.A. Bailey, *Rays and Initiations*, (Lucis Publishing, New York, 1970), 214-215.

The secret for all aspirants is to cultivate the attitude of the onlooker and of the silent watcher, and, may I emphasise the word silent. Much true magical work comes to naught because of the failure of the worker and builder on matter to keep silent. By premature speech and too much talk, he slays that which he has attempted to create, the child of his thought is still-born. All workers in the field of the world should recognize the need for silent detachment and the work before every student who reads these Instructions must consist in cultivating a detached attitude. It is a mental detachment which enables the thinker to dwell ever in the high and secret place and from that centre of peace calmly and powerfully to carry out the work he has set before himself. He works in the world of men; he loves and comforts and serves; he pays no attention to his personality likes and dislikes, or to his prejudices and attachments; he stands as a rock of strength and as a strong hand in the dark to all whom he contacts. The cultivation of a detached attitude personally, with the attached attitude spiritually, will cut at the very roots of a man's life; but it will render back a thousandfold for all that it cuts away.[25]

---

25 A.A. Bailey, *A Treatise on White Magic,* (Lucis Publishing, New York, 1974), 559-560.

4

Meditation Teachers

The Bodhisattva path

A major purpose of meditation is to equip oneself to become a Bodhisattva, a selfless server. This is an inevitable result of the self-analytical tools provided by the meditation-Mind. The consequent refinement of the attributes of mind, and drawing upon the impressions from the higher Mind, happens via the development of the *chakras* above the diaphragm.

As one awakens the qualities of Mind, it is concomitant to bringing into perspective the stages of development of the Bodhisattva path. The ten Bodhisattva stages (*bhūmis*) are canonical for all Mahāyāna schools, though there may be some equivocation and debate concerning the nature or existence of an eleventh, Buddha level. These levels of Bodhisattva activity represent the states of attainment from past lives of accomplishment. These stages therefore relate to the levels of possible meditational accomplishment or insight for any life. They clearly delineate what is and what is not possible to attain in that life, based upon what has been developed previously. These stages of spiritual growth can also be viewed in terms of the Initiation path of the disciples of the Masters of Wisdom. The ten *bhūmis* then refer to the attainment of the first five Initiations, with the eleventh referring to taking the sixth Initiation, the making of a Chohan of a Ray. This is but another way of describing Buddhahood for the few graduates from our planetary school that are selected to stay on because of planetary need, rather than moving upon one or other of the cosmic paths that lead away from this little planet of woe.

The entire process concerning gaining enlightenment is exemplified in Buddhist Cosmology and epitomised by the symbolism of the *stūpa*, which presents the needed information of the mode of visualisation in three-dimensional terms. It delineates the nature of the constitution of the inner realms.[1] Buddhist meditation is often formulated along these lines, and similar concepts aught to be part of the itinerary of each meditator.

It would be helpful for all that aspire to gain deep meditative insights to presume that he/she is a Bodhisattva functioning at one or other of the Bodhisattva levels, or at least be an aspirant thereto. One should thus endeavour to analyse some of the information extant concerning the nature of such a path and thereby to ascertain, as far as possible, to which Bodhisattva or Initiation level one may belong. This sets the paradigm of what is achievable in the field of meditation for that life, if one is honest in one's appraisal and can weed out somewhat the excess baggage of medieval thinking presented in the texts.[2] This will allow the setting of realistic goals in one's meditative life. The path can then be set firmly upon acquiescence to the requirements set forth by the Council of Bodhisattvas for entry into their ranks. It necessitates following and maintaining a disciplined lifestyle that will truly produce results in this life, and also set the stage for future lives of service activity. The attainment of Bodhisattvic purpose thus delineates the goals for meditation in any particular life. The *arhat* path of self-absorption for the sake of one's 'own enlightenment' is not a path to be espoused, nor to be deemed as anything else but as that which is illusory.

There are five Initiation levels that produce the perfection of a human unit, the making of a Master of Wisdom, and ten Bodhisattva stages *(bhūmis)* before the attainment of Buddhahood. For each pair of *bhūmis*

---

1 The section below supplements what has already been presented about the *stūpa* in Volume 4, chapter 5, of this series.

2 Much concerning the teachings re the qualities ascribed to Bodhisattvas in the Buddhist texts is redundant and often misleading. The true nature of this path no longer needs to be 'ear whispered'. That information now can be supplanted by the new presentation concerning the Initiation path presented in this treatise, which brings the doctrine of the stages of Bodhisattvic development into the modern epoch.

one Initiation is attained. The first of each pair of *bhūmis* relates to passing tests whereby the respective Initiation can be gained, and the second to the consolidation of the qualities related to the attainment of that specific Initiation. Detail concerning these Initiations will be provided in the fifth and sixth chapters of this book.

The first two Initiations are Initiations on the threshold to enlightenment. The third constitutes taking the *ālayavijñāna* Initiation, whereby the mysteries of the domain of the *ālayavijñāna* and the Sambhogakāya Flower are revealed. We thus have the awakening of the Clear Light of the Mind. The fourth Initiation is the *śūnyatā* Initiation, where the goal of *sūtrayāna* teachings of the *buddhadharma* is realised, and produces the ability to reside in the Void. The fifth Initiation is that of the *dharmakāya* revelation, where the Initiate comes to govern the qualities of the lowest level of the *dharmakāya*.

After that we have the tests related to the making of a Buddha, or Dhyān Chohan, which is attained at the sixth Initiation. Of these Initiations the first five will be described, as words fail to portray the achievement beyond this, except in symbolic, allegorical, or metaphorical terms.

Buddhists can correlate the information presented in the texts on the Bodhisattva *bhūmis*. They must however be prepared to untangle the knots concerning the description of the Bodhisattva qualities, because the accounts presented are idealised and exoteric, thus they only portray the gist of the real.

The three *lokas*

To comprehend the nature of the levels of attainment, or dimensions of perception *(lokas)*, as portrayed in Buddhist texts, one needs to analyse the symbolism of the *stūpa*. In his description of the spire discs surmounting *stūpas*, Adrian Snodgrass states:

> The levels of the spire are correlated with the Stations. As in the above, these are usually counted as ten, but there exist alternate lists. One of these enumerates nine true Bodhisattva Stations followed by a tenth stage, which is that of Buddhahood...[3]

---

3 Snodgrass, Adrian, *The Symbolism of the Stupa*, (Motilal Banarsidass, Delhi, 1992), 334.

> The uppermost layer of the spire's horizontal courses represents the Heaven of the Final Limit of Form. In the Theravāda formulations this heaven, as we have seen, is the dwelling place of the Non-Returners (anāgāmin), those who are in the penultimate stage before the attainment of the final stage of the arhat, the Worthy, he who has entered nirvāṇa. This is to say that the Akanṣṭha Heaven is the place where Non-Returners achieve Enlightenment. This heaven is the locus of liberation.
>
> The Mahāyāna texts similarly teach that the Akanṣṭha is the place where nirvāṇa is attained. It is in this heaven that all Buddhas have attained Awakening. "The idea that the Bodhisattva attains his supreme Enlightenment when he is reborn in the Akanṣṭha Heaven... recurs throughout the *Laṅkāvatara (-sūtra)*."[4]

There are three main levels to *saṃsāra* that engrosses the attention of meditators, via which they must aspire. All levels are incorporated as the world of form, the domain of sense-perception that we all know so well, which form the basis to our subjective experiences.

The first level is the realm of desire (*kāmaloka*), the desirous and emotional conditionings that govern the forms of action and thought dispositions of the many. This realm becomes the first major object of focus for analysis for the contemplative one. The associated Watery *saṃskāras (prāṇas),* with their muddied complexion, are most difficult to master. The process of mastery constitutes the bulk of the tests concerning overcoming obstacles preventing the development of the Clear Light. The teachings about the theriomorphic deities as explained in Volume 5 of this Treatise come to the fore here. This incorporates the accomplishments garnered through the entire path of yogic austerities (*tapas*).

The second main substrata of consciousness is designated the realm of form (*rūpaloka).* This realm constitutes the domain of the concrete mind, which reifies, thus makes more dense, concretising all concepts and images from high strata of thought. They are regimented into set patterns of mind, ideas and formed concepts, based upon past impressions. Stored *bījas* of all types of thought that can be recalled, must here be sequentially and correctly dealt with if any train of thought is to be

4 Ibid., 335.

brought to a fitting conclusion. There are four sub-planes to this domain of concretion, denoted in the texts as the Heavens of the first, second, third and fourth meditations. With respect to this, Snodgrass states:

> Above the six heavens of the World of Desire are the heavens of the World of Form. The beings dwelling in these heavens are no longer subject to desires or passions, but nevertheless still possess forms of an etherial nature. The World of Form is divided into the Heavens of the Four Meditations (catur-dhyāni-bhūmi), which correspond to states of consciousness attained in meditation. An ascent through these heavens is a passage to ever more refined and rarefied levels of consciousness and a withdrawal of consciousness towards its Centre. The World of Form comprises eighteen levels, three in each of the first three Meditations and nine in the fourth. The five highest of these levels are called the Pure Abodes (suddhāvāsakāyika), and the uppermost of these is the Heaven of the Final Limit of Form (akanṣtha), which is the heaven of the Non-Returners (anāgāmin).[5]

As the 'World of Form' here is the domain of *manas*, of the mind in its own Fiery Element, of pure thought life, and thus the world of ideas, so it is natural that it is also perceived as the realm of meditation. We must remember that all is a formulation of mind, and it is fitting, therefore, that a great deal of the meditative and contemplative life of the meditator concerns a proper analysis of the contents of that mind. It begins with the most concrete rationalisations, focussed almost exclusively within the world of petty concerns (the level of the first meditation), leading to more lofty and oft exalted scientific and philosophic pursuits (the level of the fourth meditation). The entire domain of the Six Realms of experience, and the various varieties and possibilities of rebirth in any of the Bardo states comes to the fore in these various meditation states. Much is locked away in the *bījas* of past life expression that can be brought to light here and honestly appraised. Proper comprehension, and hence mastery of what constitutes life in *saṃsāra,* is the onus of contemplation at this *rūpaloka* level.

The six heavens of the world of desire have a direct reference to the types of experiences associated with the Six Realms of Buddhism.

5 Ibid., 330.

The focus here is the *saṃskāras* developed via the six petals of the Sacral centre, and their relationship to the other main *chakras* below the diaphragm. All attributes concerning the field of desire therefore need to be analysed and transformed at this level of expression.[6]

The symbolism related to the eighteen levels is relatively straightforward. Each triad refers to an aspect of body, speech, and mind (the *prāṇas* derived from one's corporeal, emotional, and mental environment) for each level of expression of the mind. Concurrently we perceive the qualities of the three *guṇas,*[7] as expressed in developed *saṃskāras,* for these levels of mind.

The four empirical levels (sub-planes) of mind are:

1. The most concreted, associated with collecting the information derived from the five sense-consciousnesses, via the physical (Earthy) environment one resides in. Our concern is thus with the input of pure sensorial or empirical data from what Buddhists call the sixth sense. The focus of consciousness is upon that which is most desired.
2. The sum of the Watery afflictions associated with the emotional body, integrated with mind, hence the mainstay of the desire-mind (*kāma-manas*) developed by the normal person. All forms of emotional perturbations of mind (*kliṣṭamanas*) thus come to the fore, distorting clear rational thought.
3. The level where the mind (*manas*) comes to its own and its specific Fiery qualities are developed. Here the desire-mind is dominated by mind, and rationality produces many transformations of thought.[8] Pure logical thought divorced from the emotions therefore often

---

6 The subjective nature of both the Six Realms and the qualities of the Sacral centre have been explained in depth in the previous volumes of this treatise and therefore needs no further treatment here.

7 *Guṇa:* positive quality, virtue, a property of all created things. Literally 'fundamental quality'. All objects in the manifest world (*prakṛti*) are structurally composed of the three *guṇas: sattva, rajas,* and *tamas.* In the physical world, *sattva* embodies what is pure and subtle (e.g., sunlight), *rajas* embodies the activity (e.g., a volcano), and *tamas* embodies heaviness and immobility (e.g., a block of granite).

8 See Volume 1, chapter 1, under the heading 'The five main attributes of mind', where the technical terms for these attributes of mind: *citta, vijñāna, manovijñāna, manas,* and *ālayavijñāna* are explained.

manifests. The logic obtained is however naturally orientated towards the physical world, hence much that is subjective in nature can be reified, concretised. Syllogisms and rationalisations of all types abound in the mind at this level of expression.

4. The junction between the concreted and abstracted levels of mind. Here high revelations can be brought into the visual perspective of the mind's eye. These revelations can incorporate past life impressions, as well as those images and idea-forms that have been projected into the minds of individuals from the domain of the Sambhogakāya Flower or beyond. The 3 x 3 qualities attributed to this level therefore relate to the process of summarising the information obtained from the previous three levels, plus their integration with what is obtained from the three sub-planes of the abstract Mind.

The third main level of mind is designated the *arūpaloka*, the formless realms. Each of the various levels of the *arūpaloka* represent objectives of meditation that aspire to higher domains of revelation. The meditation therefore progresses from one subtle level to the next through the development of the Will-to-Love, which allows mastery of the type of substance associated with it. It then produces the related visualisations and experiences. These formless realms are increasingly subtle veils that obscure the full vibrancy of *śūnyatā,* and express the lowest reflex of the Buddha Mind.

Snodgrass states:

> Beyond the Heaven of the Final Limit of Form is the third of the Buddhist Worlds, the Formless World (arūpa-loka), which includes those states of manifestation that do not possess any vestige of form but are nevertheless relative in that they are still subject to the workings of causation. The Formless World includes four heavens, which once again correspond to stages of meditation:
>
> 1. The Heaven of Limitless Space (ākāśānantyāyātana), attained in meditation by the negation of all physical phenomena.
> 2. The Heaven of Pure Consciousness (vijñanāntyāyatana), in which empty space is negated.
> 3. The Heaven of Nothingness (akiñcayayatana), in which Pure Consciousness is negated.
> 4. The Heaven of Neither Consciousness nor Non-Consciousness

> (naivasaṃjñānaṃjñā-āyatana), in which this heaven both Consciousness and the absence of Consciousness are negated. In this heaven the mind is severed from both Consciousness and the non-Consciousness of nothingness. This heaven is the uttermost limit of the domain of manifestation; "beyond" this realm lies the unmanifested, the world of the Buddha, immutable, eternal, totally unconditioned and free from the workings of causality.[9]

These four Heavens correspond to the three sub-planes of the higher, abstracted mental plane, plus that which is the nexus between *śūnyatā* and *saṃsāra*. These are the true planes of aspiration and of revelation for all meditators, wherein they reside in various states of absorption (*dhyāna*). The first of the realms of abstraction (the first *dhyāna*) is denoted 'Limitless Space' because there the meditator is freed from all constraints of form, thus can instantaneously fly in all directions of his mindscape. Abstract deduction of many streams of revelation or images can thereby be made at once.

The next *dhyāna* level is denoted 'Pure Consciousness', because here we have the domain of abstracted consciousness in its own pure element, as *bodhicitta*, the Mind of enlightenment. It is the domain of the Sambhogakāya Flower *(tathāgatagarbha)*, and of all the impressions from the revelatory *bījas* stored in its immaculate form.[10] It represents the first of the three levels of enlightenment, the other two being *śūnyatā* and the *dharmakāya*. For most upon the path of meditative realisation, this is as far as they are able to travel. It represents the loss of the concept of the personal-I.

The third *dhyāna* level is denoted the 'Heaven of Nothingness'. This level represents the domain of the most rarefied substance of the abstract Mind, wherein normally no thought sequences abide. It is a quiescent state of *manasic* substance that serves to reflect the expression of the *dharmakāya* into manifestation. This level is that of the natural state, or Clear Light of Mind.

The final *dhyāna* level is denoted 'Neither Consciousness nor Non-Consciousness'. It relates to the *śūnyatā-saṃsāra* nexus, where neither

---

9 Snodgrass, Adrian, *The Symbolism of the Stupa*, 330.

10 The resplendent nature of the Sambhogakāya Flower was explained in Volume 3 of this treatise, where we saw that it is a domain of liberating insight.

the 'non-consciousness' of *śūnyatā* nor the conscious states related to *saṃsāra* reign supreme. Rather, a dynamically established *dhyāna* exists in the Clear Light that is utterly quiescent and luminous, thus receptive to the impressions from *dharmakāya*.

Meditation instructors—Part A
General concepts and Rinpoches

In parts A and B of this synopsis I shall deal with the main meditation instructors that teach Westerners within the Tibetan and Hindu streams. There are many Westerners that similarly teach, however, their information is generally derived from the above two categories of instructors. Therefore, what is said about the Tibetans and Hindus also incorporates the Western teachers, even though variations of the related information may be evident. Some teachers are egotists, whilst most are genuine Bodhisattvas trying to provide an enlightening service to those that come their way for instructions. The quality of teachings presented depends upon the Bodhisattva level they have attained.

Advanced teachings from the most awakened instructors are generally beyond what beginners upon the path are capable of comprehending. Such teachings require serious, consistent mental effort and discipline which most beginners are not willing to exert. Neither are the neophytes to the Initiation path capable of correctly undertaking the types of sacrifices associated with yogic austerities. By 'austerities' here is not meant practicing the yoga *āsanas* (body postures), but rather disciplines of body, speech, and mind; specifically the observation of emotional control. Such austerities require conversion of cherished *saṃskāras* that the beginners will rarely seriously tackle, even though they might comprehend the theory. Therefore, less awakened teachers suffice for them. Lifetimes of effort are required before they are capable of treading the higher Bodhisattva *bhūmis*.

There are generally only a relative handful of third degree Initiates, and beyond, incarnate that need to fully awaken their enlightened status in that life. They require specialised meditation instructions via serious heuristic metaphysical quandary. The instructors capable of meeting the true needs of such advanced aspirants are rare indeed. To help produce enlightenment, the type of *karma* possessed and the accelerated rate of comprehending the subtleties of intricate *dharma* of the candidate must be understood by the instructor. The education can then be wisely directed by the awakened instructor. Consequentially the instructor must know the type of information presented in this series, because those capable of attaining enlightenment in that life must be directed via many avenues of development simultaneously, psychically, as well as meditatively. The teacher must understand the arenas of limiting *karma*, as they always signify key factors in the training of students. By 'limiting *karma*' is meant any susceptibility to *saṃskāras* that will take considerable time and effort to overcome.

Any karmic situation (e.g., relationship issues) also needs to be cleansed before the proper course related to liberating Fires can proceed. The student's Ray disposition, and hence Ashramic affiliation, is another factor to be taken into account. The Ray line: the personality Ray, that of the Sambhogakāya Flower, and thus also of Ashramic standing within Hierarchy, determines the field of service the student will unfold, and the mental proclivities developed. Past life *saṃskāras* were engendered under such Ray activity and will affect the life of the disciple. Students that have emotional reactivity rarely last the course needed to transmogrify their vulnerabilities.

Most charismatic teachers that have large audiences are lower level Bodhisattvas. This is because their charisma appeases the emotional idealism of the adherents, who are generally aspirants, probationary disciples, and sometimes those preparing for the first two Initiations. The charisma itself often betokens a form of egotism.

I will avoid discussion of Theravādin sources, as the focus is upon the Mahayānā in the Tibetan context. Those following the Chinese or Japanese forms of the Mahayānā, such as Zen Buddhism, should be able to extrapolate information that can apply as criteria when seeking preceptors.

Care should be taken in selecting the teacher one wishes to obtain high meditation teachings from. Though many volumes have been written about Bodhisattvas, much information concerning them is glamoured and exaggerated. As previously stated, much is mythologised, to the degree that contemporary Buddhists would struggle to recognise advanced Bodhisattvas in fields of activity other than Buddhism. In the past when a high level Lama disincarnated, his disciples expected him to notify them in some way as to where he would be reborn, so that the child could be found and the *dharma* dispensation (the lineage tradition) that all are accustomed to could continue. The concept presented is that the Lama or great *yogin* will return again and again to be reunited with his similarly reborn disciples, always in a similar situation to preside over the monastery that has become that one's seat of power. Hence we have the present day Rinpoches[11] who are believed to have incarnated in that position for a continuous sequence of lives.

Such succession of similar or exact external circumstance however does not comply with the law of *karma*. If a person were to incarnate in an identical position over and over again his experience in mastering the material world would be curtailed, circumspect, thus antithetical to gaining enlightenment. Necessary qualities derived from living in the West would not have been mastered, or that related to being in a female body. Neither could the accumulations of knowledge from all cultural situations and religions be gleaned. All such belief systems and lifestyles have much to present to any evolving consciousness-stream. Curtailing a mass of knowledge pertaining to the development of great wisdom prevents the oncoming of enlightenment. To become truly enlightened one must have mastered every possible situation arising upon the physical plane. The truncating of this possibility would also occur for the many that would be forced to reincarnate with such a 'blessed one' because they are karmically tied to him. The hustle and bustle of Western materialism is certainly a challenge for those who need to maintain a meditative lifestyle whilst they are manifesting Bodhisattva activities. Such activity also needs to be mastered if certain resilient first Ray qualities are to be developed. This is essential for gaining the higher Bodhisattva *bhūmis*. All on the path must have wisely integrated a vast range of experiences to be able to master all of the vicissitudes of life that are the basis to enlightenment.

Without such mastery, the continuous recitation and study of Tantras and meditation texts will not produce the desired results. The *chakras* will have not been sufficiently honed to safely receive the intensity of

---

11 Meaning 'precious ones', being incarnations of former holders of seats of power in any of the many monasteries in Tibet, or founders of religious sects, or great *yogins*, or authors of the sacred texts.

the incoming energies, for the *nāḍīs* need to be properly primed for such a concourse, necessitating a foundation of correctly sequenced *bījas* of mind from both the *iḍā* (intellectual, *manasic*) and *piṇgalā* (contemplative consciousness) streams. Here the *iḍā* stream would effectively be underdeveloped, because these *prāṇas* are principally developed via Western incarnations, whilst *piṇgalā prāṇas* are principally developed via Eastern rebirths.

There are sound reasons for the existence of a world wherein high meditative states and enlightenment are gained outside of the Tibetan Rinpoche system. These reasons need to be better understood. The sequence of rebirths for all humans, be they spiritually highly accomplished Bodhisattvas or those preparing to enter this stream, must manifest in such a way that balanced rebirths in both hemispheres are necessary.[12] Generally for the spiritually advanced the process is that one or two lives are spent in a country wherein opportunity for serene contemplation, utilising the highest possible Tantras and teachers available, would be instigated. Tibet clearly manifested the best opportunity for such incarnations in the past. The Bodhisattva would then develop and stabilise the *saṃskāras* of the philosophical, meditative equipoise, and accompanying revelations that come from clear visioning, of residing in the natural state of Mind. This equips him/her for what will often be a strenuous life of service in the West, wherein great empirical achievements are to be made in any field of activity.

Thus we have the appearance of the great innovators, the artists, writers, musicians, scientists, cultural and political leaders, that have brought about the Western industrial might and scientific breakthroughs over the course of the centuries. Such Western movements as the Renaissance, the Reformation, the Industrial Revolution, and the accelerated march of science, were brought about precisely by the group incarnation of former great *yogins,* Rinpoches, and the *maṇḍalic* structure of the disciples with which they work.

If the highest level Bodhisattvas, which Rinpoches are said to represent, did not incarnate in this way, then nothing of any consequence would have ever evolved in the Western hemisphere. We would have

12 For the background reasons of the necessity for this refer to Volume 1, chapter 4, of this treatise: '*The West and the East, the Mahāmudrā of the Two Truths*'.

seen the manifestation of a cultural, religious, and scientific backwater that perpetually suffers a dark age. We should note that the period called the Dark Ages in the West (roughly speaking from the time of the dissolution of the Roman Era in the fourth-fifth century of the common era to the period of the early Renaissance in the fifteenth century) corresponded to the golden age of Buddhism, wherein the great religious philosophers flourished in such centres as Nalanda in India. This was followed by the period of the propagation of Buddhism to Tibet, by such great Ones as Padmasambhava, Vimalamitra, Rin-chen-bZang-po, Atiśa, Marpa the translator, etc.

It is easy to deduce that the onus of Bodhisattvic activity lay in the East during this time, and moved towards the Western hemisphere during the fifteenth century to the present day. The work of Tsong-ka-pa (1357-1419) signified the culmination of that epoch. He consequently incarnated at the beginning of this transition period to instigate necessary reforms in Tibet because of widespread debasement of Tantric practices. He founded the (celibate) Gelugpa school, after which many of the great Ones could begin to focus the onus of their activity in the Western hemisphere.

Great Bodhisattvas, and the individuals with which they work, obviously can incarnate alternatively in Tibet and then in the West to push along the course of civilisation. There is, however, a very limited supply of such great Ones, and they are prompted by wise consideration of the compassionate needs for all on the planet, and not just for a relative few in Tibet. Their planning incorporates entire epochs of historical development of our civilisations, involving many millennia of activity for any cycle of accomplishment. The process is akin to the enlightenment of a human unit, where the entire human race can be viewed in terms of a *nāḍī* system with its *chakras* and vitalising *prāṇas.* There is an *iḍā* circulation, a *piṅgalā* circulation, as well as an inevitable *suṣumṇā* direction. Nations, as well as the international situation, can also be rationalised along these lines. The situation is further complicated by the fact that all can be viewed as reincarnating *jīvas,*[13] each possessing a lifespan that undergoes the

13 *Jīva:* An integrated conscious entity embodied by a life force.

stages of childhood, adolescence, maturity, old age and death, as well as possessing a male or female gender. There is spiritual age, integral interrelated karmic associations, as well as streams of lives other than the human to consider. The nature of the basic greed, selfishness, and materialistic competitiveness, producing national aggression upon other nation states, gives us a general idea as to the true spiritual age of most nations of this planet. People come into incarnation within those nations and undergo forms of collective cleansing, similar to the way that *saṃskāras* are developed and transformed in a human unit.

The proper rectification of massed *saṃskāras* is part of the meditation of advanced Bodhisattvas. Such vast streams of *saṃskāras* will take significant time for humanity to correct. The Bodhisattva cannot work alone, so arenas of priority must be ascertained with the help of the entire Council of Bodhisattvas. Once the collective decision has been made, then each member of this Council takes action, according to their Ray disposition upon the task at hand. Multifarious are the factors to consider, and always the wisest decisions must be made, that sometimes will take millennia to work out. Religion is but one factor conditioning any civilisation-stream, and many Bodhisattvas focus upon other arenas of service. Consequently, all move forward along their evolutionary path. As each individual's path is metered according to their capacity to travel to greater light, so all beings are helped to progress towards liberation. The most advanced Bodhisattvas often manifest in comparative obscurity, unhindered by the glamour and clamouring attention that recognition of such a one by the religiously inclined produces.

We see, therefore, that the meditative considerations of the enlightened are vaster than most upon the path to liberation conceive of.[14] The projection of the *buddhadharma* is but one factor of many that must be weighed in consciousness. The *dharma* can of course be rephrased in many ways, as the language of enlightenment takes many forms, via many religious and philosophic streams, as well as through all cultural attributes.

A principle of enlightenment is to follow detailed observation and analysis of all that one's *karma* confronts one with. To fully

---

14 Much more concerning what such considerations are will be revealed in the later chapters of this book.

understand or appreciate anything, one must follow thoughts through to conclusion, and develop the links thereby to the abstracted realms of Mind. Eventually, the portal of the *śūnyatā-saṃsāra* nexus must be found. One must think logically and in depth upon all issues, utilising the Tantras at hand.

To dissipate energies through laziness of thought, producing an inability to reason conclusively, thus manifesting ineffectual thinking, is little more than the parable of someone asking a blind person to guide him. One must check regularly one's thoughts and meditation sequences, as there may be errors in thought all along the way to enlightenment. Instantaneous checking and rechecking is the way expressed on the path to an enlightened Mind, for this betokens the mastery of the art of humbleness in thought, word and deed. One can then reason conclusively, developing intricate pathways and *maṇḍalas* of revelatory thought. The ritual of meditation facilitates this process and must be cultivated.

Meditation instructors—Part B
Guruparamparā

All of the previous themes are part of the meditation of a great One before he/she chooses rebirth. This depends also upon personal *karma* that such a one may have with respect to any grouping (minor or major *chakra* within the collective human form) that is presently incarnate, and also with respect to what has been planned by the Lords of *karma*. The Bodhisattva acts as an agent of *bodhicitta* within that nation's *nāḍī* system, acting to purify coarse *prāṇas* within the general system, and to direct human life-streams from lower *chakras* to the higher ones in the general body. For this to happen the demons of illusions, pride, separateness, etc., must be overcome by each human unit as well as collectively by the masses. Inevitably, all *prāṇas* from the *maṇipūra chakra* must be directed to the Heart centre and there transformed into the qualities associated with the constitution of its petals.[15]

---

15 These centres were explained in all the earlier volumes of this treatise, therefore the reader should refer to these books for detail, and accordingly endeavour to transpose the information to include the evolutionary progress of a country or civilisation. History will one day be written along these lines, which will produce many revelations presently unknown to our historians.

The great Ones that have manifested innovations, yogic prowess, and writings that have inspired generations of disciples, will thus rarely incarnate again in the religious dispensation of which they were founders or major innovators. If they do so, it will be in a different arena of that religious dispensation that needs their specialised attention. Compassionate duty demands that such ones are born wherever the need is greatest, according to the dictates of the combined meditation of the Council of Bodhisattvas. We will normally find, therefore, that an important disciple will succeed as the Rinpoche to take the seat of power established by that great One. Generally such a one has sufficient background *karma* and knowledge to play the role, and can thereby continue the succession of the teaching lineage, or *guruparamparā*.[16]

The succession results in a corresponding, diminished level of esoteric acumen in the preceptor, plus quality of students, than what was possible with the great One. Over a number of lives, therefore, unless a reformer incarnates, one would normally perceive a gradual reification of doctrine, with corresponding lack of esoteric acumen in the current custodian of the lineage. With respect to the technicalities concerning how Rinpoches are chosen, it is easy enough for thoughts and impressions to be given by the guru to a candidate as to which of his former possessions to choose. The unenlightened supervising this process are unaware of the telepathic impressions, and are thus easily swayed.

All things have their natural cycles of birth, maturing, debilitation, and consequent death. This necessitates the birth of a new venture based upon the best of the past, but vitalised at a higher level of expression. For instance, in this way we see the general trend of the progressive evolution of the *buddhadharma*. Because of karmic considerations,

---

16 *Guruparamparā:* lineage tradition of a *guru*, or spiritual preceptor. The word '*guru*' is coupled with *paramparā*, meaning 'an uninterrupted series or succession'. An important consideration in Buddhism and Hinduism. It is needed where the most important information was not written down, but were 'ear whispered' from the guru to students, through a lineage or series of beings that have evolved to take the place of the preceding guru. It is especially important in Tantricism. There is an exoteric stream of *guruparamparā*, of those who succeed each other in time in the material world. We also see an esoteric stream of a succession of spiritual teachers, each possessing greater accomplishment than the one below, and are thus capable of leading those below them to where they reside.

generally the former most important students of the guru (great One) will move on to wherever he goes, leaving the younger ones to fulfil the continuation of that lineage. Therefore, the older the lineage, then generally the more dogmatic and rigid the teachings provided by its exponents become. It produces a process of slow dying (degeneracy) of the lineage, contrary to the general trend of the religion. This process happens in stages similar to the flowering of a minor *chakra* in a human unit, which is then superseded by another more important one. The former guru and major students move on to form a larger *chakra*, whilst the exoteric lineage successor continues to embody the functions of the minor *chakra* that was formerly awakened by the guru. So the entire Inner Round of *chakras* are developed, and then surpassed by the awakening of the potencies of the major *chakras*. These *chakras* have their own geometrical circulation with other centres. We have a similar demonstration with various lineages that represent minor *chakras* in the main corpus of Buddhism. They awaken, and then come to be supplanted as the focus of development shifts ever to higher vistas, leaving the former focus to wane.

The true lineage is esoteric, following the graded rebirths of the *maṇḍala* around the great One as he steps from one arena of activity to the next. The esoteric functions manifest via the meditations of the reincarnated students in whichever country they happen to be. The field of service may not even be Buddhist oriented, but high Bodhisattvic activity manifests nevertheless.

We can see that inevitably a degeneracy must manifest regarding the occupation of that seat of power, which is the cause for the present lack of true highly accomplished Bodhisattvas in the chosen Rinpoches seen in the current Tibetan world. The system no longer serves the purpose that it once did in Tibet, because the entire Western world has now opened itself up to the *buddhadharma,* and many great Ones can find opportunity to gain enlightenment via Western bodies, in accordance with the precepts of the Mahāmudrā of East and West.[17] The yab-yum process is now producing the child of that union.

Many Rinpoches are deemed living examples of being near-Buddhas, however there are various levels of Rinpoches in the system. Not all,

17 See Volume 1, chapter 3, of this *Treatise on Mind.*

therefore, are taken to be reincarnates of the highest level Bodhisattvas, manifestations of the *dharmakāya* for all to gain succour from. Others are seen to incarnate to fulfil relatively minor appointed roles in a succession of rolling incarnations.

Only Rinpoches that are high level Bodhisattvas should have the wherewithal to give guidance productive of liberation. The problem lies in the fact that the signposts for liberation have changed since Tibet was an independent country, and the highest level Rinpoches are unlikely to represent what they were said to be reincarnates of. One hopes that Bodhisattvas were chosen to fulfil these roles. The selected ones are often victims of the situation, similar to the laity who in turn worship them. They are trapped in layers of beliefs and expectations that they must follow, even if incapable of properly fulfilling their anointed roles, because they are unable to meditatively rise to the appropriate level of the symbolic *stūpa* spire assigned to them. They may have never come close to tasting the bliss-state of the Akaniṣṭha Heaven, or the *arūpalokas*, but the position generally can uplift them to aspire higher than they would have otherwise done. What they can carry forward of the *dharma* also generally suffices because of the limited spiritual level of their audience. This then establishes another level of *guruparamparā,* where these younger Bodhisattvas establish strong teaching relationships to the supplicants they feed spiritually. As that Bodhisattva travels up the *bhūmi* ladder, so they pull the devoted ones up with them, thereby developing a *guru-chela* relationship with many.

Though Bodhisattvas do occupy seats of power in Tibetan Buddhism, those that have been enthroned are generally younger in spiritual age than what the popular imagination purports them to be. Impossible lineages have been consequently attributed to those who are made to mimic roles of great illustrious forbears, because of belief that they are their reincarnates. When a more advanced but physically younger Bodhisattva comes to them for spiritual guidance, then real problems will arise in that Bodhisattva's training. The malaise of the system is consequently demonstrated, as often such a one will not be recognised as being exemplary or needing specialised training. Stultification of spiritual progress for the young Bodhisattva is then often the case.

A great illustrious One from a past cycle will have long moved on to a more befitting role, challenging that Master's full development of 'skilful means' for uplifting all in the world. Higher, deeper meditative insights and the next rung of the ascent of the *bhūmis* must still be accomplished by the Master. There is always much more to do in the world and means to serve than being an object of worship for devotional monks, lay people and the Western sycophants who are enamoured by Rinpoches and Tulkus. The entire world's civilisation needs changing, and much indeed must be done to bring true equanimity of wealth and resource sharing for all people upon the planet. Here then is the onus of focus for many of the great Ones, rather than religious development *per se*.

Overall, we see that much needs to be meditated upon concerning changes to be made to rectify the inadequacies of the roller coaster ride of the present Rinpoche system. Courageous steps need to be taken to effect the actual changes, if the outer structure is to better express the reality of the manifesting inner *dharma*. The religion needs to demonstrate the expression of a high level of wisdom in all its activities. For this reason, the truly wise must govern its seats of power. The entire system must progress to embody a higher *chakra* in the corpus of Buddhism. If the Rinpoche system cannot reform and adapt to the way the *buddhadharma* actually manifests in truth, then the possibility of abandonment altogether as something not worthy of the refined nature of the *dharma* should be considered. Gautama certainly did not instigate such a politically corruptible system amongst his monks.

The few high level Bodhisattvas that do incarnate into this system will be found to try to reform it, as in the case of His Holiness the Dalai Lama. Less advanced Bodhisattvas will work within the constraints of the teachings, avoiding any perceived inconsistencies to wisely educate those in their care. Their onus will be to preserve the better attributes of this form of lotto-like selection process for the spiritually gifted. The system is restricted almost exclusively to men, which thereby denigrates women by largely denying the possibility of the role of high spiritual stature to them. In fact, the reality is generally the opposite nowadays in the domain of the Council of Bodhisattvas, because of the lowly status of women and the cultural victimisation demonstrated against women in many societies. Surely the need to assist the plight of so many feminine victims of our societies will offer much scope for many Bodhisattvas to try to ameliorate. Many of the most advanced of them, therefore, incarnate into female bodies, a reality not yet reflected in the patriarchal Buddhist world-view and hierarchical system.

Women often bear the drudgery of most of the menial labour upon this planet, but are often found to be the most genuinely compassionate, religiously inclined people. This fact needs to be better recognised and rewarded in our ecclesiastical societies. Buddhists should think more about this issue.

If a teacher is hallowed and worshipped simply because a belief system obliges the worshipper to do so, then what guarantee exists that such a one actually is enlightened and can direct the earnest practitioner through all of the stages to liberation? The tradition merely reifies the proscribed doctrines promulgated in the texts, for which the keys for true esoteric comprehension may have long been lost. There is no guarantee that there has been an unbroken succession of liberated, awakened transmitters of the *dharma*. *Guruparamparā* is then a belief system that potentially sows the seeds of abuse of prospective practitioners. Practitioners need to develop their wisdom and open their eyes to see and properly discern the true worthiness of the one before whom they supplicate themselves for teachings.

The vast compassion of great Ones prevents their continuous incarnation into one or other religious *cul-de-sacs*. They need not be physically available in order to rightly educate their many students. The true relationship is subjective, and exists upon the mental plane, wherein telepathy and accredited visions are the method employed by the awakened Ones. The relationship persists no matter where a disciple has incarnated, and is greatly facilitated after the demise of the form.

Not meditating deeply upon all issues that affect our world produces a lack of vibrancy in one's mental space. It results in an intensity deficit that will block the 'high voltage' energy associated with enlightenment to manifest. The generation of receptivity to such energy is necessary for all that are to overcome complacent religious beliefs, with a view to enlightenment. The intensity of the radiance of the aura possessed betokens a true meditation instructor. The salutary gift waves of Light and Love uplifts the subtle bodies and consciousness of all that are receptive to the presence of such a one. There is a good reason for the radiance of the great Ones depicted in all religious imagery. The capacity to bear intense energies is far beyond mere charisma, and aspirants would do well to try to see the true signs of worthy ones—in their general reticence to speak overtly, the quietude of their demeanour and of the serenity by means of which each spoken word is articulated by. For those that have not developed clairvoyant vision, the radiance of the aura is indicated by the sometimes fiery disposition and intensity of articulation of a many-layered wisdom, but always backed by spontaneous humbleness. Sometimes the reactionary tendencies of junior disciples in training will block the capacity to rightly handle their quota of the energy transmission. Thus the great Ones are normally in retreat, with their presence buffered by their senior students that help tone down the energies. Charlatans that disguise themselves as great Ones, however, can also be 'protected' by their senior students. The difference being that in the first case the aspirants are protected thus from the high energisation, and in the second case it is the central teacher that is being protected from the desirous clamour of the devotees. Discernment of the difference is not easy for neophytes.

Aspirants therefore should enquire as to the wider knowledge base of a prospective preceptor before choosing to follow such a one. Lethargy of thinking is also bred via continuous recital of religious material by those who only possess an incomplete understanding of the intrinsic meaning of the *dharma*. A pure, one-pointed religious base may seem to have sufficed in the past to gain enlightenment, nevertheless practical knowledge in worldly affairs was always important. The enlightened one often became advisor to kings and princes, concerned with the political problems of the day, and also needed to assist in instructing the laity in all matters. The input of enlightened advisors familiar with all aspects of human affairs in the complex world of today is similarly much needed, especially in the world of government.

Our universities excel in breeding savants of knowledgeable things, but the development of enlightened wisdom is not their forte. Advanced religious practice based on developing wisdom is the answer, but the graduates of this training fail society if they cannot meet its true needs, if religion is all they know. Again we see that high Bodhisattvas need to be exponents of many disciplines in life if they are to truly serve in today's world with its technological advances, *viz* the computer age. Where are they to be found nowadays? Meditation practitioners cannot advance to lofty domains of awakening if genuinely enlightened ones cannot be found as instructors. Practitioners, however, should not be bound by sentimentality or ignorant devotion to pedantic religious formula.

True seekers must always be open to suggestion and to ardently seek the highest way via the best teachers they can find. They must not be content with mere beliefs that ascertain religious ontologies absolutely true because the tradition demands it so, or because the lineage of the teacher is shown in the texts. The texts rarely present more than a symbolic or mythological account interwoven with actual happenings of what may have transpired in the past. The lineage purported is thus not true in detail, nor is it possible for the same entity to continuously reincarnate to sit upon the same seat throughout the centuries.

The *karma*-formations of meditative unfoldment by students, producing resultant activity, must be carefully deduced by the guru. Where, however, are the teachers in the mainstream Buddhist world that can trace such karmic pathways and properly teach the consequences?[18] What are the repercussions of events that follow all forms of mental activity, and how does one project the necessary outcome into the flow of purposeful existence? These are always underlying questions to all meditative streams that are to effect enlightening conditions in the world. The meditative process allows one to trace *karma,* to discover one's purpose in life and to assist others to discover theirs upon the upward spiral to *dharmakāyic* bliss.

Proponents of the Buddhist religion generally too rigidly structure their doctrines. They must become more fluid and protean, according to the way that the meditation-Mind actually manifests. A settled structure may be needed for instructing neophytes, but the upper echelons of the Buddhist Hierarchy must continuously adapt to meet the challenges of the new. There must be an interrelation with modern society in such a way that those governing us will desire to actively seek out advice from the wisest in the religion. True social engagement is the order of the day, rather than purely exoteric religious practice.

The fact that Buddhism has a name suggests stability, which is based upon a rigid adherence to doctrines established many centuries ago and reified into the system we now possess. There is much ritualistic show, which is appealing to the great many observers who are attracted to the

---

18 My book *Karma and the Rebirth of Consciousness* needs to be consulted concerning this subject, as it aims to rectify misconceptions as to how *karma* actually works.

religion, especially in its Tibetan flavour. The religion is thus steeped with glamour, but this has caused many to observe its doctrines that would not normally have done so. The influx of many new ones to the *dharma* is a welcoming advent, but their education must meet the needs of the brightest, as well as the beginners. The loss of true comprehension of some *sūtras* and most Tantras thus needs to be rectified by the fluid, esoteric methodology of the enlightened. The Buddhist mindscape must therefore expand towards high enlightened achievements, through overcoming its attitudes based upon too careless an interpretation of the texts, and the belief in exoteric dogma. The prospective for appropriate change has always existed in the religion, and hopefully it will continue to do so. Modern trends, such as that denoted by the term 'engaged Buddhism', are manifesting in the correct direction. This development however still needs more enlightened guidance.

The prophecy that this present fourteenth Dalai Lama is the last of the line, that there will be no more to succeed to that high office after him,[19] may not ring true due to political connivance and the high demand for such an institution from the laity. The days of the Rinpoche system as presently construed is however numbered. There is little point for continuing their offices if reformation does not happen. Neither biographical myths, or medieval thinking should be the basis for determining *guruparamparā*. Such seats of power need to be filled by those who have proved themselves enlightened through their literary output and the life lived based upon the way they manifest Bodhisattva activities. This must be seen from the context of the world's true needs. The *buddhadharma* must be the motivating or driving force behind all considerations. The Rinpoche system may still serve the lay Buddhist devotee steeped in traditional values and more primitive folklore beliefs,

19 See, for instance, the article posted on the BBC World News: Talking to reporters in the northern Indian city of Amritsar, the Dalai Lama emphasised his desire to make the Tibetan leadership more democratic. '"As early as 1969 I made clear the very institution of the Dalai Lama is up to the Tibetan people", he said. He outlined other methods to appoint his successor as well, such as one similar to electing the Pope where senior lamas would choose the next Dalai Lama. The Tibetan spiritual leader also raised the possibility of himself naming a new Dalai Lama while he is still alive, a proposal he outlined in Japan last week'. Source: http:/news.bbc.co.uk, Wednesday, 28 November 2007.

however, worship of those who have not proved themselves enlightened must end. The glamour of the accomplishments attributed to such reincarnates must be demystified.

The state of affairs concerning this entire system is specially exemplified in the course of actions re the Karmapa controversy, as explained in such books as *The Buddha Cries! Karmapa Conundrum.*[20] The happenings related to who is to occupy the 16th Gwyalya Karmapa's seat at Rumteck exemplifies the malaise of the Rinpoche system. That some high officials in Tibet were awakened in the earlier epochs of their history may undoubtedly be true, however, the lack of wise coherent activity amongst the various monasteries in Tibet before the Chinese invasion, and their inability to prevision the awful consequences of infighting in the face of the Chinese threat, indicates a dearth of enlightened attitudes then also. Be this as it may, Tibet produced Lamas of great enlightened luminescence throughout its history, and they existed even in that epoch, but their wisdom was not acquiesced to.

There will always be room for improvement in all things, necessitating the need for reformation, including the office of the Dalai Lama. The Chinese invasion of Tibet actually forced upon the entire Tibetan nation the need to properly re-evaluate everything concerning themselves, of the isolationism they then deemed important, based also on a perception of the supremacy of their religion over all others. A form of a humbling process was consequently imposed upon them. They were forcibly admitted into the wider world at large, to which they exported their religious system, for the world's general benefit. However, the Tibetan system also suffered the widespread absorption (particularly by the monks) into the massed degeneracy of Western societal and cultural advances, such as television. Much can be said concerning the benefits, and also forms of degeneracy, that have befallen upon the religion since its migration into the Western world. The *karma* underlying the undeniable horrors accrued by the actual invasion and the loss of self-government of the Tibetans over their country could also be meditated upon.

Nothing is permanent, all is transient, and we must move on to

---

20 Maheshwari, Anil. *The Buddha Cries! Karmapa Conundrum,* (UBS Publishers' Distributors Ltd. New Delhi, 2000).

generate the ability to honestly see all things as they actually are, in the right order and sequence for their establishment, maturation and consequent death. Reasons for reform of the Rinpoche system should now be obvious. Problematic conclusions could also be drawn from the fact that an exoteric doctrine was promulgated from Gautama's time onwards. The demarcation between the few enlightened, worthy ones and the great number of unenlightened that bore positions of power and made decisions for the affairs of state needs to be noted. Theirs was the onus to listen to the enlightened who Knew and conveyed their ear-whispered gnosis to those they deemed worthy. Prosperity ensued when this advice was put into practice. Misfortune always comes when wise advice goes unheeded.

The proper development of the meditation-Mind reveals all. True meditation teachers know the lie of the land with respect to the nature of awakening *chakras*, and understand fully the intricacies of the necessary *karma*. In the future, those encumbered with the position of high office in Tibetan Buddhism will have proven they can do so. For instance, true prescient prevision will unequivocally show who is the rightful heir to Rumteck.[21] Where is the enlightenment observed in the cacophony of voices from the many Rinpoches arguing over this issue? This is but one of the problems that presently besets the religion.

Another issue is the untimely selection of the young boy found in Tibet for the position of the Tashi (Panchen) Lama's seat, and who has now vanished due to Chinese interference. We see squabbling over political issues within the system, but little wisdom and insight regarding the true signs of the incarnation of those at the highest Bodhisattva levels. Despite this there are some successes, the Dalai Lama, for instance, certainly serves as a beacon for study of one who is engaged in true Bodhisattvic activity.

The Chinese invasion of Tibet and the fleeing of the leading proponents of the religion to the Western hemisphere meant also that changes had to occur in the way that the religion expressed itself and its teachings. It signified a time when the more esoteric doctrines had to be revealed and made available to widespread detailed scrutiny via

21 The seat of the Karmapa, to which the present contenders are excluded, because of the controversy, and for political considerations of the Indian Government.

the methods of the Western scholastic tradition. Bodhisattvas will recognise the need for appropriately changing the mode of teaching the *dharma*, including that related to gaining enlightenment via meditation procedures. Some changes were indeed made by the Rinpoches and the graduates of the Tibetan spiritual universities (the Geshe training of the Gelug, and Shedders for the Nyingma) in the decades of the Tibetan diaspora, to accommodate Westerners requiring *dharma*. Many new centres were accordingly set up in the West, and a vigorous publishing agenda came into being. However, more needs to be done to critically appraise the nature of the doctrines themselves so that it better meets the astute deductive abilities of the best Western minds. In some ways such thinkers compromised their abilities of adequate appraisal by being indoctrinated into the Rinpoche show, and because of the challenge of the complicated esotericism of the extant doctrines, to which the Rinpoches were said to be the custodians. This was unavoidable, and facilitated these scholars to provide good translations of many Tibetan texts.

The *karma* of the fact that Tibet salvaged the Buddhist religion in the face of the Islamic hordes that swept through India more than a thousand years ago came to bear here. Tibet sent their scholar-translators to retrieve the manuscripts from ruin, and became the bastion of the *buddhadharma* the Muslims could not destroy. The Western world provided a similar role for those fleeing Chinese persecution. The Tibetans returned the *dharma,* with considerably developed improvements and specialised elaborations, to the outside world for safe keeping at a time when it was being persecuted in their own land. A new genre of Buddhism developed in Tibet because of the Muslim invasion of India, and consequently a similar development will occur in the West because of the Chinese Invasion of Tibet.

Problems arise when the role of the past enlightened ones are interpreted as if they apply to the current teachers. The question of who one should go to for meditation instructions is thus of the utmost importance for all who truly wish enlightenment. Teachers that are esoterically blind cannot serve this function. If the desire is to follow tradition and the conventional methods of interpreting the *sūtras* and Tantras, then the currently available teachers will suffice. If enlightenment is sought, then the seeker should eliminate the shackles of conventionality and the blindfolds of parochial thinking. They must truly look at the nature of the teacher, teaching method, and teachings involved. The office of the Rinpoche was useful in the past, but now we should move on to appropriate a new form of teaching dispensation for those seeking the way to liberation.

There was always a gradual release to exoteric revelation of esoteric secrets, according to a provisional plan, as were, for instance, the earlier promulgation of the Tantras. The unenlightened know not the portent of the process of revelation, but the enlightened do, and work consciously with their united plan for the gradual education of humanity. All revelatory explanations will then be found through a systematic study of the available texts, when applied via sound meditative insights. *Guruparamparā,* esoterically understood, will then be the means forwards to great revelatory heights and liberation at the behest of the Lords of Shambhala.

Meditation instructors—Part C
The concept of a Tulku

With respect to the term Tulku, Chögyam Trungpa explains the meaning in the following way:

> To understand the doctrine of *'Tulkus'* in Tibet, it is necessary first of all to understand the Buddhist attitude to 'rebirth'...While we remain more or less enmeshed in a selfhood regarded as our own, past and future lives are continually being produced by those forces which still bind us to worldly existence. In the case of a *Tulku,* however, the forces which produce his existence are of a different order. Something, or someone, that has no 'individuality' or *ego* in the ordinary sense decides to work on earth for the sake of all beings. He (or 'it') therefore takes birth over a certain period of time, in a series of human individuals, and it is these who are named *'Tulkus'.*
>
> The influence in question may emanate from any archetypal sources of Wisdom, which is the stable essence of the Universe, or else of Compassion, which is Wisdom in operation throughout countless world systems. So it may be said of a Tulku that he is an emanation of Manjusri, the Bodhisattva of Wisdom or of Avalokitesvara, the Bodhisattva of Compassion; the Dalai Lama is known as an incarnation

> of the latter. In Tibet, a great sage such as Milarepa, known to have passed quite beyond the bondage of created things, is said to extend his influence over various lines of such incarnations...In some instances a man of advanced spiritual development, but short of final liberation, dies before accomplishing a certain task and returns to complete it. Another kind of incarnation is known as a '*Tulku* of benediction': when a certain well beloved Lama dies, his disciples will ask another Lama who has been closely associated with the deceased (the latter, as often as not, will be the presiding Lama of their school) to locate his spirit; as a result of this, the Lama, though he does not return in person, confers his blessing upon the one who is to carry on his teaching; the person thus designated for the task will then reincarnate the departed Master in the sense of perpetuating his spiritual influence.
>
> Multiple incarnations, of which an example was given above, most frequently occurs in fives, of which one in particular will embody the visible presence of the departed Lama, another his powers of speech, and yet another his powers of thought; again, one will represent his activities and another his qualities.[22]

The belief expressed in the quote above is that Tulkus[23] can incarnate into multiple beings in the form of the speech of one, the mind of another, and perhaps the form of another. This is an erroneous belief because the Sambhogakāya Flower-*tathāgatagarbha* cannot separate itself in this way. There is a singular individuality for each human consciousness-stream. It is the major quality that distinguishes us from members of the animal kingdom. The *sūtrātmā* (Life cord) that connects the Flower to the mind of an incarnate personality is highly inviolable, as it must convey the stores of *karma* from Flower to personality, as well as the new *saṃskāras* generated, with their karmic expressions for the future. This does not allow for a fragmentation of that karmic purpose into differing Life-streams. Karmic purpose would become aberrant and destroyed in this way. High grade Bodhisattvas may have evolved past the stage of bearing a 'Soul', nevertheless they are bound by the exigencies of the law of *karma*, and are eminently wise in the way they act.

22 Chögyam Trungpa, *Born in Tibet,* (Shambhala Press, Boston, 1977), 270-271.

23 They are considered Bodhisattvas of high degree.

A highly enlightened being may indeed overshadow or energise many people at once, but it would not be possible for him to incarnate his different qualities to be these people. Also, each *tathāgatagarbha* embodies a different stream of *karma,* and these streams would be unduly muddled if a soul was to separate itself to produce simultaneous multiple incarnations. The law of *karma* is exact and the actual expression of such a belief of multiple incarnations would inhibit this law from manifesting correctly.

When it is stated that: 'Multiple incarnations...most frequently occurs in fives, of which one in particular will embody the visible presence of the departed Lama, another his powers of speech, and yet another his powers of thought; again, one will represent his activities and another his qualities', then what is really exemplified are incarnations viewed in terms of the five sense-consciousnesses of an individual. An error has arisen because of the belief of an amorphous life stream, one that can even flow into animal forms. The logic therefore arises along this line: 'if it is possible for the consciousness-stream to be so diffuse, so why not also split it up into five different streams that can incarnate into five different human personalities?'. The fallacy of this concept can be viewed in the light of the revelations in my book *Karma and the Rebirth of Consciousness,* denoting the impossibility of the rebirthing principle of human consciousness being so diffuse. It cannot, for instance, be reborn into animal bodies, unless the human form is considered such a body. The earlier volumes of this treatise emphasised that individuation was necessary for *karma* to function as it does. The consciousness-stream therefore is not as amorphous as supposed, and is directed by a Sambhogakāya Flower. This 'Flower' *(tathāgatagarbha)* precludes the expression of such co-mingling. It needs its karmic-field intact, unitary, with the associated *saṃskāras* directed by it from life to life until liberation is attained.

Light is the unifying substance of body, speech and mind, whilst supramundane light is the adamantine expression of the one divinity. Light diffracts into the multifarious aspects of the unitarity, pristine awareness and is known as the substance of consciousness. Although light is one and many, it is not deluded into three, five, or more consciousness-streams of separately incarnated mind's eyes. Each such eye sees via light a slightly different image when viewing the same object, because the nature of the image is then filtered through different minds. Each mind views the same object of perception differently from other minds. The mind is not designed to collate more than one set of five sense-consciousnesses, derived from a single set of sense-perceptors. Certainly it can construe things in terms of the five-ness of things, but it is not designed to collate images derived from a multiplicity of physical eyes, for instance. It cannot deal with fifteen, or twenty-five or any multiple thereof, of incarnating persona, of differing world scenarios and opinions. Such a concept of 'split personality' is a definition of madness. Why would the mind complicate and compromise its receptivity, spontaneity, and automatic retrievability of information, making such enlightened functioning exceedingly difficult, even if it could do so? How can *saṃsāra* be instantaneously integrated with *dharmakāya* under such an awkward situation?

Such a collation necessitates moving from one mind-stream to another, and then trying to correlate all forms of actions, visual inputs, sensorial outcomes and reactions, as well as *manasic* modifications and thought impulses. It necessitates instantaneous correlation of *saṃskāras* from diverse streams and continuously analysing their interrelated karmic consequences far into the distant future. Only the naïve, who know nothing about the functioning of an enlightened-Mind could assert that such an abstruse, convoluted activity is what an enlightened one would actually choose to continuously do. The enlightened one can ascertain the content of a disciple's mind at a glance and rapidly move from one such mind to the next, but there is much more to such a one's service work than continuously experiencing their sense-impressions and *manasic* input. Such a form of unskilful means to an end is thus not chosen by any enlightened being.

A much more important and viable method of educating the many is for each individual disciple of the Master to overcome many obstacles on their individual paths to enlightenment, all based upon the conversion of past life *saṃskāras*. High perceptions are then developed as each meditates upon how to best serve their target groups of people along specific Ray lines wherewith they are equipped to help them. Here the disciples are properly educated to gain the next steps upon their

Bodhisattva paths, and likewise the people they have *karma* with. The methodology is time honoured, effective, serves the greatest number with the least effort and properly allows the enlightened Mind to function as it must.

All truths and expression of consciousness states manifesting under immutable laws are easily perceived by the Eye (i.e., the Third Eye) that has been properly trained to do so. Its accomplishment facilitates the straight line of abstract Reason, and manifests from the zone of enlightenment through the *antaḥkaraṇa* (the consciousness-link) direct to the quiescent and receptive mind of the incarnate personality. The law allows only one such link per incarnating *jīva*, not two or three differing personalities existing in other localities in space. This ensures no tangling-up of impressions or mixing up of differing *karmas*. The manifestation of a split-personality is severely curtailed through this means of incarnation. Each incarnate individuality is a separate incarnation of the one kind of substance; universally dubbed divine, yes, yet they exist as separate incarnations and/or manifest as Souls. The term *Soul* means the human compassionate element capable of attaining *nirvāṇa,* as explained in Volume 3 of this treatise. Each Soul is a uniquely manifesting, radiating sun of Life, and obeys certain wholesome laws that do not permit their personality vehicles being 'split' into different fragmentary entities.

There is only one radiant illuminating sun incarnating via an incarnate personality, and for this reason the enlightenment of that individual is possible, following the way of *karma*. There is a reciprocation in the process of the conveyance of *karma*. It manifests from the source of illumination and stores of *bījas* needed for expansion and assimilation to the vehicle that is the way of expression, and returns as the consequences of expression of that *karma* via the consciousness-link that exists between the two. Such a link may not be broken or interfered with unless the Sambhogakāya Flower chooses disincarnation of the personality expression. Such is the law, otherwise all we would see is mass-scale insanity, with all forms of other people's minds scrambled in the brain's awareness.

To the untrained mind, little more is viewed than the incarnate form, and as a consequence much can be imagined concerning 'it'.

When someone's mind views a person's form, then what the mind imagines to exist is not the actual reality. It is not able to identify with the consciousness incarnate in that form. Anyone, in fact, is capable of being imputed to be an enlightened one by the unenlightened, because the process of enlightenment is still a mystery to them. The process can thus be romanticised, exaggerated, and mythologised because the laws or constraints governing its manifestation are not cognised. Neither are the available texts able to convey to the unenlightened the true nature of the permutations of the tests and processes that govern the way an enlightened Mind must behave.

The concept of Tulkus is thus skewered by unenlightened minds when it is stated that an enlightened being can pour into a system of vacant units (minds) impressions that must uniquely govern those units, in the sense of being direct incarnations of that being.[24] The implication is similar to that of pouring a bucket of water into a quantity of unitary receptacles that are equal to a mass of Tulkus. The 'water' here being consciousness or any other divine attribute of the enlightened One. This concept then produces a number of versions of the one individual, like little puddles of water created by the bucket, all said to be aspects of the one originating consciousness. The nature of the form has not been properly accounted for, nor how enlightened beings incarnate, the mechanisms utilised, or of the way *karma* would work in all of this. This view would make one enlightened consciousness suddenly take on a number of new opportunities to amass more *karma*, thus keeping such a one very far from the attainment of Buddhahood. What if any of these unenlightened Tulkus made karmic mistakes that would necessitate the overshadowing enlightened one to incarnate into hell (or other) states? We get a muddle of thinking because there is no real concept of the true mechanism of rebirth, resulting in truths being twisted to suit a political agenda disguised in a religiosity that produces only a facade that veils the real.

The Buddhist system of mathematics has little meaning when they think one can pour a bucket of water into smaller containers, and by thus spreading it around say it is equivalent to a unit (being many

24 This is possible from one perspective as we shall see later, but not in the case of each such unit being the actual incarnation of the great One.

numbers in the context of simply being a one). As a numerical system it states that one can equal five, ten, or any number of Tulkus. A system of proportions and scale relies on numbers and equivalence, whilst the process of *karma* also relies on measurements (numbers and the process of counting). For example, this one time event equals this unit, producing a certain quanta of one unit of repercussion.

Similar is the thinking that destroying one insect is equable to the action of killing a person. However, the *karma* of killing one person is not equivalent to the destruction of even a thousand insects. This holds true, even if we look further down the track and consider the large number of insects that would have been its progeny if its life was not unduly terminated. Though composed of similar material substance, insect and a human are not the same. Similarly, though two human units are constituted of similar components, they cannot bear the same consciousness-stream, no matter how one imaginatively tries to make it so.

The type of *karma* ensued from one person killing another does not equal the death of one thousand insects killed in a matter of course in one's life, as each death is karmically equated to the cause of the exact death of an entity. One precise bundle of *saṃskāras* representing a certain type of *karma*, or of aggregates of *karma,* is what concerns us here. The individual unit of that *karma* equals the individual form that the killing of one thousand insects took or takes. The sentience stake of killing an insect relates to perhaps one petal of a very minor *chakra* in the human unit, and it is there that we would find the karmic repercussions. The example, however, is that of killing, and in the field of compassion the action can be weighty because little unloving acts can easily grow into a torrent of unkindness. The compassionate Mind must work at all times in the case of a Bodhisattva. One can easily see via this small example the tangled, complex karmic web that would be woven if it were at all possible for a Bodhisattva to manifest via a host of simultaneous personalities. The unenlightened mind may think that in such a case a Bodhisattva could manifest compassionate acts through many vehicles at once and thus the world would gain much. However, the enlightened One can near simultaneously impress many disciples with thoughts of right action, and produce similar results without impossible karmic entanglements. In such a case, each disciple would be free to act upon the thought impression, utilising their own free will, and hence they will reap the karmic consequence.

Karma ensures that what ensues is the identical expression of what was sown. Similarly, each human unit taken as a Tulku will manifest unique forms of *karma* that only that individual can later cleanse. If an enlightened one therefore were to occupy simultaneously many such vehicles, then the karmic consequences would be terrible for any would be Bodhisattva. There would be, for instance, three or five or more distinct lines of *karma* to cleanse in a future life, producing an excessive and staggeringly complicated web of karmic interrelations with the rest of humanity. An enlightened one would certainly not wish to work off such unnecessary *karma*. The reticulation of *karma* with a multitude of different beings is thus also a major consideration here.

Intelligence requires a system of separation. That with which we choose to separate must be crystal clear and not of the turbulent Watery nature, which can be quite muddied. The sequence of human incarnations bearing the life essence of any soul, or a great One, similarly necessitates separations, clearly distinguishing one incarnation from the others.

The incarnating process is something like a buoy (the *tathāgatagarbha*) which moves according to waves and eddies of the water currents that support it (of the last thought that made any decision) but stays in a singular place, fulfilling its primary task as a light source and a warning of danger. Note that one cannot draw the margin of logic correctly in a Watery (emotional) environment, and in itself this prevents logical assumptions to be carried through to ascertaining truth. The eddies and currents of desire-mind (*kāma-manas*) place logic on uncertain footing, and all too often these little perturbations of thought are allowed a say in otherwise sound rationale. Trying to understand truth in the water that the buoy gets swayed by (this or that syllogism or concept) is what complicates many Buddhist thought-streams. It is better to look to the buoy, for there is the prime source of revelation. Too much relies upon the basis of assumptions derived from poorly understood *sūtras* and Tantras, often producing a lack of skill in discriminative wisdom. The bony structure supporting the entire syllogism or logic is generally correct, but the detail of the interpretable strata of thought is often askew. Thus the true relationship between all beings and considerations pertaining to *saṃsāra* can go awry. What Buddhism lacks is a current Buddha to clarify the resultant rhetoric.

There is therefore a lack of the 'birds' of far-sighted vision that can fly above *saṃsāra* in the domain of enlightenment. It does not need a thousand points of view from the denizens swimming under the water of *saṃsāra,* for that part of the ocean that the buoy delineates is the great illusion. The buoy functions like our eyesight in the way that our eyes separate all forms and yet synthesises them into a complete panorama. Conceptualisations of what lies beyond the buoy are really unthinkable to those swimming in the water beneath it, though what lies beyond the buoy is a possibility for all future *karma* to process. There lies the air, wind and the warming sunshine that condition the motions of the water's currents. In these elements there lies enlightenment.

Also, the logic would presume that one cannot precisely predict the amount of water on the other side of the buoy, however often one side expresses the vastness of an ocean (of *karma).* Just because things are illusional does not mean that they cannot be properly comprehended. As soon as something is illusional it can be mutable, and can flow into anything around (so the logic goes). But this factor is only partly true, because illusional things are far more determinable than most consider. They follow certain laws and rules concerning the behaviour of the substance involved, and how it conditions a consciousness. When we are talking about the forms of *karma* (Rinpoches, Tulkus, Lamas, and laity), we see that interchanges between forms of illusion are generally predictable, but the laws governing their interrelation are exact. These laws consequently must be understood, and in the lack of precise understanding lies the folly of many thinkers. The more illusional and immersed in *māyā,* compared to subtle reality, the more formed is the action - making the outcome generally predictable, and producing the karmic ramifications. Laws manifesting from the subtle domains that govern the Bodhisattva are precise, with easily determinable effects. They also obey rules of thought and conduct which are long established avenues of skilful means determined by aeonic-long tradition. Economy of action via compassion governs all that they do. They waste not time or energy in activities that predictably will fail or are unsuited to the need. It is best for Buddhist thinkers to better comprehend the nature of such rules of action and also the laws of group evolution (explained in the later chapters) that condition all upon the Bodhisattva path. They are bound by them, and this in itself prevents successive rebirths in the way imagined for the great Ones by Tibetans.

Because Buddhists discredited the form, they did not develop a true understanding of the nature of that form and of all the ways its illusionality manifests. They therefore have not properly understood the significance of numbers and the ramifications of the calculations of (cyclic) time. There are no parameters developed allowing a proper comprehension of the concept of one, the spaces between it and the next number. We therefore can have one Tulku, and then maybe five. Then if twenty five, or five thousand could be similarly logically deduced, why not five million, all containing aspects of the consciousness of the 'original' enlightened being. How many times can the consciousness of the enlightened one be divided and put into the minds of receptors is any one's guess, when considering the extended logic of this system of Tulkus. Is this but a version of the mathematics of infinitesimal fractions?

Obviously the concept becomes very diffuse and absurd when large numbers of possibilities are contemplated, so Tibetan philosophers try to limit the concept to a Tulku of mind, another of speech, etc. But why not one also for each and every *chakra*, or mental-emotional trait of an individual? We are, after all, looking to zones of residence for consciousness-states, whose sheer complexity would necessitate an entire *maṇḍala* of Tulkus incarnating to make the complete corporeal individual, the entire illusion of it all. A little clear thinking here will show us that such entire *maṇḍalas* must incarnate, if any component part is to be manifest, such as the Tulku of mind, or of speech, otherwise there is an incoherent organism that will not properly integrate the resultant impressions obtained from *saṃsāra* with the overshadowing enlightened One.

It is something like a person's head functioning without its bodily support, or the heart without the bloodstream it acts as a pump for. Clearly the proponents of the Tulku system have not properly considered the nature of the *maṇḍalas,* by which an enlightened One must manifest, and which such a One must utilise for service work. Much more powerful and effective is the incarnation of such a One with the entire *maṇḍala* of his/her disciples incarnating together to manifest the potency of the *maṇḍala*. Such group incarnations are often depicted in thangkas of the great Ones, such as the Gelugpa Hierarchy manifesting around Tsong-ka-pa. Such a concept veils the potency of the Hierarchy of enlightened being, or ultimately the constitution of Shambhala. There is really no point to creating an unpalatable form of such a *maṇḍala,* as espoused by the Tulku concept, even if it were possible.

There is, however, a truism to the concept of Tulkus, because an enlightened Being can overshadow serving disciples and give them impressions, visualisations and streams of enlightened consciousness-states. In the yogic texts such impressions are often described in the vein of 'gift waves from the guru'. The disciple of this calibre is sufficiently awakened for the enlightened One to utilise the vehicle for the necessary work to be done. Such activity is a common *modus operandi* for the enlightened, where conscious cooperation between disciple and guru is the leitmotiv and the disciple never for a moment loses his or her own individuality. The disciple thus is a conscious co-operator, so that the purpose of the enlightened One is made manifest, and also the disciple is trained and tested upon the road to great wisdom and liberation.

There are also cases of divine embodiment, where the overshadowing enlightened One may partly or fully overshadow the cooperative disciple in order to bring about certain effects within the human kingdom without having to incarnate. However, overshadowing also obeys certain laws, with the individuality of the embodied one still being distinct from the Master. The *karma* is entwined but distinct. The disciple's mind momentarily vacates its vehicle so that it can be used by the overshadowing One. In this case the individual is specifically trained to fulfil the desired purposes.

Here then is the basis from where the myth of the Tulku has been derived. The myth now needs to be rectified, so that people are empowered with truth, and *karma* is no longer engendered by the perpetuators of the Tulku concept. There is also the amassed *karma* of those that gain from the ignorant veneration of the laity who give undue attention and resources to those thus venerated.

When negating concepts of 'self', Buddhist logicians have fallen prey to an extremist viewpoint, as explained in the earlier volumes of this treatise. Consequently, they have missed the significance of the

Soul-form which I have termed the Sambhogakāya Flower. As they have no boundaries for the framework of 'one' and what it contains, Buddhists unbind the units of 'body' in their thinking. But in reality, they cannot do this because the aggregates remain to propel another being into individual incarnation. All cellular constituents are karmically bound to the successive incarnating individualities, as explained in Volume 4 of this treatise. The cellular units that for instance once incorporated Milarepa cannot therefore arbitrarily be divided to manifest into five different individuals at any one time, *karma* simply will not allow it. This then is another reason why Tulkus cannot be. The incarnation process and the *karma* that guides it is tied to the concept of individuation. *Karma* necessitates a singular 'I' that manifests volitions in the fabric of space, by means of which an exact reaction can be calculated and ascribed to the consciousness of that 'I' to experience, even if it reincarnates.

Every incarnate human is unique and responsible for his/her own *karma*, otherwise the law of *karma* would be chaotic and impossible to administer by the agents of *karma*. What these agents are, how they function, or the necessity for their existence, is barely conceived of by those that avow belief in this law.[25] Thus ignorance infiltrates at the deepest level of the presented doctrines relegated to *karma*, and is made to appear as wisdom. Law governs everything in the universe, and that law is a logical extension of the processes governing the expression of Mind.

Most religionists will ignore those things that do not fit with their reality structure. They have built up their ideas with the impulse of an emotional pull or desire for the familiar religious landscape into which they have been born. They are generally so staid that they will disallow anything other than what they think should be with respect to their inherited belief system, or their own personal reality. Their thoughts are detailed and circumscribed by the boundaries of the religious tradition into which they were born.

Having evolved through such a religious structure, the ontological framework of most monks' minds are constructed of limited perspectives

---

25 They are the feminine *deva* kingdom, briefly explained in the earlier volumes of this treatise.

and support the general thought-structure of the society of which they form a part. Whatever does not fit as part of the *cul-de-sac* of such a thought-landscape is then relegated into a place of unreality in their belief system. It is made to be inconsequential, not worthy of rigorous analysis, thus not contemplated upon. Complacency then reigns supreme in the accumulated beliefs, which suffice for those absorbed in their daily lives of devotion, rote learning and *pujas*. The possibilities to true inroads to enlightened reality is thus stifled or perverted through lack of a proper systemic enquiry upon all possible leads to liberation.

The building of a true *maṇḍala* of what actually constitutes enlightenment becomes impossible under the above constraints. Mere belief is not good enough to verify truth as it actually is, even if validated by centuries of tradition. Those ensnared by the context of such a belief system do not see the changing parameters that have evolved over the centuries that in turn alter the needed accomplishments to be attained by prospective candidates for enlightenment. They do not perceive how the system becomes corrupted and concretised over the passage of time. Nor is there comprehension of the true meaning of the religious texts they study and continuously reiterate in their oblations. They are so busy looking to the past, which they comprehend but little, that they see not the evolving spiritual advancements of the present. They are not capable of making the true links from the past to the future trends of the enlightened Mind. Tradition alone suffices, stifling progress. Much therefore must change in the minds of the earnest candidates seeking enlightenment as they practice the art of meditation. Revelations and visions will abound in the minds of those that block not the impressions that come, and rightly interpret, under the watchful Eye of a competent instructor.

Great Ones must continuously incarnate to progressively cause changes in the course of the traditions for the better, closer to the paradigm of the ideal. Such is the context of the Bodhisattva vow. Bodhisattvas, spread your wings, fly over the mindscape of the traditionalists and land where concepts must change. Change thereby the course of the flow of the consciousness-stream of the integrated *maṇḍala,* so that the all can be lifted to the liberation for which all aspire. So be it. Oṁ.

Meditation instructors—Part D
The Hindu guru

Having expounded at length on the *buddhadharma,* a note should be provided concerning the other main branch of meditation teachers, the guru concept found in Hinduism. This subject is complicated because of the various forms of yoga professed, such as *hatha, bhakti, kriya* and *rāja* yogas, plus the many teachings of the different *ācharyas* and gurus.

As Buddhism has reformed the Hindu yoga system, laying the emphasis on wisdom *(prajñā)* rather than *śakti* (psychic power),[26] one can make a categorical statement that it is better to seek a Buddhist teacher rather than a Hindu one for high meditation teachings. However, things are not that simple, as karmic connections leads one to find the reincarnate teachers one has *karma* with from former lives, and if such a teacher has chosen a Hindu birth, then the guru will be found there. Certainly many Bodhisattvas have chosen such vehicles of service.

Great care should be taken in seeking out a guru in this system because of the focus upon psychicism. This focus easily leads to the development of left hand practices, of the development of psychic powers to control and to manipulate the many. Thus the veiled (and often not so veiled), self-centred, egoistic black magicians abound among those that utilise the Hindu Tantras. This is especially so in the case of those who are seen to debase the psychic purity of their *nāḍīs* with drugs. Such methods may offer quick access to the lower *siddhis*, but are rarely accompanied by the expression of a high moral fibre and yogic discipline based upon compassionate ideals. It is a foolish, delusional path that keeps one perpetuated in the fields of *māyā,* resulting in births into the various hell states as the karmic due.

The desire for demonstrable *siddhis* via which to inspire, bemuse and intrigue the devotee to follow the 'god-like' *yogin* is great. Such miracle-making can attract great swathes of devotees and sycophants. Spiritual platitudes and reiteration of the written doctrines of the sect the teacher belongs to suffices for the crowd of adorers. Liberation from *saṃsāra* is however not found through the demonstration of the lower *siddhis,* and often much *karma* is created thus by the perpetuator. High

---

26 The differences have been explained in the previous volumes of this *Treatise on Mind.*

level consciousness cannot be served by this means, but certainly the ignorant devotional masses can gain images of that which to aspire, and which will better their lives. This of itself is of service to the many, as the water (of the *dharma)* seeks its own level. In this case, this level is that of the pools and lakes of *saṃsāra's* bounty and societal livingness. The high mountain pools created by the torrents of revelatory wisdom must yet be sought. The lofty heights of revelation that the Clear Mind provides in the breezes of the rarefied environment of the mountaintop of experience will then be known. *Siddhis* become meaningful, but veiled, and the supramundane states of enlightenment are revealed, the greatest of which are wisdom and boundless compassion. It should thus be stressed that great *yogins* along the white path have arisen in the Hindu system through utilising strenuous yogic practices with the right motive and loving devotion to positive concepts of divinity.

It is important to seek a guru well versed in the *rāja* ('kingly') yoga system of Patañjali,[27] living an exemplary life serving others, and who eschews drugs. Look always for the signs of wisdom and compassion in all of such a one's undertakings. The path of the awakened Heart centre must be evident. Care must be taken to not be glamoured by the number of followers a guru possesses. Masses of devotional followers rarely betoken high spirituality. More often it indicates one who is well placed to feed the desires of the masses by well chosen platitudes and the showy demonstration of some minor *siddhis.* If the seeker is awed by the appearance of the manifestation of objective phenomena, then all they will receive is the superficial attributes of the path of light.

There are also many fakirs and psychic showmen who exist to coax financial resources and sexual favours from the gullible. Egotists abound upon the religious path, yet here and there will be found the hidden true light-bearers, sincere guides, the wandering *yogin* who is a devotee of an enlightened one, or very rarely, the appearance of such a one. They generally will not be so well known because a highly placed spiritual teacher needs the freedom of relative anonymity in order to serve best, and to develop high perceptions. Such a one must have passed the appropriate Initiation tests that produce the required humbleness

27 The aphorisms of which are aimed at controlling and developing the full powers of the mind.

in motive, and skilful means in the wise application of the *dharma.*

In the Hindu system *guruparaṃparā* is rarely based upon the concept of the individual reincarnating again to play the same role. Rather, the successor is generally chosen by the guru before disincarnating. This system is more equable than the Tibetan one because generally the most worthy successor is chosen. The esoteric form of *guruparaṃparā* then has a better chance of manifesting. The chances of the central doctrine of the sect being reified by unworthy savants in positions of power are greatly diminished. However, the base level of the doctrine purported is also at a lower level than the equivalent Buddhist version, because of the semantical and ontological distinctions between the two religions. The religious card in the Hindu system is not so open to political abuse as has been the Rinpoche system in Tibet.

One should also be aware of some of the more egregious yoga practices. The strenuous postures of *hatha* yoga should be avoided, but some *āsanas* are useful as a prelude for *rāja* yoga, and then only to make the body supple enough so as to be able to sit comfortably for extended periods with an erect spinal column. *Bhakti* yoga (the yoga of devotion) likewise should be viewed as a prerequisite for the development of *rāja* yoga. There are many devotees of pure *bhakti,* especially the worship of Kṛṣṇa (Krishna, the embodiment of the second Ray in the Hindu mythos), and the forms of his manifestation, such as Nārāyaṇa. Devotion to such deities as a means to salvation from earthly woes, to assist one's course in life, is extremely popular in India.

Such schools as the Bhakti Vedānta, have merit. For those who's karmic predilection lies therein, it is appropriate for that life and can be a rich, ecstatic reward along the *piṇgalā* line of development, stimulating the awakening of the Heart and Solar Plexus integration. Pure devotion as a means to salvation from earthly woes is important because of the polarisation of humanity to the Waters. Such Watery expression in its higher connotation (the downpour of the principle of Love) is exemplified in this second Ray solar system. This energy is thereby the driving force of the evolutionary process. The Waters from the cosmic astral plane manifest as *bodhicitta,* and pure *bhakti* facilitates its development. It produces a heightened joy, exhilaration in service to (or even 'union with') deity and to humanity. When coupled with the development of the astute reason of the Mind in a later life, then *bodhicitta* is the outcome. The yoga of knowing the Mind in all of its variations is thus the next progressive stage for such a devotee. The *bhakti* therefore must later develop the *iḍā* line that produces the fruits of *rāja* yoga, and hence enlightenment. *Rāja* yoga without the *bhakti* foundation produces the seeds of the black magician. The proper development and integration of the *iḍā* and *piṇgalā* lines produces the goal for all life.

The teachings of the Sikh gurus should also be noted as worthy ones, where similar yogic accomplishments as with the *rāja yoga* system of Hinduism is gained.

There are many other forms of meditation teachings found in the West, but most derive from either of the two above religions, and therefore need no comment. Some derive from other religions, such as the Kabbalistic system. The Kabbalah is a worthy study, but there is also a predilection for left hand practices in that system because of the emphasis upon ritual whereby elementary forces are evoked, or the *chakras* are forcibly awakened. Masonic tradition also manifests via much ritual. Masonic symbolism veils many esoteric Mysteries worthy of revealing to earnest candidates.

To make an appropriate deduction as to whether a Teacher is worthy to follow, one should take care to analyse the purported motives of the instructor, noting whether there is the appearance of egotism, as well as the degree of compassionate focus. The compassionate stance is the *sine qua non* of all genuine teachers. Without compassion versed in a well reasoned method for gaining enlightenment, no true progression can be made upon the path to liberation for the all. Bodhisattvas can be found everywhere, and all have much to teach to any that wish to follow their way.

Follow those who have the ability to teach you how to best assist alleviating humanity's woes, as they are the worthy ones indeed. There can be many such teachers upon the way to liberation, so one can always move on once a teaching has revealed its jewels. In the Heart and within the Head centre will the true guru be found, and the mechanism that will maximally awaken both centres is the true path. In serene meditative poise are the instructions from the inner guru revealed.[28] The outer teacher must integrate with the demonstration of the inner delight. The two must become One; one method of instruction, one path of realisation, revelation and accomplishment. The *suṣumṇā* path is then awakened and liberation ensues. Such accomplishment is no easy task. It is well worth the seeking, the travail and deliberation of meditative focus. True yogic *tapas* then is yours—to liberation. The Buddha-Mind is inevitably the realisation. It has no bounds.

Oṁ.

28 The 'inner guru', or 'great One', in reality will be seen to be a Master that heads one of the Ashrams of the Hierarchy of Light, or a senior student of such a one.

An excerpt from Plato's Theaetetus

Socrates. Then you will be obliged to me if I help you to unearth the hidden truth of a famous man or school.

Theaet. To be sure, I shall be very much obliged.

Socrates. The uninitiated are listening. Now by the uninitiated I mean the people who believe in nothing but what they can grasp in their hands, and who will not allow that action or generation or anything invisible can have real existence.

Theaet. Yes, indeed, Socrates, they are very hard and impenetrable mortals.

Socrates. Yes, my boy, outer barbarians. Far more ingenious are the brethren whose mysteries I am about to reveal to you. Their first principle is, that all is motion, and upon this all the affections of which we were just now speaking are supposed to depend: there is nothing but motion, which has two forms, one active and the other passive, both in endless number; and out of the union and friction of them is generated a progeny endless in number, having two forms, sense and the object of sense, which are ever breaking forth and coming to the birth at the same moment.[1]

---

1 Quoted from *The Works of Plato,* selected and edited by Irwin Edman. (The Modern Library, Random House, Inc., New York. 1956.)

5

The first two Initiations

Introductory statements

Initiation is the means to the revelation of the mysteries of being/non-being. The first two Initiations are Initiations upon the threshold of enlightenment. Their purpose is to awaken properly the way of the Heart centre, and to set the candidate firmly upon the Bodhisattva path. They are preceded by the path of aspiration and that of probationary discipleship.

An aspirant is one that has become unsatisfied with pain and suffering because of attachment to the transience seen in the world around, and seeks something 'other' to satisfy an inner yearning to find the meaning of life's mysteries. The aspirant therefore often starts the search by beginning to read informative scientific and educational material, attending lectures etc., along conventional lines. Later the realisation comes that many perplexing forms of psychic phenomena, and the nature of what may exist after the death of the form, lie unanswered. Therefore, answers are sought in spiritual circles, going from teacher to teacher seeking out the truths, stopping only when a specific teaching offers the most palatable solution. The aspirant then often becomes a staunch advocate of that brand of logic.

Other aspirants may start from a religious background, earnestly applying him/herself to the doctrines, manifesting goodwill and charitable actions in accord with the information presented in the sacred books and interpreted by a religious preceptor. They enquire not the deeper meanings of the teachings, rarely questioning incongruences in the logic because the basic doctrine suffices to fill their cup. Many lives will be undertaken at this level of development until there arises a deep inner discontent, a wanting of something more, and a desire to better equip oneself to help the needs of others in the immediate community and the world around. They therefore get involved in social issues and movements, organisations to produce change, to fight against social injustice and environmental degradation. They also come to find disquiet in mere belief systems, beginning seriously to enquire as to the inner meaning of religious dogma. Esoterically, they knock thereby at the door of the Hierarchy of enlightened being, and therefore attract the notice of one or other of the Masters of Wisdom. Their sincerity in action based upon compassionate motives, and their ability to use their minds to appropriately discern truth, allows the Master to choose them as accepted disciples upon the probationary path.

This choice happens via the Sambhogakāya Flower, so the disciple concerned is generally not aware of the process. Nevertheless, that person's *karma* is then adjusted so the increased opportunity presented facilitates moving forward towards greater light and service. Inspiring thoughts also enter into the disciple's consciousness, helping to engender lofty ideas, idealism, and creative action. Resultant service work then manifests, whereby the aspirant becomes accepted as a probationary disciple, and is prepared to enter the initiation path. This process of direction happens upon the inner realms, with the individual rarely being aware of his/her spiritual status. The candidate simply follows the impulses to serve and to seek mental and emotional improvements.

More than one life generally passes at this accepted stage whereby that consciousness-stream learns various disciplines, and strengthens the resolve to serve. Finally, the life appears wherein the tests producing the first Initiation are possible. Generally by now the candidate is seriously following a specific religious discipline and is often confronted with serious life-style questions, or else he/she is a zealous advocate of some organisation involved with rectifying planetary or social imbalances.

The tests manifest in five stages for each of the Initiations, but these will not be dealt with in this introductory teaching. Suffice to say that at each level increasingly entrenched *saṃskāras* must be appropriately mastered. They also relate to the qualities of the five planes of perception, and mastery of the *saṃskāras* of each of the sense-consciousnesses in turn for each of the Initiations.

The major tests will be illustrated through recourse to Biblical symbolism according to how Jesus embodied the process, as his entire life was an outward demonstration of the stages of the path leading to the fourth Initiation. Considerations concerning Initiation from a Buddhist perspective were presented in Volume 5. That account was not exhaustive and can be correlated with the information presented below, to provide a more complete view of the subject.

For the first Initiation the candidate is often not aware of being tested, nevertheless must pass through certain difficult psychological and life circumstances satisfactorily. The circumstances are focused upon physical plane livingness and control of the bodily form. For the second and higher Initiations a teacher is found that can lead the candidate successfully through the trials. Here conscious cooperation is needed to pass the necessary tests. For the second Initiation the emotional and psychic world must be appropriately tackled, with the factor of the dark brotherhood's adversity being a constant determinant. The *karma* of the disciple's past mistakes in the field of religion, of wrong psychic projection, and while in positions of power over others must be rectified through countering such adversity. For the third Initiation the battle shifts to the arena of the mind and mastery of its qualities.

The Biblical account

There are five major steps of spiritual accomplishment that each person must consciously undertake to develop subjective perceptions and to gain enlightenment before one can become as *perfect* as the 'Father in Heaven',[1] as far as demonstration of control of the form is concerned. (There are many further Initiations that must be passed before a candidate can be equal to a planetary Logos, if such is the interpretation of the term 'Father'.) Here the 'Father' represents the Monadic *(dharmakāyic)* aspect of a human unit that the attainment of the fifth Initiation reveals. The five Initiations refer to the progressive

1 *Matt. 5:48.* 'Be ye therefore perfect, even as your Father which is in heaven is perfect'.

mastery of each of the five Elements, and consequently are related to the development of each of the five wisdoms of the Dhyāni Buddhas. As the first two Initiations are really Initiations on the threshold, they veil the two higher Initiations accomplished within systemic space upon our earth (the sixth and the seventh). The sixth Initiation is the level of accomplishment of a Buddha. The seventh allows the Initiate to hold high office within Shambhala (the Kingdom of 'God') for the relatively few that are required to stay on the earth rather than enter into cosmic space after attaining the sixth. We thus have:

Initiation	Chakra	Plane	Wisdom
First	Base/Sacral	Physical/Etheric	All-accomplishing
(Veiling the seventh Initiation)			
Second	Solar Plexus	Astral	Equalising
(Veiling the sixth Initiation)			
Third	Throat	Mental	Discriminating Inner Vision
Fourth	Heart	Buddhic	Mirror-like
Fifth	Head/Ājñā	Ātmic	Dharmadhātu

Table 1. The five Initiations

The process is exoterically revealed for all people to see by the major incidents in the life of Jesus. They represent steps constituting Initiations that access various levels of the Mysteries of the Kingdom of 'God', and must be undertaken by all that wish enlightenment. As each Initiation is successfully undertaken the meaning of the statement in *John 10:34* becomes increasingly clear: 'Is it not written in your law, I said, *Ye are gods?*' The corresponding revelations will bring one into closer contact with the divine, eventually evolving one into a 'God', manifesting divinity. This is but a Theistic way of stating that all have the Buddha-nature within them. *Romans 8:14-16* states:

> For as many as are led by the Spirit of God, they are the sons of God. For ye have not received the spirit of bondage again to fear; but ye have received the Spirit of adoption, whereby we cry, Abba, Father.
>
> The Spirit itself beareth witness with our spirit, that we are the children of God.

Being 'led by the Spirit of God' means following the Initiation path of mastering *saṃskāras,* refining perceptions, and transmuting base substance into ever-increasing, subtler energy states. Thus one raises consciousness to the higher dimensions until the Clear Light of the Mind stands revealed, and the Void can be experienced as the base to the *dharmakāya,* which here can be equated with 'the Spirit of God'. Mastering each Initiation level carries one up the planes of perception, ever closer to the domains of manifesting divinity, until eventually one becomes a resident of Shambhala, a 'son' of the planetary Logos, and imbuing consciously the spirit of *dharmakāyic* bliss. Following this Spirit thus leads one ever higher to subtler planes of perception, until freedom from *saṃsāra* allows one to travel the far reaches of cosmos. Bondage to *māyā* is overcome as one enters into the 'Spirit of adoption', by first being adopted by a Master of Wisdom, to enter into his Ray Ashram and there learn all of the requirements of Bodhisattvic service according to Ray type. Later one is 'adopted' by the Lords of Shambhala, to be received by the One Initiator (Sanat Kumāra[2]), to which the term 'Father' here refers—to whom 'we cry, Abba'. The mantric cry awakens perception of things divine. It helps to liberate us from the trammels of the form. Its energy liberates *kuṇḍalinī* at the appointed time.

'The Spirit itself beareth witness with our spirit' because it is that which Initiates us into the Mysteries at every step of the way to Shambhala. 'Our spirit' here is what drives us to develop the will to overcome all obstacles along the path of Love-Wisdom. Self-will must be transformed into good will, then the Will-to-Love, the Will-of-Love, and finally Divine Will, as explained in Volume 4, chapter 7 of this series.

The term 'sons' does not just refer to the fact that we, as everything else, are an effect of the Creative process of the planetary Logos (the

---

2 This great being, the 'Ancient of Days', the 'Eternal Youth', will be explained in the final volume of this series, *The Constitution of Shambhala.*

meaning of the term 'God' here) when the entire earth system was formed. It also refers to the esoteric consideration of this term, being synonymous with the Hindu and Buddhist concept of an accepted disciple of a guru. Such a one is titled a 'son', in that the guru is the Father of all that will proceed in the disciple's consciousness, once the teachings are properly followed. The disciple will eventually grow up to fill the shoes of the guru and play a similar role for the new students that will come for teachings. Thus we have the concept of *guruparamparā.* Similarly in the Biblical phraseology we see that those that are led by the 'Spirit of God' (i.e., the instructors from this divine Source) will be entitled to be called 'sons of God' in a similar manner that Jesus was.

The concept of 'son' also has a direct reference to the Love-Wisdom principle (being the second aspect of the trinity of Will, Love-Wisdom, and Divine Activity[3]). Christ-Jesus was the direct empowerment of this principle, and at that time was overshadowed by the cosmic Lord of Love, thus becoming an Avatar, uniquely 'the only begotten son of God'.[4]

The terminology may differ between the Christian and Buddhist religions, and the emphasis may be along different lines of expression (the *iḍā* versus the *piṅgalā* line in the field of religion), but they both are aspects of the one universal religion that are rayed out into manifestation in different parts of the world, to perform their roles in the one Plan emanating from Shambhala. They exist to enlighten humanity according to the nature of the constitution *(chakra)* wherein the religions were formed. The symbolism of the terminology of both religions can therefore reveal similar revelations concerning the principles to be awakened via the Initiation process. Initiation integrates the two views into one common embrace that reveals the hidden Mysteries of being/ non-being, of the Kingdom of 'God'.

When talking to his disciples, who were Initiated into these Mysteries, Jesus explained:

> And the disciples came, and said unto him, Why speakest thou unto them in parables? He answered and said unto them, Because it is given unto you to know the mysteries of the kingdom of heaven, but to them it is not given, For whosoever hath, to him shall be given, and he shall have

---

3 Personified as the Father, Son, Mother.

4 *John 3:18.*

> more abundance; but whosoever hath not, from him shall be taken away even that he hath. Therefore speak I to them in parables: because they seeing see not; and hearing they hear not, neither do they understand.[5]

The enigmatical statement: 'For whosoever hath, to him shall be given, and he shall have more abundance; but whosoever hath not, from him shall be taken away even that he hath' refers to the premature development of psychic powers. Those who are given to know these Mysteries are developing supersensory perceptions through applied meditation and other practices provided by the teacher. This happens in a safe way, according to following spiritual law via compassionate undertaking (the healing of the sick, etc.). Others, however, that are followers of religion, but do not obey the law of Love (Jesus' special commandment[6]), thus are self-centered and selfish, fall into the danger of left hand practices, if the lower *siddhis* are developed by them. Therefore it is best for their own good, and for the well-being of others, that this propensity be taken from them—by keeping the major portion of the doctrine from them. Less troublesome *karma* is developed all around, which betokens the love of the wise teacher.

All aspects of life, be they religious, scientific, artistic, social or governmental, can rightly be termed spiritual or divine, for all express the qualities that help bring us to the fount of realisation, and thus to the source of Life. The word *spiritual,* therefore, signifies that which can lead the person, race, or nation, one step further in its evolutionary development, that one step closer to conscious revelation of the immanence of divinity. Thus to be 'spiritual' does not necessarily mean manifesting an endeavour along the lines of an organised religion, system of philosophy, yoga, or meditation discipline. Fundamentally it implies a question of relationships, the response to the need of the other being, humanity, all upon the planet, of communal growth to enlightenment. 'No man is an island', nor is any aspect of life more divine than any other. Each entity that evolves does so as an aspect of the Body of 'God'. That the greater encompasses the lesser, and the lesser embraces the greater, is an ancient adage conveying a truth

---

5 *Matt. 13:10-13.*

6 *John 13:34.* 'A new commandment I give unto you, That ye love one another; as I have loved you, that ye also love one another'.

that Jesus tried to indicate when he washed the feet of his disciples. The unit cannot achieve its purpose without vibrantly implicating and uplifting all others, for the entire environment causes and takes part in that achievement. All must therefore share its reward.

Such is the result of the quest for divinity. Any development that increases the perception of divinity within human consciousness can be considered a minor Initiation. Such minor Initiations concern a series of graded steps that signify eventual mastery of the associated principles that produce the attainment of the overriding Initiation, revealing the mysteries of a new realm or dimension of perception. Similar forms of Initiation also effect the lesser kingdoms of Nature, and that of the *devas*. Initiation, therefore, concerns the stages of development of consciousness in a holistic manner so that it becomes increasingly embracive in a multidimensional momentum. This allows the inner reality (divinity) to expand and embrace the outer universe, until eventually there is no distinction between the two. That is one explanation of Initiation. There are many others, and we can see that the subject is necessarily somewhat abstruse, as it concerns much that is of a subjective nature, plus an understanding of the nature of manifesting Divinity. It is the process of revealing the path to Shambhala wherein the Lords of liberating Life can be found.

The Initiations defined

All ancient religions, and many modern religious sects and metaphysical systems, revealed their mysteries to the novitiates by means of a graded series of Initiations. The subject is well commented on by a number of authors, thus this information will not be restated. The more esoteric implications of the process will however be explicated, relating it to modern times by utilising the symbolism found in the Gospels.

The first five Initiations are:

The first Initiation–the Birth of the Christ in the cave of the heart.
The second Initiation–the Baptism in the Waters of the Jordan.
The third Initiation–the Transfiguration.
The fourth Initiation–the Crucifixion.
The fifth Initiation–the Ascension/Revelation.

The basic terminology and concepts that can be found in the writings of A.A. Bailey and H.P. Blavatsky are utilised here. Rudolf Steiner in his *Gospel of St. John* uses a similar terminology. He states, for instance, that:

> In a certain form of oriental initiation, seven degrees can be distinguished and these seven degrees were designated by all sorts of symbolical names. The first was the degree of the "Raven," the second that of the "Occultist," the third of the "Warrior," the fourth that of the "Lion." Amongst different peoples, who still felt a kind of blood relationship as the expression of their group-soul, the fifth degree was designated by the name of the folk itself; thus among the Persians, for example, an initiate of the fifth degree was called in an occult sense, a "Persian."[7]

In relation to this, Steiner says that Nathanael was an Initiate of the fifth degree because the Christ says to him 'Behold an Israelite indeed, in whom is no guile'.[8] These five Initiations are effectively subdivisions of the first three Initiations explained in my exegesis. The *Raven* is the aspirant, who is a scavenger of spiritual information. The second stage, the *Occultist,* refers to the probationary disciple, wherein the process producing high revelatory vistas in one's inner Life has begun to be mastered. The *Warrior* is an Initiate that is mastering the entire material domain, with which he must battle, thus is a disciple at the first Initiation level. The *Lion* is an Initiate of the second degree in whom the energies of the illumined-consciousness are definitely dominant, and the faculty of pride, of self-hood has been mastered and made subject to the esoteric lore of group development. (The symbolic pride of which the lion is a member.) The entire psychic Watery world has thereby been conquered. Myriad are the *saṃskāras* of desire-mind that have to be overcome at this level. The *Israelite* (etc.) corresponds to one that has attained the third Initiation. The Initiate is called by the title of his/her country, for by having full identification with the Soul-form, the Initiate effectively channels everything associated with the group-Soul of the nation in the related field of service.

---

7 Rudolf Steiner, *The Gospel of St. John,* (Anthroposophical Press, U.S.A., 1962), 79-80.

8 *John 1:47.*

The term 'guile', meaning cunning intelligence, has reference to that which is developed by the dark brotherhood. That Nathanael has 'no guile' is an esoteric way of saying that he has no darkness, nothing deceitful (i.e., evil), within him and therefore is enlightened. This is a trademark of the Initiate of the third degree. (One who is fully identified with the consciousness of the Sambhogakāya Flower.) The full statement concerning this meeting with Jesus illuminates this:

> Jesus saw Nathanael coming to him, and saith of him, Behold an Israelite indeed, in whom there is no guile! Nathanael saith unto him, Whence knowest thou me? Jesus answered and said unto him, Before that Philip called thee, when thou wast under the fig tree, I saw thee. Nathanael answered and saith unto him, Rabbi, thou art the Son of God; thou art the King of Israel. Jesus answered and said unto him, Because I said unto thee, I saw thee under the fig tree, believest thou? thou shalt see greater things than these. And he saith unto him, Verily, verily, I say unto you, Hereafter ye shall see heaven open, and the angels of God ascending and descending upon the Son of man.[9]

The fact the Jesus saw Nathanael under a 'fig tree' immediately informed Nathanael that Jesus was a higher Initiate than he, as this was the tree of Initiation. It was synonymous to the *bodhi* tree under which Gautama sat to gain his Initiation (enlightenment). Only an Initiate of similar or higher degree could have witnessed his Initiation, and as Jesus was not of a similar degree, Nathanael knew that he was of greater attainment. Knowing the import of that (because his own Initiation was a very high achievement at that time) Nathanael without hesitation said 'thou art the Son of God', signifying a fourth degree Initiate or higher. A fourth degree Initiate has achieved that level of abstraction from the material domain (*śūnyatā*) that would allow him to be directly educated from the Kingdom of 'God', to be a Shambhalic recipient. Consequently as an Initiate, he was not just 'an Israelite', but 'the King of Israel', the spiritual ruler of all Initiates in Israel at that time.

Because Nathanael immediately recognised the veracity of what Jesus said, Jesus indicated that Nathanael himself is due to move on to the next Initiation level where he 'shalt see greater things than these'.

---

9 *John 1:47-51.*

This was therefore not just in reference to seeing the things (miracles) that would lead to Jesus' crucifixion, but also to the development of greater inner vision (further opening of the Ājñā centre), whereby he will see 'heaven' revealed (the domain of the Hierarchy of Light) and 'the angels of God ascending and descending upon the Son of man'. The angels are the *devas* with whom Initiates of the higher degrees directly interrelate with, in cooperative service. The nature of the interrelationship between the *deva* and human kingdoms, the feminine and masculine principles in Nature, will thus be revealed.

Note that Jesus uses the appellation 'Son of man' to describe himself, stressing thereby his humanity, that he must, like everyone else, struggle with all of the issues associated with the path of Initiation. It also refers to all of humanity, who will in time be Initiated into the way that the *devas* administer unto them, as well as to all the kingdoms of Nature. The implication is that Nathanael must yet be fully awakened (Initiated) into the mysteries of the forms of activity of this kingdom.

The first Initiation

The *first Initiation* is a reenactment within the Initiate's consciousness of the birth of that which is the embodiment of Love-Wisdom: 'a Saviour, which is Christ the Lord'.[10] He was born in Bethlehem in a manger, surrounded by beasts of the field, and was 'wrapped in swaddling clothes'.[11] This occurs in one when the overshadowing Soul and personality are tentatively attuned, and the Soul is first able to penetrate the cave of darkness that is its instrument.[12] It impregnates that instrument with the 'true Light, which lighteth every man that cometh into the world'.[13]

The development of this Light within the Initiate determines his/her path in the world, and is the source of all subjective joy, revelations and mystical experiences. The path of Initiation produces liberation. It determines the levels of attainment *(bhūmis)* of the Bodhisattva

10 *Luke 2:11.*

11 *Luke 2:7.*

12 The personality.

13 *John 1:9.*

path, starting with the qualities developed by the one who has 'entered the stream' of enlightenment. This entrance stage can be considered synonymous with that developed by probationary disciples for the first Initiation.[14] There are ten of these Bodhisattva stages, two for each Initiation, therefore dividing each Initiation into two parts. As previously stated, the first part relates to the qualities developed as one passes the tests, and the second part relates to the consolidation of the qualities developed and the preparation for the next level. This produces five major Initiations preceding that of becoming a Buddha at the sixth Initiation.

I shall not here labour to unravel the exoteric teachings concerning these Bodhisattva levels as found in the texts, as this would require a volume in itself. Rather, the qualities associated with each Initiation will be divulged, allowing the earnest Buddhist student to make the necessary correlations and refinements to what is found in the texts, if desired.

The beasts of the field surrounding the newborn child in the manger symbolise the Initiate's animal and desire natures, which are tamed, and can therefore serve as witnesses for the presence of the Christ. The 'swaddling cloth'[15] symbolises the Initiate's material sheaths that still surround and limit full freedom of expression and movement. He/she has not yet learnt to journey inwards and outwards to all dimensions and directions in time and space, unfettered by the corporeal form.

Standing before the newborn child, in adoration and joy, were those who symbolised all aspects of divinity, the qualities of the Hierarchy of enlightened being. They thus witness the installation of a new member to their ranks.

In terms of being an enlightened quality of consciousness, as well as the incarnate son of 'God' by the means of this birth, the awakening Christ-aspect could be made objectively manifest in the world. The incarnation of Jesus was the first real step in establishing the kingdom of Heaven, the New Jerusalem, on earth. It is something for which all Initiates are now actively working. The historical Christ

---

14 These ten stages of the Bodhisattva path are explained in sGam.po.pa's *The Jewel Ornament of Liberation*, translated by Herbet V. Guenther, (Shambhala, Berkeley, 1971).

15 *Luke 2:12.*

thus came to sow the first seeds of a new epoch of Love, wherein a world-tree of interrelated disciples in all nations and creeds would be actively and holistically working for common goals based upon similar compassionate understandings and realisations. The symbolic implications of those that surrounded the newborn Christ-child are:

- *Mary and Joseph*–the (natural) father and mother of Jesus represent humanity, and all of the elements and qualities associated with it. The Christ-child must ascend out of the ranks of the human kingdom, whilst the Initiate's early training and development depends much upon the type of environment and cultural situation that he/she is born into.

- *The shepherds from the fields* symbolise Initiates of the first two degrees, who tend the flocks of the Lord. Jesus thus said that 'I am the good shepherd'.[16] It refers to his ability to lead such 'flocks' to the domains of liberation.

- *The angels* that gave the shepherds 'good tidings of great joy',[17] and the 'multitude of the heavenly host',[18] represent the entire angelic *(deva)* kingdom, and all members of the subjective realms of perception. They bear witness and play their inner plane roles in assisting the spiritual progress of the Initiate concerned.

- *The Three wise men of the east*[19] are Initiates of the first three degrees, as symbolised by the gifts they brought for the Christ-child; gold, frankincense and myrrh.

- *Gold*–the most noble of the metals, for it never tarnishes or corrodes. Coupled with its sun-like qualities, it symbolises the Sambhogakāya Flower. Gold thus refers to the Initiate of the *third degree* that has fused his/her consciousness with that form. Such a one is able to enrich the spiritual child by applying the wisdom and knowledge gained upon the path of Light.

---

16 *John 10:14.*

17 *Luke 2:10.*

18 *Luke 2:13.*

19 *Matt. 2:1.*

- *Frankincense* is a resinous gum with a bitter taste. It was used for sacrificial fumigation, and burns with a steady flame for a long time, freely giving off a delightful aroma. The symbolism concerns the emotional realm (the bitter taste) and its purified expression (the delightful odour) as gained by the Initiate of the *second degree.*
- *Myrrh*—an aromatic resin used for embalming, and also an ingredient in the oil used for anointing. This concerns the dense physical body, which is the direct concern of the Initiate of the *first degree.*

These rather expensive gifts symbolise the normal beneficence given to a new Initiate by the Hierarchy of Light. It is part of an ennoblement and alignment process associated with the threefold body. They allow the potency of the divine impression associated with the mystical vision to inundate the Initiate, without it being distorted in any way.

The three wise men stand as hierophants sponsoring the candidate for Initiation, and represent the aspects of his/her personality nature, which must be purified and aligned if a vision of the Christ-Light is to be received so that its implications can be known. They enable a direct experience of 'God'. The presence of Deity was indicated by the *star* that 'stood over where the young child was'.[20] This is esoterically the 'star of Initiation', of the 'one Initiator'—Sanat Kumāra, as described in *Initiation, Human and Solar* by A.A. Bailey.

The meaning of the term 'east', referring to the direction inwards to the Heart of Life, was detailed in all the earlier volumes of this *Treatise on Mind.*

- *Bethlehem* means house of bread, the symbol of material prosperity and nourishment. It signifies that the first thing a candidate for the first Initiation must be able to do, is to adequately provide for all his/her material needs and produce a healthy body; for it is the foundation that will allow divinity to grow and flower. Little can be accomplished if the person is constantly ill, or has not the physical means to serve. One must be able to help oneself before

20 *Matt. 2:9.*

others can be helped. This Initiation occurs when the overshadowing Soul (Sambhogakāya Flower) and personality are first tentatively attuned, and the Soul is able to penetrate and illumine the cave of darkness that is its instrument, allowing the spiritual aspect to continually triumph.

The way of compassion

The statement concerning Christ-Jesus being the good shepherd needs further elucidation, as it exemplifies the attitudes and qualities of all Initiates of the higher degrees. *John 10:14-16* states:

> I am the good shepherd, and know my *sheep,* and am known of mine. As the Father knoweth me, even so know I the Father: and I lay down my life for the sheep. And other sheep I have, which are not of this fold: them also I must bring, and they shall hear my voice; and there shall be one fold, *and* one shepherd.

The path of Initiation brings the Initiate to the halls of Shambhala, the domain of the One Initiator, who utilises the rod of Initiation that projects high voltage energy into the Initiate's *chakras* during the Initiation ceremony. This facilitates the transformation and transmutation of substance, helping to draw the Initiate to the higher domains of liberated life. They then become the Initiate's normal place of residence. There the Initiate experiences the higher Mysteries of being/non-being, to 'know the Father'. The revelation concerning the nature and activities of the liberated Ones ensues. The term 'Father' also refers to the One that is the Initiate's preceptor, or Hierophant (whereas we earlier used the Sanskrit term 'guru').

All Initiates progress along the road of sacrificial compassion, therefore they 'lay down' their life for those that earnestly aspire to follow them. Such 'laying down' of one's life does not just mean undertaking the path that inwardly produces the crucifixion experience, which Jesus demonstrated exoterically because of his *karma,* but also repeatedly incarnating because of the Bodhisattva vow to never cease striving until all sentient beings have been released from suffering.

'A flock of sheep' is here interpreted in terms of a particular Ashram of a Master of Wisdom (a fifth degree Initiate), consisting of the younger Initiates and probationary disciples administered to. They are all governed by the same Ray and sub-ray. The concept of 'sheep' here is not viewed pejoratively, of being a blind follower, but rather it symbolises aspirants with a gentle disposition upon the white path, that are obeying group laws. These Ashrams stand as the departments within the Council of Bodhisattvas, the Hierarchy of enlightened being.

The Christ (the head of this Hierarchy of Light) directs the united spiritual evolution of all Ashramic groups, not just the members of the Jewish religion at the time of Jesus (this particular 'flock'), or those that later styled themselves 'Christians'. He must bring them all to his Father, the Lord at Shambhala, and 'they shall be one fold'—one Hierarchy of enlightened being, with 'one shepherd'—the Christ (signified as Maitreya in Buddhism[21]), who embodies the Love-Wisdom principle for all upon this planet. This energy governs the activities of all Bodhisattvas. They are disciples of this One in a similar way that they followed the Buddha, who held this office of Christ, the most senior member of the Hierarchy of Light, 2,500 years ago. The Buddha has left the earth for his cosmic journey, thus his role was taken by the One we now call the Christ. The role of the Christ therefore represents an office within the Council of Bodhisattvas, which oversees all of their activities.[22]

Initiation is an effect of the evolution of consciousness. It is that which is the result of the expansion of consciousness into new arenas of Light, bringing with it new revelations. The revelations manifest outwardly as a life lived in an exemplary fashion, which stimulates people towards the engendering of Light (by the example of the Initiate's actions). The Light becomes translated into vision by the empirical mind. This allows the subjective purpose of the Christ, and therefore of the Will-of-Love, or Divine Will (the *dharma* of which the Initiate is the custodian), to unfold and affect the outer world.

In *Matthew 23:11*, Jesus stated: 'But he that is greatest among you shall be your servant'. The 'greatness' in humanity (the Initiate-consciousness) can only be developed in the field of service. The efforts of all Initiates, according to their varying capacities, is to raise the

21 The term Maitreya means 'loving-kindness'. He is the embodiment of the great Love of all the Buddhas, and is to be the next Buddha.

22 This subject shall be explained in Volume 7 of this *Treatise on Mind*.

conscious awareness, and to wisely relieve the suffering of all those in need. The expression of their service necessitates generating an expanded consciousness and compassionate sensitivity to the sufferings and needs of others. They constantly develop the various skills needed to be more embracive of ever larger groups of beings. They must therefore meet the demands of a great diversity of problems. They become the 'greatest among you', and are irresistibly propelled by a motivation or driving urge to do, help, or create, for they are subjectively inspired by the Christ-consciousness that is ever-growing within them.

This Christ-consciousness is synonymous with the term *bodhicitta,* and which has also been denoted in terms of the energy of *buddhi.* Much was written about the latter terms in the previous volumes of this series. For elucidation, however, we can look to the explanation of *bodhicitta* by Marion L. Matics:

> The Sanskrit word for the thought of Enlightenment, Bodhicitta, is a simple compound consisting of *bodhi*, which is Enlightenment, and *citta,* which is thought. Each of these words possesses an overwhelming depth and implication of meaning, for Bodhi is the release from suffering which is understood only by the Buddha who has achieved it, and Citta is any single idea, or the individual mind, or (in some schools of Buddhism) a kind of quasi-universal cosmic mind. The compound word "Bodhicitta" contains compound ambiguity and shifting nuance of meaning, for the simple Thought of Enlightenment is operative on three levels of definition to which Citta is susceptible. It is (1) the simple thought or idea of Bodhi; (2) the consciousness which is permeated with this idea, which results in the total transformation of one's personal life because it is so dominated; and (3) it is the force of the thought which thus turns one's life completely upside-down (as any thought is a force insofar as it results in action). Consequently, Bodhicitta (like Citta) partakes of a quasi-universal aspect, because in the latter sense, it is a force let loose in the universe to work for the good of all....Without initial Bodhicitta, the Bodhisattva (or even a Buddha for that matter) could not exist...
>
> Bodhicitta is the womb of Sunyata and of Karuna. It is twofold in its effect, bringing forth the flower of Emptiness and the perfume of Compassion, and in this way, it corresponds to the dual factors of permanency and potency found in all of its major symbols. Sunyata (the Void) is its expression on the absolute plane, and Karuna (pity

> or compassion) its active manifestation on the level of phenomenal relativity....as soon as Bodhicitta has arisen, its practice becomes twofold: (1) *bodhi-pranidhi-citta*, the Thought of Enlightenment; and (2) *bodhi-prasthana-citta*, the departure, or march towards Enlightenment. Once one has taken the vow, the karmic potency of the vow falls upon all successive incarnational experience.[23]

Only by constantly endeavouring to serve and help the evolution of the kingdoms of Nature, to relieve the various categories of suffering, fostered ignorance, depriving, enslaving ideals and tendencies, can a person gradually come to be Initiated into the Mysteries of enlightenment and the Kingdom of 'God' (Shambhala). It should be noted that the Initiation process entails the development of groups of beings, seen as units. The concern is not upon individuals *per se,* for the concept of the singular 'I' becomes translated into universality in the higher dimensions of perception. It becomes merged into the whole, the unification of diversification into Oneness, and then the extension of That Oneness into the ineffable Void. The entire *maṇḍala* of being/non-being (e.g., of an Ashram) progresses as a unit whenever any aspect of that *maṇḍala* moves upwards and onwards to more embracive Light and perspicuity. All are in fact organs within an evolving organism moving together in time and space. The concept of separativeness, of 'I-ness', happens only within the limits of a human consciousness, and as that consciousness transcends the bounds of its limitations, the 'I' concept dissolves into the all.

All is expressed as energy, and that energy is Light, which when seen in terms of absolutes becomes Darkness, Void *(śūnyatā),* for it turns into shadow all lesser forms and streams of light. One's singular consciousness thus becomes absorbed into the realms of Light by the drive to Initiation. Here reside the Hierarchy of enlightened being, composed of the sum of such accomplished beings within our solar sphere. The constituency of this Hierarchy spirals onwards and outwards into the vast vistas of cosmic Space.

---

23 Marion L. Matics, *Entering the Path of Enlightenment,* (The Macmillan Company, New York, 1970), 33-9.

Service is the key to the development of the Initiation experience, and constitutes a scientific mode of release from the vicissitudes of the personality nature and its vacillating, intensely self-aware, self-assertive, state of being. It is the door to the awareness of the universal, to that which is comprehensive of the whole, via selflessness and all-embracing compassion. It thus leads one to the embrace of the Christ-consciousness and the ineffable Light that it expresses.

Like all else in Nature, Initiation is governed by group laws, for all entities have interrelationships with every other being. Nothing can be done by one without affecting the other accordingly. One thus cannot advance upon the ladder of evolution without drawing the interrelated *maṇḍala* within which one resides up that ladder. This concept is exemplified by the words of the Christ: 'if I be lifted up from the earth, will draw all men unto me'.[24] Note that this is but a form of the Bodhisattva vow. All Initiates are inwardly impelled by the driving force of *bodhicitta* to never cease striving until all sentient beings have been delivered from suffering.

These interrelationships are the esoteric basis to the necessity of service as a means to divine realisation, for only by giving out what one has received inwardly can one's brothers and sisters be adequately stimulated to travel towards Light. Only by the transmission of that Light can one progress. Only by travelling together in service to one another and to 'God's Plan' (the *dharma)* can true desirelessness and Love be engendered. Desirelessness, in its turn, means complete receptivity to the energy streams associated with the all-embracive Whole, and Love is focusing upon the means of its expression.

Initiation is self-engendered and should not specifically be seen as a reward given for work well accomplished. The Initiation ceremony comes as a consequence of successful mastery of *saṃskāras* and resultant service work by the candidate. It is the result of the increasing ability of the Initiate to withstand ever increasing intensities of Light. The Initiate has thereby reached steadfastness in new fields of awareness, new worlds of experience. Such accomplishment effects the inclusive recognition of the attainment by all enlightened Beings, allowing this

---

24 *John 12:32.*

one to be embraced by their united Mind. It becomes his/their offering (to 'God') and leads to a more embracive field of service, the door to which is opened by the hands of all those that have come before, and with whom one must serve. In fact, one Initiates oneself in the base realisations before one is Initiated into the Mysteries.

The first Initiation continued

Those that are preparing for or have undergone the first Initiation are the *little children* that Jesus constantly referred to, for as soon as one humbles oneself in the field of compassion by becoming a true server in the mundane world, one enters the world of illumined consciousness to be tested for this Initiation. They are yet but 'children' in that world. A new sense of values and type of experience has manifested, and consequently, the world is seen with a sense of awe, wonderment, and heart-felt adoration for the divinity sensed everywhere. All aspects of life, effectively become the new 'child's' parents, stimulating, encouraging, teaching, and embracing him/her in their benevolence. The Initiate is still young in the subjective experience, only just born into the consciousness of the Christ, into the path of Love. This Initiation allows the development of the mystical life, one of devotion in service to Deity in any of its many names and forms, leading eventually to union with, or embodiment by, Deity.

Jesus stated that 'except a man be *born again,* he cannot *see* the kingdom of God'.[25] He is here referring to the birth into the new type of relationships and world of experience that enlightenment brings. These experiences become real and increasingly impelling, but the Initiate of this degree is only able to see as a spiritual child and cannot fully enter into that life. In answer to Nicodemus' question concerning this second birth (for he thought only in terms of physical birth, as most on the earth still do), Jesus qualified it by the statement: 'Except a man be born of water and *of* the Spirit, he cannot enter into the kingdom of God'.[26] Here *water* refers to the astral realm, to our emotional and desire nature, and also to the great oceans, the waters, out of which all Life

25 *John 3:3.*

26 *John 3:5.*

originally emanated—to the Waters in the Womb of the great Mother. This refers to the *first birth* and signifies that all individuals must be born in the Waters of substance before they can ascend to the Life of the Spirit. It also has reference to the type of cleansing associated with the second Initiation.

The Sanskrit term for one who is thus born again is *dwija* ('twice born'). It is the physical regeneration obtained by the consciousness of one who is able to meditate and contact a ray of 'the intelligible Light' emitted from the spiritual Sun, which is *Brahman,* the supreme universal principle.[27] René Guénon states that:

> The conception of a "second birth", as we have already pointed out elsewhere, is one of those which are common to all traditional doctrines....Water is looked upon by many traditions as the original medium of beings, by reason of its symbolism, as we explained earlier on, according to which it stands for *Mula-Prakriti;* in a higher sense, by transposition, water is Universal Possibility itself; whoever is "born of water" becomes a "son of the Virgin" and therefore an adopted brother of the Christ and his co-heir of the "Kingdom of God". On the other hand, if one realizes that the "spirit" in the text just quoted (*John 3:3-7* - author's note) is the Hebrew *Ruahh* (here associated with water as a complementary principle, as in the opening passage of Genesis) and if it be remembered that *Ruahh* also denoted air, we have the idea of purification by the elements, such as is to be met with in all initiation as well as religious rites; and moreover, initiation itself is always looked upon as a "second birth", symbolically as long as it only amounts to a more or less external formality, but effectively when it is conferred in a genuine manner on one duly qualified to receive it.[28]

The word 'Spirit' above refers to what passes through the Intuitional (*buddhic*) plane of perception, for the quality of this realm is synonymous

27 This is basically a paraphrase of part of page 145 of the book by René Guénon: *Man and His Becoming According to the Vedānta,* (The Noonday Press, New York. 1958). Brahman is the ultimate principle in Vedic beliefs: attributeless, unmodfiable and does not move. 'He' is absolute reality (*sat,* existence, *chit,* consciousness, and bliss, *ānanda),* the causeless Cause, the supreme Spirit in the universe.

28 Ibid., 145.

with the term *wind* that Jesus used to exemplify the statement:[29]

> The *wind* bloweth where it listeth, and thou hearest the sound thereof, but canst not tell whence it cometh, and wither it goeth: so is every one that is born of the Spirit.[30]

This refers to the *second birth*, birth into the spiritual realms, into the type of consciousness that the Initiation process affords. In the first Biblical quotation it is indicated that a person that is 'born again' will be able to *see*, that is, perceive the Kingdom of 'God' clairvoyantly, or with his Mind's-eye. One that is 'born of water and of the Spirit', who has attained the higher Initiations will, however, be able to *enter* the Kingdom of God and thus find his/her place in it. These are two different types of attainment and they indicate the difference between a child, the Initiate of the first degree (who can 'see'), and an adult that has grown in stature and accomplishment (the Initiate of the higher degrees), who is able to *enter* into that Kingdom and work consciously with its energies.

The Monadic aspect is 'the Spirit (Buddha) within' that governs the entire Initiation process. This process thus concerns the way of Monadic return (to cosmos). Initiation is the gain of its sacrifice by being 'planted' in the soil of the cosmic dense physical plane. The consequence of the Initiation process is the making of a Buddha, which happens when the human unit has so completely identified with the Monadic or 'Spirit' aspect that liberation into the Waters of cosmic astral space is accomplished.

Prior to this, however, the Monad manifests a link with the Sambhogakāya Flower via the Śūnyatā Eye at the Heart of the Flower, described in Volume 3 of this *Treatise on Mind*. The entire doctrine of *nirmalā* and *samalā tathatā*[31] explained in the same volume unveils the reality of this Buddha nature *(tathāgatagarbha)*. The Initiation process

29 The term Spirit can also refer to the highest, Monadic aspect, governing a human unit; hence Spirit-Soul-form, are the three attributes each human answers to.

30 *John 3:8.*

31 *Nirmalā tathatā:* Suchness (the condition of the *tathāgatagarbha*-Sambhogakāya Flower) apart from pollution (*saṁsāric* defilements). *Samalā tathatā,* Suchness (the *tathāgatagarbha*) covered over, or concealed with impurities. (This is the normal condition of the human Soul, the Buddha within.)

therefore is that which causes the condition of *nirmalā tathatā* (Suchness) to come to be, so that a liberated Buddha can return to freely travel the vast reaches of cosmic space, according to the dictates of compassionate Law. The way of Initiation, therefore, is what liberates consciousness from the thrall of *saṃsāra*. It then liberates the Sambhogakāya Flower, and eventually produces the appearance of a Buddha. As such a One is propelled into cosmos as a consequence, the journey ahead still represents a graded series of elevations into ever vaster Revelatory spaces, as the cosmic Initiations are sought and passed.

Each person that is 'born anew' is given an experience of *buddhi* (*śūnyatā*) by his/her own *illumined* Soul (even if only momentarily so), which stands midway between the 'waters' and the 'wind'. Effectively, a person's own Soul (a spiritual Sun) provides the first Initiation, for the person has to come to be receptive to the directing impulses emanating from that form. The first Initiation gives the person an insight into the type of consciousness (the abstract Mind) that this Soul-form expresses, for as *John 3:13* states:

> No man hath ascended up to heaven, but he that came down from heaven, even the Son of man which is in heaven.

The 'Son of man which is in heaven' is the Christ. From another perspective it is the Soul-form, and when it comes down from heaven (the higher mental plane), it fuses with the consciousness of the personality, thus enlightening him. It initiates one into the Mysteries thereof. This then allows ascension to the higher subjective planes of perception. This phrase also has reference to the entire incarnation process, for all personalities descend from 'heaven', the domain of the Sambhogakāya Flower, to the material realms to undergo evolutionary experience. From there they must learn to ascend again in consciousness and become enlightened. Even the 'Son of man which is in heaven', the Christ, had to undergo this process.

The next phrase asserts that the lifting of the serpent in the wilderness by Moses happened in a similar fashion that the Son of man was to be lifted to heaven.[32] It thus depicts the internal (serpent)

---

32 *John 3:14*. 'And as Moses lifted up the serpent in the wilderness, even so must the Son of man be lifted up'.

energies that must be awakened by the Initiate in order to ascend to heaven. The aspirant slowly awakens to the nature of these internal energies whilst living in the wilderness of our material civilisation before being able to be 'lifted up' upon the symbolic cross. The entire raising of *kuṇḍalinī* is hinted at here. (Note that the entire paean of evolution is hinted at in the above two verses.)

Many Initiates of the first degree are not consciously aware that they have been Initiated, because Initiation occurs on the subtle levels of perception. The information has to seep into their brain consciousness, which is often so much conditioned by the impressions from the three-dimensional illusional world that these inner plane happenings become obscured. (Though a vivid dream impression might betoken the fact, the Initiates have not yet learnt appropriate interpretation.) Nevertheless, new impulses and motivations, a new life, has begun to pulsate within them. This is because the subjective, intuited realisations always manifest outwardly as urges or promptings towards some accomplished work or motivation to serve. It generally impels them to seek to discipline themselves so as to attain a greater beauty and harmony in life. They develop a new sense of relationship as they become increasingly attracted to the inner Voice and visions of the mystic.

An Initiate of the first degree has started on that lengthy eliminative journey that will result in the transmutation of base substance, gross desires and appetites, into gold, the elixir of life, the nectar of immortality (to use alchemical terminology). But until this accomplishment happens, he/she still works in the 'caves' of the earth, in semi-darkness. The Initiate's 'eyes' *(chakras)* are just starting to open, and often he/she vacillates from light to darkness, being generally still strongly attracted to former material pursuits. (Though the belief may be otherwise.) Often such a one does not appropriately respond to the Light and subjective promptings from within. Thus the Christ-consciousness, not yet having the access to enter freely, overshadows and nurtures the young Initiate in its embrace.

Many today have undergone this Initiation, have turned about in their focus of consciousness, where their entire approach to life is no longer self-centred and turned down towards the personality, but instead is turned upwards to divinity and universality. It means a reversal of their entire psychic constitution from being focused below the diaphragm to above where the Heart and Throat centres reside. Eventually, the awakening of the Head and Ājñā centres become the onus of attention.

Such reversal is now happening within the collective consciousness of humanity. It is an effect of the influx of potent subjective energies beginning to be poured upon the planet from Shambhala because of humanity's progress over the recent centuries. It is seen in the present mass unrest, constant movement, fervent intellectual and spiritual impetus to effect positive social and environment changes, as well as the undertaking of spiritual pursuits. The means to the accomplishment of this reversal will precipitate the reappearance of the Christ/Maitreya. It is part of the process that will confer the first Initiation upon humanity in general, and must be accomplished within them before the Christ-form can manifest exoterically before their eyes. It is that which will allow people to recognise Him for themselves, despite the conflicting claims of the many who in effect say 'I am He'. It means a reversal of the entire psychic constitution of humanity and a reorganisation of the force-fields associated with the planet.

The role of such drugs as marijuana in this material world has often served as the eye opener, introducing etheric vision to a limited degree, mostly to the youth. By this means the indication (and indication only) of the nature of the first Initiation, from the viewpoint of an altered perception, has been given to many people. Thus, the use of hallucinogens has been of value by helping to break the bonds of materialistic thought in some of those that are now active in fostering the New Age (often seen as alternative) living styles, based on sound motives and true vision. We, for instance, have the realisation that the production of one's own food is the basis to stability and security in a very economically and emotionally unstable world.

However, drugs are not the means to enlightenment, for their effect upon our physiological and psychic constitution is often detrimental. There are many evils incurred through their abuse by the emotionally insecure and those that have not realised the limitations (and destructiveness) of this type of experience. The use of all forms of drugs will be superseded as the collective visions[33] of the people concerned

33 The ability to see clearly the true causes and results of the strife and chaos in the world (or in society), and what must be done to overcome those conditionings.

gradually lead them closer to understanding Nature's laws and natural rhythms. The collective action of all Initiates on the earth will thereby gradually pave the way for the appearance for the coming Christ. By 'Christ' here is meant the externalisation of the entire Hierarchy of enlightened being, who together embody the principle of enlightenment that the term 'Christ' implicates. By then many aspirants will have questioned and discarded the need for drug induced intoxications and opted for that which provides direct experience of the spiritual domains, coupled with certain knowledge.

There are no magic, instantaneous routes to enlightenment by means of agencies external to one's own inner powers and resources. Certain types of experience and knowledge may be gained in this manner, but these are of a psychic nature and have little to do with the higher realms of enlightenment. The path of Initiation does not work in that way. The only true means of divine Realisation is to master the corporeal nature (body, speech, and mind) in its entirety.

All forms of drugs must be abandoned if the person is to be illumined and become fully aware of the nature of the Mind. Illumination is an expression of the Light of the Soul. It is incurred by the meditation process (which elevates the person to the realm of the Mind, wherein resides the Sambhogakāya Flower) and only by this means can the undistorted visions occur that will allow the Christ-consciousness to be recognised for what it is. Drugs prevent that Light from manifesting by distorting its reflected expression. The white light that is sometimes seen under their influence is a reflection on the etheric realm (and thus the etheric counterpart of the brain) of the astral light.

Each person must learn by stumbling through the pitfalls and lures, the glamours and beautiful deceptions of the psychic realms (and drugs exemplify those realms), to find the path to Light and Life. This is particularly so for those that have undergone their first or second Initiations. Initiates of those degrees are always psychically (astrally) receptive, and for the second Initiation drugs are eschewed.[34] This receptivity denotes the source of their major glamours, innovations, vision, and problems, especially as they are nearly always at first

34 This statement refers to those who are consciously working on this path, rather than reincarnate Initiates that have not yet found their true path in the life.

unaware of being thus attuned. In fact, to determine the difference between emotional or psychic, and mental or illumined realisations, is difficult for them. Learning to do this is thus part of the training that leads to the third Initiation.

In this stage of evolution, the Initiate is especially susceptible to glamorous ideals and beautiful dreams of all types. He/she must learn to become aware of their nature and to differentiate the real from the unreal, the beautiful but distorted, from the true Vision, often beautiful but never distorted by personality reactions. This always means the abandoning of all types of drugs; physical, mental, emotional, psychic, or social. Only then can true spiritual vision manifest.

The second Initiation

When the person has definitely responded to the compassionate energy from the Heart centre; is strongly aspiring for identification, or contact, with concepts of Deity or liberation; and can successfully control desires and emotions by utilising the thought process in a definitely constructive manner, then the *second Initiation*, termed the *Baptism* in the waters of the river Jordan, can be realised. Water purifies, dissolves and washes away the stains and dust of the outer and inner life of the being. It cleanses and revitalises. It also signifies our fluid and often turbulent emotional and desire natures. Having cleansed and refined these attributes is what the undertaking of this Initiation refers to. The person is submerged in a purifying stream of Life and emerges triumphant into the Light of day: 'and lo, the heavens were opened to him, and he saw the Spirit of God descending like a dove, and lighting upon him'.[35] The concept of the *dove* is that which incorporates the energy of internal peace, then serenity, upon this path. This is an effect of the Initiate's work upon calming and transforming the volatile emotional *saṃskāras,* so that effectively the spirit of peace is the outcome.

The Initiate is now able to work at times consciously in the realms of the Soul ('the heavens') in preparation for the third Initiation, as its secrets are gradually revealed, 'opened to him'. Therefore the 'Spirit of God', potent Spiritual energy, can now descend upon the Initiate, figuratively

35 *Matt. 3:16.*

speaking, in the form of a *dove*. This bird implicates the *peace* which is the keynote of the *Christ-force*, and which is the unique energy of the Initiate of this degree (as well as those with greater attainment). This energy must be utilised to quieten emotional turmoil, overcome the delusions and life-style problems of those with whom one is concerned. The bird flies in the *air*, which symbolises the intuitional realm *(buddhi)*.

The true nature of Deity is not yet fully revealed, though the unseen *Voice* of its Presence is definitely heard. (For it is That which manifests as the conscience, that has always subjectively impelled the Initiate towards Light.) Now it is in the form of a mantra which sums up his qualities and point of attainment, saying:

> 'This is my beloved Son, in whom I am well pleased'.[36]

The mantra is also a mechanism for the projection of the potent energy of divinity to the Initiate's consciousness. In this case, it is the energy of being 'pleased'. The phrase 'well pleased' impresses upon the highest aspect of the emotional nature. With this the Initiator is satisfied, for in the Initiate of this degree the emotions have been refined, cleansed and consecrated to divinity. The Initiate is now a 'Son', an accepted agent of the Love of His Father, which is the energy that *buddhi* conveys.

Peter demonstrated being tested at the level of this second degree when he attempted to walk upon the *waters* to the Christ.[37] He, however, lost his faith, his mind was no longer pure in its intent (as it was assailed by the turbulence of his emotions), thus he *sank* (was immersed in the Waters). The Christ however saved him, and together they walked to the boat, which symbolises the mental body or Mind that exists above the Watery world. This could carry the Christ-principle and all the elements associated with spiritual life (the apostles) across the Waters. The Christ-principle therefore guided the lower man away from his emotional nature, and thus the Waters were calmed, for Peter had gained faith in the assurance of the presence of the Christ within and without himself as his guiding principle throughout life. Thus it must be with all those that are to undertake this Initiation, and the surety of the presence of the Christ-principle *(bodhicitta)* is the revelation accorded.

---

36 *Matt. 3:17.*

37 *Matt. 14:29.*

Nowadays, such cleansing is also associated with the fires of the mind, for humanity in the past 2,000 years has evolved considerably the ability to think, as evidenced by the present technological civilisation. People have to learn to use the mind to cleanse their most troublesome, incessant desires. The ancient method of Initiation, as was then symbolised by the Baptism experience of Jesus, should therefore be modified for this Era. It is more a Baptism of Watery Fire-mist, because both Water and Fire are purificatory, and must cleanse the desire-mind of the Initiate concerned.

The process that leads to this experience produces considerable emotional turmoil and also much of the zeal that a life dedicated to emerging ideals and aspirations normally engenders. Up to the attainment of the second Initiation therefore, the disciple often suffers much, with considerable rearranging and changing of life's activities. We can also, however, find that fanatical adherence to a particular approach to divinity that may last a lifetime or more. The person has many illusions and is carried away by all types of desire. He/she is generally a devotee of a religious sect or of a personage that can offer some spiritual guidance in any of the departments of life. He/she often finds what they feel is their guru or Master and is 'initiated' by means of an exoteric ritual or ceremony. This may or may not signify the taking of a true inner Initiation. It depends upon the state of the disciple's equipment of response, the attunement to inner reality, as well as whether the guru is valid or enlightened. If so, the guru is in communication, at-oned, with the spiritual Hierarchy, the Kingdom of 'God', and is thereby an outpost of Their collective meditative expression.

Generally, the second Initiation is difficult to attain because people find the *saṃskāras* of strong emotions and desires very hard to master and to convert into forms of compassionate idealism. Also, some of the most difficult *karma* of the candidate, concerning mistakes in past lives of overzealous fanaticism, malice, cupidity, inquisitional activities, etc., are reserved to be experienced so that tests signifying mastery of the associated difficulties can be met. If the Initiate can master these *saṃskāras,* by rightly handling the reciprocal *karma* of such actions from the past, then some of the requirements for the Initiation may have been met. (They may, for instance, be the target of a powerful group's enmity, or of financial skulduggery, to which they must respond with wisdom in an emotionally controlled way.) One must be able to undergo many personal difficulties in life situations, and to transform the resultant emotions into compassionate, loving attitudes within a group context, before this Initiation can be passed. Such tests for Jesus were not portrayed in the Gospel story, he simply suddenly appears at the river Jordan to be baptised.

The effects of former black magic activities, malice, abuse of power and psychic projections, sometimes being derived from far distant past lives, must also be annulled. This then concerns the development of certain psychic perceptions, and the awakening of the *karma* with the dark brotherhood that must also be dealt with on a psychic level. The inner war between the dark and white brotherhoods begins to open up within the candidate, who now needs to learn the weight of psychic self-defence via the process of cleansing and converting ancient *saṃskāras* at this level. A teacher well versed in this inner world is needed to assist the candidate master the cunning wiles and psychic projections of his adversaries. The white brother becomes an expert in the use of the Rays of Light, compassionate insight, and in the advanced stages, mantras, to convert the dark ones to the path of Love-Wisdom. In this 'war' there is no such thing as death *per se*. Conversion is the name of the game, and it is relatively easy for the dark foes to actively intensify the base natures of most disciples: pride, selfishness, cupidity, separativeness, the critical mind, etc., to become the victors in this battle. Few are those that consequently master the requirements to pass this Initiation test at the appointed cycle. Many subtle forms of desires and mental-emotions are revealed, but generally so strong are the *saṃskāras* that most have great difficulty to convert and refine them all. True group Love, for Hierarchy and humanity, is the outcome, and sacrificial service becomes the leitmotiv of the Initiate's activities. Love of the internal Life is the joy of the service work accomplished. This is how one moves up the steps of the path, the domains of perception and ranks of Hierarchy towards Shambhala. One evolves by laying down his/her life in service for all and thus progresses along increasingly subtler, vaster and more esoteric lines. Eventually the entire path moves from the earth as the main sphere of activity to cosmos, as the higher Initiations possible upon this earth are attained.

The degree of the inner attainment and outer service (or 'works'), *karma,* astrological auspiciousness, plus the development of the subjective group to which one belongs, all determine the worthiness for Initiation. As Initiation is a group happening, it affects and includes the entire spiritual Hierarchy, and eventuates upon the subjective levels of perception. For:

> The kingdom of God cometh not with observation: Neither shall they say, Lo here! or, lo there! for, behold, the kingdom of God is *within* you.[38]

At present, this is the only place that it can be found, so there is no need to seek personal utopias outside the human system until that Kingdom is found internally, becoming the focus of one's meditation. The external manifestation (utopia) is the accredited extension of that which is *within,* the result of the works that emanate from the heart. No amount of external seeking or name calling will cause the Christ or 'the kingdom' to be revealed until the divinity within is realised, be it in the aspirant, or society as a whole. That which allows this Kingdom to manifest outwardly is when the world disciple works to change our civilisation from within to reflect what has been established through meditative practice. This involves the manner of the reappearance of the Christ (the externalising Hierarchy of Light) and the foundation of the New Jerusalem.[39] It can be ascertained that those that shout lo! the Kingdom is (only) in this system or in that religion, have certainly not found it.

Speaking of the *'day when the son of man is revealed'*,[40] which is

---

38 *Luke 17:20-21.*

39 The *Revelation of St. John* is concerned with this subject of the externalisation process of the Hierarchy of Light in the form of this descending Kingdom of 'God'. *Rev. 21:2-3* thus states: 'And I John saw the holy city, new Jerusalem, coming down from God out of heaven, prepared as a bride adorned for her husband. And I heard a great voice out of heaven saying, Behold the tabernacle of God *is* with men, and he will dwell with them, and they shall be his people, and God himself shall be with them, *and be* their God'. This is a happening that the entire Hierarchy is presently working for, though it might take another millennia or so before Shambhala is exoterically manifest. Further detail will be provided in Volume 7 of this *Treatise on Mind.*

40 *Luke 17:30.*

the result of the Initiation process, Jesus stated:

> 'In that day, he which shall be upon the housetop, and his stuff in the house, let him not come down to take it away: and he that is in the field, let him likewise not return back'.[41]

Here the *housetop* symbolises the Soul, the *house* symbolises the sum of the personality-nature, and the 'stuff in the house', the various qualities of the personality with its emotional, mental, or sensual bias: its myriad thought-forms, glamours, desires and urges. The first portion of this verse can therefore be reworded: 'he that is illumined and identified with his higher Mind (or Soul), let him not regress into his lower nature to again get involved with it, by coming down from that high place to take it'. The *field* is the field of service whereupon one must manifest compassionate works. In doing those works, one can no longer desire or revert to one's old type of consciousness, with its sensual, materialistic pursuits and habits.

The following verse then states 'Remember Lot's wife', who did so, and was thus turned into a 'pillar of salt'.[42] She was made bitter, hard, crystalline, materialistic. It is certainly an infertile bed for the germination of the seed of the Christ-consciousness/*bodhicitta.*

To be granted *eternal life,* the disciple must *'lose his life'*[43] by manifesting the sacrificial service work that demonstrates *bodhicitta.* The personality desires and ambitions must be lost in order to gain the Initiations that will allow this *eternal life* to register in consciousness, driven by the Spirit of 'God', as manifesting divinity (enlightenment). Then the Kingdom of 'God' shows itself internally to the Initiate and begins to manifest externally.

The bed referred to in the phrase: *'there shall be two men in one bed'*[44] refers to the mental realm, which is dual. One of the two men relates to the personality that is dominated by the intellect, and the other to the Soul upon the higher, abstract Mind. Both the Soul and

---

41 *Luke 17:31.*

42 *Luke 17:32.* See *Gen. 19:26* for the reference to Lot's wife.

43 *Luke 17:33.*

44 *Luke 17:34.*

the personality reside in the *bed* of the mind/Mind, which is utilised and developed by their integrated action. The Initiate of the first degree is still subject to the types of illusion associated with life in the dense material world, which is sometimes beautiful, though often violent and painful. The ordinary person (or personality) is almost entirely dominated by them. The *bed* therefore symbolises a realm (the mental) wherein the phenomena associated with the dense physical life is engendered and experienced, and is that which the Initiates of the lower degrees are desirous of fully mastering. Only through the development of the qualities pertaining to the Mind can Initiation be successfully attained. To do so, both aspects of mind must be integrated and linked by means of the consciousness-link (the *antaḥkaraṇa),* as there is a gap in consciousness between them. The Initiate must work to consciously bridge the gap if the higher perceptions are to be obtained.

Luke 17:35 states: 'Two *women* shall be grinding together; the one shall be taken, and the other left'. Here the word *grinding,* and also the reference to women relates symbolically to the emotional realm and desire nature. It keeps us tied to the wheel of *saṃsāra* (of birth and death) which 'grinds' away life after life. It relates to the totality of the activity associated with the material world, the third or Activity aspect of Deity, the womb of the great Mother (Nature). The verse also infers that there is a relation between the Initiate of the second degree (who has feminine characteristics in relation to Initiates of other degrees) and the average person. Both are 'grinding away', but for different motives, one to eliminate material *karma,* and the other because 'she' is completely enmeshed in it.

Luke 17:36 states: 'Two *men* shall be in the field; the one shall be taken, and the other left'. The meaning of the word *field* was explained above. As this field is that of service, so the 'two men' here must refer to the relationship between Initiates of two differing degrees who are involved in active service in the world. By inference, they are Initiates of the first and third degrees, where they are considered masculine because of having to develop the Mind to control physical and mental plane activities, rather than being focused upon the emotions.

The Initiate of the first degree has learned to control that associated with the dense physical world, which is most concrete and material.

Consequently, much (masculine) material force and driving energy must be utilised to do so. The Initiate of the second degree has learned to control the vacillating, ever-changing emotional body, which is here considered feminine. The Initiate of the third degree must learn to control the potent, fiery energy of the mind, thus must develop the *will* to do so, which is considered masculine.

The mystery of who is taken and who is left in the phrases 'the one shall be taken' and 'the other shall be left' is found in the difference in meaning of the phrases *'the one'* and *'the other'*. 'The one' relates to one whose consciousness is fully identified with the one source of inspiration and is one-pointed in his aspiration. He is taken, for he is able to tread the 'narrow razor-edged path', the path to enlightenment and Initiation. The phrase 'the other' relates to one who is dual in consciousness, still subject to the vicissitudes of the emotional world, still wavering in his aspiration, and therefore is not able to see clearly the distinction between the One and the other, and consequently cannot be taken, cannot attain Initiation.

In the case of verses 34 and 35 of *Luke chapter 17*, 'the one' relates to the person responsive to the energies of the Soul (and thus to the Hierarchy of Light), and in the case of verse 36 it relates to an Initiate of the third degree, who responds to the 'Spirit' (the Kingdom of 'God'). The chapter finishes with the phrase:

> And they answered and said unto him, Where Lord? And he said unto them, Wheresoever the body *is,* thither will the eagles be gathered together.[45]

The concept of eagles refers to Initiates. They 'fly' high in the domains of being/non-being to perceive a vast panorama, and can spot their spiritual 'prey' from a great distance with very finely attuned perceptions. Specifically, it refers to Initiates of the fourth degree, that have mastered the Airy Element *(śūnyatā),* the high point of attainment for the members of Hierarchy in Jesus' day. Jesus took this Initiation when he mounted the cross at Golgotha. Thus, whenever one is ready to be trained for Initiation, there will be high Initiates around to administer to one's spiritual needs. Those who were fourth

45 *Luke 17:37.*

degree Initiates during his epoch have since moved on to take their sixth Initiations, and consequently are Chohans, Lords of the Rays of Life. The eagle also refers to an awakened third Eye, the Ājñā centre, which has two lobes of petals, which can be likened to wings. Because of the multidimensional far sightedness of this *chakra,* its development is likened to an eagle's vision.

The Light within one in training for the *Baptism Initiation* has revealed the mists and fogs in the cave of darkness that is the personality nature. The candidate has begun to recognise them for what they are, the glamours, delusions and illusions that have been the focus of attention for much of that life, with their enticing, clouded, semi-illuminating expression. The candidate is being freed from the emotional attachments to the lower self. The Light of the Soul flickers with increasing brilliance in consciousness by way of the mind, and perceiving this, the Initiate seeks to know the way to greater Light. The mind must be used with understanding to reason out the way, but emotions and their consequent deceptions still sometimes influence his/her actions. They colour that which is perceived as an ideal, until the individual sees beyond it, and becoming disillusioned starts anew on another higher cycle of endeavour. The 'ideal' here is the highest aspect of the emerging plan that can be sensed and expressed through service and meditation.

We see that the Christ-consciousness is fostered through trial and error, by constant experiment with the resultant experience. It concerns the registration of that experience and its active expression, until it no longer serves the emerging sense of purpose, or motive for existence. The most useful elements (or seeds) of that experience must then be extracted and the rest catalogued as memory. This then becomes part of a pattern, a continuum of realisation, which serves as an incentive or catalyst for further discovery. The seeds must be planted in the bed of compassionate understanding (the field of service) and made to grow outwards and upwards to Light.

One ascends the summit of attainment, and from that exalted point of vision one sees a new mountain in the distance with an even higher peak to climb. This leads to higher and subtler realms of experience, to broader expansions of consciousness, where things are seen in greater perspective. It always means strenuous work and service to humanity, the engendering of true unselfishness and compassion, of following in the footsteps of the Christ, until eventually the 'face of the Lord'[46] is known.

Initiates of this degree often lead a dual life and are confronted with the fight between their higher and lower self (the battlefield of *Kurukśetra* in the *Bhagavad Gita)* to which St. Paul testifies:

> For I know that in me (that is, in my flesh) dwelleth no good thing: for to will is present with me: but *how* to perform that which is good I find not.
>
> For the good that I would I do not: but the evil which I would not, that I do.
>
> Now if I do that I would not, it is no more I that do it, but sin that dwelleth in me.
>
> I find then a law, that, when I would do good, evil is present with me.
>
> For I delight in the law of God after the inward man:
>
> But I see another law in my members, warring against the law of my mind, and bringing me into captivity to the law of sin which is in my members.
>
> O wretched man that I am! who shall deliver me from the body of this death?
>
> I thank God through Jesus Christ our Lord. So then with the mind I myself serve the law of God; but with the flesh the law of sin.[47]

As the 'law of God' increasingly gains the upper hand and the 'law that is in my members' is no longer dominant in the life of the person, then he/she can walk in the footsteps of the Christ and participate in what Paul calls 'the fellowship of his (the Christ's) sufferings'.[48]

After this period of vacillation, the Initiate at last realises that he/she walks not alone, that the Christ[49] is always present, and those that also have been inspired by this Presence, who have always subjectively and objectively inspired and helped, have ever been there at the right time when help was needed, and when he/she could give. This is an important realisation at this stage in the Initiate's journey; that he/she is not, never

---

46 *Luke 1:76.*

47 *Romans 7:18-25.*

48 *Phil. 3:10.*

49 The Christ here also stands as a generic term for the entire Hierarchy of Light.

was, and never will be alone, but walks in fellowship with all Initiates. They are the Initiate's true brothers and sisters. All that are treading the path to enlightenment share (in varying degrees) the dispensation of the Christ's compassion, and thus of His sufferings. Together they work so 'that the righteousness of the law might be fulfilled in us, who walk not after the flesh, but after the Spirit'.[50]

This law (as an ideal) is the highest attribute of the Hierarchical Plan (the *dharma)* that forms within the Initiate's consciousness. It impels the spiritual person to fulfilment, and is also the esoteric cause for the conditionings that manipulate the realms of form and human interrelations. It allows the plan to be made regarding how best to serve, whether or not one recognises the source of one's inspiration. This is determined or modified by the Ray quality, thus by the department of Life to which the Initiate belongs.

General considerations of Initiation

The ability to work with the Plan, and the fulfilling of the law, leads ever to further experiences that will make one realise, as Paul eventually did:

> I am *crucified* with Christ: nevertheless I live; yet not I, but Christ liveth in me; and the life which I now live in the flesh I live by the faith of the Son of God, who loved me, and gave himself for me.[51]

The Initiate's personality desires become completely and utterly abandoned to the need of the hour. The perception as to the cause and relief of all suffering, and the ability to help, grows. The Initiate becomes ever more inundated with the Christ-consciousness and shares a measure of the burden of his cross. Eventually the Christ lives perpetually in the Initiate, there is no separation in consciousness, for she/he is now also a Christ.

We see in these few quotations the transformation of a person who is at first in constant battle between the higher and lower self, to being so completely inundated with the Christ-force that one is 'crucified' with Him. For it is only by this means that all must 'come in the unity

---

50 *Romans 8:4.*

51 *Gal. 2:20.*

of the faith, and of the knowledge of the Son of God, unto a perfect man, unto the measure of the stature of the fulness of Christ'.[52] This 'fullness' being interpreted here as that of complete integration into the corpus of the Hierarchy of Light, who are the embodied Christ-principle *(bodhicitta) in toto.*

The faith of the Initiate becomes absolute, as the knowledge of the 'Son of God' manifests within. This happens as compassionate meditation is applied, producing service in the world, as well as a constant refinement of the entire personality in conjunction with ever-increasingly practical subjective and objective experiences. The path of Initiation produces *knowledge* of what Hierarchy is and its relation to Shambhala. The path of integration with that kingdom makes a person 'perfect'.[53] It is a perfection equal to the 'measure of the stature of the fulness of the Christ', and not just to be like him.

From the above we see that Initiation is not so much an event, but rather, an eternal process of becoming into new fields of revelation and Light until the Initiate and the Christ-principle are in fact at-*oned,* and the Head centre of this planet stands revealed.

The *first Initiation* results in freedom from the control of the physical body and its appetites. Many of those that fanatically adhere to regimented or peculiar ideas and ideals about food, breathing exercises, body postures, and environment, are Initiates of this degree, or are on the path of probation, and are therefore under observation by those responsible for the Initiation process. Later on, after it has served its purpose, such fanaticism fades away, for then the Initiate knows that one can neither eat nor starve one's way to heaven, and that it is more important to have a balanced approach to all aspects of Life.

The symbolism of the Christ's first miracle at the wedding feast by turning water into wine in *John Chapter two,* indicates the nature of the first Initiation. It begins with the phrase: 'there was a marriage in Cana of Galilee; and the mother of Jesus was there'.

The *'mother'*, as previously mentioned, symbolises the material world, the realms of form, with which the Initiate of this degree is much

52 *Eph. 4:13.*

53 The perspective taken here, therefore, is that Hierarchy is the 'Son' of 'God', where 'God' represents the Lord governing Shambhala.

concerned, for he/she is Initiated into its Mysteries. It is significant, therefore, that Mary was the one who told Jesus that there was no *wine* at the feast (by which the desires of the body are satiated). Our desires must be fulfilled, then consummated and transformed by means of our ability to sip the energies, the 'wine' of the Divine. Our dense vehicles must be perfected and consecrated, married to the Christ-energy. We must become intoxicated with the Divine if we are to achieve the higher Initiations, after which the body will no longer serve as a focus of our attention. Wine is therefore also symbolic of the 'Blood' of the Christ (the energies associated with his enlightenment) which gives life, nourishment, and vitality to every cell in his body.

His answer to her is appropriate: 'Woman, what have I to do with thee? mine hour has not yet come'.[54] This means that the time for the general descent of the Christ energy upon humanity (the bridegroom) and the material world (symbolised by His mother, and also by the six water pots), had not yet come. However, it was imminent, as the bridegroom would soon be married in the presence of the Christ, as will also humanity at the beginning of the New Age with his reappearance. World-wide brotherhood, a sense of oneness, prosperity and sharing, are obvious benefits that such a 'marriage' would confer upon us.

Despite, or because of his answer, Mary set about the task that would result in the descent of the Christ's energies—the preparation of the pots with which to receive them. This showed that her faith and ability to visualise the potency and nature of the Christ-force was then already steadfast, that she was an Initiate.

The question *'what have I to do with thee?'* is profound, for she gave birth to, and nurtured him. Thus with her (or with Mother Nature) lies the whole foundation to the Initiation process. It implies an intense questioning as to the nature of enlightenment and how its gradual appearance will affect the life of the aspirant in the material world. We have the tremendous upheavals and rearrangements that will cause all the resultant activities. It concerns the entire relation of the enlightenment-consciousness to this world, which the aspirant must work out individually. The first Initiation is not possible until the probationer, who is still feminine in nature: possessing an emotional,

54 *John 2:4.*

vacillating desire-mind, is able to think seriously about evolution and the nature of the Christ-force (compassion) and his/her relationship to it. That enquiry must become so deep as to have reached the higher Mind and obtained a definite link. Until then, the Waters of the fluid emotions, and the energies that manifest through the etheric body, cannot be turned into wine, into the Blood of the Christ.

This Blood is effectively the energy from the sixth sub-plane of the cosmic astral plane, manifesting as the Divine Love *(bodhicitta)* dispensed by the Hierarchy of Light. Its energy is viewed as a wine-red colouration, which is also found in the skull cups held by the Wrathful Deities of Buddhism. It finds its grounding in a purified, consecrated astral body (the 'pot'). This effectively happens at the attainment of the second Initiation, and for which this marriage feast is but the symbolic preparation.

His mother prepared the pots, and her realisation was such that she could tell 'the servants' (those elements and forces that are responsive to the body nature) that 'whatsoever he saith unto you, do it'.[55] The entire body was thereby put in complete control of the directive energies of the Christ. (At this stage, these energies signify the manifestation of the intuition.)

In accordance with his instructions, they 'set six pots of stone'.[56] The number six, as well as the stone, symbolises the entire manifest world, the six days in which Creation was actually carried out ('God' resting on the seventh),[57] and the six points of the interlaced triangles of the seal of Solomon. The actions of the guests symbolise all the processes and forces that are undergone within the body of the Initiate of this degree during the wedding feast. The people partaking in this feast symbolise the entire manifest world, as ruled by:

- *The Christ* and his disciples—the Soul and its energies.
- *His mother*—the corporeal body or form nature, as well as the *deva* kingdom, Mother Nature.

---

55 *John 2:5.*

56 *John 2:6.*

57 Referring here to the opening passages of the book of *Genesis.*

- *The bridegroom*—who is ruled by his heart, thus the candidate for Initiation, and the bride (who is not mentioned, for the Christ and His disciples symbolically take her place).
- *The governor of the feast*—the mental principle.
- *The servants*—already explained, they are the dispensers of the intoxicating wine, psychic energy, *prāṇa*.
- *The guests*—the body of desire, who are revelling, as this aspect is not yet fully controlled by the Initiate.

The *water pots* symbolise receptacles of the emotional body, and of *prāṇa*, as are people's corporeal forms. (Being receptacles of *prāṇa,* they also thus symbolise the six main *chakras* below the Head centre, which concerns the Initiate at this stage.) These pots of stone were to be set 'after the manner of the purifying of the Jews';[58] that is, these pots were *purified and consecrated to 'God'*. Each of us must do this if we are to undertake the first Initiation; we must all purify and ceremonially consecrate to 'God' our physical bodies. Only then can water be added 'to the brim'[59] and the person be inundated to capacity with vitality *(prāṇa).* In turn, this can be *converted to wine,* to the spiritual beverage that intoxicates the bridegroom to the extent that the physical body falls below the level of focus for consciousness. Note that the *'good wine'* is served at the end of the feast and not at the beginning.[60] The end of the feast symbolises the actual attainment of the Initiation.

This section finishes with the statement: 'This beginning of miracles did Jesus in Cana of Galilee and manifested forth his glory (as does the first Initiation for the first time in a person) and his disciples believed on him'.[61]

All the disciples of the Christ are necessarily present at the Initiation. They take part by witnessing it and adding their energies ('believed on him'), for no new Initiate can arise in their ranks without greatly

58 *John 2:6.*

59 *John 2:7.*

60 *John 2:10.*

61 *John 2:11.*

affecting the group. As one is admitted, so another must ascend to greater heights, manifesting forth 'his glory'. All evolves as a unity, and miraculous indeed is Initiation into the Mysteries of Life.

Jesus then went to Jerusalem, 'and found in the temple' (the human body, which is the 'temple of the Lord') 'those that sold oxen and sheep and doves' (that is, the human animal-like passions) 'and the changers of money sitting'[62] (greed, desire, etc.). He then made a scourge of small cords and drove them all out. This is what all that will undergo the first Initiation must do regarding their passions, desires, and 'beastly' qualities.

The *second Initiation* results in the freedom from the control of the emotional nature and selfish desire for material things and comforts. The Initiate learns to control what is known as the astral body, and is given the eventual understanding of its properties by working upon the astral (fourth dimensional) realm of perception.

The first two Initiations are termed Initiations of the threshold, for they lead to eventual conscious Soul realisation (enlightenment), when one has finally mastered the qualities of the three worlds of human perception. In the case of the first Initiation, the Initiate is indirectly (via the Soul) Initiated by the Christ, who acts as the Hierophant in the place of the 'Father', the planetary Regent (the One Initiator, Who acts as the Hierophant for the higher Initiations). In the case of the second Initiation, the Initiate is directly Initiated by the Christ.

Though most Initiates of the first two degrees are not generally aware of the subjective happenings that condition them, or of their spiritual status, much of their sleep life, however, is concerned with the subjective planes of perception. There they are either being taught spiritually, gathering experience, or helping others.

People should learn to cultivate an attitude of awareness during their sleep life. They should carefully observe subtle impressions, and analyse their dreams, for much real knowledge concerning their subjective relationships could thus be gained. For example, during sleep and/or deep meditation, one at this stage could come to know one's Master, by means of a symbolic presentation, or by direct contact.

Often during deep sleep people leave their bodies and meet others with whom they are subjectively involved, and sometimes they

---

62 *John 2:14.*

prearrange to meet again in waking consciousness (synchronising times, place, right circumstances etc.). This especially happens when people have unfulfilled work to do together. In such cases, the personalities concerned, rarely remembering contact during sleep, experience the manifesting physical plane happening as fate or destiny. Often much beauty comes from such 'chance' meetings. Nothing, however, that happens on the earth is chance, everything is prearranged, for 'It is easier for heaven and earth to pass, than one tittle of the law to fail'.[63]

All happenings, meetings, and fateful consequences are the result of inner promptings (and *karma).* Where Initiates are concerned, they manifest in such a way that the spiritual Law is fulfilled, and opportunity to proceed to the next step upon the Initiation path is furthered.

The Soul/Sambhogakāya Flower also utilises the symbolism of dreams via images that are part of the person's emotional and mental equipment to teach or inspire. It incorporates into them the symbols of the Mysteries, the qualities of the Law as it is applied from its own realm of perception. This is because the Soul is considered to be an Initiate of the third degree.

Examples of the Soul-infused type of dream are often seen in recurring dreams. These are generally peaceful, revolving around a key theme, of which the dreamer can intuit the meaning. Sometimes the precognitive dream is also similarly inspired. Such dreams are generally accompanied by a voiceless Voice that explains the dream and yet has origins far beyond it. People should learn to listen to this Voice speaking to them from the silent recesses of their heart, not only in dreams, but throughout their waking consciousness.

If an important dream is not remembered, or its meaning was not understood, then nevertheless, later the person is strongly urged to do a certain action motivated by conscience. One may also have a series of revelations about some subject that has been perplexing, or upon which one has silently brooded upon in the past. (The Soul will always find the means to convey the teaching that it knows the personality can utilise.) Many creative people of genius get their profoundest inspiration after they have slept on their problems. This is a guarantee that they have been Initiated at one or another level in past lives. In the latter part of

63 *Luke 16:17.*

the evolutionary growth of disciples, they are able to directly receive instructions through meditation.

Obviously, not all dreams are of an exalted type. It takes much careful observation, reflection, and meditation to distinguish the difference between:

1. The subconscious mind chattering (calling forth images stored within its realm).
2. The desire-mind or intellect twisting or directing the dream along the lines of its own conditionings, producing images that are sensually appealing.
3. Distorted sensation, with intermittent glimpses of the real, and true astral or mental visions and experiences.
4. A projection into the mind by an extraneous entity, not necessarily with altruistic intent. There are many mischievous and malevolent entities in these realms that the Initiate must learn to discern.
5. Teachings from enlightened sources.

Eventually, the result of fruitful meditation will allow one to consciously gain awareness about all inner plane happenings. The full import of the meditator's service work will then be multidimensional, and the physical plane may not be the main arena of activity at all. Much is accomplished by the Initiate upon the higher dimensions through meditation that is designed to affect others via the mental plane, and also to cleanse the psychic atmosphere from negative influences. This will allow others to function in a way so they can be receptive to inspired and creative thoughts.

Though the major Initiations are accompanied by ceremonies undertaken on the subjective planes, the process is nevertheless non-static and continually happening, leading ever into new, freer realms of revelation. There is always a vision imparted (in the first and second Initiations) that seeps down into the brain-consciousness. It gives the Initiate a revelation pertaining to the inner life (of Hierarchical activities) that becomes part of his/her equipment of response, upon which the Initiate can draw in times of difficulty. When there is no such vision it is reasonable to presume that Initiation has not been undertaken. In the life or lives that follow such an Initiation experience, the actual experiences may not be remembered, but the awareness, the fundamental changes in consciousness that they have produced is recapitulated at the appropriate turning of the wheel (cycle of experience) of the person concerned. The higher Initiations are directly experienced.

For the first Initiation, the vision emanates from the plane of the Soul, the higher mental plane, and for the second Initiation an impression from the plane of at-onement (intuition, *buddhi,* the fourth plane of perception) is experienced. This generally provides revelation of the fact of divine ordering; that there is One universal Life that is far more abundant *(see John 10:10*[64]*),* replete with the myriad lesser lives inhabiting a multidimensional space transcending what can be cognised by means of the intellect via the five senses.

64 'I am come that they might have life, and that they might have it more abundantly'.

Lift the Hydra high
Oh disciple.
High into the sky,
away from the lair,
the stench
and the muddy desert pool
where he resides.
Rise from your knees
and triumph.
Oh conqueror!
So you aspire
and fly arrow-like
to the mountaintop
of illumined Being.

Who sees the vision,
who visualises the seeing,
who, who seeing Knows,
and who knows what seeing is?

6

The Third, Fourth and Fifth Initiations

The third Initiation

Those preparing for the third Initiation have stabilised their emotions to the point that it no longer rules their activities in any way. They are mentally focused, and use the sharp analytical thought processes to assist humanity in the fields of service governed by their Ray line. A contemplative meditative lifestyle and accompanying service work is a deeply established habit. They have passed the second Initiation in a former life and compassionate understanding of the needs of those around is deeply ingrained. They may or may not be religiously motivated; nevertheless there is a deep inner attunement to impressions coming from their own Souls and from the Hierarchy of Light. If their Souls planned for them to be awakened, they will appropriately meet an emissary from Hierarchy that will help advance their path by revealing subtleties concerning their inner plane contacts. They will then undergo the tests that will prepare them for the awakening of *kuṇḍalinī.*

Their meditative focus will have shifted away from the *chakras* below the diaphragm to those in the chest, and to the Head lotus. The objective is to awaken the 1,000 plus petals of this centre and to produce an alignment with the overshadowing Sambhogakāya Flower. Methodology similar to what was explained in Volume 5 of this treatise will be pursued. At the third Initiation, the Head lotus and the Sambhogakāya Flower become integrated, and for all intents and purposes are One. Therefore, we see the death process manifesting for what people consider their personality. The ego, or concept of 'self', must die so that the enlightened consciousness can rule. The tests associated with the third Initiation thus revolve around this death process. They produce the *ālayavijñāna* enlightenment, which provides full freedom to function in the domains of Mind (the *ālayavijñāna).*

The Eye can be opened and the third Initiation, the *Transfiguration at the Mountaintop,* can be undertaken when:

- The personality has achieved integration of its constituency.
- Body, speech, and mind have become a functioning unity under the impetus of the higher Mind and inspired by the flowering of the service work ahead.
- The gross aspects of the body nature have been transmuted.
- The emotional and desire nature are purified, transformed and working in accord with the mental principle.
- The mind is abstracted and receptive to the guiding impulses of the Christ, standing here for the entire Hierarchy of Light via the domain of the Sambhogakāya Flower.

As a result of the process, the personality light wanes and the greater transcendent Light waxes stronger, so that the interrelated triangle of light between the combined Head centres, the pineal and pituitary glands, and the light of the Sambhogakāya Flower shines vibrantly. Providing that the corresponding refinement of substance of the sheaths has occurred, this then facilitates the descent of Monadic energy to the Base of Spine centre.

The Light of revelation that then occurs reveals the Christ for what He truly represents. Such revelation is symbolised in reference to the vision that confronted Jesus' disciples on the mount of Transfiguration. There he was:

> transfigured before them: and his face did shine as the sun, and his raiment was white as the light. And, behold, there appeared unto them Moses and Elias talking with him. Then answered Peter, and said unto Jesus, Lord, it is good for us to be here: if thou wilt, let us make

> here three tabernacles; one for thee, While he yet spake, behold, a bright cloud overshadowed them: and behold a voice out of the cloud, which said, This is my beloved Son, in whom I am well pleased; hear ye him. And Jesus came and touched them, and said, Arise, and be not afraid. And when they had lifted up their eyes, they saw no man, save Jesus only.[1]

We could interpret this to say that the bright white light of the spiritual Sun shone before them, and in that light they could see visions of the Christ and its significance.

Here on the mountaintop of experience, on the summit of corporeal or physical attainment, three of His most beloved disciples behold the vision of the subjective Christ, and also of the prophets Moses and Elias. The three disciples symbolise the three aspects of the personality which have to be perfected and aligned before the Christ-force can overshadow them:

a. *Peter,* meaning 'rock or foundation', symbolises the *physical body.*

b. *James,* whose name is said to derive from 'Jacob', meaning 'he supplants', and who is (with John) noted for his fiery zeal, thus symbolising the *emotional or astral body.* (The potency of its desires and glamours, for instance, generally supplants the other characteristics of the personality nature.)

c. *John,* meaning 'the Lord has spoken', symbolises the *mental body.*

Moses and Elias (Elijah) were the two Old Testament prophets who were said to have never died. When Moses had 'died', for instance, it is said that 'his eye was not dim, nor his natural force abated'.[2] (He thus still retained his spiritual powers and was active in the objective world.) Elias was taken to heaven in a 'chariot of fire'.[3] He therefore symbolises the psychic constitution of the spiritual being, who possesses an intricate, fully vivified *nāḍī* and *chakra* system.

---

1 *Matt. 17:2-8.*

2 *Deut. 34:7.*

3 *2Kings 2:11.*

Moses the lawgiver (his name means 'saved from the water') came down from Mount Sinai (the pinnacle of empirical attainment) with the 'tablets of testimony' bearing the Ten Commandments, whilst 'the skin of his face shone'.[4] He therefore symbolises the abstract Mind bearing the ten commandments gained through clear, rational thought and communion with the divine, the Mind of 'God'. These commandments represented the highest moral code and guide for people to live by at the time, to be later superseded by the 'new commandment' of Love from Christ Jesus.[5]

The fact of when 'they had lifted up their eyes, they saw no man, save Jesus only' signifies that what Jesus symbolised upon the mount is the energy of the Sambhogakāya Flower, to which the disciple at this Initiation fully awakens. This Soul form is the instructor of the twelve (apostles) that signify the awakened Heart centre.

The people mentioned above symbolise all the attributes that must be perfected and aligned in the spiritual person who stands upon the mountaintop when the third Initiation is to be undertaken.

1. The physical body	Peter
2. The emotional body	James
3. The mental body	John
4. The etheric body	Elias
5. The higher mind	Moses
6. The Sambhogakāya Flower	The Christ-Jesus
7. Life Itself (the Spirit or Monad)	The Presence (of 'God')

For this reason, and to express the enlightenment that Initiation affords, Peter wanted to make three tabernacles[6] to enclose and convey the energies associated with the Christ, Moses and Elias. They symbolise

4 *Exodus 34:29.* The story of Moses thus symbolised the time when the 'chosen people of God' *(1Kings 3:8, Psalm 105:6)* had the capacity to throw consciousness-links upwards to the domain of the higher Mind and to receive instructions from the domain that Mind veils.

5 *John 13:34:* 'A new commandment I give unto you, That ye love one another; as I have loved you, that ye also love one another'.

6 *Matt. 17:4.*

the equipment needed to channel spiritual energies to the world. As soon as that wish was expressed by the *rock,*[7] the foundation stone of Christ's church (that is, by the common people, whom Peter embodied in his name), then the 'bright cloud of the Father' could overshadow them. This cloud refers to the sum of the energy fields of the Hierarchy of enlightened being that are a constituency of the Kingdom of 'God'. This Kingdom was thus indirectly revealed to them, in the form of that which veils the potency of the Lords of liberated Life. Jesus' disciples would eventually come to know that Kingdom by meditating upon the revelations which the light revealed.

The highest and lowest attributes of those concerned were at that moment united, and Jesus' third Initiation was undertaken. In a similar manner, the humanity of our era will also undertake this Initiation when together they express the same wish as Peter, to make known the energies of the Christ (the spiritual Hierarchy upon our planet).

The unfathomable Voice of the Presence of 'God' then spoke, saying: 'This is my beloved Son, in whom I am well pleased: hear ye him'.[8] Note that this statement is the same as that given in the Baptism Initiation,[9] except that now the phrase 'hear ye him' is added. Deity is more than pleased with the action of the 'Son God', for now the Initiate has grown in stature and is able to be *heard* in the world. He is able to use the powers of the Mind, of reason, and of the written and spoken *word*, to near perfection. That ability is exactly what this Initiation signifies. The Initiate is now a force to be reckoned with in the world of ideas. He is able to succinctly present to people their highest ideals and aspirations, and the means of successful achievement.

This Voice frightened Peter, James and John, as it was a mantra that was at once the keynote for Initiates training for the third degree, and also signifies the highest possible quality or state that they could then attain. When their vision was broken, they were led down from the summit and admonished not to tell anyone 'until the son of man

---

7 *Matt. 16:18.* 'And I say unto thee, That thou art Peter, and upon this rock I will build my church; and the gates of hell shall not prevail against it'.

8 *Matt. 17:5.*

9 *Matt. 3:17.*

be risen again from the dead'.[10] They were not to reveal the *secrets* of what they had seen until the Christ-force could walk again amongst humanity, for only then could people understand the secrets of the Initiation process, and thus the Mysteries of being.

These secrets have been hidden in parable form and can now be gradually revealed to us, for the planetary Christ, humanity (the 'son of man' everywhere born amongst men), is now 'rising from the dead'. It is emerging with an altered vision from out of our present materialistic civilisation. Though the lords of materialistic and avaricious might are presently at their apogee of power, the factors to topple their egregious effects amongst humanity are already in place. It will take time, but the unified human consciousness will ascend to the summit of the mountain where the eternal Voice of the Presence of divinity can be heard. They will be guided by the Christ-Light in their minds, the efforts of the entire Hierarchy of Light, born everywhere amongst them. The Christ will thus again walk amongst us.

This will be seen figuratively, in terms of the mass advancement towards compassionate considerations in human consciousness. It will manifest effectively in terms of the mass incarnation of the Bodhisattvas that embody the Christ-light, *bodhicitta*. It should also be seen factually in terms of the direct incarnation of this Avatar of Light and Love, as the promised Messiah, or Buddha of the religionists. However, this One will do so only after humanity has been fully prepared for this event by his disciples, the Bodhisattvas working in all departments of Life. Those who in the past have undergone the third Initiation and can see clearly how the 'Son of man' (the Christ in all of us) is to be 'risen from the dead' (from within our own material natures) will thus greatly facilitate this work.

The third Initiation marks the attainment of freedom from the control of the Initiate's threefold personality, giving the revelation of the nature of the Soul and its purpose in the scheme of things. One that has undertaken this Initiation is said to be enlightened or illumined. Illumination is an objective for nearly all systems of meditation or metaphysical philosophy extant today. Nearly all such systems give rules for the training of spiritual aspirants, rules of living, things to

---

10 *Matt. 17:9.*

abstain from, things which must be done, methods of body postures, and a disciplined form of meditation. Often, complete devotion to the guru and his instructions is taught.

In the past (and for many nowadays) all this was necessary, for people needed a format and set of rules to cling to that prevented them from erring through sluggishness, or by succumbing to the temptations of the flesh, as well as guiding them on the path, rightly or wrongly, according to the rules concerned. Humanity has now evolved in consciousness, as has the aspirant. We should no longer need authoritarian discipline imposed upon us by a guru or religion to impel us to serve. The new form of yoga that will be taught by the enlightened is the higher, unsurpassed yoga[11] of (or akin to) the Dharmakāya Way. This Way leads the Initiate away from Soul-consciousness to that absorption associated with the Spirit aspect (the *dharmakāya).* For those on this Path, it will be understood that the aspirant has in many former lives undertaken various paths to realisation, and that there can be no true salvation unless all people be 'uplifted'[12] with him/her. Such a one is guided by a fluid inner impetus to serve, to develop wisdom and to strive for liberation from *māyā,* the prison-house of the form. The person will work out the appropriate disciplines needed, and will then innately be guided to the awakened Teacher, who has similarly striven, and has developed the liberation sought. One's *karma* will unfailingly lead one thus, once set upon the path in the correct direction.

The Dharmakāya Way impels one to ride the allurements of *saṃsāra* to *nirvāṇa,* to discover that one is but the vehicle for the other,[13] then within the Void to discover the qualities of the universal Mind that is the *dharmakāya*. It requires one to tread the Bodhisattva path in full. It will therefore be understood that though prescribed rules and the various codes of discipline in the meditation digests may be useful, they are not necessary for the enlightenment process. Nevertheless, the

---

11 The word yoga comes from the Sanskrit root *yug,* meaning union, with whatever is the object of meditation. The Sanskrit name for unsurpassed yoga is *anuttarayoga.*

12 *John 12:32.* 'And I, if I be lifted up from the earth, will draw all *men* unto me.'

13 See the *Mulamadhyamakakārikā* of Nāgārjuna, which according to Garfield states: 'There is not the slightest difference between cyclic existence and nirvana. There is not the slightest difference between nirvana and cyclic existence'. From: Jay L. Garfield, *The Fundamental Wisdom of the Middle Way,* (Oxford University Press, N.Y., 1995), 331.

time-honoured rules of the road will condition the life of the Initiate, who will innately follow his/her own inner promptings and conscience. The impetus of these 'inner promptings' were gained through many lives of experience. Unhesitatingly, the outward life will be prompted or impelled towards the attainment of enlightenment, and that life will be offered in service to humanity and to the *dharma* (the Law of 'God').

Enlightenment is accomplished by means of compassionate understanding, as indicated by the statements of Jesus, and is the way of the Bodhisattva path. It implies that the personality becomes non-attached to objects, emotions, ideals, the vision of the 'beloved', or whatever is desired. It implies that service becomes the keynote of his/her aspirations and all activity is relegated to that arena. It implies an instinctively spontaneous attitude to all life's events, an outward gesture that is all-giving yet asks nothing for itself. It implies living in the world and meeting outer obligations, yet always keeping a firm inner command of the streams of contemplation, to the soundless-Sound of the guru within. It means utter fearlessness and an ability to meet head on every aspect of life, to plunge into the thickest morass and then emerge triumphant. One then grows like a radiant lotus blossom from out of the mud of the swamp to greet the morning sun with its petals. It means an instinctive following of the Buddha's middle way, the intuitive understanding of his Four Noble Truths and the Eightfold Path, combined with the demonstration of the multifaceted compassion that Jesus embodied.

One cannot achieve enlightenment without first building a vibrant mental body that is controlled and rightly directed, so that it becomes an expression of the higher Mind. It is then receptive to all the guiding impulses that are the expressions of divinity. These impulses must be regulated by the thinking mind to skilfully benefit the world. All systems of divine realisation must allow for the fact that people possess minds that must be developed to their full capacity before enlightened aspects can begin to be expressed. This is pre-empted by the present world-wide information explosion that illumines humanity. The intellect becomes humanity's most useful tool for advancement when coupled with Love, to produce wisdom. When bereft of Love, then a path of unbridled materialism, egotism, separateness, and destructive, rapacious selfishness follows.

As all personality attributes are developed, one inevitably becomes master of them. By experiencing all aspects of Life one inevitably masters Life. Only after mastering the process of Life can one be truly compassionate. Mastery allows the fostering of enlightenment. The new system of spiritual development will therefore necessitate a complete mastering of the entire Life process by an individual that has experienced what Life can teach—the fruit of which is the development of compassionate-understanding. Such understanding necessitates:

- A complete *spontaneity* in meeting the effect of all Life's forces.
- A *desirelessness* as to the way it affects the personality life.
- A complete *fearlessness* in meeting and overcoming all of the challenges and obstacles preventing the Spirit within from manifesting without.
- A complete *harmlessness* in thought, word, and deed; the result of developing compassion for all sentient beings.
- An adamant *faith* in the providence of 'God' *(karma)* and the righteousness of the fulfilment of the Law that will enable the person to 'move mountains'.[14]
- A complete *obeisance* to instructions from the bearer of the Christ-principle as to the way of Initiation leading to liberation.
- The development of the *Will-of-Love* that will draw the many into the One, and then direct that One to the highest cosmic Magnet via the cosmic astral plane.

We therefore have the method of gaining enlightenment along the seven Ray lines indicated by these key terms: spontaneity, desirelessness, fearlessness, harmlessness, faith, obeisance, and Will-of-Love, from the seventh to the first Ray. These terms therefore should be subjects of serious contemplation by all desiring enlightenment.

The monastic form of man-made rules of conduct and codes of

---

14 *Matt. 17:20:* 'Verily I say unto you, If ye have faith as a grain of mustard seed, ye shall say unto this mountain, Remove hence to yonder place; and it shall remove; and nothing shall be impossible unto you'. See also *Luke 17:2-6, Matt. 6:25-34.*

ethics that were the mainstay of religious teachings of the past will be superseded as people become increasingly ready to tread the higher way in the new epoch. Generally speaking, the more esoteric, mystical and yoga based schools of teaching develop the mental alertness and loving reception to the needs of others. It is the basis to the comprehension of the beginning stages of this higher path. In furthering the development of this process, then the 'Spirit within' will inevitably lead them to the esoteric schools, or teachers (such as those based on the writings of A.A. Bailey), wherein exemplary guidance will be forthcoming. Upon the higher path, the qualities developed produce the elimination of the *karma* associated with the material world which is concurrent with undertaking the higher Initiations.

Jesus' temptations in the desert

The three different *temptations* that Jesus successfully resisted in the desert, after he had fasted for 'forty days and forty nights',[15] relate to the temptations that each person must successfully overcome if the first three Initiations are to be obtained. The number forty (40 = 4 x 10) is significant in that here it numerologically relates to that which is the perfection (the number 10) of the 'square' (the number 4), the tabernacle or foundation stone of the personality nature, the material world. It can also refer to the four corners of the 'Throne of God', the four quadrants of manifest space. This is the substance of the 'temple of God'.[16] It allows the energy of *buddhi* (enlightenment) to inundate the form.[17]

The *first Initiation* is related to the temptation of the bread:

> And when the tempter came to him, he said, If thou be the Son of God, command that these stones be made bread.[18]

---

15 *Matt. 4:2, Luke 4:2.*

16 *1Cor. 3:16, 17, Rev. 11:19.*

17 Note that *buddhi* is the fourth principle (and plane of perception), the first principle is the etheric form, the second is the emotional body, the third is the mental body, then *buddhi*. The dense physical body is not a principle, it is an automaton of that which manifests through the *chakras*.

18 *Matt. 4:3.*

The nourishment and well-being of the dense physical form by means of food, the bread that is the symbolic body of the Christ, is that with which the aspirant of the first Initiation is primarily concerned. It implies proper control of the corporeal form, thinking not only in terms of gross foods, but also of subtle, subjective *(prāṇic)* energies as well. The aspirant is concerned practically with the transmutation of the 'stones' of substance into the bread of life, with how to turn that associated with the material world and bodily nature into spiritual substance, into resources that the divinity within can use.

The *'tempter'* here is not something that is in itself evil (despite the fact that the word 'devil' is used in the following verses), but rather, that which is the gain of an aeonic involvement with the material world and the weight of the sum total of the related experiences. It can be considered the voice of the entire personality nature, in contradistinction to that of the Soul. This voice asked for an objective miracle to assist in fostering bodily well-being, a major concern for the aspirant at this stage. The aspirant must, however, learn to view the form as a symbol of the divine. The 'tempter' thus helps one to realise the esoteric, or real, significance of the bread that will produce that transformation in consciousness.

The transmutation of stones into bread, into living vital energy, is part of the compassionate undertaking of every Initiate, no matter of what degree, and is the *raison d'etre* for the process of incarnation. The entire purpose of incarnation into a body of 'clay' and the corporeal world, is to transform and transmute it from one kingdom to the next, and thus lift all to heaven. This is done by imbuing substance with the seeds of intelligent life, the qualities of the mind that bind the human form into a coherent whole.

Esoterically, the concern is with the quality of the *prāṇas* that vitalise and incorporate the form. Inevitably, the five *prāṇas* must be converted to the Void Elements[19] by working upon one's base *saṃskāras,* their transformation and transmutation into the attributes of enlightenment and liberation. The entire enlightenment process is concerned with this purpose, as has been detailed in the previous volumes of this *Treatise on Mind.* The first degree Initiate is at the beginning of being able to command the 'stones' representing the corporeal form to be converted

19 Explained in Volume 1 of this series.

to the bread of Life. In essence, this is the meaning of *salvation,* thus the undertaking of a Bodhisattva. The aspirant to the first Initiation must begin this transformation process with full awareness as to the implications of his/her actions.

Jesus, who was then in much need of bodily nourishment, was thus forced to look deeply into the nature of being and its interrelated energies, as to what was truly needed to sustain his form. Being aware of the esoteric significance of bread, he could answer without hesitation:

> It is written, Man shall not live by bread alone, but by every word that proceedeth out of the mouth of God.[20]

The question of humanity's essential divinity: 'if thou be the Son of God?'[21] is one that looms large in the aspirant's mind, and also to a lesser extent within the mind of the Initiate of the first degree, thus this query is repeated in *Matthew 4:6.* Though having had experiences to support the claim, the Initiate is nevertheless unsure and thus often walks in distress and much darkness, as first the material and then the spiritual attracts his/her attention. Jesus, however, could avoid this question, as it was obvious that he was a 'Son of God' by the very fact of being so tested. The demonstration of his command of the transmutation process was thus unnecessary. He therefore gave the correct esoteric answer that is needed by all those that succumb to this temptation (of unnecessarily or profanely exhibiting one's spiritual powers, knowledge, or abilities), that the eating of bread is inconsequential if the person is not attuned to 'every word that proceedeth out of the mouth of God'.

---

20 *Matt 4:4.*

21 In the Christian ontological sense, the appellation 'Son of God' is considered unique to the Christ. From an esoteric viewpoint, however, it can be applied to the Soul aspect of all Life, for the Soul is the receptacle for the Spirit of 'God'. Each Soul is a 'Son' or divine spark of 'God', the expression of His 'Seed' (the *tathāgatagarbha,* or Buddha-womb) impregnated into the Womb of the substance of the mental plane, which is the Divine Mother. It is the divinity in us, which we must eventually come to know and thus be abstracted into. All Initiates who are consciously identified with this aspect are 'Sons of God' in a direct sense, and average humanity, indirectly. From this perspective the Christ can be considered uniquely the 'Son of God' in that He embodies the World Soul, the *anima mundi,* by being the head of the Hierarchy of Light.

These 'Words' (in the form of the person's conscience) first lead one to the Path, and it is the Word that one must staunchly learn to follow if Initiation is to take place. The Word is the living bread. When the person is able to respond to it in every action, and the transmutation process has begun in earnest, the Word being thereby made manifest in the form, then we have the appearance of the phenomenon of an Initiate. The dense substance of the corporeal body, thus also the mineral substance, with which the first degree Initiate is primarily concerned, can begin to be rightly utilised and etherealised.

The 'Word of God' at the beginning of John's Gospel is equated with the Christ-energy. From this Word (mantra) all things were made. It was the Life that was 'the light of men', which 'shineth in the darkness' that 'comprehended it not'.[22] The embodiment of this Word is what was described in the earlier volumes of this treatise as the planetary Logos. Mantra is the mechanism whereby the seed *bīja* of what is to be can be made to expand and flower, like a bud lotus, into the entire *maṇḍala* of being/non-being. All things thereby come into manifestation, and the life imbued into the *maṇḍala* then manifests in terms of light (consciousness) which begins to overpower the darkness of ignorance. As it does so, wisdom evolves, and the Christ-light *(bodhicitta)* awakens in the form of the Bodhisattva that works to liberate all. Such a Bodhisattva was John the Baptist, 'the man sent from God' that 'came for a witness, to bear witness of the Light, that all through him might believe'.[23] This Light is this energy that directly sustains the life of the disciple. Thus we have the meaning of the opening passages of this Gnostic gospel revealed. It is a simplified version of what was detailed in the earlier volumes of this *Treatise on Mind* in Buddhist terminology.

Amongst humanity there are many tens of thousands that are on a probationary path in preparation for attaining the first Initiation. For this reason, this temptation (of effectively asking 'stones be made bread') now directly affects them in terms of the myriad consumer items

22 *John 1:1-5.* 'In the beginning was the Word, and the Word was with God, and the Word was God. The same was in the beginning with God. All things were made by him; and without him was not anything made that was made. In him was life; and the life was the light of men. And the light shineth in darkness; and the darkness comprehended it not'.

23 *John 1:6-7.*

they must deal with. Each item manifests a version of this tempter's allurement, that the disciple command these material objects to fulfil all their needs. They must learn to resist the allurements of the material contraptions and glamorous images relating to the 'body beautiful', designer wear, and unlimited comfort, to pass these tests. It is all but an expression of the scientific and technological commandeering and exploitation of the mineral kingdom for our needs, and also Humanity's world-wide concern for an adequate food supply ('bread'). This is especially so in light of the effects of the population explosion, the desertification of our arable land and the destruction of much of our natural resources. We see, therefore, that:

a. The question of our essential divinity is one that now (again) seriously confronts us. The scientific community, especially in the fields of physics and biology, and also the parapsychological investigators, have thus probed the borders of the psychic, the phenomenal, and the supersensory realms. Some of the properties of such phenomena have come to light, but garbed in modern terminology. The results of modern archaeological research, in conjunction with the study of comparative religion, mysticism, mythology, astro-astronomy and science is posing perplexing questions for the orthodoxy. Theologians are beginning to seriously probe the similarities of the world's scriptures and are utilising their minds with increasing effectiveness to investigate the real meaning of their sacred texts. They are thereby producing an effective religious revival in the West. The torrent of books that have been published on these subjects in the past few decades is a good gauge, indicating the intensity of the fervour of answering the question of how to transform substance into 'living bread' by humanity. It is 'living' because it not only concerns bodily nourishment, but also mental and spiritual food as well.

b. We still have to solve the problem of how to adequately feed the world's population. The reason for this is that humanity still have not yet learned to utilise the 'Word of God' as compassionate understanding. Selfishness, cupidity, and iniquitous resource sharing abounds everywhere. From the point of view of the expression of energy, we see that the lower correspondence of that Word (the Blood of the Christ) is *prāṇa*. It is the subjective, intoxicating 'wine' that vitalises all foods, and feeds our subtle bodies. Humanity must learn to rightly utilise all energies, including *prāṇa*, that emanate from the (spiritual) Sun. They must adapt them to their needs in a way that all members of the human race equally benefit, rather than trying the self-defeating method of grandiose 'miracle-making'. Modern technology is used in egregiously destructive ways to aggressively exploit natural resources so that a relative few can make enormous profits. For example, nowadays there is the prolific use of pesticides and herbicides, many of which are poisons and environmentally destructive, whilst genetically modified plants with unknown consequences are aggressively fostered. They claim that these factors are needed to increase the productivity of the land. These may have short term benefits, but actually foster long term disastrous consequences. Such methods do reap enormous profits for the megacorporations, who then accrue significant lobbying power to sway legislators. However, nowhere is it proven that such methods are more productive than community and organic farming methods that do not have any egregious side effects. The modern vast agri-businesses are literally examples of the attempt to 'command... stones be made bread'. Other arguments against the use of such chemicals are that those used generally produce a few showy harvests and then weaken the resistance of plants to their enemies, or poison the earthworm population, or environment in general, destroy the bee population, or rob the soil of some of its essential nutrients.

The next temptation is associated with the emotional body and the *second Initiation.* We start with the statement:

> Then the devil taketh him up into the *holy city,* and setteth him on a pinnacle of the temple.[24]

We saw that the *'holy city'* is the 'city of the living God, the heavenly Jerusalem',[25] Shambhala, that exists on the subjective realms. It is inhabited at its lower levels by the Hierarchy of enlightened being and the kingdom

24 *Matt. 4:5.*

25 *Heb. 12:22.*

of the Sambhogakāya Flower. Shambhala is the esoteric correspondence to the 1,000 petalled lotus, the *sahasrāra padma* at the top of the head.

There is an interesting ontological query here as to how 'the devil', being the epitome of evil,[26] could actually enter that City and show Jesus anything. The inference, therefore, is that the pinnacle of the temple that is referred to here is that of the Jerusalem of Jesus' time. We can also deduce that Jesus was not carried there bodily, but astrally; thus the temptation referred not so much to the concept of the death of the physical body, but rather to reversion to indulge in the emotional-mental qualities associated with *saṃskāras* that by now should have been mastered.

If the *temple* is taken to represent the temple of the body, then the 'pinnacle of the temple' will be seen to be the etheric counterpart of the *pineal gland.* The pineal gland is situated above the spinal column (thus is a pinnacle) that houses the *iḍā, piṇgalā* and *suṣumṇā nāḍīs,* through which the *prāṇic* energies must flow that are to liberate the person. It also provides the ability to esoterically vision and to see multidimensionally when viewed as being the externalisation of the *sahasrāra padma.* The relationship between the Head and *Ājñā* centres with the pineal gland thus awakens the Third Eye when the meditator is in command of the processes involved.

The candidate in training for the second Initiation must endeavour to reside on this pinnacle if there is to be progress. There the entire bodily and emotional processes can be viewed in retrospect, but the Initiate can still listen to the voice of temptation, which:

> Saith unto him, If thou be the Son of God, cast thyself down: for it is written, He shall give his angels charge concerning thee: and in their hands they shall bear thee up, lest at any time thou dash thy foot against a stone.[27]

To dash one's 'foot against a stone' means, symbolically, to be so glamoured with the material world and the form nature that one's spiritual direction is hurt. Here the feet are related to the intellect, for to utilise them one must direct the vision to where one wills to go and

---

26 Signifying the members of the dark brotherhood, which the Initiate of the second degree is in the process of directly confronting.

27 *Matt.* 4:6.

then proceed. There must be a clear thought-form as to the destination, as well as to the terrain immediately ahead.

Until the candidate is healed of the tendency to focus materialistically, much time and spiritual momentum is lost. The *angels* who have been given 'charge' concerning the Initiate are members of the Hierarchy of enlightened being, as well as referring to the *devas* that regulate the dispensation of people's *karma*. They are Initiates of higher attainment, and walk in the 'fellowship of his (Christ's) suffering'.[28] They will certainly 'lift' Initiates up if they should so fall, for to help is a fundamental law of their being, but Hierarchy can only do this if there is a willingness and ability of candidates for Initiation to help themselves.

The lure of astral plane glamour, of psychicism, or the concretion of the mind, is still possible, even when the lofty vision that is seen from the 'pinnacle of the temple' has been attained. The Initiate is still able to 'cast himself down'. What tempts him/her to do so, however, is not so much concern for the nourishment of the body, but the *glamour* of being an all-important healer, teacher, or a messiah in the world. Thus pride, and the development of psychic abilities, can lead to such a one's downfall. The subtle whisperings of the dark brotherhood constantly pillage the disciple with a never-ending stream of such thoughts. They must be strenuously resisted, and the dark ones made impotent through the countering projection of the Rays of light, and strong internal resolve to prevent such qualities developing. When the factor of prideful endeavour in any form is defeated and the dark brotherhood thus converted, then this Initiation is possible.

The angelic kingdom and many of the laws of Life are known, but candidates often use this knowledge in a distorted manner. They become glamoured by the thought of being 'closer to God' than the people around; by the sense of eminence; by the importance and quality of the work done and the over-emphasis of their place in the scheme of things. This tendency is so strong that candidates often become fanatical and subjectively assertive, rash and impulsive. Indeed, Initiates working for this degree are often well known personalities in the world, and great is the temptation to be involved in self-glorifying complacency,

---

28 *Phil. 3:10*. 'That I may know him, and the power of his resurrection, and the fellowship of his sufferings, being comfortable unto his death'.

which would relegate to others the necessary work of 'salvation' *('in their hands* they shall bear thee up'), whilst they act out self-centred dreams. Initiation is not gained in this way, thus 'Jesus said unto him, It is written again, thou shalt not tempt the Lord thy God'.[29]

Only through centering oneself in one's fundamental being (the divinity within) by constantly resisting the temptations of the flesh and the desire nature (thus the zeal and fanaticism that this often engenders) can the person gain the second Initiation, and glamour be overcome. The candidate must obtain the golden mean, the middle way, between all extremes.

The gist of this temptation is placed on an intellectual level, for the mind is to be fully utilised if the disciple is to overcome the lures and vicissitudes of the emotional body. Both the devil and Jesus, therefore, quote religious scriptures ('it is written') which must be mentally analysed for the integrity of their concepts regarding the problem at hand. Also, we see that 'the tempter', with its fundamental emotional-desire basis, no longer suffices to tempt the person, but the devil is substituted instead. As well as representing the forces of evil, 'the devil' is identified with the misdirection of the energies of the mind, of knowledge itself. (For example, the misapplication or perversion of the context of religious scriptures for temporal gain.) This is important, for by now the various deceptions, illusions, and qualities of the mind are a force to be reckoned with.

The *third temptation* concerns attaining the third Initiation, thus the overcoming of illusion. Concerning this, *Matthew* states:

> Again, the devil taketh him up into an exceeding high mountain, and sheweth him all the kingdoms of the world, and the glory of them.[30]

If a 'high mountain' signifies the undertaking of the third Initiation, then an *'exceeding high mountain'* can only signify that which exceeds this Initiation, thus taking the fourth and higher Initiations. The focus is thus upon the fourth plane of perception *(buddhi),* to which the Initiate of this degree comes to be receptive, and concerning which,

---

29 *Matt. 4:7.*

30 *Matt. 4:8.*

the Initiate in training for the third degree is given a vision. Only from that exalted realm of being can 'all the kingdoms of the world' and the glory of them be seen in perspective. Only there can the properties and interrelationships of the seven Ray departments in the body of Deity be seen as a unity. The vision is profound, for the Initiate can see in a moment of time, in the form of living streams of light, all of the undertakings, qualities and ailments of the entities within those kingdoms. (The *world* incorporates all realms of perception and localities of existence, subjective and objective.)

Again, another ontological problem arises, because that which is evil has not the ability to attain this great spiritual height. In fact, the level of attainment associated with the third Initiation is beyond the capabilities of those of the left hand path. There is a parting of the way after the second Initiation. The dark brother cannot manifest the lofty thoughts to enter the higher domains of the abstract Mind that the white brother can. The dark brotherhood have their own form of higher Initiations, but they lead ever deeper into domains of materialistic power. The exceeding high mountain implicated here therefore has a materialistic bias, referring to the highest pinnacle of the domain of the empirical mind possible. This involves the ability to reason and to vision with the mind's Eye (the Ājñā centre). Visualising through the third Eye then, and seeing the glory of the interlocking system, the candidate for the third Initiation is confronted with the illusion of power, as indicated by the continuance of this verse.

> And saith unto him, All these things will I give thee, if thou wilt fall down and worship me.[31]

The phrase 'if thou wilt fall down and worship me' refers to Initiates that are in training for their third Initiation, for they are often involved in the various meditative practices that allow the development of the qualities needed to unfold the serpent power. They can therefore listen to the oft enticing deceptions associated with the development of psychic power *(siddhis)*. Here, therefore, 'the devil' takes the attributes of the *serpent,* and thus the *kuṇḍalinī* that resides at the base of the spine

---

31 *Matt.4:9.*

(the foundation or base of the 'pinnacle of the temple'). People need only to 'fall down' in consciousness to the base *chakra* and worship *kuṇḍalinī*, 'the devil' there, and consequently gain *siddhis,* the power that will allow them to psychically command all the kingdoms on earth. They need only to meditate exclusively upon that *chakra* in the hope of raising the potent forces associated with the most material aspect of our subtle form. Enlightenment, however, is not gained in this way. *Kuṇḍalinī* will only produce bondage to the material world and disrupt the form nature, even destroy the person physically or psychically, if unduly tampered with.

The premature raising of *kuṇḍalinī* is a subject that most books on yoga meditation strongly warn against. This is the way of the dark path that leads to unmitigated evil and sorcery, which is what 'the devil' asked Jesus to do. The personal will must not be used in this manner to force *kuṇḍalinī,* but rather the Divine Will of the 'Father' (the Monad) must be invoked instead. This energy must descend down the spinal column in order to wed with the feminine *kuṇḍalinī* (the 'Mother'). The result is the conjugal embrace of the Wisdom and Compassion of female and male deified forces, as symbolised in Buddhist art. The compassionate union of all into One produces the high Mind-space of revelation.

The vision provided by 'the devil' was not just in terms of possessing great psychic power over others, but also the material possessions, vast monetary reserves and political power that such a one can accrue, once this path is followed. Great is the karmic cost however, as it produces a mass accumulation of suffering and misery for the victims of such rapaciousness. Quite clearly the Initiate at this level of development knows the fallacies of this left hand path, nevertheless, the vision of what it portends in its entirety is accorded to such a one. It invokes an attitude of deep compassion and resolve to overcome all evil upon this world, to unwaveringly follow the plan as to how best to accomplish this end. This third temptation thus shows the direct opposite of that to which Initiates aspire for with their innermost heart, and for which they have worked for many lives.

Generally, the reason given by those desirous for spiritual power, but unwilling to follow the path of right transformation of undesirable *saṃskāras* (thus being tempted by 'the devil' to prematurely awaken *kuṇḍalinī*), is to purport one way or other to help people, to become a healer, etc. They claim thereby to be enlightened. However, the subjective motive of such people, when scrutinised, is to obtain the *siddhis* that would make of them 'gods', or to be treated as such by devotees and the general population. They wish material power, wealth, fame, glory, and to control the denizens of the various kingdoms of Nature. They thus develop great cunning and devious scheming to meet those ends.

In many ways this temptation recapitulates a similar one offered to Eve by the serpent in the garden of Eden. She succumbed to this temptation and was thus ousted ('fell down') from the garden. Because of this, humanity gained rulership over 'all the kingdoms of the world'.[32] The Initiate has evolved by means of experience in all these kingdoms and has completely mastered the life-process in them all. For this reason, he/she can endeavour to appropriately raise *kuṇḍalinī* and to rise up to the Kingdom of 'God', to be liberated. The Initiate thus regains the direct communion with the divinity that humanity lost when they 'fell' from Eden.

The Initiate has eaten from the fruit of 'knowing good and evil' in the midst of the garden of Eden, and as a consequence has opened the eyes *(chakras),* that makes all such ones 'as gods'.[33] Esoterically, the trees of this 'garden' represent the *nāḍī* system, where the flowers are *chakras,* whilst the central tree represents the *suṣumṇā nāḍī.* Having originally tasted its fruit, Adam and Eve were ousted from the garden of Eden (the astral plane) into dense manifestation via their etheric forms, which then consolidated a dense body. The Initiate of the third degree

32 See *Genesis Ch. 3 ff.*

33 *Gen. 2:16-17, 3:2-6.* 'And the woman said unto the serpent, We may eat of the fruit of the trees of this garden: But of the fruit of the tree which is in the midst of the garden, God hath said, Ye shall not eat of it, neither shall ye touch it, lest ye die. And the serpent said unto the woman ye shall surely not die: For God doth know that in the day ye eat thereof, then your eyes shall be opened, and ye shall be as gods, knowing good and evil. And when the woman saw that the tree was good for food, and that it *was* pleasant to the eyes, and a tree to be desired to make *one* wise.' Note the significance of the tempting 'serpent' here to the serpent power of Hindu and Buddhist yoga philosophy, which conveys psychic powers when evoked, and which indeed will make one wise when appropriately evoked to awaken the *chakras.*

reverses this process by discovering the *suṣumṇā* path, and awakening the powers of the Head lotus. Again, the etheric body is consciously resided in, with the dense form being seen to be the illusional body of appearance. Esoterically, the Initiate has thereby become Adamic, able to 'name,' to possess esoteric, mantric command over all there is.[34]

Temporal power, be this in the physical world or in a subjective realm, is part of the great illusion, of the wheel of birth and death.[35] It cannot be a part of the Initiate's aspiration. Images of the service that could be accomplished with wealth and privilege often have a subtle bias of personal possession and gain. By 'personal possession' is meant the idea that one 'owns' the wealth and resources that are in one's possession, rather than it merely representing units of *karma* appropriated through one's relationship to the whole, and really belongs to the all. One can only be a wise manager of these resources, so that the greatest benefit for the all can be accrued. Wealth may come as a consequence of karmic situations, but is not to be visualised as part of a *maṇḍala* of subjective desire.

Everything, in and of itself, comes as part of an expression of temporary movement into our possession before it moves elsewhere. The *karma* of every phenomenal thing must be appropriately assessed. Transience is the order of the day. Desirelessness for the personal 'self' will be a *fiat accompli* when the limitations of whatever such a 'self' may be is fully comprehended. To serve others, Initiates must often overcome obstacles and lack of resources, or limitations of time etc. They come to understand the nature of the tests involved, the gains accrued through hardship and appropriate struggle. Nevertheless, despite the lack of resources, service is provided to others by means of being the living example of what can be accomplished.

Myriad are the tests associated with wealth and its relation to desire, personal pleasure, and material comforts. The tests related to the first Initiation, which were focused upon the physical domain, simply move to the realm of ideas and concepts of great service at the third Initiation

34 *Gen. 2:19.* 'Whatever Adam called every living creature, that *was* the name thereof'.

35 In Buddhist philosophy, this wheel contains Six Realms; the human realm, the animal realm, that of hell, of desire wrought hungry ghosts *(pretas)*, of jealous titans *(asuras)*, and the realm of the gods.

level. The third degree Initiate must come to be indifferent to concepts of personal wealth, everything must be subjugated to the service at hand. Thus finances are not to be eschewed, but rightfully appropriated and consecrated in service to 'God' and humanity, by fulfilling with it the plan of Hierarchy for that cycle.

The Initiate knows, through many painful experiences, that all is transitory and concepts of individual possession leads to the pain of rebirth, suffering, and death. It was certainly not part of the ambition of Jesus (though it was an integral part of the Jewish concept of the work of a Messiah). He thus stated:

> Get thee hence Satan: for it is written, Thou shalt worship the Lord thy God, and him only shalt thou serve.[36]

Here we see that the Initiate forces this entity back whence it came by directly using the will. All Initiates endeavouring to realise the third Initiation must do this if they feel *kuṇḍalinī* stirring, and their motives are not 100% pure. If not done so, then their unreadiness will be emphasised, their subjective desires and uncontrolled passions reinforced. This leads to spiritual destruction, the inadvertent following of the methods of those on the left hand path, to effectively 'worship the devil'. We therefore have the last and most dangerous of the temptations to overcome, one that needs much application of energy to do so. If premature awakening proceeds, a direct command is needed—'get thee hence Satan'. The entire power base of the forces of evil must be finally defeated on all of its levels: physically, psychically and mentally. Every aspect of one's psychic projections and subtle whisperings in the mind must be overcome. The Initiate must conquer the entire concept of 'self', and produce that self-lessness that transcends space and time.

The statements following this demand, 'for it is written' (again quoting the Law), and 'thou shalt worship the Lord thy God', indicate that the Initiate must focus his/her entire attention upon gaining enlightenment. The focus is therefore upon the nature of divinity, upon that which emanates from the kingdom of Souls, Hierarchy, or the *dharmakāya*. *Kuṇḍalinī* can only rise without catastrophe when one

---

36 *Matt. 4:10.*

is so identified with the Divine Will as to have absolutely no personal will left that could distort the vision, plan, or energies concerned; when 'God only' is served. The Initiate's three-fold vehicle will then be properly consecrated and purified. There will be naught that can hinder its journey to the highest spiritual centre after it has fused with the energies of 'the Father', producing the 'divine Son'—enlightenment.

In the terminology presented by the Gospels, 'the Father' is thus the dynamically active, 'masculine principle', the Will energy that descends from above. The completely cleansed, consecrated, threefold vehicle of the Initiate becomes the passive, receptive, Son. The *māyā* from which the Initiate evolves is considered the Mother. Such an Initiate is consequently a 'Son of God', and stands as the Christ-principle, a force of positive change amongst people everywhere.

The phrase *'get thee hence Satan'* also indicates the means of dissipating all the *karma* associated with the personality nature in the material world.[37] The third Initiation can only be undertaken when the person is freed from the repercussions of past actions and no longer has any *karma* that can bind him/her to the realms of glamour and illusion. This leads to complete freedom of movement within the precincts of the kingdom of Souls (the higher Mind). There is then naught that can restrict this freedom, forcing one back into the world of personality reactions (unless so chosen, as an act of compassion, in an endeavour to relieve world *karma).* This statement is therefore an injunction that motivates every action regarding the effect of the *past* life or lives (which the person had once *lived,* but no longer has a validity in the present or the future). The Initiate is consciously eliminating or transmuting the associated *saṃskāras.*

The elimination of Satan has far-reaching implications when applied to the salvation of the substance *(karma)* of the three planes of human endeavour. It implies the means to complete the transmutation process that was begun when the Word was first responded to (resulting in the first Initiation), and which will make the person the 'living Word', or 'bread of life', giving nourishment to all.

Many of those in power, and the thinkers of the world, are on a

---

37 See also chapter 8 of my revised book, *The Revelation,* where the concept of Satan was related to *karma.*

reciprocal, though lower octave of expression than the Initiate in training for this degree. They therefore have similar illusions, with similar thoughts of channelling energy (of Fire), militaristic or monetary, to amass financial or territorial empires, or to secure world dominance. They often express similar motives to those of the Initiate that succumbs to this temptation, such as 'for the benefit of humanity in general', but, if scrupulously examined, the motives fall far short of the ideal presented.

This temptation, therefore, concerns cleansing the mental body, overcoming illusions, the subjective desire for power, and also the pride that such illusions produce.

The fourth Initiation: the Crucifixion/Renunciation

This Initiation frees one from all self-interest and provides the revelation of That which the Soul-form veils. From the time of the transfiguration, the Initiate has continued to grow in the experience of the Divine, with his/her consciousness becoming ever more embracing in its expansion, for the Soul-Light continually grows. This is paralleled in the life of Jesus by his ability to perform increasingly greater miracles.

By now old sensual habits have been renounced, material desires, glamours, and illusions overcome. Even all that one considers essential to one's existence as a personality, all sense of ego, has been renounced, for the fundamental unity with all other 'selves' has been realised. The entire body nature is now a purified, consecrated vehicle, via which the unifying impulses of divinity manifest. Accordingly, the Initiate has become illumined and radiates that light as a world server. Because of conspicuous desirelessness, purity in motive, and dedication to the demonstration of the unfolding Law within, another renunciation or sacrifice on the path of enlightenment can occur upon the domain of the Sambhogakāya Flower. It renounces its existence as a mediating form between the Monad and the personality. It has been the acumen of life and focus of spiritual being till now, but the purpose for continued incarnation in the material world has been gained, as far as the derivation and transformation of *saṃskāras* are concerned. There is no further need for it to contain the experiences gained from *saṃsāra*. It (the 'Son') therefore is abstracted into its essence, to the 'Father' (the Monad), which takes direct control of the Initiation progress.

The Sambhogakāya Flower is the intrinsic 'transformation body' *(sambhogakāya)*, in its aspect as a qualified energy source that consubstantiates the result of the incarnation process with That which is true Being, the Monad or Buddha within, via the domain of Mind. The Soul is the instrument of perfection that has stood between the personality and the Presence (of 'God') for unknown ages, and has slowly grown in beauty and wisdom until it has become perfected and fully vibrant in pulsating, living light.

This Flower is the most sublime of subjective forms, the ultimate form of manifest being, yet it has served its purpose, as it cannot adequately express the potency of the Monadic-Light, the *dharmakāya*. The Initiate has fulfilled the task of being a unitary *cell* in the Body of Deity, and is now to be liberated from that exalted, though still limited, state of consciousness. The Initiate is now to tread the higher Way, to be abstracted into the immutable formlessness of the Void *(śūnyatā)*, which will inevitably come to reveal the ineffable potency of the *dharmakāya*. The former life as such a 'cell' is extinguished. Its essence becomes at-oned with the cosmic all pervasive embrace (or embraciveness) that is beyond time or space. (Which is but one way of describing *śūnyatā*.) It can be conceived as being both being and non-being (or neither, or that from which either can manifest), via which a universal Mind is veiled. Such a Mind is beyond conceptualisation by an ordinary mind.

Metaphorically, the consciousness that was formerly limited to being a 'cell' in size now becomes an organelle, a vaster unitary entity. Further progression, such as evolution to being an organ, or abstraction into the energy dynamics of the body (e.g., as 'nerves'), or into the fluid vascular and circulatory system is then possible. All being an expressed part of the 'Body of God', when viewed in terms of transcended correspondences.

From another perspective, the fourth degree Initiate becomes absorbed as a spark in the ocean of energy that constitutes the immeasurable Mind of 'God'. The term 'God' is equivocal and can be interpreted according to the angle of vision of the interpreter. It should be re-emphasised that the term is used in this text as an ontological concept of That which is incognisable by the mind (as verifiable experience) and yet which one intuits to be the inexplicable causeless Cause, the Father of all-Being (the Ādi Buddha, Vajrasattva), of time and space, of all there is or is not. It thus is the embodiment of universal Mind *(dharmakāya).* To realise 'It', one must become devoid of any quality associated with any philosophical, conceptual acumen of 'self', or thought of any tacit teleological phenomena or noumenon to which we may aspire. It is not an 'empty' mind that is here espoused, but a Mind that is held steady in ineffable Light, and in that Clear Light (that is transmogrified *saṃsāra)* is the Knowledge of what directs it all. To do so allows one to develop the capacity to not just become 'like God', but to be 'equal with God'.[38]

This indeed is the outcome of the path of Initiation, as one eventually becomes a Buddha, and travels on, ever onwards to encompass ever vaster domains of space, and that space is cosmic Mind. The concept of 'God' (and all such concepts) then becomes not devoid of meaning—for That becomes starkly Real—but inexplicable in terms of words and thought patterns. Metaphors, symbols, similes, and the context of those words, only allude to the Real indirectly, by inference, and therefore only veil, limit, or circumscribe concepts associated with the incommunicable.

In the process that leads to this Initiation, the meditator has learnt to bypass the Soul by having built consciousness-links *(antaḥkaraṇas)* to the spiritual triad *(manas, buddhi, ātma),* the planes of enlightenment that are rapidly becoming the Initiate's true home. They are the domains of the three levels of enlightenment: the *ālayavijñāna, śūnyatā,* and *dharmakāya* enlightenments. As a consequence, the Sambhogakāya Flower is no longer the onus of meditation. It can not bear the energies pouring down from the triad. It thus enters into a phase of radiant glorification, then a finalisation that can be likened to a supernova explosion, where the essence of all that it contained is absorbed into the Monad via the Śūnyatā Eye. This Monadic presence is the true human unit, a cosmic unit of Life that is a Buddha that leaves the confines of the earth-Womb after the higher Bodhisatttva *bhūmis* have been trodden. These *bhūmis* relate to the taking of the five higher Initiations, where a Buddha appears after the fifth.

The work of the candidate for the fourth Initiation has made potent

38 *Phil. 2:5-6.* 'Let this mind be in you, which was also in Christ Jesus: Who, being in the form of God, thought it not robbery to be equal with God'.

the fiery Light at the nucleus of the radiant Sun, which is the Soul-form, to such an extent that the substance composing its form has become intensely radiatory. Its energy field has then been brought to its critical state, annihilating the form. (This symbolism relates to that which brings about a nuclear explosion in the atomic world.) The Initiate is left utterly alone, devoid of all contacts associated with the former state of being: from the domain of enlightenment, the world of the personality, and also the comforting light of the Soul. That into which the Initiate is abstracted has only just become a home. Such a One has become a baby born into a new cosmos, of overpowering vastness. The Initiate is brought to the darkness that existed before the appearance of things to experience aloneness, separation from all that is familiar and what was formerly a comfort zone of activity. It 'momentarily' manifests as a form of meaningless, desolateness, and then expands into all-encompassing knowingness of the unitariness of the All—the Void experience depicted so well in Buddhist eschatological doctrine.

It was such an unspeakable state of experience that confronted Jesus, that it caused him to cry out at His death on the cross (in the ninth hour[39]): 'My God, my God, why hast thou forsaken me?'[40]

The demonstration of the livingness of 'God' was crucial to the exuberance of his dispensation, the central dynamo of his being, his only true companion, and now for one brief moment he knew what it was like to be without 'God'. He thus knew directly of That which was the root of evil and of its relation to the Law. He stood in darkness, where there was once light. He stood alone, bereft of all guidance, and yet that darkness was eternal Life.

The verse following immediately after Jesus 'gave up the ghost': 'and the veil of the temple was rent in twain from top to bottom',[41] explains in symbolic terms exactly what happened to him. Here *the temple* was not his Body (for it was not torn asunder), nor even the temple of Jerusalem, but the temple of the Soul, and it was the 'veil' of this temple, its outer form, that was rent.

The information provided in Luke is similar to that given in Mark.

---

39 *Mark 15:34.*

40 *Ibid.*

41 *Mark 15:38.*

We find the statement that in 'the ninth hour':

> the sun was darkened, and the veil of the temple was rent in the midst. And when Jesus had cried with a loud voice, he said, Father, into thy hands I commend my spirit: and having said thus, he gave up the ghost.[42]

Here the Light of the 'sun' (symbolising the Soul of Jesus) was occluded, not by the clouds created by intellectual fogs and miasmas, for these did not exist in him, but by the potent intensity of the immutable Light of the Spirit aspect (the Father). Its intensity is such that it is completely incomprehensible to the intellect. It is absolute, the unknowable, the *dharmakāya,* that puts into shadow all lesser forms of (intelligible) light. The night sky, which veils the potency of countless billions of radiant stars and galaxies, is the symbol of this. It concerns the Spirit aspect of a person, the start of that cosmic journey that produces complete Identification with the Father. Therefore, it is that to which Jesus could now (after the crises of darkness) unhesitatingly and with full understanding proffer His Spirit.

The number *nine* here ('the ninth hour') refers to the Initiation process, for esoterically, there are nine of these associated with solar evolution preceding the level of becoming a cosmic Man, a planetary Logos, the Lord of Life for a planetary system. They relate to the nine months (or 'hours') of gestation in the Womb of Nature. The phrase therefore signifies the time of undertaking of an important Initiation by Jesus.

In the garden of Gethsemane, the night before the crucifixion, Jesus knew he must give of himself utterly to do the will of his Father,[43] which the Initiate learns increasingly to do from the third Initiation onwards. He thus told his disciples that his 'Soul is exceeding sorrowful even unto death'[44] and three times prayed and stated the same words: 'Father, all things are possible unto thee; take away this *cup* from me; nevertheless not what I will, but what thou wilt'.[45] Three times he affirmed his absolute faith in the divine providence of the Kingdom

42 *Luke 23:44-6.*

43 *Matt. 26:36-44.*

44 *Mark 14:34.*

45 *Mark 14:36,* and see also *Luke 22:42* and *Matt. 26:39.*

of 'God'. The word *cup* here symbolises the Soul, which has been the receptacle of all Love and Light rayed into it from the Spirit. It has been filled with the result of the Soul's manifold experiences for ages, both in the human and angelic realms, and has given abundantly of that Love and experience to all beings.[46] Now, what was left—the Unknown? Jesus knew this veiled his next revelation, and yet it was also a source of inner distress to sacrifice that which was his most cherished possession.

The Divine Will

We saw previously that Jesus was ready to completely abandon any inkling of personal will so that the Divine Will could be accomplished. He had to sacrifice everything to fulfil the objective of that Will. After He completed the above prayer 'there appeared an angel unto him from heaven, strengthening him. And being in an agony he prayed more earnestly: and his sweat was as it were great drops of blood falling down to the ground'.[47]

The angel is an emissary from Shambhala, conveying unto Jesus potent energies that 'strengthened him'.[48] This strengthening process is effectively a consolidation of the Divine Will manifesting in Jesus, for this Will, the first Ray aspect of Deity, must be developed by the Initiate if advancement into *śūnyatā* and then the *dharmakāya* is to be achieved. Receptivity to this Will of the Father is therefore what liberates one from the thrall of *saṃsāra*. By this means the highest energies can be expressed on earth via the medium of the Initiate. To do so, he/she must completely eliminate any vestige of personality will (desire-ambition). Divine Will is essentially the Destroyer-Regenerator aspect of Deity, and causes the tearing asunder of the 'veil of the temple', effecting the liberation of the Initiate from the trammels of the material world. This liberating energy transmutes our base elements into the elixir of immortality. It is therefore the energy that must be invoked if the fourth Initiation is to be accomplished.

---

46 See also *Luke 22:20,* which states: 'This cup is the new testament in my blood, which is shed for you'.

47 *Luke 22:43-4.*

48 In Buddhist terminology this angel would be termed a *ḍākinī.*

Divine Will can only proceed from a vehicle that is already vibrant in its expression of Love-Wisdom and fully endowed in compassionate action. This Will is expressed as the power that can cause the objective appearance of phenomena and then its subjectivisation. Compassion must be the basis of its expression if the person is to travel upon the right hand path. Divine Will is the direct exponential expression of energy that can eliminate all obstacles barring the consummation of the (evolutionary) Plan. The strengthening of Jesus was therefore one of the momentous points in his life, of which the *crucifixion* was the aftermath. It was subjectively accomplished at Gethsemane. This was symbolised by the potent imagery of the sweat that fell as 'great drops of blood', and which happened objectively on the cross.

This Blood was effectively the descent of wine-red cosmic astral energy that is the driving potency of *bodhicitta*. It was poured into the substance of the earth by means of the expression of the 'sweating' of this Blood. It was the end result of a cosmological process that awakened the *bīja* of the cycle of Love for this planet within the context of the era of developing mind. It is something for which his brother Gautama laid the foundation for through his wisdom teachings based upon a conception of the nature of *śūnyatā*. The experience of *śūnyatā* is what is attained at the fourth Initiation at the death of the Soul-form. Jesus demonstrated exoterically the symbolism of the method needed to be attained by Initiates if they too are to experience the Void. He thus exemplified the full rigour of the Bodhisattva path, which led to his crucifixion. It was this energy of *bodhicitta* (the Will-of-Love[49]) that was poured into the substance of the planet, that will eventually cause the liberation of all sentient beings. This is the esoteric interpretation of the Christian concept that Jesus died to atone for our sins, as first uttered by John the Baptist:

> The next day John seeth Jesus coming to him, and saith, Behold the Lamb of God, which taketh away the sin of the world.[50]

---

49 The Will-of-Love is the compassionate drive empowering the activity of the Bodhisattva, whereas Divine Will adds the Shambhalic impetus preparing the Initiate to travel upon the cosmic paths away from earth evolution.

50 *John 1:29*. See also *1John 1:4-7*.

After this sacrificial act we then have the explosion of the *prajñāpāramitā* teachings of Mahāyāna Buddhism, that properly explicate the doctrine of *śūnyatā*. All it needed was for those that followed Jesus to be reborn in the Buddhist religion to push forward the next step of the Hierarchical plan for the education and the liberation of humanity. We are now at the dawn of the next major expansion of the *maṇḍala* that developed from this *bīja*, in the new second Ray era that is poised to supplant this present ruthless epoch of mind, once humanity have digested the effects of massed selfishness and materialism. The future for humanity portends well, though the process necessitates educative suffering, as massed evil *karma* is adjudicated and cleansed from the face of the earth.

In his past Incarnation, the Christ-Jesus completed the revelation of the nature of Love, which has been given to humanity since the beginning of evolution and has slowly unfolded within them. In fact, all was planned since before 'the foundation of the world'.[51] He also gave us an insight into the nature of Divine Will as it can be expressed by humanity. This is also part of the context of the seventeenth Chapter of John's Gospel.[52]

By means of his 'strengthened agony', Jesus could express the first Ray energy in such a way that the collective 'third eye' of humanity can eventually be opened, though almost imperceptibly so at first. It

---

51 *John 17:24*. 'Father, I will that they also, whom thou hast given me, be with me where I am; that they might behold my glory, which thou hast given me: for thou lovest me before the foundation of the world'.

52 Careful reflection of this chapter will well reward the earnest student concerning the nature of the relation of the high Initiate to the disciples that have formed around him. (In this case demonstrating the twelve petals of a Heart centre.) He is 'glorified in them' *(John 17:10)*. 'I have given them thy word, and the world hath hated them; because they are not of the world, even as I am not of this world' *(John 17:14)*. This is because they are all members of the Hierarchy of Light, Bodhisattvas that have come to change people for the better, as a consequence they can only expect enmity from those that fear change. Nevertheless, Jesus prayed to his Father 'not that thou shouldest take them out of the world, but that thou shouldest keep them from the evil' *(John 17:15)*; to protect them from dark brotherhood predations ('the evil'), whilst manifesting service work for humanity. We also have such phrases as 'And the glory which thou gavest me I have given them; that they may be one, even as we are one: I in them, and thou in me, that they may be made perfect in one'. *(John17:21-22)*.

laid the foundation for the expression of the energies and revelations that will produce the future bringing down and anchoring on the earth of the City of 'God', the New Jerusalem *(Shambhala).* It has allowed the expression of the energy that will give humanity the opportunity to manifest 'greater works'[53] than were accomplished by Jesus. This will eventually bring about such radical changes upon the earth that 'a new heaven and a new earth'[54] will be formed. It will be part of the effect of the exoteric manifestation of the heavenly City. The foundations for this will be accomplished in the new era, when everywhere small groups will be able to demonstrate the energy of Will in a unified manner, and not just singularly, as in the case of the world's past ages.

The incarnation of the Head of the Hierarchy in the form of Christ-Maitreya will bring the revelation of what the Divine Will really means, as far as it can be expressed by humanity. Though the seed to this revelation has been slowly developing during the past 2,000 years (particularly so since the twentieth century), people still little realise what this, the 'Father' aspect of Deity signifies. They think of the will in terms of its destructive, war-like attributes, or in the form of strong desire. They know of the will to achieve or to overcome obstacles, a stubborn determination in the face of adversity, usually manifested via materialistic or egoistic objectives. These forms of self-will are embryonic states of the will, and have far yet to evolve before the Divine Will can manifest. They must be translated into the Will-to-Know the all, good will, the Will-to-Love, and then transmuted by consciousness into the Will-of-Love *(bodhicitta).* The Will can then be used to directly master the properties of substance (the development of *siddhis)* and to direct the evolution of lives in space. From this then derives the Divine Will that allows one to master the eternal verities of space and time.

The collectivisation of the Will by a nation or group of nations to

---

53 *John 14:12*. 'Verily, verily, I say unto you, He that believeth on me, the works that I do shall he do also; and greater works than these shall he do; because I go to my Father'. So it has been and will continue to be, as the millennia pass and the Initiations that were possible in Jesus' time become superseded. Thus greater accomplishments ('miracles', *siddhis)* were fulfilled, for instance, by the great *yogins* of India and Tibet. Nothing is static, everything evolves together, and the evolutionary Light marches on towards Shambhala.

54 *Rev. 21:1.*

achieve an end, rather than around a charismatic figure, is another development of the will worthy of consideration. It was, for instance, the will to win of the allies, to prevent the human race from falling into abject slavery, that defeated the Axis nations in the second World War. It was a collective (almost one-pointed) force that was generated. That force was comparatively unselfish, thus differing from personality will, which is effectively an expression of strong desire. This unselfishness united the entire world to fight a common evil, and therefore produced victory. It is said to have caused a downpour of energies from the Kingdom of 'God' that strengthened the determination, insight, and courage of those that were fighting for the common good.[55] The force was then channelled by the collective vision of what the world would be like under the domination of the Axis powers, versus the free world that would be produced by the allies if they had won. This was the major vision that allowed the allies (the 'forces of Light') to be victorious, for the force of Will is always associated with a long-range vision of the accomplished work. It is a force that synthesises and abstracts, that inevitably means the death of the form (of which the destructive potency of modern explosives is an agent), freeing the life within and allowing it to expand in consciousness.

Divine Will concerns the whole, rather than the individual or group. Desire-ambition on the other hand, ever feeds the form, and is separative in its effect, for the object of desire is taken from all else by the one who desires.

Groups of Initiates will later evolve in our nations to mobilise collective force via mantra to produce certain objective creative effects that will be considered magical, impossible by average humanity. The use of collective will to establish *maṇḍalas* of power for altruistic purposes will be based upon sound esoteric knowledge of all principles concerned. In this way work the Hierarchy of enlightened being, and upon a vaster scale, a Logos and His immediate emissaries.

When the same type of energy and motivation that defeated the Axis nations is again generated by humanity and constructively put to peaceful and mutually beneficial purposes, then nothing can prevent

55 See the book by A.A. Bailey, *The Externalisation of the Hierarchy* (Lucis Press, New York, 1981) for detail.

the exoteric manifestation of the 'City of God'. This then portends the united journeying of humanity into the immensity of the astounding universe. Certainly the invocation of such a unified Will by those of good will, and visionaries, is again sorely needed, because the forces of evil have insidiously struck back. This has happened mainly via the tyranny of the Western banking system and the debt-ridden fiat money they propagate, coupled with the Corporate and militaristic power of the Fascist[56] hegemony of the USA and its allies.

The cross of Life

There is a literal gap in consciousness between the lower and abstract minds that has to be bridged by means of the construction of the consciousness-link, the *antaḥkaraṇa,* before the third Initiation is possible. This represents the onus of attainment of primordial substance, moving from that which is truly empirical to that which is capable of transcending the bounds of time limitations, to integrate many aspects of thought into a oneness. It represents the proper deification of substance. The mechanism is the evolution and development of the man-plant, of the consciousness bearing principle that could transmute concretions of form into the lighted substance of Mind.

At the fourth Initiation there is a similar 'gap' to bridge, between Mind and that which is no-mind (the Void). As this is accomplished, then the complete death of the 'self' concept happens, even that of the subtle form of the 'self', the Soul. Yet at the same time lucid awareness remains. This bridge that integrates *saṃsāra* with *śūnyatā* I call the *śūnyatā-saṃsāra* nexus in the earlier volumes of this *Treatise on Mind.* We see here that the Void is not empty, in the nihilistic sense. It is replete with the essence of Mind, but that Mind is stilled, is simply observant, residing in its natural state. Thus it is Void of images or objects of perception. The intense (cool) luminosity of the energy field that underlies all space is experienced. The term for this energy field in

56 Fascism is the merger of Corporate power with government, where the moneyed elite rule over and dictate the life of the great majority. Under the façade of democracy, a powerful elite of demagogues thereby rule our Western nations. This avaricious force, 'the evil', must once again be strenuously fought by all means available by all those bearing the energy of good will.

Buddhist Sanskrit is *bodhi* (the state of being enlightened, presciently aware and serenely cognisant). It is a compassionate (blue) energy because it is an aspect of the integrated universal whole, the oneness that is the All.

When turned towards *saṃsāra,* then the substance of mind *(citta)* is organised by it, according to the object of focus. Thus we have the term *bodhicitta,* the compassionate universal Mind that is made potent to organise *saṃsāra* into a *maṇḍala* of oneness. This is the state of readiness or non-dual alertness that is the *śūnyatā-saṃsāra* nexus. It is the compassionate Mind absorbed in its own serene field of energy dynamics that moves not, unless there is a need to act. The dynamic non-movement (dynamic because it is an intense energy field on its own level) of the space of this Mind depicts the Void *(śūnyatā).* When there is an object of action there is the appearance of the phenomena of *saṃsāra.* When attuned to the zone whereby space is organised, there is the universal Mind. The domain of the spiritual triad represents the cosmic ethers, wherein exist the *nāḍīs* of a Logos. They provide a vast stream of revelation for those that can correlate the *nāḍī* and *chakra* system of a human unit to that of cosmos.

The *śūnyatā-saṃsāra* nexus is the junction that interrelates the two domains of Mind. The limitations that *saṃsāra* represents to a conscious mind must become transmogrified, and the result abstracted via the experience of that which is void of mind into the universal Mind. What is accomplished in *saṃsāra* therefore is not lost, it is not annihilated, simply stripped bare of its phenomenological aspect and abstracted into a vaster domain of Mind. The attributes of mind inevitably become Void Elements (*bījas* of revelation) that contain the imprint of whatever was. They can be resuscitated in a future time to produce what must be upon a subtler, transformed level of expression.

Up to the third Initiation the person principally learns to express the force of Love. First personality love, and then the Will-to-Love, and finally the Will-of-Love. This brings the Initiate within the portals of the Hierarchy of enlightened being. From the third Initiation onwards, it is the force of will that the Initiate must consciously embrace. This eventually enables him/her to stand within the Council Chamber, the Head centre of the planetary Logos (Shambhala) and therein gain Initiation.

As stated, by his emphasis upon detachment to all material things the Buddha paved the way for the Initiation of Renunciation, allowing Jesus to embody it by manifesting the glorifying act of sacrifice by dying on the cross. By this Jesus manifested the next stage of the will's development—receptivity to the Divine Will.

The symbol of this ultimate detachment, as well as the originating attachment, the *cross,* is a very ancient symbol, long antedating the Christian era. It has always referred to the material world, to the burden of the physical body, to the earth and the four directions in space. Jesus therefore died upon the cross of materiality, the cross of his passions and desires, and sacrificed them for humanity.

The originating appearance of a cross is the effect of the expression of the Divine Will by a creative Logos to establish the four directions of space that must be conquered and circumscribed by a self-limiting sphere of activity, if a world sphere is to occur. Thus the earth is symbolised astrologically by a plain cross, enclosed within a circle. Once established, the four cardinal directions of the cross come to be guarded (protected) by cosmological entities, the four Guardians of space. Thus we have the four 'beasts' of the book of *Revelation*[57] and the four Maharajas of Hinduism and Buddhism. This entire philosophy is vast and lies outside the scope of this present treatise.

What Jesus did when dying on this cross was to counter the expulsive creative process associated with material evolution, thus producing the triumph of its purpose. He became liberated from the *maṇḍala* of formed space originally set up by the creative Logos, embodying thereby the gain of it all, the countering mantra to concretion.

The meanings of the directions of the arms of this fixed cross have been adequately explained in the previous volumes of this treatise. The *northern* direction represents the direction upwards to divinity, the Kingdom of 'God'. Alternatively, it represents the descent of the Life stream into manifestation, to where it reaches a quiescent point from which activity can commence. The *eastern* arm represents the direction inwards to the Heart of Life. (The Hierarchy of enlightened being.) The

---

57 *Rev. 4:6-9.* Speaking of the throne of 'God': 'And before the throne *there was* a sea of glass like unto crystal: and in the midst of the throne, and round about the throne, were four beasts full of eyes before and behind'.

southern arm represents the descent of the creative process downwards into the field of activity represented by the little ones toiling in strife (all sentient beings). The *western* arm represents the outward direction to humanity via the act of Bodhisattvic service.

The east-west polarisation (representing the two hands of the crucified one) point to the two modes of religious development on earth. One leads to inward contemplation and meditation (espoused by Buddhism)—the revelation of the inner 'God'. The other leads to outer observation and devotion to the works of 'God' (the focus of Christianity and the other religions of 'the book').

They join near the point where the crucified one was stabbed by the spear of the soldier (representing carnal, ignorant humanity). The spear was aimed inwards towards the heart, and the objective was to see if the crucified one had died. This symbolises the inner quest for the principle of Life, the Void (*śūnyatā*) that signifies the death of all personality attributes. The one on the cross, however, represented the outward method that was exemplified in Jesus' life. Humanity can choose either method, but they use crude methodology to do so—the spear wielded by the soldier. It signifies the use of elementary will to try to pry open the heart to see what it reveals. At this level the knowledge gained was minimal, releasing the Blood of Life mixed with water.[58]

The religious dispensation that flowed from the Heart of the Christ caused both the compassionate, enlightening doctrine (Blood), plus that which dilutes the doctrine and mixes it with the distorting desire principle (water). Blood and water thus symbolise the properties of the *buddhic* and emotional realms of perception. The highly purified, receptive, and aligned emotional body utilises the creative imagination. It then waters down the richness of *buddhic* perception (the Blood, *bodhicitta)* so that people engrossed in the *māyā* of the world can be stimulated by the story of Christ-Jesus' sacrifice. This *māyā* (delusion) is the effect of people's basic emotionality, and was symbolised by the *vinegar* that the soldier gave the anointed one on the cross, the taste of which literally killed him.[59]

58 See *John 19:34.*

59 *John 19:29-30.*

The northern point of the cross represents the Spirit aspect of the crucified one. The point of juncture between all the arms represents the Soul aspect; and the southern arm, where the feet were nailed together, symbolises the matter aspect. The feet walk upon the plains of the earth, from which the gain of *saṃsāric* activity is derived. Though the crucified one is personally liberated, the Bodhisattva vow ties him/her irrevocably to *saṃsāra,* where compassion is directed to uplift those thereon that are bound to *māyā*. In this line of vertical descent we therefore have the triune Spirit-Soul-form that is the integral reality of a human unit.

By being nailed, the two hands and feet were bonded to the form of the cross, immovable and fixed in space, whilst the head was crowned with the thorns resulting from the accomplishment of the Bodhisattvic service amongst humanity. The 'thorns' represent the effects of the critical minds, ignorant reactions, and animosity directed towards the transforming agent in their midst. They cannot bear the thought that their opinions and approaches to divinity may be fallacious, or of what this agent represents. Their thoughts and desires but serve to feed the separative 'self' concept, whereas the Bodhisattva has come to liberate them from such concepts. Therefore, the threat to their complacent attitudes must be 'crowned' in this way. It becomes a laurel of honour for the enlightened one, the spiritual king in their midst. It is the reward that blind, ignorant humanity dispenses to those that come to raise them beyond the vales of illusion and self-engendered suffering. Thus is the lord of Life, the compassionate one, effectively sacrificed upon the tree of knowing of good and evil. It is the long eventual gain, and atonement for Eve's initial eating of the forbidden fruit in the garden of Eden.

The head esoterically depicts a circle symbolising the Ineffable, from which comes a vertical line, showing the descent of Spirit into matter. This is the *sūtrātmā* or 'Life-line', the thin stream of spiritual substance that gives each cell in 'the Logoic Body' Life and an apparent nominal 'separate' existence. In humanity we see that a point of balance has been established that has allowed the 'God within' to expand in consciousness. This provides humanity a horizontal life of expansive inclusiveness and a giving outwards of Light and Love to the kingdoms of Nature. (Symbolised by the outstretched arms of the Christ on the cross.)

Eventually all Life is drawn back to divinity by means of projecting the *antaḥkaraṇa* along the line that the *sūtrātmā* descended.

The Heart of Jesus has sometimes been pictured as a flower *(chakra),* a many-petalled rose, ever-expanding and rapidly growing in opalescent splendour as it bathes in the light of the spiritual sun. It gives that light as colour, nectar and perfume, for all to behold and enjoy.

The crucifixion is the result of the work of the Christ within us,[60] and also of the planetary Christ (the Bodhisattva), who can vow: 'And I, if I be lifted up from the earth, will draw all *men* unto me'.[61] This uplifting is the result of a definite non-materialistic scientific approach whereby *'all men'* will eventually be transfigured and transfixed upon the fixed cross of the heavens. It refers to a state of consciousness that is withdrawn and steadfast in purpose, and yet it is a state of all-pervasive and all-giving boundless compassion, of looking ever-downwards (to those in pain). It produces the flow of spiritual force and Love onwards and outwards to humanity. It is effected by means of the Blood of the Christ emanating from the heart, hands and feet: from the wounds inflicted by people on the one upon the cross:

- His *Heart*—the source of active compassion, the experiencing of the causes of the suffering of others, revealing the realisation of the means whereby the sufferings can be remedied.
- His *Hands*—with which he must heal and give.
- His *Feet*—which must take him over hard and stony ground to wherever he is needed.

All the while the Initiate refuses to move from the cross of self-sustained suffering and joy, until all within the embrace of his/her compassionate-Mind have been unfettered from their chains and have been lifted and exalted. Such is the Path of the Bodhisattva that eventually produces the highest bliss. All who wish to follow the Christ must bear the burden of this cross.

---

60 *Col. 1: 26-27. 'Even* the mystery which hath been hid from ages and from generations, but now is made manifest to his saints: To whom God would make known what *is* the riches among the Gentiles; which is Christ in you, the hope of glory'.

61 *John 12:32.*

For many lives the spiritual being gradually mounts this cross, as symbolised by all the events from the scourging to the crucifixion of Jesus. The Initiate must undergo each stage internally, until eventually at the fourth Initiation he/she is impaled upon it. The renunciation process is then complete. The Initiate cannot travel north to higher revelation, for the groundwork for full residence in Shambhala has not yet been laid. Further travelling the direction east is not possible, because full residence in the Heart of Life has already been established. The Initiate cannot travel south because *saṃsāra* offers no appeal. Travelling west is also not possible because the little ones the Initiate has come to serve have rejected the gifts offered, and have thereby placed the crucified one upon the cross.

The Initiate thus responds to all four directions in an equanimous manner, truly following the middle way in all activities. However, from the elevated position upon this cross of sacrificial service, the Initiate has always looked downwards upon those of the world and their sufferings, and has striven to relieve that suffering by showing them how to focus upon Love and Light. By turning one's back upon the source of one's own advancement, one paradoxically advances. Humanity are unresponsive to the effect of the energy of Love at the level the Initiate knows of it, and yet skilful means must be used to somehow educate them, despite their reticence to change. The difficulties encountered upon such a path, and the observation of the path of pain and woe pursued by the ignorant, becomes 'the fellowship of the Christ's sufferings' for the one upon this cross.[62] He/she cannot be taken from it until those that can do so have appeared. The Initiate thus becomes a steadfast, adamantine, vehicle of Love and active service.

The crucifixion experience thus signifies the essence of the *Great Symbol (mahāmudrā)*[63] actively portrayed by the Bodhisattva. Every

---

62 *Phil. 3:8-11.* 'Yea, doubtless, and I count all things *but* loss, for the excellency of knowledge of Christ Jesus my Lord: for whom I have suffered the loss of all things, and do count them *but* dung, that I may win Christ...That I may know him, and the power of his resurrection, and the fellowship of his sufferings, being made conformable unto his death; If by any means I might attain unto the resurrection of the dead'.

63 *Mahāmudrā,* literally 'great seal'. The Great Symbol, referring to the state of the attainment of Buddhahood. It is a *mudrā* (gesture) because realisation of the

life becomes a renunciation, a sacrificial ritual of active enlightenment, unfolded in such a way that the greatest benefit is accrued by the greatest number possible, as gauged by karmic limitation. Every action becomes a *mudrā*[64] of the path to enlightenment, it becomes the symbol of the path itself, for all to view and partake of. The Bodhisattva path is thus fully demonstrated by the Initiate of this degree.

The Initiate's vision is now turned to the fundamental source of being/non-being, as the former types of identifications and attachments no longer exist. Freedom from *saṃsāric* allurement is a *fiat accompli.* Standing at the intersection of the arms of the cross, the Initiate can relate one arm to the other with equanimity. This Lord of Compassion, stands steadfast in the ability to merge the qualities of 'this' and 'That', being and non-being, form and space, the inner and the outer universe. All dualities, perceptible or imperceptible are merged. The Initiate can meet the needs of others without being karmically knotted in the transaction. Fundamentally, therefore, the fount of the Initiate's activity is the Void of all knowable attributes and qualities, equated with *śūnyatā.*

The sacrifice of everything for the benefit of all, the one divine Life, produces death of all (limiting) forms, be they subtle or gross, that separate one from union with That which is the source of Love in this world. In Buddhist Tantricism, such union is symbolised by the *yab-yum* (copulative) position assigned to their highest Buddhas of meditation (such as *Vajrasattva)* with their complementary female energy. It is also the *yin-yang* conjugation of the Taoist philosophy, and

---

three bodies of a Buddha in one is sealed in supreme unchanging bliss. It involves realisation of enlightenment in one lifetime through the 'seal' that integrates the masculine compassion with the feminine wisdom aspect. In the Kagyu tradition, it denotes the experiential attainment of the Buddha-Mind. The absoluteness of being/non-being, which unites all duality, male and female into a unity, completeness. This Symbol can be depicted as the cypher zero, and involves the sum of the entire cause-effect world play, as it impresses itself upon consciousness. Note that a 'seal' also signifies a *chakra* that is completely mastered, hence 'sealed' during the process of gaining Buddhahood. Attaining the fourth Initiation (the *śūnyatā* enlightenment) is effectively the realisation of the Great Symbol, that is carried to fruition at the sixth Initiation (Buddhahood).

64 *Mudrā,* A hand gesture signifying a state of enlightenment.

the *Śiva-Śakti* union of the Hindu Tantricism.[65] In such union is the Will-of-Love known to Initiates wrought.

The concern here is not sexual union known to humans, as that is but a metaphor of the process where the masculine (human) principle weds with the feminine *(deva)* principle. The concern is the process that produces the union between units of two self-conscious kingdoms in Nature. The marriage begins at the fourth Initiation and is consummated at the sixth. The *iḍā* and *piṅgalā nāḍīs* in Nature thus wed to liberate *suṣumṇā*. Having been utterly emptied of any vestige of personality will or desire, there is naught but complete receptivity to the omnipotence of the Divine in such Initiates. This 'omnipotence' is to produce the mergence of these two parallel streams incorporated within the one body of manifestation. Bliss is produced when it is expressed through the personality vehicle, fecundating it with the *dharma*. This bliss is but the ability to command potent energies that can influence far larger numbers of beings than ever before, both physically and on the subtler levels of perception. Being totally consecrated to the task of enlightening others, fourth degree Initiates can begin to consciously express the Divine Will.

The fifth Initiation: the Ascension/Revelation

This Initiation is generally called the *Ascension*, but is more correctly termed the *Revelation*, because the Initiate becomes a resident of Shambhala, the seat of the highest spiritual energies, and experiences the revelations pertaining to *dharmakāya*. The purpose of the multidimensional universe, the variegated interrelation of the various kingdoms of Nature, and the mode of expression of the Mind of Deity, are revealed. Knowledge of the laws of being/non-being is then wielded with effectiveness along the sub-ray line the Initiate embodies. The Initiate can say as Jesus did: 'All power is given unto me in heaven and

65 Such union, as far as the Buddhist philosophy is concerned, is well explained by Lama Anagarika Govinda in *Foundations of Tibetan Mysticism*, (Samuel Weiser, Maine, 1982), 97-98. It is one of the most valuable works on Tibetan philosophy presented to the West.

in earth'.[66] The knowledge of the cycles and conditionings associated with the three worlds of human perception, as well as every Element and force, can thus be commanded and utilised to benefit all. Such a one is termed a Master of Wisdom, a Jīvanmukta, or fully awakened one.

Further background information will now be presented concerning the planes of perception *(lokas)* so that one can comprehend what is actually mastered, and what the Initiate comes to be liberated from. There are seven planes constituting the sub-planes of the cosmic dense physical plane. Through these planes all Life in the solar system must progressively evolve. Of these, the lowest three are relegated to *saṃsāra.* The domains of *saṃsāra* are patterned upon the reality of how cosmos is organised. *Saṃsāra* is but the mirror image of the Real, where the fourth plane of perception, *buddhi (śūnyatā),* represents the mirror, hence the Mirror-like Wisdom of Akṣobhya, which qualifies the nature of *śūnyatā*. This Wisdom can reflect the attributes of cosmos into *saṃsāra* without adulteration, in accordance to the truth of the fact of the ancient hermetic axiom 'that which is above is as below'. *Saṃsāra* is built upon the paradigm of the Real, 'the above'.

Figure 3 (on page 280) summarises the information concerning the planes of perception. What is represented are the seven sub-planes of the cosmic dense physical plane. These seven sub-planes are also termed the seven systemic planes because they constitute the planes of perception delineated and circumscribed by our solar Logos at the beginning of the evolutionary process *(mahamanvantara)*, through which all incorporated lesser lives evolve through to Buddhahood. Above the seven systemic planes stand the seven sub-planes of the cosmic astral plane, through which *nirvāṇees* from earth spheres such as the one we presently reside in travel to various stellar destinations to gain the higher Initiations that will enable them to become Logoi. Above the cosmic astral are the seven sub-planes of the cosmic mental, wherein the 'Mind of God' exists. This is subdivided into a concrete and abstract portion, as is our systemic mental plane. With planes of perception beyond this I shall not herein deal.

All of the planes are divided into septenaries. The three *saṃsāric lokas* are the dense physical, the astral, and the mental. Of these, the mental and the dense physical are dual. The dense physical has four

---

66 *Matt. 28:18.*

etheric sub-planes, and three earthy. The etheric sub-planes contain the *nāḍī* system of a human unit. The mental possesses three higher, abstracted sub-planes and four concreted, whilst the second sub-plane of the abstract mental is the domain of the Sambhogakāya Flower.

The fourth plane of perception is *buddhi*. The three planes of perception above *buddhi* are termed *ātma, anupādaka* and *ādi*. *Ātma* and *ādi* are also dual. The five alchemical Elements (Earth, Water, Fire, Air and Aether) constitute the substance of the five lower planes of manifestation, whilst the substance of the higher two are too rarefied to be part of the reckoning of empirical minds. The manifestation of the five Elements concern the planes of causation, wherein the *karma* of the sum of *saṃsāra* conditions evolutionary space.

This manifestation of *karma* by a Logos that utilises substance from a past evolutionary space is considered the first Outpouring of the Creative impulse of Deity. The base substance emanates from the plane *ātma*, and is eventually resolved therein. This third plane of perception (counting from above down) is the plane of emanation and resolution of *karma*. This is an important consideration. It is organised by means of rotary activity causing the formation of the planes of perception incorporated into the globes of activity whereon Life must find scope for evolution. This substance is *Fiery* in nature, and concerns the evolution of the way of mind by means of the consolidation into the forms that the various streams of life come to occupy. It is an aspect of the work of the *third Logos*, the *Great Mother*, and has as its basis the unfoldment of the five instincts and senses. The third Logos externalises Herself upon the *ātmic* plane (the fifth from below upwards). From *ātma* thus manifests the primordial *karma* that instigates all conditioning activity of the lives manifesting upon these planes. *Karma* governs by way of the evolution of all attributes of mind/Mind, which is the fifth principle counting from above down. It is also considered 'the fifth' when counting from below up, when the major subdivisions of the planes of *saṃsāra* are taken into account. We thus have the concrete dense, the etheric subdivision, the astral, the concrete and abstract subdivisions of the mind.

The second Outpouring represents the emanation of the streams of conscious Lives that are to undergo evolutionary attainment by utilising the substance built into the *maṇḍala* of a Logoic Body of manifestation. This emanates via the plane *anupādaka,* and it also incorporates the Monadic Life governing the evolution of each human unit. These streams of differentiated consciousness are the lighted Lives, the expansive unfoldment of the *Son* in incarnation. This outpouring of the myriad Lives constitutes the various kingdoms of Nature, thus the emanation of the *Creative Hierarchies.*[67] These Hierarchies en-Soul all forms. In turn they activate the petals of the *chakras* in the Logoic body. Their activity is controlled at first by the Solar Plexus centre, and later, by the twelve petals of the Logoic Heart centre, of which the Hierarchies are emanations. This concerns the awakening of consciousness, the spiral-cyclic motion that governs the work of the *Son or Second Logos,* externalised upon the plane *anupādaka.*

The third Outpouring emanates from the first Logos (as per Figure 3)—the *Father* or Will aspect, externalising Himself upon the first plane, *ādi.* This Will, or Fiery Life, is the abstracting impulse of the *Father.* At first it helps produce the Individualisation process of an animal kingdom into the human by means of the formation of the kingdom of the Sambhogakāya Flower upon the higher mental plane. Consequently, we have the evolution of the fourth kingdom in Nature along the path that leads to Initiation. This outpouring then involves the nature of the descent of Logoic Mind into manifestation at the appropriate cycle to assist in the liberation of the Lives undergoing evolutionary progress. For the third and subsequent Initiations of humans, such energy manifests via the Rod of Initiation held in the hand of the One Initiator (Sanat Kumāra), the Lord governing Shambhala. This is part of the ceremony of Initiation which fully awakens Initiates into the Mysteries concerning the level of attainment *(loka)* that they have mastered. In this manner, humans eventually become embodied Deity.

There is a vast philosophy hidden here, much of which remains the secret of Initiation, but a significant amount has been revealed

---

67 Of which there are twelve to this solar system. Five have passed into obscuration, and seven find space for evolutionary attainment via these planes of perception. They are explained in *Esoteric Astrology* by A.A. Bailey. Humanity represents the fourth of these counting from below up and the ninth from above down.

in the books by A.A. Bailey,[68] and somewhat previously by Helena Blavatsky. More shall be provided in my future books. It is important in this era of revelation for prospective Initiates to consider that for which they aspire, and which is veiled under the rubric of the terms 'enlightenment' and 'liberation'.

Each Initiation signifies the mastery of one of the planes of perception. The first Initiation accedes the Initiate comprehension of the mysteries of physical plane activity, and the nature of its etheric substratum. The second Initiation produces revelation as to the nature of the Watery astral domain, the qualities of the lesser *siddhis,* the nature of life in the heaven and hell states of the various religions, and the way that Love governs the evolution of the all. The third Initiation produces mastery of the domain of mind/Mind, including the mysteries associated with the Sambhogakāya Flower and the *ālayavijñāna* environment it resides in. The fourth Initiation produces mastery of the qualities of the fourth cosmic ether, thus comprehension of the mysteries of the *chakra* system embodied by a Logos. The *nāḍīs* purveying this system convey various cosmic energies that the fourth degree Initiate becomes cogniscent of in this *śūnyatā* environment.

By mastering the qualities of the *ātmic* plane, a Master of Wisdom has consequently gained revelation of the sum of the processes concerning evolutionary Life. This includes full access to the nature of the Logoic Mind that brought to fruition the first Outpouring and all consequent events to the resolution of the *karma* of manifestation. We then have the basis of the nature of the *dharmakāya* experience at this (the lowest) level of its expression.

The information concerning the planes of perception can best be visualised as a series of concentric spheres of increasingly rarefied substance around a globe such as our earth. At first glance, we see that Figure 3 posits three outpourings of the Creative Essence from the Triune Deity.

---

68 See, for instance, *Initiation, Human and Solar,* and *The Rays and the Initiations,* both published by Lucis Press. A wealth of information is provided therein, for which this exposé is but an introduction.

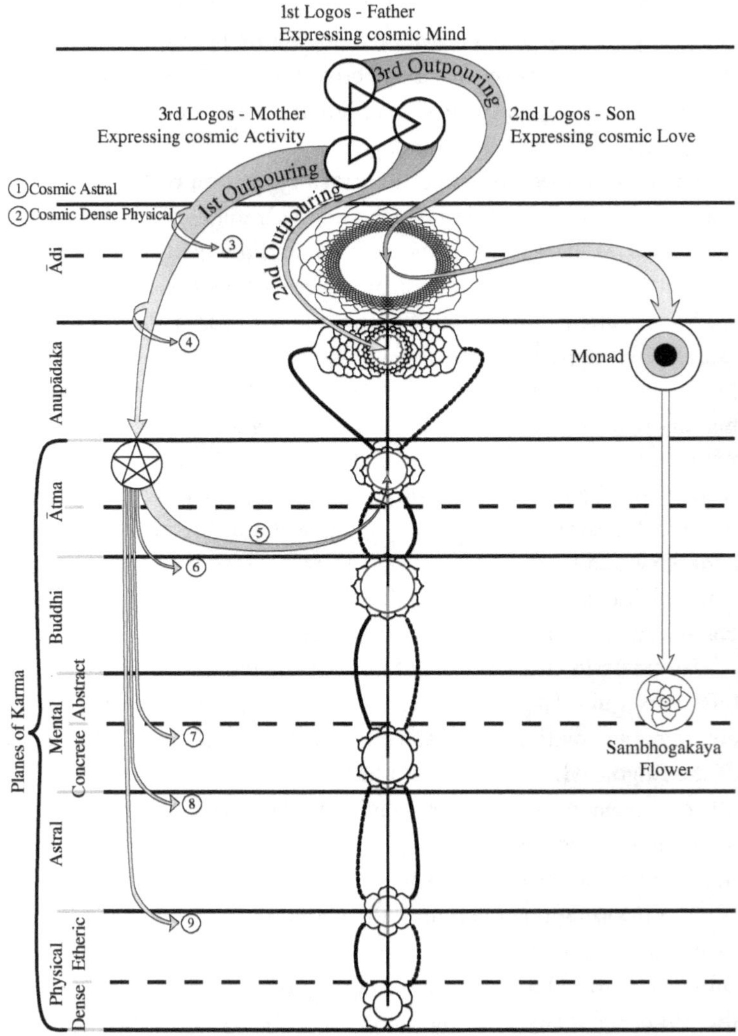

Figure 3. The three Outpourings

The figure shows a linear representation of the *chakras,* simply depicting the *chakras* that are the foci for the respective planes of perception, rather than where they actually exist. Like in a human body, their places of locality are the (cosmic) ethers. With respect to the constitution of Shambhala (the planetary Head centre), we see that the *ātmic* plane controls the potency of the planetary Throat centre, but the respective *prāṇas* are absorbed in the outer tier of petals of the Logoic Head centre, termed the Solar Plexus in the Head. The plane *anupādaka* governs the activity of the planetary Heart centre and the associated *prāṇas* are absorbed in the middle tier of petals of the Logoic Head centre called the Heart in the Head. The Ājñā centre upon this plane is simply the organ of vision of the Logos that is focussed via the Heart or Throat centres in order to govern the sum of planetary manifestation. The liberated lives that occupy these two centres then govern the evolutionary streams of the lives of the *chakras* situated below the diaphragm. The plane *ādi* supports the Throat in the Head, which integrates all of the energies in the Body of manifestation of the Logos and coordinates them with cosmic Purpose.

Notes to the Figure:

1. The *cosmic astral plane*, which is the sixth of seven cosmic planes counting from above down.
2. The *seven systemic planes*, whereon humanity finds scope for evolution in this solar system. These planes are sub-planes of the cosmic dense physical plane. The seven are divided into four etheric *(ādi, anupādaka, ātma* and *buddhi)* and three concrete (mental/Fiery, astral/Watery, and the Earthy etheric/dense) sub-planes. Each manifest as septenaries. The five planes from *ātma* down are termed the five planes of Brahmā (the Mother). Here the five sense-consciousnesses are developed and the Mind is evolved. The qualities of the five instincts are also developed.
3. Plane 1: *Ādi*. Initially, the first Outpouring establishes the primary substance of the sheaths of the increasingly dense matter of the seven planes. This substance is very tenuous for the first two planes of perception, and this outpouring of the forces of the Mother only properly comes into effect upon the third, or *ātmic* plane. This is symbolised by the pentagram enclosed in a circle, which implicates the five-ness of the domains governed by the Mind, from where we get the Wisdoms of the five Dhyāni Buddhas. *Ādi* is the plane of

the Father, where the full Head lotus (Shambhala) of the planetary Logos is found. It is integrated with the Ājñā centre upon the second plane. This Eye becomes the main organ of expression to empower and organise those evolving in the Body of manifestation of the Logos. The Head lotus provides access to those the planetary Logos has connection with in the solar system and in cosmos. The *Third* Outpouring proceeds via *ādi* to help effect the Initiation process of the various kingdoms of Nature. The lowest level of expression of Shambhala is found upon the *ātmic* plane, where the Creative Word of the Logos emanates from.

4. Plane 2: *Anupādaka.* Here resides the Monadic aspect of the human, or fourth Creative Hierarchy. The Monad is the Spirit or Father attribute to the human Life-stream. Each is intrinsically a Buddha that gains its omniscience as the human unit that is its vehicle (the *tathāgatagarbha, viz.* the Sambhogakāya Flower) undertakes its evolutionary journey and undergoes the Initiation process. At the sixth Initiation the objective for the sacrificial act of the Monadic Impulse has been fulfilled and a Buddha can return back into cosmic astral space. *Anupādaka* is the domain upon which the Lords of Shambhala are primarily focussed.
5. Plane 3: *Ātma.* Here the *maṇḍala* of the Logoic Thought Form first takes shape, which is known in Buddhist texts as the *dharmakāya.* It is objectivised by utilising past *karma* and is organised by means of mantra to which the *devas* that embody the substance of all forms automatically respond. Thus are the reverberations in the fabric of space set in motion that condition the appearance of all forms. The fifth degree Initiate masters all mantras associated with the Ray line that such a one is the custodian of. The appearance of a Master of Wisdom is the objective of human evolution. Such a one directs the evolution of *manas* in systemic space by cooperatively working with the governing *deva* lives, and by comprehension of mantras that are the basis of the higher *siddhis.* The next step, Buddhahood, generally necessitates leaving the familiar world of the planetary sphere far behind, as a path is chosen to follow that leads to far distant cosmic shores.

6. Plane 4: *Buddhi.* This plane represents the middle between extremes, the place of integration of all the energies that sustain *saṃsāra.* It is the fourth cosmic ether, whereon can be found the *nāḍīs* and the *chakras* that govern life in *saṃsāra.* The energy fields conditioning this plane are the basis to the experience of *śūnyatā* by the fourth degree Initiate. This is also the plane of actualisation of the planetary Heart centre, the Hierarchy of Love. They are the mechanism whereby Logoic Love can direct the planetary manifestation via the ability of the human (or fourth) kingdom in Nature to develop Bodhisattvic attributes. They are the dynamic, driving impetus behind all group participation. Compassion, the shedding of the Heart's Blood for the welfare of others, rules all on this plane. The members of this Hierarchy also embody the all-embracive radiance of Mind. These two attributes, compassion and *manasic* radiance are the basis to the expression of *bodhicitta.*
7. Plane 5: *The mental.* This plane is divided into an abstract portion, consisting of three sub-planes, and a concreted portion, consisting of four sub-planes. The Sambhogakāya Flower upon the higher mental plane, and its link to the threefold Monadic Form upon the plane *anupādaka,* are depicted.

   The third degree Initiate gains full revelation of the nature of the Fiery intent of *manas* upon this plane. The Logoic Solar Plexus centre functions here to govern the evolutionary development of all the streams of life in Nature's kingdoms. This Initiation is accomplished when the energy of the third Outpouring (directed by the Monadic Word) descends to the Base of Spine centre and awakens the feminine *kuṇḍalinī śakti.*
8. Plane 6: *The astral.* This plane is effectively the organising field for all of the energies that drive the factors of *saṃsāric* life to its fruition. It is therefore practically synonymous with the etheric substratum of the dense physical. Here the Logoic Sacral centre functions to appropriate the forces of Logoic desire to see the evolution of all lesser lives through to their evolutionary goals. With the advent of human desire bodies, these energies become incorporated into the *saṃskāras* of their attachments to attributes of

saṃsāra. Thus the Bardo realms, the heavens and hells that humans reincarnate through, are formed. When the Watery *saṃskāras* that produce such realms are consciously controlled, then the second Initiation is possible.

9. Plane 7: *The physical*. This plane is also dual, with four etheric sub-planes containing the *nāḍīs* and *chakras* directing the forces underlying all physical plane evolution. There are also three dense sub-planes (the gaseous, liquid and concrete). Attachment to the illusional forms constructed via their agency is what must be mastered to pass the first Initiation. Desire for the allurements of material plane living must therefore be overcome. The *chakra* in the Body of the Logos governing this plane is that of the Base of the Spine. The awakening of the potencies of its four main petals then conditions the evolution of the four kingdoms that evolve by means of dense forms: the mineral, plant, animal, and human.

The Master of Wisdom can transmute gross substance into a body of living Light. He has the yogic experience and occult knowledge to be able to (if needed) directly create and project an illusional, though tangible, body of appearance via which service work can occur.[69] Supramundane *siddhis* are his to command. Jesus demonstrated the qualities of such attainment after his resurrection. In *Mark 16:12*, for instance, it is stated that Jesus appeared in another form to two disciples as they walked and went to the country. Also, at the end of the Luke Gospel, on the third day after the crucifixion, and directly after Jesus had risen from the tomb, he went with two disciples in a form they did not recognise. Only later, after he had symbolically re-enacted the last supper,[70] were 'their eyes opened', that is, they saw his true form (clairvoyantly) and hence they knew him, and 'He vanished out of their sight'.[71] The two disciples immediately sought out the other disciples to tell them the good news that Jesus had risen from the dead. As they spoke, 'Jesus himself stood in the midst of them' and said 'Peace be unto you', immediately dispensing the type of energy (of peace) that he was

---

69 The term for such a form in yogic texts is a 'transformation body'.

70 *Luke 24:30-32*.

71 *Luke 24:31*.

blessed with at birth.[72] They were, however, 'terrified and affrighted, and supposed that they had seen a spirit',[73] for the idea of a physical return of a man they knew to have undoubtedly died was beyond their comprehension. (They were not Initiated into the higher Mysteries.) He however stated 'Why are ye troubled? and why do thoughts arise in your hearts? Behold my hands and my feet, that it is I myself: handle me, and see; for a spirit hath not flesh and bones, as ye see me have'.[74]

After having convinced them of the actual solidarity of his form, that he indeed had complete control of the process of birth and death and of all the laws governing the material world,[75] he could say that he completely fulfilled 'all things...which were written in the law of Moses, and in the prophets, and in the psalms, concerning me'.[76] That is, he completely fulfilled all Biblical prophecy concerning the coming Messiah, as well as the qualities and properties associated with the nature of a Christ and of the enlightenment-process, which were 'written in the Law'. He was a perfect example of a perfected man, who was thereby a 'Son of God'.

Similarly, the Master of Wisdom is literally the demonstration of 'the Law' (the *dharma)* of 'God'. He regulates the law of the *karma* for all within his Ashramic domain. The Master is the central point of the entire *maṇḍala* that is his particular Ray line of service. All that flows through that *maṇḍala* is analysed and projected by him, in accord with his part of the general plan that emanates from the Council Chamber of Shambhala.

Yogically, the production of a transformation body is possible because the etheric form consisting of the *chakras* and the *nāḍīs* is the true form of a human unit. The physical appearance is an automaton built from the quality of the energy fields that are the *chakras.* The yogic process of the higher Tantras gradually etherealises the form, because of the purity of the life, right breathing techniques, and mantric command of the forces

---

72 *Luke 2:17.*

73 *Luke 24:37.*

74 *Luke 24:38-9.*

75 For further proof of his physicality 'they gave him a piece of broiled fish, and of an honeycomb, and he took *it,* and did eat before them' *(Luke 24:42-43).*

76 *Luke 24:44.*

pertaining to the form. (Signifying the mastery of the Creative process that is one of the secrets bequeathed at the level of the fifth Initiation.) The body can then be made to appear or disappear at will. It has been transformed. Jesus had created such a form, thus his body disappeared in the tomb,[77] and consequently appeared when he wished it to. The process involved activating certain *chakras* via appropriate mantras that attracted the needed substance to them for the form to appear. The foundation for this process was laid by his earlier ability to feed the 4,000 people with the small number of loaves and fishes[78] he possessed. The technique to materialise these loaves and fishes (mantric command of the associated *deva* lives) is the same as what was needed to make his own bodily form appear after it had, to all intents and purposes, died.

These quotes are provided because though Jesus embodied the fourth Initiation for the world, he could also demonstrate many of the qualities of the fifth, especially after his death on the cross. This is because he had also passed many of the tests for the fifth Initiation.

Amongst Tibetan *yogins,* such ability that Jesus demonstrated is a well known accomplishment. Dudjom Rinpoche states:

> So it is that great accomplished masters may make themselves disappear from the view of ordinary disciples and then, after a long time has passed, they may make themselves reappear, and then remain present for a long time. They may be invisible in some places and visible in others simultaneously. In one place they may demonstrate transference [of consciousness after death], and in another, the act of taking birth. In these and other ways their manifestations are infinite. Thus, once upon a time, Virūpa thrice appeared bodily after disappearing; Jālandharipā similarly reappeared five times; and the great Kriṣṇacārin, after passing away in Devīkoṭa and being cremated by his disciples, reappeared elsewhere in his former body and acted to benefit the world.[79]

77 *Luke 24:2-3.* 'And they found the stone rolled away from the sepulchre. And they entered in and found not the body of the Lord Jesus'. For differing accounts of the story, see also *Luke 24:22-25, Matt. 27:60-28:1-8, Mark 16:2-7,* and *John 20:1-8.* These accounts convey differing symbolic perspectives of the fundamental teaching.

78 *Matt. 15:34-39, Mark 8:5-9.*

79 Dudjom Rinpoche, *The Nyingma School of Tibetan Buddhism,* trans. Gyurme Dorje and Matthew Kapstein (Wisdom, Boston, 1991), 473.

The fifth Initiation builds upon the attainment of the fourth, in that it is the result of further reception to Divine Will in such a way that the Fiery Mind of 'God' *(dharmakāya)* comes to be appropriately expressed for the planet. The Master has become an awakened petal within that Mind. He demonstrates its Cognition in the forthright expression of the karmic weave for the planet according to Ray considerations. The way of the cross, however, remains in the Master's Heart, but he[80] has moved northwards towards the Kingdom of Shambhala, as a completely integrated member of that Kingdom. The Master of Wisdom is an executive member of the Hierarchy of enlightened being, under whom the fourth degree Initiate is the true prototype expression, as well as being a junior member of Shambhala.

The Master works via a triad, where he is the Father aspect, the first point of an Ashram governing a sub-ray of light for the planetary dispensation. Under him, as the second point or 'Son', works an Initiate of the fourth degree, whilst an Initiate of the third degree (who is generally very close to taking the fourth Initiation) exemplifies the functions of the Mother aspect of deity for that Ashram. There is then a further gradation of nine Initiates (where the youngest is often directly working for the third Initiation) to complete the twelve petals of a Heart lotus. The first seven of the twelve also embody the qualities of the seven Rays for the Ashram. Effectively, the Ashram of a Master then extends outwards to incorporate the sacred number of 108 Initiates altogether. All embody the same sub-Ray quality, but also there are generally members from other Ashrams that have interrelated functions that play a role in that Ashram's development. All activity within the Hierarchy happens according to the Ray purpose of the various Ashrams.

Little can be here presented concerning the nature of the work of an Initiate of this degree because much of this work is an integral part of the Initiate's standing within the Council Chamber of the Lord of the world. It concerns the dissemination of that part of the plan for the evolution of all kingdoms of Nature, which the Master helps to formulate. Interplanetary and cosmic interrelatedness, as well as psychic protection for the residents upon the earth, are all within the Master's

80 In the coming epoch, many Masters will exist in female bodies, however, the past has been a generally masculine disposition.

ken. More detail shall be provided in Volume 7 of this treatise, *The Constitution of Shambhala,* where the qualities of the various Ashrams are detailed.

The way of the Initiate

After his crucifixion, having bodily reappeared in the room where the remaining eleven disciples were, and having proved to them his physical reality in a transformation body, Jesus told them that he had fulfilled the prophecies concerning the appearance of the Jewish Messiah. As a consequence, 'opened he their understanding, that they might understand the scriptures'.[81] This meant that he awakened ('opened') their eye of vision, allowing them to see in full the esoteric implications of the various scriptures. The disciples could then derive true spiritual knowledge from them with complete understanding, allowing them to wisely dispense that comprehension to all that could receive it. No longer did they need to rely on the interpretation of the exoteric context of the scriptures and parables.[82] The parables however protect truths and revelations of the highest order from the pejorative assumptions of the uninitiate, who have not yet the capability to rightly utilise them.

The word *opened* here is of significance, for it is the same word that is used in yoga and occult texts associated with awakening the lotus blossoms that constitute the various psychic centres in us. Clairvoyant and spiritual perception of increasing exponential order manifest as the powers associated with the highest *chakras* are developed. Many function in a partly opened (semi-awakened) state to produce the normal waking consciousness, but are not fully 'opened' to awaken the paranormal states of perception called *siddhis.*

To 'open their understanding' thus means producing revelations concerning broader, subjective implications of the subject at hand, and implicates stimulating the opening of the various *chakras* of the disciple concerned. The ability to do this in the right order for each individual (so that 'they might understand the scriptures') is the

81 *Luke 24:45.*

82 *Mark 4:11:* 'And he said unto them, Unto you it is given to know the mystery of the kingdom of God: but unto them that are without, all *these* things are done in parables'.

functioning that qualifies the Master with regard to the neophytes in his charge. He can with certainty aid their spiritual development, for he knows exactly what lies ahead of them, what energies they must develop and express, and what must be done to overcome all hindrances to the engendering of enlightenment.

Only higher degree Initiates possesses the spiritual Will that can help produce awareness of new fields of revelation and service in the disciple that are consistent with the overriding plan, the Law of 'God'. All systems of meditation require the acolyte to obey implicitly, with unwavering faith the instructions from the Initiate of higher degrees, once the spiritual acumen that can distinguish the Initiate from those that are merely teachers has been developed. For all intents and purposes, the Initiate and the Christ are at-oned in consciousness and the disciple knows this to be true through verifiable experience, for the awakened (Christed) Initiate resides in the deepest recess of the disciple's heart.

The following phrase, 'And said unto them, Thus it is written, and thus it behoved Christ to suffer, and to rise from the dead the third day',[83] should instantly revert our minds to the three temptations in the desert. In each of them Jesus answers the 'tempter' with the phrase 'it is written', and here again we have the same statement, implying his successful resistance to another such temptation. We saw that these temptations were concerned with overcoming the limitations of the threefold personality nature, which allowed him to undertake the first three Initiations. At the next Initiation level, however, *saṃsāra* now no longer concerns the candidate, for there is nothing left whereby he/she can be tempted by its conditionings.

What the candidate is now tested with is that which arises from the realised standing concerning the type of path that the Initiate is best able to tread. The associated temptation is of such a subtle type that it is just hinted at in this verse, which effectively comprises the differences between the ideals of Hīnayāna and Mahāyāna Buddhism. In the Mahāyāna, the path pursued is that of the Bodhisattva. In the Hīnayāna, the *arhat* path is exemplified. In the *arhat* path, enlightenment is sought purely for the sake of the individual concerned, the object being one's own release from suffering, and thus of the need to incarnate

83 *Luke 24:46.*

again. The idea concerns being liberated from *saṃsāra* by staying perpetually in *nirvāṇic* bliss, wherein *saṃsāric* life is disdained to obtain enlightenment (*nirvāṇa,* the fourth Initiation) with a subtly selfish motive. With this approach, true enlightenment is not possible. The concept has a limited validity in terms of the third Initiation, where union with the Sambhogakāya Flower is achieved, providing a form of 'personal *nirvāṇa'.* Of necessity, the enlightenment-process governing the Soul will however propel the *arhat* on, as there is no such thing as individual enlightenment, or its supposed *nirvāṇa.* All beings constitute an interrelated unity, which has its source in being/ non-being, and which continues beyond human ken. An *arhat* must inevitably reincarnate again, because compassionate development must unfold, as the nature of That into which one is abstracted will carry one onwards as a Bodhisattva, for all journeying leads to the Heart of Life.

Jesus had developed the spiritual acumen to know without any hesitation the fundamental illusiveness of the *arhat* path, that there was actually no other choice for him but that of a Bodhisattva, for he had 'risen from the dead' and had returned to speak of it. (This allows him to undertake the fifth Initiation.) The 'dead' refers not so much to the realm of disincarnate entities, as to the entirety of *saṃsāra* and every entity in it. They are still attached to the ever-dying, transient realms of illusion associated with the three worlds of human perception. Therefore it incorporates the kingdom of Souls, from which the Initiate of the fourth degree has risen. As a Bodhisattva, Jesus fulfilled his esoteric obligations. He then 'blessed them' and was 'carried up into heaven',[84] to receive the revelation that awaited him.

It is interesting to note that this Gospel concludes with the statement that his disciples 'were continually in the temple (which as we saw above, is the 'temple' of the Soul), praising and blessing God. Amen'.[85] This tells us that the general achievement of Jesus with regard to the apostles was to confer upon them the illumination that the third Initiation affords.

The Initiate of the fifth degree is embodied light and takes the guise of the 'light of the world'. He is liberated from the realm of form, is in contact with the highest spiritual energies (which register in our dense world as

---

84 *Luke 24:51.*

85 *Luke* 24:53.

Love, Light and Life), and can use these energies to effect the liberation of all sentient beings. In fact, he can effectively say as Christ-Jesus did:

> I am the light of the world: he that followeth me shall not walk in darkness, but shall have the light of life.[86]

This light can illumine the three worlds of human perception with the Light of the 'living Father'.[87] A difference between an Initiate of this degree and the Christ, however, is that the light the fifth degree Initiate embodies is qualified by one of the sub-rays of seven Rays, whilst the Christ utilises each Ray line with equal facility. He embodies the silver-white Light that is their united interrelated potency. Basically, the Master becomes guru to a disciple because the disciple's Soul-Ray, and the Ray quality the Master embodies, are congruous. Accordingly, the Christ is the Master of Masters.

From the above we see that an Initiate of the fourth specifically embodies the energy of Love. He/she is consequently a Lord of Compassion. The Initiate of the fifth degree adds mastery of Light to this Love, thus expressing all of the attributes of the dual Ray of Love-Wisdom. Thus he is a Master of Wisdom. The Initiate of the sixth degree (a Chohan, or Lord of a Ray line) has a direct affinity with Life Itself, a term which is relatively meaningless to all still incarnate in the realms of form. (These realms are esoterically considered the realms of transformation and the perpetually dying.) Sixth degree Initiates are fully integrated with the Monad, having fused both *deva* and human attributes of their constitution into a unity. Such a one is a resident at the Heart of Shambhala, as well as being an executive member of the Hierarchy of Love, involved in all major decisions concerning the evolution of all kingdoms in Nature.

The energies of Light, Love and Life are tangible substance to the expanded consciousness of Initiates of these degrees. Their expression in the world becomes the force of the Will-of-Love, and its lowest reflex as the goodwill that unites people into a joyous community, enabling people to grow properly towards spiritual maturity.

The future attainment by Jesus of the higher Initiations was

---

86 *John 8:12.*

87 *John 6:57.* Integrate here *1John 1:5,* where he says that 'God is light'.

prophesised by the statement accompanying his birth at Bethlehem. '*Glory* to God in the highest (the gain of the attainment of the fourth to sixth degree Initiates) and on earth peace (the effect of the attainment of the third degree Initiate), and the method whereby this is accomplished, good will toward men'.[88] (This is the gain of the attainment of the second degree Initiate.)

The entire Gospel story then fulfilled this prophecy. The *peace* mentioned here is not just quietude, where people live in fellowship with others in such a way that no strife or discord arises. It also implies developing a tranquil mental state and peaceful bodily conditions that allow the highest spiritual energies to manifest, and to be unequivocally recognised. It means a complete relaxation of the cognitive process, so that which fundamentally IS, can be expressed. Peace is that state of being, therefore, that allows enlightenment to manifest, for it is devoid of distorting, clouding, or perturbing elements. It does not mean inaction, but rather, necessitates compassionate activity. It is an action wherein the friction that causes pain and suffering (the various noises of materialistic life), is not possible, for no discords are produced. By this means 'God' can be 'glorified'. This glorification process involves the descent into a controlled emotional body of the effects of the Will-of-Love, and that which is known as Life. Eventually, we have the type of peace manifesting that is experienced in *śūnyatā*.

Note that the difference between 'noise' (from disharmonious activity) and the harmonics of Sound (mantra), is that between destructive vibration, and peace-engendering, creatively building frequencies of liberating possibilities.

The Initiate of the fifth degree has mastered ordinary intellectual perception, and his mind is used only as an instrument of service. Indeed, it cannot be otherwise, for there is now an unbroken beam of Light connecting the Mind of such a one to the highest attribute of being/non-being signified as Shambhala, and then to cosmic Mind. There is no mental-emotional reaction, nor is there a Soul toning down the force. The Master's outer life is one of perfected rhythm in service, where the intellect has become automatic (like the instinct is with us), below the threshold of consciousness.

---

88 *Luke 2:10-14.*

The rising of Lazarus

The symbolism associated with the cross is one method of describing the process associated with the attainment of the fourth Initiation. Another, perhaps more ancient method, is that associated with *resurrection from a crypt or tomb* after a period of internment for a number of days. This is depicted in the Gospels by the story of *Lazarus,* who was 'raised from the dead' by Jesus.[89]

Though we are not told about his life, the symbolism in the Gospel of John is clear enough to the Initiated. Lazarus died to his personality nature so that he might be raised triumphant from 'the dead' (the ephemeral, ever-dying situations associated with the material world), Initiated into the Mysteries of the Kingdom of 'God'. He rose into the world of spiritual values and eternal being. He therefore had undergone the same process in secret that Jesus was demonstrating for the public gaze, to be risen from the dead, from the cross or cave of matter. The cave, or tomb, symbolises the depths of the material world, which is hard, rocky and unyielding. The Christ was born in the cave of the personality nature, the bodily form, and was therefore eventually resurrected from it. 'Jesus wept'[90] in recognition of Lazarus' achievement and of what he also must eventually do. It was an expression of spiritual gratitude, love, deep subjective joy resulting from a recognition of the profound spiritual event that was taking place, and understanding what the process involved. Jesus thereby demonstrated 'how he loved him'[91]—in the form of the expression of the Christ-force (the energy of Love) that allowed Lazarus to attain his Initiation. The weeping was thus not because Lazarus had physically died, even though this is what appeared to all others, for Jesus plainly told us:

> This sickness is not unto death, but for the glory of God, that the Son of God might be glorified thereby.[92]

The dialogue in *John 11:10-16* indicates just how uncomprehending the disciples of Jesus were as to the real nature of what was happening to

---

89 *John 12:1.*

90 *John 11:35.*

91 *John 11:36.*

92 *John 11:4.*

Lazarus. Jesus told them that 'Our friend Lazarus sleepeth; but I go, that I may awake him out of sleep'.[93] This means that he was experiencing an altered state of consciousness that was profoundly different from that which we term 'waking consciousness', and was out of the body to do so. 'Then said his disciples, Lord, if he sleep, he shall do well',[94] thereby telling Jesus that they felt there was no need to undergo a dangerous journey to Judea (where the Jews sought to stone him[95]) for such a seemingly insignificant reason. Then follow the statements:

> Howbeit Jesus spake of his death: but they thought that he had spoken of taking of rest in sleep. Then said Jesus unto them plainly, Lazarus is dead.[96]

To speak 'unto them plainly' means to awaken their comprehension as to the real significance of the event, which allowed Thomas to enthusiastically say 'unto his fellow disciples, Let us also go, that we may die with him'.[97] To thus 'die' was an event they were all working towards in their consciousness. Going to the cave where Lazarus was entombed therefore allowed them to play their subjective parts in the Initiation process. Lazarus was 'dead' because he had died completely to his personality nature. It no longer conditioned his perception, for after this Initiation only the Life of the Spirit-Monad could work through him.

The period of internment in the crypt varies according to the Initiation undertaken. In Jonas' case, this was for three days and three nights during which he was in the belly of the 'whale'. Because of its ancient esoteric significance, and thus to fulfil Biblical prophecy, Jesus also had to re-enact this period of internment after his crucifixion. He thus spent three days and nights in the sepulchre provided for him, the heart of the earth.[98]

---

93 *John 11:11.*

94 *John 11:12.*

95 *John 11:8.*

96 *John 11:13-14.*

97 *John 11:16.*

98 See *Matthew 12:40,* where the internment of Jonas and the 'Son of man' are directly related: 'For as Jonas was three days and three nights in the whale's belly; so shall the Son of man be three days and three nights in the heart of the earth'.

This period of three days and nights (technically three and a half days) refers to the attaining of the *third Initiation.* After many weeks of fasting and ritualistic invocative religious observances, the candidate was helped into a state of deep paralytic-like trance by his religious superiors. His body (as if dead) was normally safeguarded in a crypt or tomb that was specifically consecrated for this purpose. He was then shown the Mysteries associated with the incorporeal realms, with everything associated with his degree of attainment, whilst he was in his spiritual body. This knowledge and ability to enter into spiritual communion at will was retained when he finally resumed waking consciousness, being brought thereto by the mediatorship of the Hierophant. In Lazarus' case the Hierophant was Jesus in the guise of the Christ. Lazarus stayed in the crypt for a full four days,[99] which, accordingly symbolises the attainment of the fourth Initiation.

Note that a crypt of the size that would adequately hold a person was the only object found in the Great Pyramid of Giza, and some have investiged its use for this function.[100]

After arriving at the cave, Jesus 'groaned in the spirit and was troubled'.[101] This 'groaning' was an invocation calling forth the energies needed to bring Lazarus back into the consciousness of his corporeal form, to awaken the 'dead', that the 'Son of God be glorified thereby'. The phrase 'in the spirit' means exactly what it says, therefore the 'groaning' had nothing to do with deep personality affliction, but implies that he summoned energies from the 'kingdom of God' (the 'Spirit') to accomplish his purpose.

The ability to 'glorify God' has profound esoteric significance. (We have both 'God' being glorified and the reciprocal, 'that the Son of God be glorified thereby'.) The word 'glory' is defined in terms of the ability to shine, radiate, to provide splendour, praise, honour, admiration, or distinction to a person or thing. It is a high reputation and an honourable fame that comes from the highest achievement, something that brings

99 *John 11:17.* 'Then when Jesus came, he found that he had *lain* in the grave four days already'.

100 Such as Manly Palmer Hall and Paul Brunton, who spent a night therein and gives us an account of his experiences in his book *A Search In Secret Egypt,* (Rider, 1969).

101 *John 11:33.*

or gives renown, and resplendence. Spiritually, it is the divinity in a being, an emanation of the light that radiates from those of sanctity. It is the term for the intensity of the aura around a person. This is depicted as a circle of golden light around the head of saints in Christian art. In Buddhist representations of their great ones we see the radiant aura, in semicircles around the entire body and head. The demonstration of glory is the predominant quality associated with the expression of Love-Wisdom (enlightenment). It is exemplified by the quality of the radiance generated, thus we have the Light body of the Christ.

To 'give God glory' means esoterically to add the intense aura or radiance of the Initiate's presence in Shambhala. This glory veils the *dharmakāya*, allowing it to be expressed as an omnipotent Sun, the central spiritual dynamo to all being. Each Ray of this Sun demonstrates the wisdom of a fully liberated, enlightened being. When seen clairvoyantly, the radiance expressed shows the fundamental Ray line of the Initiate concerned. Such glory is virtually incomprehensible to all except by direct perception. The symbolism is associated with the solar discs (⊙) of the absolute deities of the various theisms, as well as the fully awakened Head or Heart lotus. Glory is the effect of the consummation, the return journeying from *saṃsāric* wandering by all sentient beings (each of which can be fundamentally considered sparks of light), culminating as the result of the transformation of base *saṃskāras* into enlightenment-perceptions by humanity.

As naught can proceed without receiving and consequently giving, so on the arc of return, glory is the divine radiance that emanates from the Throne or Seat of Power of the Kingdom of 'God' as its fundamental second Ray quality. It signifies the basic emanatory quality that in this solar system can be considered the achievement of a perfected evolution. Glory is the demonstrated potency of the 'Grace of God'[102] in the world of form, which helps liberate all Life.

Those whom Jesus loved

That it is possible for all people to achieve the fourth and fifth Initiations is shown in *John 21:20-24*. The dialogue starts with the statement that

102 *Luke 2:40, Acts 11:23,* etc.

it was broadcast 'abroad among the brethren, that the disciple whom Jesus loved shall not die'.[103] The author of that Gospel then emphasises that this is not exactly what Jesus said to Peter, but rather the words:

> If I will that he tarry till I come, what *is that* to thee?[104]

Death (as humanity understands it) is mastered by Initiates of these degrees. They have conquered all the deaths, achieved all the transmutations possible to the form, and have risen from the cross or cave of matter. They can reside in a transformation body at will. Perpetual physical life is however not an Initiate's desire; rather the fulfilling of the plan before him/her concerning how to best advance human evolution. They are part of the *maṇḍala* of Hierarchical endeavour, and act according to its overall demonstration of spiritual power.

The phrase 'what *is that* to thee?' is an injunction that informs Peter that not only is the relation between the Christ and this disciple not his concern, but more importantly, to meditate or ponder deeply on the meaning of the words 'I will that he tarry till I come' in relation to Peter's own spiritual evolution. Peter was an Initiate of the third degree (a 'son of Jonas',[105] the epitome of the Initiate of this degree and his attainment). He therefore had to think deeply about the qualities possessed by an Initiate of the fourth degree (the degree of the disciple whom Jesus loved[106]) and what his work was in the world, for that development was immediately ahead of him. The Christ was also talking about his next appearance or Incarnation (in the new age). He was therefore asking the 'disciple whom he loved' to stay on in *saṃsāra* to perform Bodhisattvic duties until the time for the reappearance of the Christ.

For this reason Peter was asked three times,[107] 'Simon, son of Jonas, *lovest* thou me?'[108] We saw previously that such Love (compassionate activity) is brought to its fulfilment in the Initiate of the fourth degree. It

---

103 *John 21:23.*

104 *Ibid.*

105 *John 21:15.*

106 Who could directly bear therefore this energy of cosmic Love.

107 This refers to the ability to master the body, speech (emotions) and mind, as all of the third Initiation must be able to do.

108 *John 21:15-17.*

is an energy that he/she is able to perfectly embody. Jesus was therefore not just testing Peter's love as faith in the Christ, but the extent of his ability to Love, to express the type of energy that would be required of the Initiate of the fourth degree. Jesus then gave explicit instructions on how to accomplish this, that he had to 'Feed my lambs'.[109] This meant that he had to convey spiritual nourishment (energies) from the Hierarchy of enlightened being to those just born into the Christ-consciousness. This is followed by the statement: 'Feed my sheep'[110] after Peter answered that Jesus knows of his love, thus of his ability to take the next Initiation. This Initiation incurs increased spiritual responsibility, meaning that one could then appropriately educate those that have matured and have attained Initiation.

That Peter would be prepared for the fourth Initiation at the end of his life is indicated by the words spoken by Jesus: 'when thou shalt be old, thou shalt stretch forth thy hands (thus effectively assuming the same position as the person on the cross), and another shall gird thee, and carry *thee* whither thou wouldest not. This spake he, signifying by what death he should glorify God. And when he had spoken thus, he saith unto him, Follow me'.[111] That is, Peter was to follow in the footsteps of the Christ, to the crucifixion experience. Peter did not, however, attain the fourth Initiation in that life and was said to be crucified upside down in Rome. This symbolises the manifest activity of the third Initiation. Andrew also was said to be crucified, but on a mutable cross. We thus have a northern pointing cross, a southern pointing one, with a mutable cross interrelating the two. Much esoteric symbolism is veiled here. Jesus' cross symbolises the orientation to Shambhala. Andrew's the activity of Hierarchy, Peter's the projection of the divine into humanity—the externalisation of the teaching dispensation from Shambhala, thus the foundation of the New Jerusalem on earth, of a universal religion. What arose instead was the debased exoteric Roman Catholic church.

We saw above that the disciple 'whom Jesus loved' was an Initiate of the fourth degree, for only such a one could explicitly convey the energy of the Love of the Christ. It is easy to see that many could confuse

109 *John 21:15.*

110 *John 21:15-17.*

111 *John 21:18-19.*

him with the disciple that 'shall not die', for 'deathlessness' is a quality attained by the Initiate of this degree. Jesus had also stated to Martha, with a specific reference to Lazarus: 'whosoever *liveth* and believeth in me shall never die'.[112] The Initiate of the fourth degree lives completely and consciously within the energy body of the cosmic Christ, and accordingly has absolute faith in the providence of 'God', to which he shall never die, for there can never be any separation in consciousness from That. All else in heaven and earth is an embodied form, which suffers change, and must die. In order to dispel the confusion between Lazarus, whom Jesus 'loved', and this particular disciple, we have the additional information in *John 21:10* that he was the one who leaned on Jesus' breast at the last supper (and who was therefore the closest to Jesus out of all his disciples).[113] As the Matthew, Mark, and Luke Gospels agree that only the twelve apostles were present at the last supper, so Lazarus is excluded here.

That this particular disciple is the author of the John Gospel (the same John that stood on the mount of Transfiguration) is clearly provided by the words: 'This is the disciple which testifieth of these things.... and we know that his testimony is true'.[114] It is obvious that only an Initiate of the fourth degree (or greater) can testify to all that happened, including that relating to the subjective domains, and experience of the higher Initiations of Jesus and his disciples.

The Love energy is best conveyed via the second Ray line—the second, fourth and sixth Rays. The great ones embodying these Rays had to directly bear the import of the new dispensation of Love of the Christ. The first of these to take the fourth Initiation was Lazarus, over whom Jesus 'wept'. Lazarus was the embodiment of the second ray line (under the Christ, who also embodies this Ray expression), hence became the future second Ray Chohan (sixth degree Initiate), known as K.H. in the esoteric literature. Jesus was the candidate along the sixth Ray line of devotion, hence he was the founder of a devotion-based religion. Logically, therefore, the disciple John, whom Jesus loved, is the one who would become the future fourth Ray Chohan (of beautifying Harmony overcoming Strife).

112 *John 11:26.*

113 His 'Sun-like' disciple, to use Buddhist terminology.

114 *John 21:24.*

There is some controversy concerning the authorship of John's Gospel and when it was written, however, modern scholarship posits it to have been written about 90-100 A.D. Be that as it may, the implication above is that John indeed was the author of the Gospel, and also, at a very advanced age, of the *Revelation of St. John* (despite the different styles of the books). Indeed, *St. John's Revelation* encodes the entire revelation accorded at the fourth Initiation to a successful candidate,[115] which John most certainly was. When Jesus taught him, he was a young man with the qualities already developed that would allow him to pass the tests that would provide him the capacity to encode the visions into the phrases that can be read in the final book of the Bible. It should be noted that the Gospels were written by enlightened people, Initiates, who may, or may not have seen the events in Jerusalem with their physical eyes, but certainly it is apparent that their third Eye was opened, and they could See.

Likewise, the various Buddhist texts were written by enlightened beings some centuries after the Buddha's *parinirvāṇa.* They were written from a viewpoint of the visions (awareness) obtained by the enlightened Mind (backed by a strong oral tradition), by one in deep meditation. The encoded revelations can then be authenticated by anyone who has developed a similar meditation-Mind.

The others that Jesus was said to have specifically 'loved' were:

a. The rich young man[116] who is supposed by some Biblical commentators to have been Lazarus.[117] In the esoteric sense, to be rich, however, is to have attained the third Initiation, wherein the Soul-form is endowed with the riches of divinity and is full of glory. The energy of Love is conveyed to such a one by the Christ to enable him/her to undertake the fourth Initiation, which Lazarus subsequently did. This Initiation allows one effectively 'to go through the eye of a needle'.[118] This 'eye' is but a symbolic rendition of the

---

115 A detailed explanation of the meaning of the chapters of *The Revelation of St. John* will come in a book that will hopefully be published later.

116 *Mark 10:17-27.*

117 For the reasoning behind this see William Smith, LL.D., *Smith's Bible Dictionary,* (Fleming H. Revell Company. N.J.)

118 *Mark 10:25.* 'It is easier for a camel to go through the eye of a needle, than for a rich man to enter the kingdom of God'.

Monad-Spirit, and its line of interrelation *(antaḥkaraṇa)* with the embodied personality.

b. The sisters of Lazarus (Mary and Martha) were loved along with Lazarus.[119] Though this indicates that they may be of the third or fourth Initiation level, this is unlikely. Here it more specifically implies that they acted as sponsors to the Initiation procedure, and thereby could share in the Love-energy that was to awaken Lazarus. (They were thus along the same second Ray line of Love-Wisdom.) Note that this verse appears after they sent word to Jesus stating, 'Lord, behold, he whom thou lovest is sick'.[120] The fact that they were unaware of the real nature of the 'sickness' ('Lord, by this time he stinketh'[121]*)* argues against them being intrinsically of the higher Initiation level. From a textual reference, therefore, the enquiring reader can decipher that they were Initiates of the second and first degrees, who can accordingly express the lower reflex of the Love-energy, its Watery aspect.

It might be of value to note here that doubting Thomas, who needed to touch the form of the resurrected Christ before he would believe,[122] proved by that action that he had yet to attain the second and third Initiations, for his emotional body (his doubts) still clouded his vision, and he needed the testimony of that which was most corporeal, or physical (to touch), before he could see. The other disciples (apart from Judas) had the capacity to attain the third Initiation. Of the twelve apostles, Thomas and Judas were thus the youngest spiritually.

The advent of the new epoch

The transformation body of Initiates of the fifth degree, whose substance has been transmuted by means of living Light into its ethereal state, is equated with the *nirmāṇakāya* of a Buddha. The related qualities are aptly described in the hagiographies of the accomplishments

119 *John 11:5.*

120 *John 11:3.*

121 *John 11:39.*

122 *John 20:24-30.*

associated with the greatest Buddhist saints, such as Milarepa and Padmasambhava.[123] Some of the Hindu depictions of their greatest Mahātmas and Jīvanmuktas offer similar depictions. Initiates of this degree (Masters of Wisdom) generally influence the external happenings of humanity from behind the scenes, by means of thought projection (telepathy), direct incarnation and via the medium of their disciples. Hence they nurture the seeds of divinity in our civilisations. They are servants of all, as they must be if they are to prepare humanity for the service arena of the Master of Masters, the Christ as the forthcoming Buddha. The Masters have travelled deep along the path of Love and the way of wisdom, and so are the executive members of the Hierarchy of enlightened being on earth.

All Initiates possess the function of miracle-making to varying degrees, and 'tarry on' in the world, sometimes incarnate, sometimes disincarnate, preparing us for the future appearance of the Christ, and therefore the externalisation of the Ashrams. In this way the Christ remains ever active, involved in the three worlds of human livingness on the earth. He is not a silent, pensive figure living in some paradise or cloud in heaven. He has not left us, but rather, has always demonstrated his compassion to us through his disciples, through those that have been Initiated into the Mysteries of the kingdom of enlightened being. In the wilderness of our cities they have actively cried out, as did John the Baptist,[124] for all people to prepare themselves for the coming of the liberating One, not by means of proselytising and zealous regurgitation of the content of religious scriptures, as many would like to believe, but by their *works* in the world. They have, often without recognition, and nearly always in the most adverse conditions, striven in the various departments of Life to enlighten humanity as to the true nature of being, and of the divinity within and without them. They have always striven to foster good will and right human relations amongst us, which must be manifest if the new era is to dawn.

The Initiates of the past who had a hand in altering the course of

---

123 See W.Y. Evans-Wentz: *Tibet's Great Yogi, Milarepa,* and *The Tibetan Book of the Great Liberation* (Oxford University Press, London), for further detail.

124 *Matt. 3:1-2*. 'In those days came John the Baptist, preaching in the wilderness of Judaea. And saying, Repent ye: for the kingdom of heaven is at hand'.

human events in any field of activity were rarely known or recognised in their times for what they were, or had accomplished. This was because they had always come to destroy old, clouded, or restrictive ideas and methods so as to install the new. This was always met with animosity, callousness, and ignorant biased reactions from those that feared change. Now, because of the large number of Initiates that are incarnating (as a multitude of innovators) these changes are happening on a vast scale through two world wars, and have been carried through the post war years. It has produced the turmoil incidental to such changes. The result is incidental, as widespread benefits of every type and description for humanity have been accrued and so shall continue. Consequently, there has been a ferocious endeavour by the forces of evil to offset this success.

Those concerned have often not been aware of their inner conditionings, but because they could express a measure of true (unselfish) Love for humanity, they could be subjectively inspired and helped in their self-initiated task towards human betterment: scientifically, educationally, religiously, artistically and culturally. In the heuristic way, through trial and error, by their own experiments and experiences in a chosen service, as well as their subjective stimulus or inspiration, people slowly come to realise the nature of Life, of Love and its purpose.

A concentrated effort along the path of Love (by a person, or the human family) leads through many points of crises, reorientations, and redirections of energy, of how best to help, etc., to a point of focussed tension that allows new light and realisations to flood the lover's mind. Humanity has produced such a point of tension during the last two world wars. This unfortunately has objectively resulted in a revelation of the nature of the power of the atom and of the awesome potential of the possible total annihilation of all life by modern methods of warfare. Many technological innovations have followed since (especially in the field of warfare), and now we live in an internet dominated world. A corresponding compassionate development of humanity, for the sufferings of all in the world, has barely kept apace. Fear mongers, and the ruthless that foster war and the aggressive rapine of other's wealth, overly dominate the legislators governing us in most capitalistic Western nations. The great need is therefore for the accumulated weight of the activities of Initiates to hasten the time of the appearance of a new era of good will and resource sharing amongst people and the nations of the world. Such consideration is synonymous with the concept of 'the reappearance of the Christ'.

The Initiates have freed humanity from much of the enslaving Victorian type of social mores and sentiment, allowing new era ideals to be taught. Also, much *karma,* and the type of fostered ignorance that would have prevented his imminent reappearance, has been cleansed by the Armageddon type of conflict of the world wars. Sadly, more wars, however, appear yet to be on the agendas of our parliaments. Their effects upon humanity are of such a grand scale that like diseases, they produce cleansing effects. Though painful, diseases can rid the body of much harmful substance that if accumulated could cause a far more dangerous reaction, or death. Pus, toxins, and decaying matter, are similarly expelled by boils in the human system. Once passed, the individual should comprehend their causes and work to prevent recurrence. The diseases should not be continually, purposefully propagated by ignoring the lessons of the past. There is therefore a necessity for humanity to unite in a common endeavour to prevent this by working to block the schemes of the warmongers and the rapacious ones.

Those that willingly or inadvertently assist the perpetuators of unnecessary pain and suffering must later pay the karmic price. None can avoid the cyclic expression of this law. The perpetuation of cycles of death, destruction, massed poverty and sickness can be stopped if humanity awaken to the need and act wisely to stamp out the root causes by electing compassionate legislators, and by rooting out all sources of false propaganda. The culpability of compromised and biased media should weigh heavy in the minds of the majority of people. The perpetuation of lying propaganda by the major media outlets should be considered a criminal activity. Information passed on as 'facts' must be properly sourced, and put in the right context of what was said or done. People must care enough to ardently seek out the sources of truth so as not to be fooled into believing lies.

The Master of Masters has undergone an even higher Initiation than the fifth, but the subject is too abstruse to be dealt with here.

In conclusion, it must be stated that:

a. There are (as previously mentioned) nine Initiations associated with the evolution of the fourth kingdom in Nature (humanity). These parallel the nine months of gestation of a child in the womb of the mother, but in this case the womb is the solar system, and the child is the collective-Christ within us all. At the tenth Initiation the attributes of a planetary Logos are gained.

b. The five Initiations that are the goal for humanity in this world period were undertaken by the Master Jesus. (Four objectively and one subjectively.) He was overshadowed (used perfectly as an instrument) by the Christ from the time of the Baptism onwards. Jesus prepared a vehicle that the Christ could use, and when the time was right, he stepped out of it so that the 'dove of peace' could enter and manifest outwardly, eventually to inundate all humanity with that energy. In a unique way, Jesus was the Christ, the 'Son of God born in man'.

This is paralleled in the Buddhist philosophy by the doctrine of the Tulku or 'Incarnation'. In such a case, Jesus can be considered a Tulku of the Christ. This doctrine was earlier explained, but the pertinent quote can be provided here, as it elucidates somewhat the nature of the fundamental mystery concerning Christ-Jesus:

> Something, or someone, that has no "individuality" or *ego* in the ordinary sense decides to work on the earth for the sake of all beings. He (or 'it') therefore takes birth over a certain period of time, in a series of human individuals, and it is these who are named *'Tulkus'*.
>
> The influence in question may emanate from any of the archetypal sources of Wisdom, which is the stable essence of the Universe, or else of Compassion, which is Wisdom in operation throughout countless world-systems. So it may be said of a *Tulku* that he is an emanation of Manjusri, the Bodhisattva of Wisdom or of Avalokitesvara.[125]

Only a basic understanding of the subject of Initiation could be presented above. It is a subject that must be of great interest to all

---

125 Chögyam Trungpa, *Born in Tibet,* 280-81.

seriously concerned with spiritual development. For further information, the reader should study the writings of A.A. Bailey, which give profound insights into this subject. Also, only glimpses as to the esoteric nature of the life of Jesus could be given, for truly, as stated:

> there are also many other things which Jesus did, the which, if they should be written every one, I suppose that even the world itself could not contain the books that should be written. Amen.[126]

This is no idle boast, especially if his many incarnations, and his work on subjective levels, are taken into account. The *Revelation of St. John* provides much detailed information in this field, if properly interpreted, as its opening verse clearly indicates: 'The revelation of Jesus Christ which God gave unto him....and he sent and signified it by his angel unto his servant John'. This is another way of saying that the Revelation (i.e., Initiation into) of the Mysteries of the Kingdom of 'God' was revealed to John by the Christ via this 'angel' *(deva* Lord, *ḍākinī)* and given to humanity in the form of the symbolism of John's book. It can therefore be interpreted as such only from an esoteric perspective by one who possesses the keys to that symbolism; by one who has been Initiated into the Mysteries.

126 *John 21:25.*

7

The Beatitudes: The way of evolution of Prime Causative Agents

Definition of Causative Agents

By 'causative' is meant that which produces a fundamental change in the structure or existence of something, or in the environment in which they reside. The concept generally implies the existence of directive Wills (also seen in terms of the expression of natural laws) that impinge or act upon that which exists, to change it. These agents can be categorised into five main groups.

1. Unconscious agents that are capable of manipulating the various categories of substance without the factor of intelligence involved. The actions come as a consequence of automated responses to stimuli manifesting in the environment concerned, through instinct, desire, or emotional projections of force. They do not comprehend the processes and laws governing their actions, they simply act in accordance with inherent predispositions.
2. Semi-conscious agents that work with the impulse of desire and mental-emotional actions. Here the actions are largely the expression of massed conditionings, or inherent tendencies, instinctive urges, brooding sentiments, fears and the like. They generally sweep over the conscious factor, impelling it to action. Little thought is actually used to meld the controlling forces into a preconceived direction, however, what is to be desired is comprehended.
3. Intelligent agents. Here the thought processes are involved. The

mind clearly formulates what it desires to accomplish, analyses the requirements necessary, the tools and materials available and the longevity of the construct. The causative activity then proceeds according to plan.

4. A prime causative agent. This is one that meditatively comprehends and can utilise all of the laws and energies constituting the multidimensional universe to create the forms desired at will. Such a one can also consciously use forces, materials, and substance other than that which is purely material. Planning ensues from the abstract Mind or the *dharmakāya,* and the *maṇḍala* that ensues evidences a multidimensionality and far-ranged purpose not possible by means of the use of intelligence alone.
5. Logoic creators. They start the entire gamut of the evolutionary process happening from first principles, directing that which is originally static and inert into motion by means of Mind. Inevitably, a myriad minds capable of becoming prime causative agents will evolve from the originating impetus.

The way of evolution and forms of action of prime causative agents has by now been significantly understood by the world's esotericists. It constitutes the evolution of Bodhisattvas and of their various grades of expression to Buddhahood. This concerns the nature of the making of a *mahāsiddha*, the treading of the higher Tantras, stripped of their complex layers of congealing veils. This necessitates the path of Initiation, the making of a Master of Wisdom, and eventually the evolution of a Logos. Indeed, the entire path of evolution is geared that way. Here I wish to present this subject from a new perspective, to unveil some of the mysteries of the esotericism ensconced in the Bible. The aim is to try to elevate Biblical studies to a level akin to Buddhist ontology, to facilitate the gaining of enlightenment. True insight as to the nature of the mysteries of being/non-being can then arise from the Gospels, as was always intended by the originating authors. It concerns the process of a developing divine 'Covenant with God'[1] that the Council of Bodhisattvas must engender if they are to become 'like unto God', i.e., an Ādi Buddha.

1 The term here refers to a planetary Logos, an evolved Buddha, consistent with the philosophy already presented earlier in this treatise.

It should be remembered here that all terms such as 'God' possess many meanings. It is entirely a question of interpretation that determines how one attributes labels to them. How to interpret these labels are generally provided by the particular school of philosophy or religious creed one ascribes to. Traditional beliefs and interpretations for all such terms will be here ignored unless valid, to allow the presentation of a more wholesome, multifarious view. The symbolism of the various religious streams can now be assimilated and incorporated into one grand religious tradition, as originally conceived by the great Bodhisattvas that originated these religious dispensations. All religious paths were originally designed to help lead people to liberation from the thrall of *saṃsāra*. They are but differing attempts by the wise 'sons of God'[2] to educate humanity as to the next way before them, according to the peculiar cultural situation and world period within which that 'son' was born. Manifested according to a prearranged plan, a *maṇḍala* of enlightenment is prepared for all humanity, not just for a relative few, an elect or 'chosen of God', as so often viewed by those who ignorantly deem themselves to be so chosen.

The causative streams of Fiery energy originate from the Mind of a Logos, and the Initiate must meditatively befit him/herself to wield them, and become a channel for the Divine Will. The foundation to understanding the history of this process of continuing revelation, or human march towards enlightenment, rests in a statement given in *The Revelation:*

> Note also, the close parallel with Moses' action when he went down from the mountain with the Tablets from 'God', with whom he had made a Covenant, to all the Israelites encamped on the plain. The difference was that most of the Israelites gave themselves to licentiousness and idolatry, whereas those who approached Jesus came

---

2 *John 10:34-35.* In reference to the charge of blasphemy against Jesus because he said that he was the 'Son of God': 'Jesus answered them, Is it not written in your law, I said, Ye are Gods? If he called them gods unto whom the word of God came, and the scripture cannot be broken: Say ye of him, whom the Father hath sanctified, and sent into the world, Thou blasphemest; because I said, I am the Son of God?' By this statement Jesus plainly meant that all could equally state that they were 'sons of God'. Here 'God' is interpreted as the Logos of this planet, 'For in him we live and move, and have our being' *(Acts 17:28).*

to hear Him and to be healed of their diseases. Moses nevertheless 'healed' the Israelites of their 'diseases' in a wrathful way, and gave them the testimony of the Law, as written throughout the rest of Exodus and Leviticus. Jesus similarly gave the Beatitudes in the rest of Luke (chapter six) and Matthew (chapters five and six). This would henceforth become the 'testimony of the Law' for the new Covenant with 'God' (or stage two of the old Covenant).[3]

The first stage of this Covenant was given to Moses in the form of the *Ten Commandments.* This story is well known, as depicted in the book of Exodus, with the Commandments being found in *Exodus 20:1-18.* These Commandments sufficed as the best moral and ethical guidance for developing humanity for many centuries, until the advent of the Buddha, and then of Christ-Jesus. His purpose was to present the next level of these teachings to humanity along the line of the Judaic tradition, in accordance with humanity's increased capacity to properly Love. (The Buddha before him rightly sprouted the seeds of the foundation of the necessary wisdom that prepared the way of Love.)

In *Matt. 22:36-40,* Jesus gave out the 'great commandment in the law':

> Thou shalt love the Lord thy God with all thy heart, and with all thy soul, and with all thy mind. This is the first and great commandment. And the second *is* like unto it, Thou shalt love thy neighbor as thyself. On these two commandments hang all the law and the prophets.[4]

Jesus also promulgated a 'new commandment': 'That ye love one another; as I have loved you, that ye also love one another. By this shall all *men* know that ye are my disciples, if ye have love one to another'.[5] The important thing here is that these commandments are statements of necessity, of what one must obey and ardently follow, if one is to become a disciple of the head of the Council of Bodhisattvas. One thereby becomes a Bodhisattva, following the Bodhisattva *bhūmis* to Shambhala. The methodology makes one a prime causative agent, an Initiated member of the Hierarchy of enlightened being. All other 'commandments' are superseded by these three:

3 Balsys, The revised *The Revelation, 401-2.*

4 See also *Mark 12:28-34.*

5 *John 13:34-5.*

1. The *Love of 'God'*, and thus identification with the purpose and qualities of the prime causative agent within our planetary sphere. The 'God' mentioned here is that concept of Deity (the planetary Logos) as explained in the earlier volumes of this treatise, and effectively equated with the *maṇḍala* stemming from the Eye in the triangle of the first Shambhalic level.[6] It is embodied by the planetary Regent, the One presented earlier as Sanat Kumāra. Here we have the proper esoteric interpretation of the word 'Father' for all Initiates, thus Sanat Kumāra (Melchisedec[7]) is termed 'the One Initiator'. This is the Father of the process undertaken by all 'sons of God', if they are to come to know 'God'. (The term 'God' can also refer to one's own Monad, the Buddha within.) Such identification necessitates the development of the type of activity that will allow one to become Initiated into the mysteries of the Kingdom of 'God' (Shambhala). Initiation involves undertaking the steps in the process of becoming a causative agent, and thus consciously becoming an aspect ('spark') of the Mind structure of that Logos. This necessitates serving the Logoic Plan or Purpose with unswerving loyalty, as did Jesus. This then incorporates awakening to the expression of the Divine Will within. Meditation upon that Plan (or *dharmakāya*) and mantric prayer to effectively bring about its purpose then becomes the leitmotiv of the expression of the Initiate. There is no other way for such 'Love of God' to be expressed.

This is aptly demonstrated in the statements of Christ-Jesus: 'For I have not spoken of myself; but the Father which sent me, he gave me a commandment, what I should say, and what I should speak. And I know that his commandment is life everlasting: whatsoever I speak therefore, even as the Father said unto me, so

6 See Volume 7 of this treatise, *The Constitution of Shambhala*.

7 Heb. 7:1-3. 'For this Melchisedec, king of Salem, priest of the most high God,.. to whom also Abraham gave a tenth part of all; first being by interpretation King of righteousness, and after that also king of Salem, which is, king of peace; Without father, without mother, without descent, having neither beginning of days, nor end of life; but being made like unto the Son of God; abideth a priest continuously'. See also *Heb. 6:20,* where it is stated *'even* Jesus, made an high priest for ever after the order of Melchisedec'. So it is for all high Initiates that bow before the One Initiator in the Council chamber of Shambhala.

I speak'.[8] This is followed by the words: 'whatsoever ye shall ask in my name, that will I do, that the Father may be glorified in the Son. If ye shall ask anything in my name, I will do *it*. If ye love me, keep my commandments.....As the Father hath loved me, so have I loved you: continue ye in my love;....even as I have kept my Father's commandments, and abide in his love. These things I have spoken unto you, that my joy might remain in you, *that* your joy might be full'.[9]

This quality of joy, followed by bliss, is the result of the unqualified, spontaneous, magnanimous service work to enlighten all beings. They come as a consequence of following the commandment of Love that is the fiat of the Lord of this world. There is then an unbroken chain of Initiates that 'abide in his love', following their portion of the instructions ('Commandments') emanating from Shambhala. This manifests according to their respective Ray lines and Initiation status, so that humanity can be glorified and lifted eventually to the Throne of the Lord of this world, to whom they will humbly give obeisance. 'Life everlasting' is the stance of the liberated Initiate that can bear the glory of the Radiance of That One in the Mind's Eye. We can then say: 'Glory be, another Buddha has evolved to tread the endless Ways of cosmos'.

2. To *love thy neighbour as thyself. John 15:13* states: 'Greater love hath no man than this, that a man may lay down his life for his friends'. By this statement Jesus did not necessarily refer to those sometimes foolish acts of heroism, wherein a person sacrifices his physical body to save the life of another, as in war time. That indeed indicates the basic type of love to be developed on the most material level. What, however, is really asked is something far harder: that one's entire life become consecrated to the service of one's fellow human beings, that every thought, word, and deed is used only to assist. In this way, through the following of the Bodhisattva vow, a person truly 'lays down his life for his friends'. Only in this way

---

8 *John 12:49-50.*

9 *John 14:13-15,* and *15:9-12.*

can the Love of the greater being, the 'gift waves' from the *guru* or Master, come to work through one. (That Master may be Jesus, any other Bodhisattva, or great Shambhalic Lord.) One then becomes truly causative of new streams of unifying, creative endeavour laid before the altar of service to humanity.

3. *That ye love one another; as I have loved you.*[10] This statement is not just a repetition of the one given above, to Love one's neighbour, but is an injunction to Love each other in the same way that Jesus Loved them—as an Initiated member of the Kingdom of 'God', so that the Love of the Father can work through them. It concerns the development of the spirit of true group consciousness, of identification with the one Mind that is the basis of all enlightened activity that will Initiate one into the Mysteries. This will indeed make them disciples of the Christ. That is, they are Masters of Wisdom in the making. Such development will allow the 'Spirit of truth'[11] to enter into them. This 'Spirit' is but an aspect of Monadic/Shambhalic Identification, which to bear its potency necessitates true group (Hierarchical) consciousness, via the developed Heart centre.

We see in the above three statements concerning the making of a prime causative agent, that the fundamental or unifying principle is the quality of developed Love. This necessitates awakening the Heart centre, allowing an undistorted flow of energy from the highest centre (Shambhala) to flow through the disciple to humanity via the mediating agency of the Christ, who is the Hierarchical Heart upon this planet. This way of Love is the basis of the new Covenant, and is more than simply following a set of rules, code of ethics, or listing of 'commandments' that rigorously limit the patterning of the minds of the aspiring ones. (As did the ten Commandments.)

To freely work within the unlimited bounds of Love is the only means of gaining ever-expanding insight into the nature of the Mysteries of being/non-being, of the entire Causative process.

---

10 *John 13:34.*

11 *John 14:17.*

The Beatitudes

Consideration of the *Beatitudes* provides further insight into the way of development of the 'new' Commandment of Love, via the undertaking of Initiation. In explaining them, some of the information concerning the Initiation process will be repeated from a different perspective. This should provide a further tapestry for understanding the nature of the path of Initiation. I have numbered the statements of Jesus from 1 to 12.

1. And seeing the multitudes, he went up into a mountain: and when he was set, his disciples came unto him:
2. And he opened his mouth, and taught them, saying,
3. Blessed *are* the poor in spirit: for theirs is the kingdom of heaven.
4. Blessed *are* they that mourn: for they shall be comforted.
5. Blessed *are* the meek: for they shall inherit the earth.
6. Blessed *are* they which do hunger and thirst after righteousness: for they shall be filled.
7. Blessed *are* the merciful: for they shall obtain mercy.
8. Blessed *are* the pure in heart: for they shall see God.
9. Blessed *are* the peacemakers: for they shall be called the children of God.
10. Blessed *are* they which are persecuted for righteousness' sake: for theirs is the kingdom of heaven.
11. Blessed are ye, when *men* shall revile you, and persecute *you*, and shall say all manner of evil against you falsely, for my sake.
12. Rejoice, and be exceeding glad: for great is your reward in heaven: for so persecuted they the prophets which were before you.[12]

The significance of these statements has never been properly understood by the world's aspirants. They relate to the twelve steps or stages of unfoldment of the Heart centre that must be awakened if a prime causative agent is to rise from the ranks of humanity. If this information here is correlated with that presented in Volume 3, chapter 2, concerning the Heart centre, it will reveal the process of

---

12 *Matt. 5:1-12.*

accomplishment eventually producing the qualities described in that chapter. These twelve steps concern the undertaking of the various Initiations. Each step also relates to a sign of the zodiac.

1. Seeing the multitudes, he went up into a mountain.

This refers to the first sign of the zodiac, *Aries the ram.* Aries is the sign of cyclic beginnings, of the formulation of the idea from the loftiest heights of the realm of the mind (the mountaintop). There we also find the Sambhogakāya Flower (the Soul). The initial stages of the path of Initiation, that of aspiration, is implicated, when aspirants begin to receive impressions of loving service from their Souls. If they are to be succoured by 'the good shepherd', the multitude of aspirants must aspire to that high domain. In doing so, impressions are received from the mountaintop of their experiential selves. This 'shepherd' refers not just to Christ-Jesus, but also any enlightened member of the Hierarchy of Light. This path then draws to them many similarly focused ones ('his disciples'), as well as the streams of thoughts that serve to inspire, and to assist the work.

'The multitudes' are thus aspirants yearning to know something about the mysteries of being and of the Kingdom of 'God'. They aim to produce a better lifestyle by living in accordance with divine guidelines. Most seek simple teachings relative to the level of devotion applicable to their daily lives. In climbing to the higher levels of the mount of Initiation, one notices a correlated reduction in the number of fellow climbers, as the lofty qualities needed to be attained are increasingly difficult. Few indeed are the expert mountaineers able to reach the summit of earthly attainment, though all have the capacity if they seriously so aspire.

The keynote for this sign is 'the focussed purpose of the one that initiates'. Upon the Initiation path the Arian becomes a 'lamb of God' that will eventually develop the Divine Will.

2. He opened his mouth, and taught them.

This refers to the second sign of the zodiac, *Taurus the bull.* Once the initial idea (from the abstracted domain of Mind, ruled by Aries) is conceived, then it must be clothed in the appropriate substance or form that will produce the necessary effects. Here such substance represents the expression of teaching that the disciples yearn for. Taurus clothes the desired form and governs the directive Eye that helps project the clothed form onwards to its conclusion. This introduces the element of desire, which is bequeathed by this Taurean sign.

This second stage of the path concerns the ability of the aspirant to begin to communicate with others as to the nature of the revelations that were received from quiet meditative moments and high points of inspiration. They develop a yearning to discipline their lives so that they can live better, more productive lives in their field of service. Such increased focus allows a Master to accept them into his Ashram as disciples.

The keyword for the Taurean is 'illumination'. Upon the path, the Taurean clothes the Divine Thought and develops the all-seeing Eye that allows the Initiate to direct the all.

3. Blessed are the poor in spirit: for theirs is the kingdom of heaven.

Those who are 'poor in spirit' are poor in the knowledge of the nature of the Kingdom of 'God' (Shambhala). At first, the Sambhogakāya Flower has only a limited and infrequent influence upon the aspirant. Even so, this is the guarantee of them eventually becoming members of the Hierarchy of enlightened being (the 'kingdom of heaven'). This third stage of the path is governed by the sign *Gemini the twins*. Gemini governs the temples of the Mysteries of Initiation, the portals of which the candidate can enter at this stage, and when entering the presence of the innermost sanctuary (the adytum), can gain Initiation.

This stage thus refers to candidates working directly to obtain their first Initiation. (Whereas the other two stages refer to the path of aspiration and to probation for the undertaking of Initiation.) Here the aspirant often struggles between concepts of divinity and aspects of the vacillating, sensual, material self. He/she lives a dual life between being 'poor in spirit' and being stimulated by impressions from the rapidly approaching kingdom of heaven. This relates to the battle between the immortal (the Sambhogakāya Flower) and the mortal (the personality) brothers associated with this sign. We also have the distinction between the abstract and concrete minds, *śūnyatā* and *saṃsāra*.

The main attention is upon disciplining the physical form, and also upon the etheric constitution of the individual wherein reside the *chakras*. This is generally achieved through focus upon issues of health and mental-emotional vitality rather than through direct esoteric knowledge. It concerns 'turning about in the seat of consciousness' with regard to the effect of the *prāṇas* within the etheric form. The candidate begins to refocus away from the seat of desire (i.e., downwards) to upwards, where the centres above the diaphragm reside.

This stage is governed by the qualities of the seventh Ray of Ceremonial Magic, of ritualised activity. Those seeking this Initiation generally work from the conventional platforms provided by the orthodox religions, focused via temples and monasteries. They are also found in large numbers in all groups associated with social and environmental activism. They can also be found as investigative journalists, teachers, members of the medical profession, scientists; wherever an outlet exists to serve people in some way.

Such practices as *hatha yoga,* adherence to martial disciplines and following ethical, logically sound, or monastic rules of conduct, are often the mode of expression for the individual at this stage. Symbolically, the seventh Ray is 'poor in spirit' in that it governs the etheric-dense physical plane, the densest and furthest removed plane from the domain of Shambhala. The seventh Ray is however the most potent of the Rays for all esoteric (magical) endeavour. All Ray lines have their strengths and weaknesses.

The keynote for Gemini Initiates is that of 'equanimous synthesis' of the diverse qualities manifesting in the path of life. Upon the path of Initiation the Gemini subject becomes the temple builder, and then manifests as the divine intermediary between that which is above and that below.

4. Blessed are they that mourn: for they shall be comforted.

The concept of 'mourning' here does not specifically refer to grievance for loss of a personal friend or property that was dear to one. Rather, it refers to the loss of things associated with the material domain, to desire, selfishness, emotionality, and sensuality, which must be transformed if the way to Shambhala is to be trod. Old, often cherished allurements, glamours, emotional attachments, habits, sensual pursuits and the like, must go. Generally, this causes a sense of regret or loss in the aspirant, producing mourning or grieving for them. Such people are comforted, in that a beneficent gift wave of vivifying Watery energy descends upon them. Also, the Hierarchy sends their agents and helpers, both on inner realms and upon the physical plane, to offer comfort and guidance. The aspiring one learns that he/she is not alone, but is part of a band of like-minded travellers, who are geared to help on this path to light and liberation and with all decisions to be made.

This statement is ruled by the qualities of the sign *Cancer the crab.* Cancer is a Watery sign, and at this stage the candidate prepares to undertake the second Initiation, signifying overcoming the vicissitudes of the Watery emotions. The disciple has to confront many old glamours, whilst many new ones associated with treading the path open up. The lure of the lower psyche, of astral plane magic, looms strongly. Cleansing and invigorating energies now pour through the *nāḍīs,* coupled with the transformation of *saṃskāras* that otherwise would keep one tied to lower psychic and emotional states. The 'crab' also rapidly attaches itself to all things desired with its claws, generally by now found in the form of appealing spiritual information or of that associated with the service arena it is focussed upon. At this stage, disciples have not yet developed an impeccably refined mind, and emotional considerations often taint decision making.

Cancer is the sign of incarnation, of repeated births into new situations and of mass consciousness. Here it provides birthing into many new mental habits and enlightening concepts that comfort the Initiate as he/she struggles with the process of adaptation to the various spiritual and service orientated challenges ahead. At this stage surrendering things desired because of new allurements constitutes many of the battles within the disciple's consciousness. Being an accepted disciple, the doors to the beneficence of the related Ashram have opened for them. The downward flow of vitalising thought-forms from the Hierarchy through activity in the arena of service of one or other of the Ashrams of the Masters of Wisdom produces many enlightening insights.

The devotional qualities of the sixth Ray now also definitely stimulate disciples. They become devoted to concepts of divinity, and to images of one or other of the spiritual teachers or guides upon the way. Everything is determined by the quality of spiritual desire and ambition, with many conflicting ideals through which one must fight. The turbulence of the emotional and desire body must now be understood and overcome, for it is with such substance that one 'mourns'.

The keynote for Cancerian Initiates is that they are 'the lighted house', carrying illumination wherever they go. They become the dispeller of the Waters, the light of the Watery lives.

5. Blessed are the meek: for they shall inherit the earth.

This statement refers to the fifth sign of the zodiac, *Leo the lion,* whose major quality or problem is the demonstration of pride, for at this stage the attributes of mind begin to be seriously confronted. Thus all of the illusions that the disciple had previously fostered must now be dissipated. Pride looms all-important because the disciple faces all past accomplishments concerning both spiritual and temporal activities and forms of creativity. Their true worth must be ascertained from an enlightened point of view. Meekness here refers to compliance to the laws of Love, whereby the hubris associated with prideful tendencies is overcome so that what must be learnt can be applied for the benefit of others. A form of humbleness thus is developed that will submit one's activities to the requirements the path imposes, so that inevitably the group (symbolised by the pride of a lion) can be best served. Forms of arrogance will not allow one to enter through the portals of the third Initiation. Intellectual prowess is fostered, but must be tempered with the way of thinking with the Heart, the awakened abstract Mind. The Will-to-Love and then *bodhicitta*[13] becomes the dominant force driving the Initiate to the enlightenment that the third Initiation signifies.

The lion here is lord or conqueror of the jungle of the material domain. The development of true meekness, where a true sense of values and knowledge of the right placement of things is known with surety and worked with, is literally what allows one to 'inherit the earth' as a third degree Initiate. Through mastery of the realms of mind, the Initiate of this degree comes to know all of the mysteries concerning the world. He/she is thus able to rule this domain with effectiveness. The mastery of the glamours and illusions preparatory for the third Initiation facilitates the task of becoming a prime causative agent. This is only possible when the objective of the process will not be frustrated by any illusions stemming from the mind and emotional perturbations, and their glamour forming tendencies.

This stage is governed by the fifth Ray of Scientific Reasoning, for this is the Ray of the Mind and of its mastery. This certainly allows one

13 Here seen as the Heart's Mind, the Mind of enlightenment. The power or force productive of awakened realisations, enlightenment that emanates from the Heart centre. Bodhicitta is the Mind of pure perfection, the authentic nature of Mind.

to rule the material domain, as is aptly demonstrated by the effects of modern materialistic science.

The keynote for Leonine Initiates is that they are 'the lights of consciousness'. They are lords of the material domain, embodying the qualities of the Soul of all Life.

6. Blessed are they which do hunger and thirst after righteousness: for they shall be filled.

The word *righteousness* means 'that which is characterised by uprightness or fine morality, virtuous ideals'. Esoterically, this word implies bringing down the energies and qualities that will impose upon the aspirant the highest virtues and stout realisations of the nature of Love, eliminating commonplaceness. The disciple can now undertake causative activities that are directly guided from the higher domains, and by the Hierarchy of Light, from which this downpour of righteousness comes. The stable base of this Hierarchy is the *śūnyatā-saṃsāra* nexus. Only from the state of being Void of all discernible attributes of mind, can one truly discern the right from the wrong, and thus manifest morally correct decisions at all times, which righteousness demands.

We see, therefore, that righteousness is a force, an energy-wave that becomes applied in one's service arena, as righteousness is only seen as a demonstrable effect. It is not something wishy-washy, or some idealistic meandering of the loving mind, as was possibly the case in the previous stages of development. The energy of righteousness from this perspective can therefore be considered to be equated with *bodhicitta*.

Those that 'hunger and thirst' for the 'Body and Blood of the Christ' esoterically seek for the Hierarchical energies, with which they are soon to be filled to capacity. This stage is ruled by *Virgo the virgin*, who gives birth and succours the Christ child. Indeed, the Christ is born in the cave of the heart when the *first Initiation* is undertaken, and the Bodhisattva vow that is the leitmotiv of his work becomes fully expressed by the time of the fourth Initiation. These Initiates come to be filled with 'the Spirit of God' (*dharmadhātu,*[14] or *bodhicitta*), for nothing else could satisfy this type of hunger.

---

14 The wisdom of superior qualities, the pristine cognition of reality's transcendental expanse or sphere of empowerment. The fundamental essence or realm of the *dharma*, the *dharmakāya*.

Virgo governs all material substance (via the *devas* that embody it all) which those that 'thirst after righteousness' strive to master and transcend.

The fourth Ray of Beautifying Harmony overcoming Strife finds its rightful place here. Through the application of the energy of righteousness the Initiate is able to produce harmony and beneficence in the midst of the chaos and conflict of materialistic life. The fourth Ray allows the highest expression of divinity to be reflected into the lowest domain. Spirit (*dharmakāya*) thereby comes to be born in matter (*saṃsāra*), and the passing of the various Initiation levels allows the Initiate to increasingly manifest that Spirit to transform *saṃsāra* into the Divine. The divine child matures into the embodied Christ-Bodhisattva, and eventually a Buddha, before consequent progress into cosmos.

The keynote for Virgoan Initiates is that they are 'the divine Mother'. They produce the Christ-child, and are the sowers for the harvest of life.

7. Blessed are the merciful: for they shall obtain mercy.

This and the next four statements are concerned with the five major attributes gained and suffered by Bodhisattvas in training for the various Initiations up to the degree that Jesus aptly demonstrated by the incidents that led to his crucifixion. This then refers to undertaking the fourth Initiation (and the veiled fifth). Everything relating to the attainment of this Initiation, therefore, is what is emphasised by the teachings in the New Testament. Obviously, very few had the ability to take this Initiation, even now there are only a relative handful of fourth degree Initiates amongst us. The whole tone of the teachings is therefore geared to educating the prospective Initiates of the second degree (being the lower reflex of the fourth). One will find a large number of disciples in training there, with their esoteric needs being foremost upon the minds of those responsible for their spiritual awakening.

Because of the significant number of candidates for the first and second Initiations amongst the ecclesiastics of the Christian religion, so we see zealotry, religious bigotry, fanaticism, intolerance, martial qualities, and even outright hatred of those who follow different sectarian views, which has so much dogged the history of Christianity. That history was also considerably influenced by the negative attributes of the sixth Ray flavour of devotion that governed the Piscean era through which the religion evolved.

As the Initiation following the second is the third, so it should be noted that the qualities to be attained for the third is the emphasis of the remaining statements of the Beatitudes. (The overall aim though is the attainment of the fourth Initiation.) The phraseology therefore is written within the context of what most concerns those of the second degree. It is designed to enthuse them to aspire to greater heights of revelation.

A purpose of Christianity was to give expression principally to the devotion-Love and sacrificial qualities needed as a foundation for the undertaking of the fourth Initiation. This ideal Hierarchical agenda was waylaid by the aberrant ones preparing for their second Initiations. In providing the wisdom attributes, Buddhism gave definitive teachings as to what taking the fourth Initiation entailed in the doctrine of *śūnyatā* and the *prajñāpāramitā*. It capitalised upon the yoga tradition whereby high meditative insights and complete mastery of *saṃsāra* could be produced. The mainstay was therefore the third Initiation, but the focus was upon attaining the fourth. The Tantric tradition that developed in the later half of the first millennium provided teachings for attaining the fifth Initiation. Christianity continued along the line of the *bhakti* tradition inherent in the concept of absolute devotion to a worship of 'God'. The mainstay was therefore the second Initiation manifested in a way that facilitated the taking of the fourth.

We can see here how these two religious traditions really compliment each other, one esoterically spiralling round the other along a general *piṇgalā nāḍī* stream of evolution.[15] Meditative insights in one tradition laid the foundation to become a wise philosopher in the other. Steadfast devotional ecstasy to a high concept of divinity (Christ or 'God') laid the foundation for later strenuous focus upon a yogic path when that aspirant was born into the Mahāyāna Buddhist stream of development. Both religious streams concurrently evolved with similar concepts of sacrificial Love. In one, the divinity in people was awakened through Love for the concept of God and the exemplar of His sacrificial Son, who was to be initiated. Buddhism on the other hand developed the Bodhisattva ideal. The teaching provided by Jesus was to so thoroughly

15 Māhāyana Buddhism is *piṇgalā-piṇgalā*, Christianity is *iḍā-piṇgalā*. Theravada is *piṇgalā-iḍā*, and Islam is *iḍā-iḍā*, where the *iḍā* line relates to reified or Theistically oriented focus, and the *piṇgalā* the inward way of the Heart. Tantra represents the genesis of the *suṣumṇā* path in religion.

sacrifice the personal-I for the Love of humanity and for 'God' that only the Christ-presence (enlightenment) remained. Buddhism undertook a thorough analysis of mind to discover its illusionality, and in doing so evoked the path of wisdom by awakening the full powers of the Heart centre in its approach to enlightenment. Because the main Mahāyāna doctrines had their genesis at a similar time as the ministry of Jesus' disciples, it allowed cross fertilisation between the religions through Initiates rapidly incarnating from one to the other. The external dissimilarity in methodology of the two religions is bridged by an internal esoteric symbiosis. The process, however, was marred by the deflection toward the left hand path by the Christian stream.

The Initiation path produces inevitable mastery of the five types of *prāṇas*, allowing the Initiate to eventually wield causative energy without undue destructiveness or dissipation of energies. The path from the first to the third Initiation effectively takes about five lives to accomplish, and a synthesising two to extract the purpose or essence of the qualities gained.[16] The true mastery of the second Initiation, however, is normally very difficult for the prospective candidate because of the stranglehold of the emotions upon the human psyche. Consequently the groundwork of much of the fourth Initiation has generally been laid before the third Initiation can be taken. Often, therefore, we find one taking the second, third and fourth Initiations in one life once the problems associated with the second have been overcome.

The first two (minor) Initiations produce creative insights into the qualities to be expressed when consciousness is centred in one or other of the five *vayūs*.[17] They are thus trial runs for the Initiations to follow. They express lower octaves of revelation wherein base human qualities (*saṃskāras*) are mastered that will later be fully transmuted in lives when the fourth and higher Initiations are undertaken. All is veiled by

---

16 This statement concerning seven lives of accomplishment to the third Initiation is perhaps idealistic. More lives are often needed because of the ubiquitous problems of the second Initiation.

17 The term *vāyus* refers to the five Winds or *prāṅas* embodying the qualities of the five Alchemical Elements which course through the *nāḍī* system. They are termed *prāna* (Air), *samāna* (Water), *apāna* (Earth), *udāna* (Fire), and *vyāna* (Aether). These five stages therefore relate to the mastery of the elemental attributes and the awakening of the associated *chakra*. See also chapter 8.

cycles within larger cycles of spiral expression. The qualities associated with the development of human consciousness manifest within the spirals and spirillæ (planes of perception) of the Logoic permanent atom of which we all are a part.

The process of enlightenment, the making of a prime causative agent, happens through spiral after spiral of interpenetrative, expansive awakening of creative application through meditative insight into the ways of the Heart. Each spiral of development has five implicit sub-spirals of creative activity, answerable to the qualities of the five *vayūs*.

The tabulation below summarises the qualities associated with the remaining statements in relation to the five *vayūs*.

The merciful	Third Initiation	**Plane of Perception**
Stage 5. Vyāna	Head centre	Ātmic
The pure in heart	Second Initiation	
Stage 4. Prāṇa	Heart centre	Buddhic
The peacemakers	First Initiation	
Stage 3. Udāna	Throat centre	Mental
The persecuted	Probationary disciples	
Stage 2. Samāna	Solar Plexus centre	Astral
The reviled	Aspirants	
Stage 1. Apāna	Sacral and Base centres	Etheric/dense

Table 2. The five *vayūs*

Some of the qualities of the higher Initiations are also hinted at in these stages, and will be mentioned when appropriate. By now the reader should be accustomed to viewing things from many levels of interpretation at once. In esoteric matters, the principle of multidimensional visioning is always applicable. They are sequences of expression of the same event upon ever-expanding, higher cycles of being/non-being.

The phrase *'Blessed are the merciful'* relates to the third Ray of enlightening, Mathematically Exact Activity. To be truly merciful one must creatively utilise the mind correctly and with mathematical exactitude to appropriately serve the plan. The quality of mercy here does not just mean manifesting a compassionate or kindly act towards an enemy, offender, or other in one's power; nor does it just mean to have pity or benevolence upon those weaker than one, or the oppressed. These are qualities easily developed by the lovingly intelligent person or general religious aspirant. It means an in-depth, meditative insight into the sources of the entire world's troubled profile, and the formulation of a plan to help one's developed sphere of concern.

Such contemplative action is governed by the qualities of *Libra the balances.* This sign represents that which balances the polar opposites signifying the extremes in life, and comes to an equilibrium, producing meditative insights into the needs of the moment. We also have the long distant view. These insights necessitate developing the meditative attributes that allow one to stand upon the clear mountainous heights where the third Initiation is wrought. To do so one must practice mercy through all the five stages of the liberation process. To be truly merciful one must carefully weigh out the pros and cons of any planned act of benevolence, with increased efficaciousness as each stage manifests. Libra is the adjudicator of the Law and carefully weighs out the mitigating factors of any given situation before acting.

The beneficence given and the energy expended must be effected in the most efficient manner, if the consequence of one's mercy is not to be abused by, or be squandered upon, those to be benefitted. The objective of such acts of mercy is to uplift the oppressed and to free them from the chains of bondage of the many delusions, the forms of materialistic, selfish, and separative attitudes that are the cause of their woes. The merciful one must also comprehend the nature of the conditioning factors in civilisation, of the powerful ones that manipulate resources, financially rape and pillage from the many, producing widespread hardships that must be countered by wise activism of the merciful. Many that suffer are the victims of the evil doing of these egregious ones.

To be truly merciful necessitates being in full control of the emotions that would tend to distort the situation at hand or the facts of the matter, and to act also from truly compassionate motives. The Initiate of the third degree is thus implicated. Bereft of the concept of ego the third degree Initiate works totally selflessly for the benefit of the plan. By extension, we also have the Master (fifth degree Initiate) working from *dharmakāyic* levels. He manifests similarly upon a vaster domain, showing beneficent mercy for the many maladroit activities of those within his Ray Ashram (and in the wider community) undergoing the training needed to take the higher Initiations. Many individual and group *saṃskāras* are brought to the surface, developed in former unruly, oft violent, heartless, selfish times, that now need to be cleansed by the disciples in his care. The Master must have merciful considerations for those personality blunders as the *karma* is woven for their rectification.

The more esoteric interpretation of the phrase 'the merciful' refers to the work of the Master of Wisdom at the Heart of any divinely ordained sphere of activity, and those that 'shall obtain mercy' refers to the disciples struggling to attain their third Initiations.

To obtain mercy means to receive the *wave of benediction* from a high source (e.g., Deity), which is definitely uplifting and liberating in its effect. This allows one to travel through increasingly higher spirals of creative activity, through the various stages of *prāṇic* circulation, and the successive undertaking of the trial runs that are the prelude to Initiation. The Initiate travels by means of such waves of merciful benediction from Deity, or the *guru* or Master, for it is the power that draws him/her ever upwards and outwards toward cosmic heights. The great wheel of the Law turns through spiral after spiral of merciful activity. As a consequence, material or limiting *karma* is cleansed, for this quality of mercy also implies the absolution of the *karma* that ties one to the entire ephemeral, material world. Such absolution is not something that is conferred by divinity, but because someone has appropriately transformed the associated *karma*. The merciful one facilitates comprehension of how to do so.

The *prāṇa* referred to here is that of stage 5, Vyāna, associated with the Aetheric Element and the *ātmic* plane. The gift waves of benediction therefore come to flood the entire *nāḍī* system of the Initiate, pushing out the remaining unruly *saṃskāras* to be transformed by the candidate. The objective of these beneficent waves of compassionate energy is to awaken the full Head lotus (*sahasrāra padma*), which happens when the third Initiation is undertaken.

The keynote for Libran Initiates is that they are 'righteous adjudicators'. They demonstrate the qualities of the interlude between all breaths of activity, and appropriately dispense the law of the *dharma*.

8. Blessed are the pure in heart: for they shall see God.

Purity of Heart implies that the qualities of the major Love petals of the Heart *chakra* are being actively expressed. As far as the Heart centre is concerned, we see that there are five petals specifically associated with the development of the Fires of the Mind (the knowledge petals), which are also related to the qualities of the five *vayūs*. They are the correspondences to the non-sacred planets, the bearers of the attributes of the sense-consciousness that need to be mastered and converted to wisdom. The remaining seven petals directly express the refined attributes of the Heart. These seven esoteric petals channel the qualities of the seven Rays. Once the attributes of all these petals are mastered, then the individual can think with the Heart and work through that centre as the major focus for all activities. Only then can the higher Initiations be undertaken.

The Initiations specifically inferred here are the second, with the overtones of the fourth and sixth Initiations. Second degree Initiates have definitely cleansed their emotional volatility and gross desires in such a manner so as to be pure in heart, to rightly follow the dictates of divinity as outlined for them in their religious scriptures, or to serve humanity in one way or another. Their astral bodies are vibrant and permeable to higher impressions, yet they still manifest as a veil preventing direct access to 'God'. As the higher Initiations are undertaken, so progressively various veils are lifted. The fourth degree Initiate stands as a pure transmitter of cosmic Love, having transcended all attributes of *saṃsāric* form that can limit the expression of this energy. The sixth degree Initiate (a Chohan of a Ray, or a Buddha) has no veils left to remove. He stands directly in a Monadic (*dharmakāyic*) vehicle (a Lord of Love), seeing 'Eye to Eye' with the Logos of a planetary system.

The Heart in the Head is inferred in this phrase, and also the qualities of the eighth sign of the zodiac, *Scorpio the scorpion*. This sign is specifically concerned with the myriad tests and trials that the candidate must successfully undergo if Initiation is to be taken. These trials specifically deal with overcoming the vicissitudes of the emotional nature. The major battles thus concern taking the second Initiation, which when successfully passed, will make one 'pure in heart'. It involves battling with and overcoming the nine-headed Hydra of desire (the gross *saṃskāras* of the Solar Plexus centre) before one can actively stand in the Heart. Inevitably, the petals of the Heart centre are awakened, there being twelve major petals and 96 subsidiary petals. Scorpio governs the energies that cause the turning of the great wheel of Life one way or the other. Many are the stings in Life it bequeaths before emotional quietude and rectitude is possible.

This stage is governed by the second Ray of Love-Wisdom, as this quality must be evoked if one is to become 'pure in heart'. The second Ray directly invokes the powers of the Sambhogakāya Flower. When done so by way of mind, the third Initiation can be undertaken and one becomes a causative agent. Then one stands upon the mountaintop where 'God' can be seen, and a dialogue is entered into with those of His kingdom. The third is the first cosmic Initiation.

Stage 4, Prāṇa and the Airy Element (buddhic plane) rules this level of development, as the Initiate must learn to channel the breath of Life throughout the entire *nāḍī* system if the Heart *chakra* is to be effectively awakened. This process happens at the time of taking the second Initiation.

The keynote of Scorpio Initiates is that they are 'triumphant visionaries'. They become sword bearers for the Lord of Life.

9. Blessed are the peacemakers: for they shall be called the children of God.

This statement interrelates the first to seventh degree Initiates in the manner outlined below. The term 'peacemakers' has a reference to the qualities obtained by seventh degree Initiates with respect to the effect of their work and energies upon the entire planetary disposition. Peace is the type of energy dispensation that they emanate. For this reason, the Christ (an Initiate of the seventh degree) is esoterically styled 'Prince of

Peace', being the embodiment of the Messiah announced in *Isaiah 9:6-7*.[18] In *John 14:27* he stated: 'Peace I leave with you, my peace I give unto you: not as the world giveth give I unto you.' However, we also have such statements as: 'Think not that I am come to send peace on earth: I come not to send peace, but a sword.'[19] This is the sword of Spirit, the energy that causes the Initiation process, via strife in the life of the disciple, that works to eliminate all of the emotional *saṃskāras* that prevent enlightenment. This produces most of the problems in the disciple's life, often causing him/her to enter a place of quiet contemplation, such as a monastery. The Buddha also did this when he left his wife and family to seek enlightenment. Family, friends and society often do not comprehend the nature of such 'antisocial' behaviour, and thus strife results. When the Initiation process manifests upon a planetary scale, such as is now happening, then we have widespread strife as an effect of the changes caused by a large number of disciples warring against the conventions of the norm in society, and to bring about the new by overcoming adversity.

To bring about peace in the midst of strife is also a function of the qualities of those training for the *fourth* Initiation, which is governed also by the fourth Ray. Fourth degree Initiates are concerned with the practical demonstration of the energies of *buddhi (bodhicitta)*. This energy works through group interrelations, wherein all aspects of strife must be effectively remedied. These aspects prevent the related service work and causative output of the group from manifesting. This needs little elaboration, as much can be collated from the previously published teachings on Initiation, and of the nature of the work of the Bodhisattva. The fourth degree Initiate is the exemplar of the Bodhisattva ideal, being able to consciously reside at the *śūnyatā-saṃsāra* nexus.

First degree Initiates are termed 'children of God', as far as the Initiation process is concerned. Those of this degree are 'child-like', still

---

18 'Unto us a son is given: and the government shall be on his shoulder: and his name shall be called Wonderful, Counsellor, The Mighty God, The Everlasting Father, the Prince of Peace. Of the increase of his government there shall be no end, upon the throne of David, and upon his kingdom, to order it, and to establish it with justice from henceforth even forever. The zeal of the LORD of hosts will perform this'. The 'government' referred to here is that of the Hierarchy.

19 *Matt. 10:34.*

to learn the lessons so aptly mastered by their elder spiritual brothers and sisters. The fourth degree Initiate stands in relation to the first degree in a similar manner as an Initiate of the seventh degree does to the fourth. Thus we have a direct line of energy transmission from the highest to the lowest:

Logos ('God')
↑↓
seventh degree Initiate
↑↓
fourth degree Initiate
↑↓
first degree Initiate

First degree Initiates are the children of this dispensation, and must reverse the process of descent of energies as they ascend to greater heights of revelation and awareness. In this way, they shall inherit the 'kingdom of heaven' and know the associated mysteries.[20]

The Initiation process concerns the development of, and receptivity to, the Divine Will. It eventually supplants self will with the Divine Will, which Jesus ardently prayed for in the Garden of Gethsemane ('not my will, but thine, be done').[21] The candidate must also be able to increasingly abide in the Love (*bodhicitta*) that is the emanatory radiance of the Hierarchy of Light, the Council of Bodhisattvas. (Termed 'The Holy Ghost' in the New Testament.)

To thus become a 'child' one must be able to draw upon the first Ray of Will or Power, as this is the energy qualification that cuts away all illusions and barriers to the highest revelations. The first degree

---

20 *Matt. 13:11.*

21 *Luke 22:42-4*, which states: 'Father, if thou be willing, remove this cup from me: nevertheless not my will, but thine be done. And there appeared an angel unto him from heaven, strengthening him. And being in agony he prayed more fervently: and his sweat was as it were great drops of blood falling to the ground'. This is actually one of the great seminal moments in world history, as the outcome of this prayer was eventual crucifixion. The angel would be called a *ḍākinī* in Buddhism, whilst the 'great drops of blood' signify the response from Shambhala, anchoring onto the physical plane the energies of cosmic Love via his agonised invocation. Great is the esoteric significance of this statement.

Initiate must demonstrate the goodwill that expresses the revelation of the glory that direct contact with the realms of Light supernal confers. He/she must be able to project the *antaḥkaraṇa* from the personal-I to the Sambhogakāya Flower, and thus to Hierarchy. As the higher Initiations are undertaken, Shambhala and the *dharmakāya* awaken to the Initiate's ken. The downpour of Shambhalic energies from the 'Kingdom of God' will produce peace on earth when enough Initiates arise that can bear the energies.

The peacemakers draw upon the energies of those that are pure in Heart (of Stage 4, Prāṇa) because it is the energy of Love that draws one to the path, to want to master the personality vehicle so that others can be helped. Effectively, it results at this stage to make one a healer in the true esoteric sense. This means that first degree Initiates begin to see the various areas of discord in the society around and resolve to do something about it. They work hard to try to bring peace in the midst of the forms of discord and strife affecting the planet. They become political activists, warriors for the environment, educators in the fields of nutritional health and for social conscience, etc. Many also become professional healers. All Initiates (Bodhisattvas) develop planetary healing capabilities, which increasingly awaken as they spiral through their Bodhisattva *bhūmis*. The accumulative work of healing the troubles, woes, and all dark (evil) *prāṇas* in the Body Logoic (thus the rectification of all diseases) by the community of Bodhisattvas is what will produce true peace upon this planet.

Stage 3, Udāna, actually underlies the entire field of the Initiation process from the first Initiation onwards. The function of becoming peacemakers necessitates the development of the qualities of the Mind, by awakening the Throat centre and by thinking with the Heart. One can then unfailingly articulate to others what is wrong, and provide the correct remedy. Causative energies can then be evoked to build constructs of service for the all.

It would be of value to the student to try to work this out for the Initiation stage they think they might be at. They should also try to account for the five minor sub-Initiations, or stages to the development of the next major Initiation for them. These sub-Initiations are along the line of mastery of the *vayūs* at the level of expression for the Initiation concerned. In Jesus's time, the focus of the world-disciple was upon undertaking the first three Initiations. The general Mahāyāna Buddhist epoch emphasised what was needed to attain the fourth Initiation, whilst in the present new cycle, the focus is upon the fifth Initiation. This necessitates an entirely new cycle of teachings and method of education, as exemplified in this series of books.

Sagittarius the archer rules this stage, because the peacemakers must be able to fire the arrows of visionary impetus to lofty heights if they are to inspire people to work in harmony for unified goals. This is accomplished in accord with their combined vision of what the future portends if their work is successful. The peacemakers need to break the bounds of previously formulated thoughts that were based on comparatively narrow, selfish, self-centered ambition and related reasoning. They must direct their arena for service work in such a way that the outcome is successful, resulting in societal and planetary harmony. They must rearrange these thought-structures on the basis of a common ground of one glorifying, unifying whole.

The keynote for Sagittarian Initiates is that of 'one-pointed direction'. They direct arrows of aspiration for the little ones, and manifest the qualities of the Avatar on the white horse riding forth to spiritually conquer the domains of materialism.

10. Blessed are they which are persecuted for righteousness' sake: for theirs is the kingdom of heaven.

The word *righteousness* means that which is morally right or justifiable, characterised by uprightness, virtue. At this stage the disciple is generally a far sighted visionary, who is concerned with the promulgation of new ideals and ethical views to humanity. These views often run counter to the established modes, mores, and rules of conduct. Aggressive reactions are thus generally the consequence because people fear change. The educational activity of Jesus is a good case at hand of the effect of high grade Initiates. He was often nearly stoned because of the fact that the teachings he gave were blasphemous to the Jewish orthodoxy of the time.

Such Initiates are always innovators. They can quite clearly see the limitations in established practices (of customs, religious observations, social inequalities, many scientific promulgations and laws), and thus work ardently and righteously to impose that which is new and better suited to meet the needs of the new generations. To do so, however, they are often persecuted by the reactionary stalwarts of orthodoxy that have much to lose if their positions of power, cherished beliefs, and financial bases are seriously challenged.

Stage 2 of the *vayūs,* Samāna, is directly implicated, referring to probationary disciples that are preparing to enter the path of Initiation and to travel the way that will eventually lead them to the summit of the mountain (Capricorn) where Initiation is possible. To do this they must seriously work upon their emotions, and to master this stage of the meditation process. The Initiate learns the code of silence to carefully and wisely meter out advice when needed, and to be silent when speaking would serve no purpose other than provoking ignorant reactions and aggressive verbal persecution. Those that fear the changes in their established belief systems, or the challenges to the selfish ways that society or an organisation is structured, are aggressively adverse to inconvenient truth. The Initiate is always a harbinger of change and of right education in the midst of those that have much personal power to lose as a consequence of the Initiate's activities. The gist of this tenth statement of the Beatitudes therefore follows through to every level of Initiation and the related service work that is provided.

The process of learning how to best overcome various forms of persecution and adversity provides many of the tests that generate wisdom. The challenges of overcoming adversity also produces the strength of the Love expressed to better help, and the Will to persevere to produce the necessary changes the work demands. Thus, eventually a Master of Wisdom evolves, who generally works hidden from the public eye, but nevertheless manifests a far-reaching service arena. Because persecution (or adversity) is so pervasive in the life of a disciple, so the remaining verses continue with this theme.

Capricorn the goat that climbs the mount of Initiation rules this stage, for now the entire Head centre is utilised. An Initiate can thus advantageously utilise all of the exigencies entailed in being a causative agent. Such a one stands at the crown of achievement for any cycle of activity.

The keywords for Capricornian Initiates is that they are 'transfiguring agents'. Upon the mountain of spiritual attainment they become the unicorn of 'God' carrying aloft the horn of plenty for all in need.

11. Blessed are ye, when men shall revile you, and persecute you, and shall say all manner of evil against you falsely, for my sake.

Here the quality of being a world server, as consistent with the symbolism of *Aquarius the water bearer,* is brought to the fore. Aquarius dispenses the Waters of Life and Love to all needy supplicants to help overcome the natural selfishness associated with this sign. The new Initiate is brought down from the lofty heights of revelation to the plains or fields of labour. Therein he/she is truly tried in the practical demonstration of all the qualities developed in the previous Beatitudes, wherein the five *vayūs* were mastered depending upon the Initiation level passed. Such Initiates battle with the sum of the fears, ignorant reactions, critical assertions, and projected animosity of those to be served.

Specifically, however, this quality of being reviled connotes the organised and massed attacks (psychically and otherwise) of the members of the dark brotherhood. Their materialistic empires and power bases are seriously threatened by the work of such fearless bearers of Love and Light. This introduces the entire subject of the nature of psychic attack and the methods the evil ones use to revile and generally hinder the work of the white brotherhood. The way the white brothers offset the effects of darkness in human minds are thus also implied here.

This verse also has a reference to Stage 1, Apāna, thus to the aspirants that enter the path to light by no longer adhering to the generalised opinions of their compatriots. Some present opinions that counter their fellow religionists, others are the dissenting voice in an organisation they are part of, and so forth. They are breaking free from the herd or mass mentality and openly posit their more broadminded and compassionate opinions, and consequently come to be reviled. They generally have not yet fully developed a proper understanding of what they are internally seeking, but are dissatisfied with the status quo. They aspire and go window shopping (an Aquarian disposition) for more satisfying teachings or service orientated vocations. The commonplace lifestyles of their friends and families no longer satisfy.

They restlessly seek more, often to the dismay of those around them, and hence the feeling or expression of being misunderstood, reviled, and even persecuted. They learn that to progress along the path to Initiation they must begin to serve a greater group than was in their ken before.

The keynote for the Aquarian Initiate is that of 'compassionate service'. They represent the group conscious ones that become world servers, exemplars of the Bodhisattva ideal.

12. Rejoice, and be exceeding glad: for great is your reward in heaven: for so persecuted they the prophets which were before you.

The qualities of the twelfth sign of the zodiac, *Pisces the fishes*, and the successful accomplishment of the work earlier planned relates to this last stage of the Beatitudes. The Initiate is exceedingly glad, as evil is vanquished for that cycle of endeavour and the fruition of the labour finally seen. The worthy candidate has been truly tested on the battlefield of life, which was mastered and the Initiation undertaken. Hierarchy exists in 'heaven', and rewards the server who becomes a saviour in Pisces. The reward denotes opportunity for greater service work, in accord with a newly unfolding plan formulated by the members of that Hierarchy. Such a plan rests upon the laurels of the accomplished task.

There is much rearrangement of energies and personnel within the Hierarchy as a consequence of this rejoicing. The prophets that were 'before you', are the Initiates of past cycles of activity who had played similar roles upon the world stage, and whose placing (seats of power) the new Initiate can now take. They can then ascend to even greater heights. This forces open the Door that allows stronger energies to descend to assist the great service.

The phrase *'rejoice and be exceeding glad'* refers to the undertaking of the first Initiation. The Initiate of this degree rejoices as he/she is finally Initiated into the first stages of the Mysteries and fully accepted into Ashramic life, with its many benefits. Indeed, the quality of Love manifesting through the Solar Plexus centre must of necessity cause such rejoicing. The statement has emotional implications, for the Watery Element has not yet been mastered.

The next statement: 'for great is your reward in heaven' refers to undertaking the second Initiation, for as in the case of Jesus' Baptism, divinity directly blesses such a one. The Initiator is pleased with the one that has emerged from the Waters, thus to enter the Fiery domain associated with heaven.

The final phrase, *'for so persecuted they the prophets which were before you',* refers to undertaking the third Initiation. This is because the *prophets,* to which the individual is compared, were Initiates of this degree. They had to identify with their higher selves *(tathāgatagarbha,* the Buddha-nature which resides in the kingdom of Heaven) in order to prophesy. Only from the realms of the Soul (or above) can spiritual truth be found.[22] From here one can hold the type of covenant that will allow one to become a prophet. This is not possible from the realms of glamour, to which those of lesser degrees are susceptible.

The keynote of the Piscean Initiate is that of 'mediatorship and sacrifice'. They represent the sacrifice of the one for the other that becomes the basis for the accomplishment of a world saviour.

A reason why the twelve signs of the zodiac are implicated in the Beatitudes is that the Initiate must master all of the qualities associated with the Heart lotus. The generation of Love-Wisdom is the key note for this solar evolution, and the development of the qualities of the petals of the Heart lotus sees to it. Initiates must learn to be fluent in all the attributes of the twelve signs of the zodiac, through which they must consequently labour. This necessitates them be reborn in each sign in turn as they pass their testings. They become glorified with the beatitude of Hierarchy manifesting through them, to uplift the consciousness of humanity. Such is the Bodhisattva way. Such is the teaching of the Sermon on the Mount.

22 The Sambhogakāya Flower has planned out that incarnation from beginning to the end within the context of all other Souls that have similarly incarnated. The future is therefore set in their collective meditations.

8

The Laws of Group Evolution

The zodiac and the laws of group evolution

With respect to the twelve signs of the zodiac and their keynotes as petals of the Heart lotus, we see that seven signs specifically relate to the progress of self-consciousness within Nature. They eventually produce a compliance to the effects of the group laws for humanity, and are associated with Ray purpose. The development of self-consciousness upon the upward way produces the path of Initiation and the evolution of the Ashrams of Hierarchy. Group evolution therefore comes into predominance. At first, these laws condition the development of humanity en-masse according to the Ray types that are incorporated within it. Later, more coherent groups evolve within humanity that demonstrate some of the attributes of the first four laws, bringing Hierarchy into existence. The process is stimulated by the Lords of Shambhala, who affect the consciousness of Soul-groups, and this effects human groups upon the physical plane. Later, there is a conscious response from the awakening disciples as the Ashrams begin to grow in number and diversify into their sub-ray groups. Loving obeisance to the dictates of the conditioning laws then manifest in the Initiate's consciousness. This is the stage humanity is at now, stimulating the need to broadcast information concerning the existence of these group laws and of the way they work.

The laws of group evolution are barely conceived of, let alone understood in the world today, but should be the subject of considerable discussion amongst disciples. I shall therefore try to elucidate upon, and provide further detail, to the information provided by the Tibetan Master D.K. in the books of A.A. Bailey.[1] The hope is to inspire further meditation, analytical deduction and application in the lives of all serious students of esoteric lore. Much can be revealed concerning the way of evolution of all lives in cosmos, and of what the future holds for the human race. These laws of group evolution will also be analysed from a different perspective in Volume 7B, chapter 2, of this *Treatise on Mind.* The introductory information presented here can correlate with what is later imparted. The laws are: The law of Sacrifice, of Magnetic Impulse, of Service, of Repulse, of Group Progress, of Expansive Response, and of the Lower Four. There are also three fundamental laws governing activity in the universe: the law of Synthesis, the law of Attraction, and the law of Economy. To them we must add the law of *karma,* and the overriding law of cosmic Identity.

The group laws concern the way of ascent into cosmos by the various groups that pass the tests of group Initiation. The era of individual progress upon the Initiation tree has been surpassed because of the large number of individuals now preparing to enter the ranks of Hierarchy. It is the way of evolution that conditions the Hierarchy of Light. The systemic third Initiation is here viewed as the first cosmic Initiation, thus the first two Initiations are Initiations on the threshold.

The order of the group laws provided by D.K. in *A Treatise on Cosmic Fire,* which condition the way of human evolution (rather than evolution in general) shall be utilised and placed upon the arms of the cross of direction in space. The first law (the law of Sacrifice) is placed upon the northeast arm of 'unity', the second law in the eastern direction and so forth to the northwest arm. The law of Attraction (one of the major laws emanating from the cosmic mental plane), of which the group laws are subsidiary, is placed upon the northern arm. Being subsidiary, the group laws are emanations of the great Lives existing upon cosmic astral levels, in which case the laws are organised according to their governing Rays.

---

1 *A Treatise on Cosmic Fire,* 1216-1222, *Esoteric Psychology II,* 87-200. (Lucis Press, 1977, 1981).

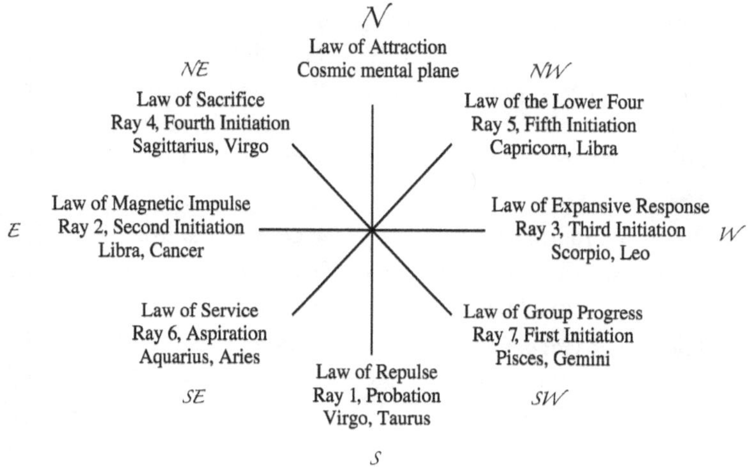

Figure 4. The group laws

Figure 4 incorporates two groups of astrological signs. The first shown for each direction is esoteric and the second is exoteric. The signs related to the Beatitudes differ from those governing the group laws, as they set the stage for the major struggles in *saṃsāra* and the field of testings preparatory to taking Initiation in Capricorn. Consequently, the signs associated with the Beatitudes are considered exoteric, whereas those governing the group laws are esoteric, and are interpreted from a higher perspective. The Beatitudes are a part of this cross as they condition the process whereby one comes to master the attributes of the corresponding law to which one is coming to be receptive in conjunction with the Initiation aspired to.[2]

The signs found in the Beatitudes governing these laws are Aries for the law of Service and the path of Aspiration, followed by Taurus

2 D.K. states: 'These seven laws lie behind all the various presentations of truth as they have been laid down by the world Teachers down the ages. It requires much spiritual insight, however, to enable the average disciple to see the correspondence or the trend of ideas which link, for instance: the beatitudes...the stages of the Noble Eightfold Path...the eight Means to Yoga...The ten Commandments. (*Esoteric Psychology, Ibid., Vol II, 163-164.*) He illustrates 'the eight Means to Yoga', whereas I shall utilise the Beatitudes for this purpose.

for the law of Repulse (the probationary path), then Gemini, Cancer, Leo, Virgo and Libra as we move up the Initiation levels.

The focus of this rendering will be the path of Initiation, from the development of aspiration to tread the path to taking the fifth Initiation. Each of the laws will be seen to refer to one or other of the stages, though in reality there are higher considerations that could also be dealt with.

1. The *law of Sacrifice* relates to *the fourth Initiation.* The governing Ray is the fourth of Beautifying Harmony in the Midst of Strife, and its esoteric name is the law of 'Those Who Choose to Die'. The symbol is 'a Rosy Cross with Golden Bird'.
2. The *law of Magnetic Impulse* relates to *the second Initiation.* The governing Ray is the second of Love-Wisdom, and its esoteric title is the 'Law of the Polar Union'. The symbol provided is two fiery balls and a triangle.
3. The *law of Service* relates to *the path of aspiration.* The governing Ray is the sixth of Devotion, and its esoteric title is 'The Law of Water and the Fishes'. The symbol is a 'Pitcher on the head of a man'.
4. The *law of Repulse* relates to *the probationary path.* The governing Ray is the first of Will or Power, and the esoteric title is given as 'The Law of all Destroying Angels'. The symbol is 'An Angel with a flaming sword'.
5. The *law of Group Progress* relates to *the first Initiation.* Its esoteric title is the 'Law of Elevation', and the symbol is 'The Mountain and the Goat'. The governing Ray is the seventh of Cyclic or Ritualistic Activity.
6. The *law of Expansive Response* relates to *the third Initiation.* The governing Ray is the third of Mathematically Exact Activity. No esoteric title is provided and the symbol is a 'Flaming Rosy Sun'.
7. The *law of the Lower Four* relates to attaining *the fifth Initiation.* The governing Ray is the fifth of Scientific Reason, and the esoteric name is the law of 'Etheric Union'. The symbol is a 'Male and Female Form placed back to back'.[3]

3 The information for these laws is derived from the chart on page 1220 of *A Treatise on Cosmic Fire.*

The Ray lines provided by D.K. in the order given for the laws start off with the second Ray line: 4, 2, 6 , followed by that of the first Ray line 1, 7, 3, and 5. We thus have a delineation between the *piṅgalā* and *iḍā* expression in Nature, signifying the distinction between the second Ray human line, who embody the way of Love in Nature, and the *deva* line that embody the way of mind.

1. The law of Sacrifice

This law is focussed via the *northeast* arm of the cross of direction in space, signifying 'unity', and relates to *the fourth Initiation*. Its esoteric name is the law of 'Those Who Choose to Die'. The symbol given by D.K. is 'A Rosy Cross with Golden Bird'.[4] The human unit must learn to sacrifice its own wishes, desires and attachment to form in order to travel upwards to the domains of liberation. The process of struggle to overcome the allurements of *saṃsāra* by renouncing transitory attachments to objects of the senses invokes the major law governing the fourth Creative Hierarchy[5] (the human Monads and Souls)—that of Sacrifice. This path will inevitably produce the sacrifice of the form of the Sambhogakāya Flowers when the purpose of human incarnations have been achieved. This is how *bodhicitta* awakens, and becomes the leitmotiv of the pledged disciple, which is the mainstay of the Initiate. It demonstrates through the potency of being able to transmit the cosmic Waters, by means of which all compassionate concerns and merciful decisions come to be continuously made.

The entire purpose for the originating aeonic incarnation of human Monads into the substance of the cosmic dense physical plane is here implicated. It concerns the redemption of the substance of the space incorporated by a Logoic form in the originating act of the creation of a planetary or solar sphere. All of the kingdoms of Nature came into existence, and by incorporating that substance in the periodic sheaths of cyclic incarnation, the human unit assists in converting it into units

---

4 These symbols shall be given but not commented upon, except to supplement the descriptions in *A Treatise on Cosmic Fire*.

5 See A.A. Bailey, *Esoteric Astrology* (Lucis Publishing, N.Y. 1968) for explanation of the Creative Hierarchies.

of intelligent activity. The process takes a vast arena of time. It is a salvaging and sanctification process of the myriad elemental lives that constitute the substance of *saṃsāra*. Freedom to travel in cosmos is 'temporarily' sacrificed by the Monadic Life so that primal substance can be 'redeemed' in this way.

Sacrifice essentially means giving up something valuable, precious, for a concept or significance deemed more worthy. For a human unit this involves renunciation of all attachments to the allurements of *saṃsāra* so that divinity can begin to reside within the temple of the human form. It means the complete renunciation of the concept of 'self' so that others can be maximally benefitted without egotism interfering. It therefore constitutes the foundation for the development of the group laws. An entire group of individuals are then stimulated towards loving interrelations via the surrender by the sacrificial ones of the sum of their egotistical posturing so that others may benefit.

Often, sacrifice connotes giving up significant or prized material possessions to the poor or needy. Such action is only the beginning of the path (dealt with in the law of Service). True sacrifice, however, means a complete reorientation of one's entire psyche for the benefit of the many. It incorporates renunciation and striving, of constantly developing more skilful ways to give. It necessitates the development of the Heart and Mind in unison to produce great wisdom regarding how best to give. Sacrifice produces the Bodhisattva vow to never cease striving until all sentient beings have been released from suffering. This inevitably leads to the crucifixion experience whereby the fourth Initiation is undertaken. It is the path taken by all who comprehend the true significance of the 'fellowship of the Christ's suffering'. It is the Hierarchical way. For this reason, this law stands at the northeast direction of Unity, as the path of Sacrifice unites all into a bond of Love and the will to serve. Unitedly they evolve their plan to do so, taking all of humanity's (in fact all of Nature's) illusions and causes of suffering into account. Vast and complex is the interrelation and interdependence of all members of humanity, and to meet their needs many of the plans may take thousands of years to accomplish. Such is the nature of the sacrifice by the Bodhisattvas to see the plans through until the last weary pilgrim has passed through the gates to liberation.

The plane of perception in which these group laws manifest to affect those in *saṃsāra* is *buddhi*, the fourth cosmic ether (*śūnyatā*), which is a major objective of the general Buddhist dispensation to experience. Such experience is also conceived of in terms of Jesus' crucifixion.

Esoterically, *Sagittarius the archer* governs the significance of this law. After the Initiation path has been instigated, the arrows of lofty aspiration can then be fired towards the highest target upon this planet, Shambhala. This goal necessitates aspiration to take the fourth and higher Initiations. The fiat of the Lord can then manifest through the service arena of Initiates developing righteousness and virtuous ideals via their specific Ray dispensation. Sagittarius connotes developing the various types of will that allows one to relinquish attachment to one or other form of *saṃskāra,* until all that is left is manifesting divinity. It signifies firing the arrows of will and purpose to ever higher goals of possibility. For the aspirant, the goal signifies the symbol of the divine, or their own Souls. For the probationary disciple it represents the precincts of the Ashram of the Master, or the service arena of the group. For the first degree Initiate it relates to aspiring towards the mountaintop experience. For Initiates of higher degrees it means firing arrows of revelation ever towards the target of the greatest source of Light and Love. This then produces the crucifixion experience.

Inevitably, the target becomes the domain of Shambhala, by paradoxically turning one's back to that august Door because the need of service to the little ones is so overwhelmingly great. One sacrifices one's own perception of progress so that the myriads can gain. The Door of liberation thereby looms large behind the Initiate, and many are the ones that are consequently drawn to it. At the appropriate time, the Lords of Life will cry out 'accepted' (into Shambhala). The cosmic paths will then open to which the Initiate must learn to fire arrows of release to far distant shores. Life upon earth is then sacrificed, so that the greater vastness can be served. The effect of Sagittarius the archer thus helps to generate the various forms of the will, leading to the Divine Will. It concerns firing arrows of one-pointed aspiration upwards through the door of Initiation (Capricorn), which produces the way of escape from the thrall of cosmic dense physical incarnation.

The development of the Initiation path turns all candidates into 'children of God',[6] because it is what makes one divine through sacrificial action. Sacrifice sanctifies, making one a Shambhalic recipient. The law of Sacrifice is a basic law that propels the evolutionary march of humanity; the sacrifice of time of a mother for her children; of the unit for the good of a family, tribe or nation; of a soldier's life at war, etc. It produces all forms of heroic actions in society, noble deeds, creative activities and the Bodhisattva idealism. It therefore conditions all of the other group laws.

The fourth Ray of Beautifying Harmony overcoming Conflict governs the law of Sacrifice and is the Ray governing humanity in general.[7] The generation of sacrificial acts amidst the conflict, struggle, egregious forms of human behaviour, to produce beneficent beauty, right human relations, and truly wholesome societies is an expression of this Ray. History abounds with the stories of those that have sacrificed their lives for human betterment, often in the most appalling conditions, and by confronting cruel, undeviating opposition. They work to overcome the selfish disposition, avarice, rapacity and materialism of humanity so that human lives are bettered upon all avenues of expression.

The sacrificial ones become martyrs, heroes, innovators, philosophers, educators, healers, scientists, and warriors of the Lord. Myriad are the unsung stories of the sacrificial acts for the benefit of others generated by people living in everyday society. Every such act is but a step towards eventual liberation from *saṃsāric* woe; a step upon the path of Light and Love that will incorporate them into the Ashrams of Hierarchy.

Aspirants for human betterment must struggle to produce a sense of harmony and beauty in their daily lives amidst the chaos, disharmony and conflict all around them. Such harmony can only be achieved if they incorporate into their surroundings others that similarly aspire. In doing so, group endeavour evolves and grows until they become crucified for the salvation of all. The energy of beautifying harmony will then flow through every pore of their beings, so as to produce the new Aquarian era of aesthetic garden cities around the globe that adequately sustain society's needs.

---

6 *Matt. 5:9, Luke 20:36,* etc.

7 They are termed 'Lords of Sacrifice' in A.A. Bailey's *Esoteric Astrology,* 35.

We can see from the above that the entire tenure of these group laws is the elevation of the little ones by those who 'choose to die' (to their material selves) so that all can progress upon the path of liberating Light and Love to Life Divine.

The exoteric sign governing this law is *Virgo the virgin*, associated with the sixth Beatitude, 'Blessed *are* they which do hunger and thirst after righteousness: for they shall be filled.' Righteousness (uprightness characterised by high morality and virtuous ideals) is a force that becomes applied to one's service arena, involving the sacrifice of time and resources so that others can be appropriately educated. Righteousness then is the force of the energy waves of the united service work of Hierarchy to cause the liberation of all lives from the *māyā* of their lives and the throes of the causes of their suffering. It is the effect of *bodhicitta* demonstrating via positive actions; a major energy governing the activities of Hierarchy. One sacrifices oneself for the common good for righteousness' sake.

Virgo here represents the Mother of all new ventures, as well as the substance embodied by the *devas*. One must sacrifice the lower *devas* (the *lunar lords)* and elementals that embody the substance of our incessant desires and emotions. A working cooperation with the higher *devas* must take their place, so that eventually a marriage, a new interrelation between human and *deva* evolutions occurs. Eventually, even concepts of being 'human' are eliminated through a fusion between the two kingdoms that happens at the higher Initiations.

2. The law of Magnetic Impulse

The *eastern* arm of the cross of direction in space representing inwards to the Heart of Life governs the *law of Magnetic Impulse* and relates to the *second Initiation*. The governing Ray is the second and its esoteric title is the 'Law of the Polar Union'. The symbol provided is two fiery balls and a triangle. To understand the nature of this law necessitates comprehension of the way that the Heart centre functions. The magnetic impulses from the Heart beat out the rhythms of the cycles of activity of Soul groups. The Heart centre only knows the way of group evolution and assesses the mode of movement in the spaciousness of consciousness accordingly. A magnet attracts all magnetic elements to it, similarly the Heart in the field of consciousness, once that consciousness has been refined enough to be affected by its attractiveness. Only when one is sufficiently established upon the path of Love, as signified by taking the second Initiation, where group consciousness is realised, can the Initiate firmly comprehend the nature of the dynamic pull of the Heart's activity. The cyclic pumping of blood to feed all manifest lives in the body is its symbol. By this means it integrates all into a unity.

The law of Magnetic Impulse is the force behind the development of the Will-of-Love, which is conceptualised by second degree Initiates. They utilise the Will-to-Love to learn to serve with the group of which they are a part. Later they all come to be united into a unified field of service via the Will-of-Love. The fourth degree Initiate, wielding the law of Sacrifice, comprehends the nature of this law via the sacrificial quest to integrate the all into the Heart of Life through the shedding of its Blood. The way inwards to the Heart necessitates the development of Love-Wisdom *(bodhicitta),* which is that which draws the many to unified knowledge of the purpose of the One Life, and to actively express its beneficence. As D.K. states:

> This Law of Magnetic Impulse governs the relation, the interplay, the intercourse, and the interpenetration between the seven groups of souls on the higher levels of the mental plane which constitute the first of the major *form* differentiations. These we can only study intelligently from the angle of the seven ray groups, as they comprise the spiritual aspect of the human family. This law governs also the relationships between souls, who, whilst in manifestation through form, are en rapport with each other. It is a law, therefore, which concerns the inter-relation of all souls within the periphery of what the Christians call "the Kingdom of God." Through a right understanding of this law, the man arrives at a knowledge of his subjective life; he can wield power subjectively, and thus work consciously in form and with form, yet holding his polarisation and his consciousness in another dimension, and functioning actively behind the scenes. This law concerns primarily those inner esoteric activities which are not primarily related to form life.[8]

---

8 A.A. Bailey, *Esoteric Psychology II,* 110.

He further states that because the solar Logos is upon the second ray path, all life in the solar system is controlled by this law.

> Under its stimulation the egoic lotuses unfold. It could perhaps be best considered as:
>
> a. The impulsive interplay between souls in form and out of form.
> b. The basis of egoic recognition.
> c. The factor which produces reorientation in the three worlds.
> d. The cause of the magnetic rapport between a Master and His group, or a Master and His disciple.[9]

This 'Law of the Polar Union' can only be realised when everything concerning personal ambition and egotistic posturing are eliminated, and focussed service has produced inner alignment with the Sambhogakāya Flower. 'Polar Union' can also be conceived if one places this law at the centre of the eight-armed cross, so that it integrates all of the polar opposites of this cross. It is the mantric Sound of the Heart of Life (Hierarchy) beating out the laws of Love that attract and galvanise all units of consciousness to organise into various groups in order to serve, to nourish, and to uplift the little ones to more wholesome arenas of activity. They can then do their 'whole duty' as they journey to the Sacred Sun.[10] It concerns the Hierarchical integration with Shambhala, producing an overshadowing beneficent Magnetic Impulse to draw all lives to the Light of the Love that glorifies the groups of conscious lives that respond. The Polar Union therefore is between the Sun at the Heart of Life and the groups of conscious response working to overcome the impediments between them and the glory of the radiant blaze at the Heart of all.

Similarly, Hierarchy stands as such a Sun for humanity, drawing to it the sacrificial groups along all Ray lines that are truly working for the benefit of all. They strengthen group resolve with intensified energies,

9 Ibid., 111. The term 'egoic lotus' here refers to the Sambhogakāya Flower.

10 Part of the Gayatri mantra: *Oṃ bhūr bhuvaḥ svaḥ, tāt savitúr vāreṇyaṃ, bhārgo devāsya dhīmahi, dhíyo yó naḥ pracodāyāt.* 'Unveil, O Thou who givest sustenance to the Universe, from whom all proceed, to whom all must return, that face of the True Sun now hidden by a vase of golden light, that we may see the truth and do our whole duty on our journey to thy sacred seat'. Translation by William Q Judge, (January, 1893) in *The Path.*

shield them with embracing Love, and help develop their wisdom and motivation to move forward upon the path.

The entire process towards enlightenment is impregnated by means of cosmic astral energies via the law of Magnetic Impulse. Magnetic Impulse involves the cyclic flood of cosmic Waters and the way they impact upon the systemic planes to cohere all separative *(manasic)* forms into a unity. *Devic* lives are thereby amalgamated into the *maṇḍala* of an earth sphere that develops via expansive response (the opposite arm of this cross) to eventually produce a divine marriage between the *deva* and human units that together serve. The entire embodied form then radiates out glory as the cosmic magnet draws all upon the evolutionary path of developing Love-Wisdom.

The attractive coherency of Magnetic Impulse finds a distorted resonance in humanity when it builds all of the attachments to the objects of desire that the creative imagination deems it needs. Thus inevitably the astral plane is built along with the myriad *saṃskāras* of desire-mind humans know so well, which becomes the field of all their misery. The causes of misery are well understood by Buddhists, as well as that the path of liberation concerns the methodology to become non-attached to the sum of this impulsive behaviour. The way of non-attachment is the basis to the development of Love-Wisdom, but can also be the foundation for the expression of much of what is deemed as evil, when directed by the separative mind. The entire battle upon the path to liberation whereby this evil is overcome (ruled over by Scorpio) concerns the movement of the disciple from the eastern to the western direction of this cross. The way of the Heart, of the awakening of Love-Wisdom, inevitably is that which will allow one to become liberated as the laws of group service are actively unfolded. Magnetic Impulse concerns the electrical interplay between all evolving groups of atomic lives. Positively charged units seek their negative counterbalances. All lives have such interactions, and the sex attraction of humans is but an effect of this law manifesting in our physical domain.

Esoterically, the ruling sign is *Libra the balances*, which governs the interlude between forms of activity, thus it works to integrate the moving spheres of activity in either pan so that they are resolved into one sphere of quietude. (The left pan contains the *saṃskāras* of the past, the burden of the *karma* of material activity. The right pan contains the future, where the *saṃskāras* come to be cleansed of impediments.) The past and the future then come to be resolved into the present that is the eternal Now.

Magnetic Impulse manifests as the deep blue of the ceaseless cosmic Breath that lies at the Heart of all outgoings and ingoings, the tides of *manvantara* and *pralaya.* We first have the Polar Union between Spirit and matter that instigates the phenomenal appearance of things, then in conjunction with the law of Expansive Response, consciousness manifests its evolutionary output. Finally, with the Law of Repulse we have the driving of all back to its originating source, carrying the gain of it all.

The fourth of the Beatitudes, 'Blessed *are* they that mourn: for they shall be comforted', governed by the sign *Cancer the crab,* is associated with this law. From this perspective, the crab attaches itself to concepts of group evolution, of the ways of Love, to become 'the light of the Watery Lives'. Old glamoured opinions about the importance of an 'I' are detached and replaced with new, invigorating concepts of how to best serve the Hierarchical Way. It is difficult to let go of separative habits of mind, so group-conscious affiliations can take their place, hence the 'mourning'. Humbleness, representing receptivity to the mantric Sound of the Hierarchical Lotus, comes to be developed in this eastern direction. Cancer represents the door to incarnation, or else to the Initiation process, the climbing up the lofty mountain associated with Capricorn, the polar opposite of this sign. Here the attainment of the second Initiation is implicated, wherein the Watery Element associated with Cancer comes to be controlled. First the probationary disciple must work upon his/her ego-seeking involvement with concepts of 'self'. The disciple must then overcome the tendency of attachments to the many material and sensual pursuits that incarnation into the Watery pools of the earth have provided. Mourning is the result of relinquishing things that have for so long been coveted. The tendency is also to harshly criticise the obvious failings in others, of other religions and philosophic presentations. Fanaticism and zealotry must be counteracted with a broadminded tolerance and wise acceptance of these faults, seeking how best to lovingly bring an amelioration of the problems. This is one of the major tasks leading to the attainment of the second Initiation.

3. The law of Service

The *southeast* arm of the cross of direction in space, signifying 'expression', governs the *law of Service* ('The Law of Water and the Fishes') and *the path of aspiration*. The governing Ray is the sixth. The path of aspiration happens at every level of expression at progressively higher stages of identification with the all for each new cycle of Initiation activity ahead. The process leads from the first to the seventh Initiation, which is the highest Initiation a person can attain upon this planet.

The associated Beatitude is: *'Seeing the multitudes, he went up into a mountain'.* The sign earlier presented was that of Aries because it signifies the initial urges, the inner promptings that cause one to aspire to achieve lofty ambitions, to walk the path to light. The general keynote of the path of service, however, is Aquarian. It is the energy of the presence of the Christ upon the mountaintop administering to the needs of the multitude of aspirants that have come to receive the living bread of Life from the serving one. His presence to draw them all up to greater heights is also an effect of the law of Magnetic Impulse, of the second Ray energy that he wields.

The esoteric appellation of 'the Water and the Fishes' implicates the Waters of Life, the energy of *bodhicitta*, that is dispensed from on high by the serving one to vitalise the 'fishes', the aspirants and disciples swimming in the murky depths of *saṃsāra*.

The key quality of the aspirant (apart from inherently selfish, self-serving motives) is the desire to serve, to help others, the planetary situation, or their concept of 'God', in some way. For this reason, they are drawn to listen to the accomplished one upon the mountaintop. What they receive causes them to devote themselves to the cause by taking up the challenge to tread the path of discipleship. They aspire to better themselves and the lives of others around them, and as they do so, the effects of the dispensation of this group law draws them to others with whom they can best serve. Together they develop as a group, learning from mistakes made, and the results of individual triumphs. They symbolically stand at the *southwest* arm of 'Understanding' of this cross of direction in space. Here is received the Living Blood dispensed by those standing upon the 'mountainous' northeast direction that have sacrificed their all for the Law.

The candidate learns humbleness upon this path because of the many difficulties encountered. *Saṃsāra* is not easy to master. Many devotional prayers, invocations and mantras are offered to deity by those beginning upon this path to gain blessings, revelations, and eventually enlightenment. Inevitably, the mantras become automatic, spontaneous, the emanation of the Heart attuned to all of the intonations of Nature.

Humbleness is the key to the law of Service that opens the gates to the advanced forms of Watery Activity upon cosmic astral shores. In humble and obeisant reverence do the members of an Ashram come to view the astounding revelations and beauty coming from the Masters of Wisdom via the polar opposite (governing the law of the Lower Four) of their southeast arm of the cross of Hierarchical activity. Humbly they aspire to imitate the forms of activity of the great Ones that are the source of their energies. Thus they serve. This way of service constitutes the entire Bodhisattva vow and resultant path. It leads to *śūnyatā* and the inevitable closing of the doors for the need to reincarnate. Bodhisattvas, however, continue to do so until as a group they progress upon the upward way. Liberation from the wheel of *saṃsāra* is the gain as they travel to the portals of the cosmic temple of Love-Wisdom. In so moving, they draw all those they are committed to serve up to the domain where they too can move on, and so the process continues, until *saṃsāra* no longer exists. They do so as part of groups, exoteric and esoteric, and so the Aquarian dispensation manifests through them.

This law, therefore, is the keynote of the age we are now entering, and increasingly more groups of inspired ones will manifest their arenas of service in all seven Ray departments of Life. Decentralised, self-initiated service will increasingly become the hallmark of the serving ones. In the Piscean era that is presently ending, the concept of service was generally centred around a charismatic leader governing a group or organisation. In the new era, however, the group members will together demonstrate leadership abilities, each with their own specialised niche that adds to the beauty of the combined venture. The *dharma,* the overall body of teachings, and the inner revelations accorded to each meditating unit become the teacher. If there is a central teacher then such a one simply becomes a guide pointing the way, a living example of what can be accomplished, and a fellow server similarly striving to achieve greater heights of revelation. Impersonality, and not the ego-posturing of the central one, becomes the way to greater light for all.

The Aquarian is ever the one bearing a pitcher of 'water' that is perpetually full, to dispense to the needs of others. The symbol of this law, however, is that the pitcher is upon the head, because it expresses the right use of the mind, the development of wisdom, and mental poise, to thus serve. Here the service work is not a burden (which carrying the pitcher upon the shoulders signifies), but rather a sense of joy in accomplishment, and from the liberation from the *māyā* of things that such service denotes. Inevitably we have that spontaneous outpouring of Love that comes as a consequence of having the Heart centre awakened, and the presence of the Hierarchy of Love pouring their blessings via the serving one. The emotional ones can thereby come to think properly about their life's activities, and also learn to appropriately serve, in accordance with group law and direction. Eventually, the consecrated group can come to be crucified upon the fixed cross of the Heavens so that all can be uplifted to the high point of exaltation. This law of Service therefore is a subsidiary of the major law of Sacrifice that governs human evolution. Service is the foundation for all of the other forms of activity associated with this eight armed cross of the group laws.

4. The law of Repulse

The southern arm of the cross of direction in space signifies the descent of energies to serve the little ones. Here the *law of Repulse* demonstrates its potency. The symbol of 'The Law of all Destroying Angels' (its esoteric title) is 'An Angel with a flaming sword'. The first Ray of Will or Power governs the potency of this law, and first manifests upon the *probationary path.* At this stage the candidates definitely react negatively to the attributes of *saṃsāra* because they clearly see the truth of its nature. *Saṃsāra* is not eschewed, but comes to be transformed so that its qualities are lifted to higher domains. We thus have the beginning of the process of the control and transformation of *saṃskāras* into enlightenment attributes. The probationer works upon him/herself to produce better ethics and response to life. In doing so, the impact upon the world around is to start to uplift the collective substance of the environment to a higher domain. This uplifting process of the all is an effect of the energy of this law of Repulse. It produces a driving forward to higher domains and greater freedom of expression of the Life that was formerly imprisoned.

The angel with the flaming sword guards the portals of Initiation from the unworthy. (It is thus a version of a Wrathful Deity.) It repulses those unable to walk the way of group consciousness. The substance of their sheaths is too low a calibre and must be burnt away—by means of the 'flaming sword'. The sword is that of discriminating wisdom and cuts away that which no longer serves a purpose.

This law is primarily enthroned upon the highest sub-plane of the cosmic dense physical *(ādi)*. It therefore ultimately concerns the purpose for the sacrificial act of incarnation in material substance for a human unit or a Logos, which is to further progress the little lives constituting that substance. It drives forward the sum of evolutionary space.

Figure 4 shows that this law is upon the opposite pole of the major cosmic law of Attraction, which concerns the cosmic pull (similar to gravity) of the lesser atoms constituting embodied forms to the greater (Logoic) sphere. All these group laws involve consciousness, and the inherent Life, with its incorporated conscious lives, that are attracted to the central Source of Being. This law fosters the ability of *nirvāṇees* to travel outwards upon any of the seven cosmic paths upon attaining the sixth Initiation.

The law of Repulse therefore governs the increased incentive towards gaining enlightenment that is the foundation of the attraction to divinity, which eventually facilitates travelling the cosmic paths. The law of Service (the basic conditioning quality of all Initiates) has become such an established fact in the life of the aspirant that it allows a Master to include the aspirant into his Ashram. The disciple can now be provided with instructions as part of the development of the group progress of the Ashram which will produce the first Initiation. The associated phrase of the Beatitudes is therefore *'He opened his mouth, and taught them'*. It is ruled by *Taurus the bull*, which clothes the substance of the ideas of candidates along the lines of what is needed if they are to progress towards light. The activities of those upon the probationary path as they progress to gain Initiation will help to drive all forward to experience the revelations of the Mysteries in the precincts of Shambhala. Probationers are thereby impelled to learn the context of the Mysteries, to master their corporeality, and to experience what the entire *maṇḍala* of the Ashram provides.

The first Ray must be developed and expressed to overcome all obstacles upon the higher way, through to the experience of *śūnyatā* and beyond. The associated quality of the will is what opens the doors to the mysteries of Initiation. The impact of strong, potent energies, as a consequence of piercing the higher strata of energy by means of service based activity, at first produces a strain upon the uncontrolled mental-emotional substance of the disciple. At this stage, however, the energy is channelled to the physical domain, often producing yogic austerities, or their modern forms of expressing control over the physical body and all aspects of desire (e.g., sexuality), the right use of money and of moderating the need for physical comforts.

As the Initiation path advances, ever greater intensities of energies are experienced and must be wisely appropriated by the Initiate. This is a direct consequence of the Initiate's ability to increasingly progress towards developing the Will-of-Love and the Divine Will. Inevitably, through right discrimination it produces the repulsion of hindering attributes of the form. As the development of the will intensifies, so more limitations to the reception of the energy expression occurs, necessitating an increasing refusal to be involved with that which does not produce manifesting divinity (enlightenment). Consequently, the nature of the Soul within the form is revealed, its governing laws are comprehended and consciously worked with.

The development of reception to the energy of the will becomes the driving impetus of the law of Repulse. It drives all of the other laws forward towards the cosmic mental plane, assisted by the general pervasive pull of the law of Attraction. For humans it is gradually developed, mainly at first as a consequence of the effect of pain and suffering. Forms of attachment to illusory phenomena are then relinquished, with the law of *karma* silently directing the outcome of each action so that eventually the right choices are made. Consciousness is then able to expand to include more of the not-self, as people learn that it is better to be loving and kind to others than to be selfish and separative. Goodwill towards others is next developed, followed by the Will-to-Love. Herein lies the foundation to the development of all the laws of group evolution arising in humanity. When the Will-to-Love becomes the Will-of-Love *(bodhicitta),* then consciousness works fully in compliance with the group laws.

Virgo the virgin esoterically rules this law through sympathetic identification with the needs of the 'child' to be born. Virgo is the divine Mother who is always pregnant, and in this case the child in her womb is the developing Initiate that will find the place of parturition in Capricorn. (The mount of Initiation, being the ninth sign after Virgo, including Virgo in the rectified[11] zodiac.) Those in her Womb must overcome the material conditionings governing it, if they are to be born out of it. The first to appear are first degree Initiates that are 'poor in spirit', still needing many teachings that will help them on their path to enlightenment as they develop via the law of Group Progress.

The association with the sign Virgo has a specific reference to the *deva* kingdom (the Mother's department). They en-Soul the substance of all forms, which incorporates the limitation of incarnation. Thus all bodies of manifestation utilise the *devas.* In the highest case, we have the building of the sheaths of the Monad. *Saṃsāra,* which is constituted of *devic* substance, also comes into perspective. The *devas* in question here are those of the fifth Creative Hierarchy, which form a symbiotic relationship with humans, in that they embody the substance of the mind, and are thus the quality of our thoughts, imaginations, dreams and meditations. They are also incorporated as the substance of the Sambhogakāya Flowers. Initiation then is a process that produces a divine marriage, and eventual fusion of the human (the fourth) and fifth Creative Hierarchies at the sixth Initiation. This process is part of the mystery of the sphinx, which has a lion's body (the masculine, human, fourth Creative Hierarchy) and a woman's head (the feminine *deva* Hierarchy). We see, therefore, that effectively, under the law of Sacrifice, each Hierarchy sacrifices its own identity in order to gain liberation from the throes of dense physical incarnation. Mergence between the two Hierarchies provides the way of escape out of the confines ('prison') of the cosmic dense physical plane. We thus have the appearance of a Buddha or Dhyān Chohan, a divine being of meditation substance that is neither human or *deva,* but rather a fusion of both.

---

11 The zodiacal wheel we are used to is exoteric and considered reversed. Once one becomes an Initiate, the wheel is rectified and becomes esoteric.

This process for the incarnate human necessitates a continuous series of renunciations, as one form of attachment after another must be renounced upon the upward Way to cosmic Bliss. Eventually, even the Soul form must be renounced, when the Initiate can stand upon the fixed cross, in the semblance of a crucified Christ, a world teacher. The Initiate then prepares to mount the cardinal cross that will cause the cosmic door to be opened to allow escape from the confines of the cosmic dense physical plane. The ability to mount this cross implies following the way of the law of Repulse through the development of first Ray attributes. The Will-to-Love, the Will-of-Love and Divine Will are espoused and expressed to make one a world Saviour. Thus the way stands clear for the final act of renunciation and sacrifice, wherein the planet as a field of activity is left behind.

5. The law of Group Progress

The *law of Group Progress,* governed by the seventh Ray, manifests at the *southwest* direction of the eight-armed cross, designated 'understanding'. Those preparing to undertake the *first Initiation* must discover this law. The esoteric title is the 'Law of Elevation', and the symbol is 'The Mountain and the Goat'.

This law manifests once a probationer has manifested a rhythm of service and the spiritual discipline preparatory to the taking of Initiation. Initiation occurs whilst the candidate is working to completely comply with this law. It produces the disciple that is no longer centred upon concepts of self. Selflessness is an essential ingredient. Even subtle forms of spiritual selfishness must go, for instance a demand that the Master or spiritual preceptor focus special attention upon them. Self-serving activities are not on the agenda. The concept of service must become an instinct. One must begin to develop abstract thinking and to clearly discern the problem that *saṃsāra* poses.

Many are the contacts with the spiritual group of world servers the individual belongs to. Some may be the disciple's personal friends, others may be unknown, or known, but serving elsewhere in the world. The groups that consciously work together consist of 'free souls' that do not submit to an authority figure directing them. Rather we have groups of like-minded individuals together to share resources, concepts and energies, so that together they can better serve. They answer to impressions from their own Souls, and from their individual internal contacts with Hierarchy. (Often they are unaware that they have so contacted the inner Teachers.)

Much concerning the path of Love, of how to give, is developed and learned through right group activity. The deadly serpent of the critical mind must totally be conquered, other's opinions and ways of service accommodated, and the sum of the group experience and the equipment to serve integrated by the group members in a harmonious way. Ego-posturing of all types must disappear. United they stand for the service at hand and each proffers well-considered help at the opportune moment. The service arena is ceaseless, producing many challenges, which must be met by all in the group. Each to their own capacity to fulfil group purpose. The logical mind must rule all group decisions, thus emotional considerations must be kept in abeyance. All decisions must come via contemplative attitudes and group meditation, wherein impressions are received that compliment the group discussion and vision.

Meditation within a group context should not be kept 'secret', as this can be a form of selfishness, but rather proffered for advice and open minded discussion, unless personal information comes that the disciple knows is not helpful in full disclosure to others. Spiritual competitiveness has no place in group evolution. Wisely must all decisions be made. All have much to contribute to the developing service. All are being trained to eventually become Masters of Wisdom, and so must be accorded the freedom to reveal the extent of the Love and light that must shine upon all. In this manner the group grows together as a unit.

Many are the Ray lines that will constitute the membership of the group, and comprehension of the qualities of other's Ray lines helps to develop a sense of camaraderie (magnetic interrelationships) that unifies the group. Right mental discriminations *(vikalpa)* produces right decisions in all aspects of the disciple's life. Advice can always be sought from other group members, as the spirit of cooperativeness has been developed, and meditation is always the guide. Personality or egoistic characteristics must be held in abeyance. Only that designed to help, based upon Love, purity of motive, and perceptive insight must come to the fore. Group unity, group meditation, and its focussed activity become the keynotes of the disciple's life, and must supersede all other considerations. The dual life of the disciple, of inward focus, inspiration, and outward service come to the fore.

As a consequence, the group will receive a downpour of energy and impressions that will guide them well upon the Initiation path. The challenges of true group interrelation and the obstacles that service work presents then pose as the tests to be passed. Once mastered along the lines that the first Initiation demands, this allows group Initiation to become possible. Above all, emotional perturbations of all types must always be stemmed at their root, their causes sought for and weeded out. Mental equipoise should be seen at all times as the central characteristic of the group, no matter the form of service work rendered to the world. (The arena of service will be characterised by the overall Ray line of the group in question.)

In all such groups there are always those that are more spiritually advanced (they are upon a higher Initiation level, and can intrinsically contact higher revelatory sources). The younger disciples should always offer respect to those with greater wisdom and listen well to well-placed advice. Such advice however must never become a dictum by the senior disciple that he/she demands must be obeyed. True loving dispassion is the key phrase here, as the younger ones can only learn from their own mistakes appropriately rectified. A heuristic approach is therefore encouraged. New ones that are attracted to the group's service arena must be similarly taught.

The group should, however, not unnecessarily entertain the existence of one whose egotism and other attitudes are destructive to the group's meditative harmony. All that enter the precincts of the group's aura come as aspirants or probationary disciples to them, and must be provided a trial period, where every effort is given to help them understand the group's verities and the way of discipleship. Those who consistently fail to comprehend the basics of group evolution normally weed themselves from the group structure because of incompatibility. However, this is not always the case, and the core members of the group should wisely discuss the needs of such candidates. Failures to pass the needed grade are many. It is better to have a small group of well versed disciples than a large group with many unruly ones, constantly waylaying important arenas of service because of the emotionality of those demanding they be served, that their egos be mollycoddled. The group should always be on guard for loving-minded tendencies—a major failing of disciples in training—where they seek to Love, to give, but with a subjectively hidden selfish motive, or because they are naïvely optimistic of another's potential, and thus give them greater credence or leeway than they should. Serious problems then arise later down the track with the group's evolution.

The third phrase of the Beatitudes, *'Blessed are the poor in spirit: for theirs is the kingdom of heaven',* also refers to *Gemini the twins* and is associated with this group Law. It is focussed upon the *southwest* direction of 'understanding'. Here we have the Temple of Initiation implicated and therefore of the ritualistic means whereby a true identification with the all becomes possible. The twins are said to consist of a mortal and immortal brother holding hands in service to each other. (Though in an earlier stage they are in conflict and are often warring.) 'The poor in spirit' are those aspirants that come knocking at the Temple gates to enter this path of Initiation into the Mysteries. Officiating therein is the immortal brother, who is already a member of the 'kingdom of heaven' and whose task is to lead the mortal brother (those that are 'poor in spirit') via graded stages back to that kingdom. Those who are 'poor in spirit' relative to the immortal brother must develop the right qualities to partake in the ceremonial activities of the group service and related meditations.

Gemini also governs the etheric double, the *nāḍī* system, the comprehension of which becomes an esoteric part of the group's meditation enquiry. More of the mysteries concerning the awakening of the *chakras* are revealed as the greater identifications with the All happens as a response of the Ashramic service work that manifests. Within the Temple, the ritualised activities eventually bring into view the feminine lives governing Nature. Cooperative activity then occurs, and many internal visions are received concerning the nature of the path. Much is revealed concerning the nature of *karma*, and of its rectification. Past lives consequently come to view, especially in relation to where the account books of ancient debts (usually perceived in negative terms) are to be settled. The higher Way is sought and then trodden. Greater mysteries are revealed, and inevitably a Master evolves when the service arena is comprehensive enough and the laws of mind/Mind are fully mastered.

The group represents the embodied Christ principle, evoking His sacrificial Blood to the degree that they are able to help the needy. (This southwest arm being the opposite arm to that governing the law of Sacrifice, the qualities of which they are endeavouring to emulate.) This Blood is rhythmically pumped according to the law of cycles, as governed by the seventh Ray of Ceremonial Activity. Such ritualised activity assists aspirants to enter the precincts of the 'Temple' wherein Initiation is possible. The higher *chakras* then awaken as *saṃskāras* of mental-emotional living are transformed.

The entire process of the evolution of an Ashram concerns the ability to develop and project *bodhicitta,* which draws participants magnetically (utilising the law of Magnetic Impulse) to the cosmic Temple that is the source of the energy of Love-Wisdom to our entire solar system. The group then travels via the northwest gate (utilising the Will-to-Good) outwards upon the way of escape to cosmos. Eventually, multifarious *maṇḍalas* for cosmic travel (space vehicles) are constructed by those of our earth Hierarchy to enable them to do so. This building process will become a major theme of the new era ahead of us.

The esoteric ruler of this fifth law is *Pisces the fishes*, which in this case is integrated with the symbol of 'The Mountain and the Goat'. The ancient symbolic representation of Capricorn as a goat with the tail of a fish is implicated. It is thus a version of Makara, the Mystery, veiled by the sign Capricorn, which concerns the nature of transition from a Watery to a Fiery constitution. We then have the evolution of *kāma-manas* (desire-mind) and its eventual conversion to *bodhicitta.* The Initiate, the sure-footed goat, is able to survive on the coarsest of material substance, can climb the hard, rocky mountain of materialism, and finally upon the summit attain the transfiguration experience associated with the third Initiation. The fish's tail symbolises the sum of the waters of sensation *(saṃsāra)* from which the Initiate evolves and comes to master as the mountain is climbed. The path of Initiation therefore properly begins in this sign and is at first focussed upon the attainment of the first Initiation, but later shifts to the third. Eventually upon this path the world Saviour arises at the end of a major cycle (the onset of *prayala),* as signified by the sign Pisces. Consequently, this is the 'Law of Elevation' because by following its precepts, it comes to elevate the humble aspirant to the highest peak of accomplishment. Understanding of the nature of the path helps make it so.

6. The law of Expansive Response

This law, which relates to gaining the *third Initiation,* is the emanation of the direction *west,* governing the field of service to humanity. The governing Ray is the third of Mathematically Exact Activity. No esoteric title is provided and the symbol is a 'Flaming Rosy Sun'.

The term 'Expansive Response' concerns the expansive nature of the Mind of the Initiate after the third Initiation has been undertaken. Not only are the vistas of the Sambhogakāya Flower revealed (the *ālayavijñāna* environment) but also some of what lies waiting in Shambhala and upon cosmic shores, to which this Initiation opens the door, as it is the first cosmic Initiation. 'Expansive Response' awakens the vision of what the future will reveal for this western direction of outward into the field of service, representing humanity. The far vistas of humanity's potential can then manifest, once the nature of the Initiation path is comprehended and ardently followed. Consequently, there is an increased effort by the Initiate to serve, to logically present the vision of the Plan to humanity, so that their expanded vision produces a vaster field of application for disciples.

The 'expansive response' is in the field of the Mind and its mysteries. All phenomena stems from mind and is resolved into it. The nature of cosmic Mind comes into view, and vast is the vision accorded (of Logoic Mind) to which the Initiate aspires.

As this Initiation is undertaken at Shambhala, so the pull of the planetary Head centre upon the Initiate and his group works to incorporate them into its sphere of activity. This then defines the nature of this group law. As one travels towards this centre, to increasingly play a role in its affairs, so Shambhala expands its response to the approaching group. The response is from above down. The Lords of Life pour increasingly intense energies into the Initiate's Mind, producing an expanded field of vision therein. All manifests within a group context.

The nature of the development of Mind by the Initiate of this degree also produces an expanded awareness of the *devas* (the fifth Creative Hierarchy) that embody the substance of mind in all its grades. There is also a natural response from these *devas* to the Initiate's service work. *Deva* and human compliment each other. The Initiate provides the driving will of the organising ability, and the *devas* the fabric of the space that clothes. The *māyā* of the evolving forms can thus be appropriately resolved into domains of the real.[12]

The esoteric ruler of this law is *Scorpio the scorpion*, and in this case it provides the energies of the fourth Creative Hierarchy (humanity, which is governed by this sign), wherein the Initiate is appropriately tested in the fields of service. Such service is now always through the use of the highly refined mind/Mind. The result is an expanded response by the human groups that the Initiate inspires and the ability to delve deeper into the realms of ideas and associated revelatory vistas. This response is thus due to vertical alignment and horizontal application. Scorpio also provides increased energisation from Shambhala. It prepares the Initiate for the attainment of the fourth Initiation and the associated crucifixion experience, as *bodhicitta* increasingly comes to be the driving force behind all activities.

The law governs an increasing field of compassionate activity for the Initiate. For the *devas,* this law manifests in a way that draws them into incarnation, to form a Logoic body, and build the *maṇḍala* of *saṃsāra* so that it will expand into the universe of possibilities it must come to be. The human kingdom then evolves consciousness, and later greatly develops its expansiveness by entering the path of Initiation as a consequence of the service arena to humanity. At first the concrete mind is developed, and then one learns to project *antaḥkaraṇas* towards the domain of the abstract Mind. This process is governed by means of the third Ray of Mathematically Exact Activity, and when driven by the second Ray, wisdom is gained. The abstract Mind is then the base for further expansion into cosmos via the continuation of the *antaḥkaraṇas* into the *dharmakāya*. The fifth Initiation is then undertaken and becomes the base for further expansions via group progress.

The law of Expansive Response for humanity therefore concerns a progressive unfoldment of consciousness to fill the sum of the domain of the *maṇḍala* originally established by the *devas*. Along the way, the prisoners of the planet, the *devas* who were incorporated as 'the

---

12 It should be noted that in this exposé the concern is with the life wherein Initiation is consciously undertaken. In a subsequent life, the Initiate may be oblivious to such knowledge and simply manifests service to humanity appropriate to the Plan.

lower four', come to be liberated through being included as part of the equipment of response of a human unit that has gained mastery of the form. Such a unit has transformed the lower *devas* embodying the associated *saṃskāras* (the *lunar pitris)* by infusing them with the qualities of Love and Mind. *Deva* Individualisation happens as a consequence, and they enter into the ranks of the greater Builders, to be out-breathed from that planetary cycle. Later they will be inbreathed into a new earth sphere as the informing *deva* lives upon a higher level and turn of the spiral of evolution. This is the way expansive response progresses.

The law of Expansive Response is the gain of the Initiate of the third degree, as he/she stands upon the mountaintop and integrates with the consciousness of the Sambhogakāya Flower. Supporting the entire progress of the path and its eventual attainments is the probationary disciple, who, responding to the law, begins to master the vicissitudes of *saṃsāra*.

The attributes of the third Ray of Mathematically Exact Activity must be developed through contemplation and meditation to produce the refinements of mind that allow one to be truly compassionate, and to act in a non-glamoured way according to the dictates of *karma*. A keen meditation-Mind must be developed that facilitates penetrative insight into the higher domains of Mind. This development was earlier related to Vyāna, which lays the foundation for the undertaking of the third Initiation. The most refined attributes of thought then come into play, producing a complete integration between Soul and personality. The group-conscious Sambhogakāya Flower, governed by the law of Magnetic Impulse, then comes to rule the life of the Initiate. It attracts to the Initiate the members of the Soul group(s) with whom he/she serves, to drive them onwards towards a goal to which they conjointly aspire. (In many cases no formal physical group has been arranged upon the physical plane, or else it is loosely structured. They are individuals bound by a common service arena, which the third degree Initiate positively influences because of such a one's highly perceptive insights and wisdom.)

The fifth of the Beatitudes, governed by the sign *Leo the lion*, *'Blessed are the meek: for they shall inherit the earth'*, is associated with this law. This concerns the elimination of the attributes of pride, of ego-posturing, so that enlightenment can take its place. Meekness, compliance to the laws of Love and group evolution, allows the generation of *bodhicitta* and identification with the consciousness of the Sambhogakāya Flowers, the Fiery lions, and earlier in the evolutionary process: the 'Lions, divine and tawny orange Flames'.[13] Leo governs the cycles of awakening self-consciousness so that the lion of Life can roar out its victory prowess. This present scientific and technological era is governed by the fifth and third Rays. Indeed, by means of scientific investigation humanity have come to 'inherit the earth'. When the normal arrogance of the mind is properly tamed so that it becomes meek, submissive to the higher verities of spirit, then the stage can be set for undertaking the third Initiation wherein the full powers of Mind are brought to fruition.

7. The law of the Lower Four

This law, associated with the northwest position of 'goodwill', relates to attaining *the fifth Initiation.* The esoteric name is the law of 'Etheric Union', and the symbol is a 'Male and Female Form placed back to back'. The governing Ray is the fifth of Scientific Reasoning, and the esoteric ruler is *Capricorn the goat.*

The concept of goodwill is here the will-to-good, which relates to the demonstration of the will that impulses evolutionary purpose to produce the 'good' for all. The 'good' refers to that which produces evolutionary perfection. The Master of Wisdom wielding this law resides consciously upon the *ātmic* plane. Thus 'the lower four' from this perspective refers to the lower four planes of perception: *buddhi, manas,* the astral and the dense planes. This law therefore concerns the means whereby a Master organises attributes of cosmic Mind and focuses them into those of his Ashram so that eventually *dharmakāya* becomes their zone of residence. All must come to be directed according to the Divine Will of the Lords of Shambhala. Streams of lives are thus coordinated into one overall organism, one *maṇḍala* of expression, flowing on through time to produce their liberation.

Normally, the concept of 'The Lower Four' refers to the sum of the personality constitution: a mind, the emotional (astral) body, an etheric

13 A.A. Bailey, *Esoteric Astrology*, (Lucis Press, London, 1968), 301.

body and the corporeal form. The mind also possesses four subdivisions of its concrete expression. We are concerned with the development of the sum of the personality, thus the expression of the *māyā* of things. When the mind is utilised in conjunction with an awakened Heart, then true wisdom can be evoked. The effects of the *law of the Lower Four* effectively produce the gain of everything that the symbolism 'the earth' conjures, by way of the mastery of mind.

The work of the Master is to overcome the limitations of the concrete minds of those in his Ashram, so that they can be receptive to the expression of concepts from the abstract domains of Mind. The Clear Light of Mind then comes into perspective and the *saṃsāra-śūnyatā* nexus discovered, wherein the disciples must learn to reside. The Master is therefore specifically focussed upon bringing all members of his Ashram to follow the laws of group evolution, to master all mental-emotional *saṃskāras* and to transmute them so that the third Initiation and the transfiguration experience is attained.

Another consequence of this 'law of the Lower Four', of 'Etheric Union', concerns the union with members of the fifth Creative Hierarchy. Here the male and female form standing back to back (the symbol representing this sign) represent the human (male) and *deva* (female) kingdoms that are polar opposites in Nature and parallel streams of evolution. Being 'back to back' they can be oblivious of each other's existence. Esoterically, they must learn to turn around and to embrace. This law thus concerns the method whereby full effective union is established. The *devas* embody the substance of the human thought and desire impulses. They are the sum of the Fiery substance of our meditation constructs, as well as of the bodies of manifestation of the Sambhogakāya Flowers. Humans generate the volition that organises this substance, and as their thoughts become increasingly refined, so the interrelation between human and *deva* become barely distinguishable, until at a certain stage a fusion, or mergence between the two streams occurs.[14] All is then revealed in the Clear Light of the Mind. This law defines the mode of interrelation between the two kingdoms, producing the inevitable results of Buddhahood.

14 Detail concerning this process is presented in my book: *The Astrological and Numerological Keys to The Secret Doctrine.*

The Master works via the domain of the Mind and with *deva* substance, utilising the laws of mind by the generation of intensified Light, and controlling Fiery substance through mantra. This is the reason why this law is governed by the fifth Ray of Scientific Reasoning. The Fires of mind/Mind are also ruled by this Ray.

The 'etheric union' implied here is also between the Monad upon the second cosmic ether and the etheric body of the enlightened human unit. This union eventually integrates the entire Head centre, which exists upon the highest etheric sub-plane. In this case, the 'male' figure is the Monad, and the 'female' is the Head centre of a human unit. The way of response between the human unit and the Monadic Self is manifested through a scientific methodology applied to the path, producing enlightenment. This process sets the conditions that inevitably produces Initiation into the Mysteries of Life. The third Initiation is at first implicated, which is the springboard to taking the fifth. The mind is thereby used to build *antaḥkaraṇas* to the abstract Mind, and then to the cosmic Mind *(dharmakāya)* in the form of a line of cosmic ascent for the Monadic Life. The nature of this ascent concerns the Mysteries of the Initiation path via the laws of Expansive Response, Sacrifice and Polar Union.

Esoterically, the sign *Capricorn the goat* governs this law, because Capricorn governs the mountain that is the sum of the substance of mind/Mind, which through the initiation process comes to be mastered by the One wielding this law. Mind, in all of its expressions, then becomes the tool for the fifth degree Initiate.

Exoterically, the sign *Libra the balances* rules this law, and the Beatitude is the seventh. The remaining Beatitudes refer to the five attributes of mind, the five Elements, etc., that come to be mastered as a consequence of following the path to the fifth Initiation. This Beatitude is *'Blessed are the merciful: for they shall obtain mercy'*. The demonstration of the type of mercy, or compassion, by the Master for those that are ensnared by the various attributes of mind produces an energisation from the domains of Logoic Mind to help liberate all *manasic* lives.

Libra governs the cycles of meditation, and of the elated yogic austerities that help bring about this process of governing all the elements and forces of mind/Mind.

The laws of the cosmic mental plane

When referring to the cosmic astral and mental planes we enter into the domain of abstract concepts and speculative curiosity for most. It represents future possibilities, yet is the basis for the existing conditions in our localised universe. These cosmic realms are the domains into which high Initiates are preparing to enter, and from which they receive energies and assistance. For these Initiates, knowledge of these realms is necessary, and for this reason the pioneering work of H.P. Blavatsky was instigated, followed by that of A.A. Bailey and Helena Roerich. We now also have my present series of works. The information is new in terms of exoteric revelation, but is timeless, existing for uncounted aeons when meditatively discovered in terms of the 'ear-whispered' doctrine. These revealed teachings are the new signposts upon the way to liberation. Coming generations of Initiates shall receive and amplify them, until what was once esoteric becomes the cultural norm, the accepted science. Such is the nature of evolutionary progress in the world of ideas. Such is the way to Shambhala.

A new era is thereby dawning, one for which the past religions and the present materialistic sciences have prepared us. The materialistic ones must, however, overcome the shackles of their concrete minds. When they can do so, the laws pertaining to a vast multidimensional universe will open for their scrutiny. These laws are immutable, they govern the mode of expression of all things. They govern the Real and fecundate *saṃsāra.*

We can now proceed with some suggestions concerning the nature of manifestation of the cosmic mental laws. These cosmic laws are given in *A Treatise on Cosmic Fire* as: the law of Economy, the law of Attraction, the law of Synthesis, plus the Sirian law of Karma. They are expressions of the four concrete sub-planes of the cosmic mental plane. We can also add another law (that is inherently triune) that synthesises the qualities of the petals of the Logoic Soul upon the cosmic higher mental plane, the law of cosmic Identity.

There are two pentads of signs of the zodiac that can be attributed to the laws from the cosmic mental plane. They effectively transcend the direct import of the Beatitudes. We should also note the limitations of language to explicate the properties of the laws under consideration.

The laws can, however, be somewhat analysed from the perspective of the *vayūs,* cosmically considered, or concerning transmuted correspondences of the instincts. To think in terms of the conditions associated with the cosmic lower mental plane one must use transmuted correspondences. Here the attributes of the consciousness known to humanity are thoroughly transmuted. From a lower perspective, for instance, pure intellect (as completely divorced from the emotions) is a basic instinct to a Master of Wisdom, and *bodhicitta* manifests similarly for a Chohan. These qualities then need not be generated or further developed in any way. Their expression is perfected and automatically manifests as the most basic characteristic of the Initiate's demeanor. Such modes of thinking are far from what general humanity rationalise by.

One must also think in terms of a vaster multidimensional scale of Logoic Service work. This is not easy, but working with laws of analogy, with the maxims of 'as above so below', 'that which is within is also without', will provide many revelations. Below is an outline providing a cosmic perspective that will aid the student to make necessary deductions.

When the concept of humanity being a 'man plant' was earlier used, it referred partly to the fact that the seven *chakras* are flowers, and therefore the *nāḍīs* act in a plant-like fashion, which conditions the entire human being. Also, the human Soul is a flower, with the spinal column of the human unit holding the three-fold central *nāḍīs* being the main trunk, and the various *chakras* supporting smaller flowers.

The main interpretation, however, is that the Monad is considered a member of the cosmic plant kingdom that is planted in the soil of the cosmic dense physical plane. This is important, as it provides a clue as to the nature of cosmic evolution, and indicates one method of comparison with the 'reality' of Life known to us in our world-sphere. The entire process of evolution from human Individualisation[15] onwards concerns the upward way of movement towards the light of the Central Spiritual Sun of the seed that was sprouted. This Sun represents the Logoic Soul upon the domain of the higher cosmic mental plane. The entire Initiation process therefore concerns the way of movement upwards to the source

15 The time of the mass appearance of human Souls (Sambhogakāya Flowers) upon the higher mental plane, by linking mind to the embryonic consciousness of prepared members of the animal kingdom, producing human units.

of that Light. The undertaking of the third Initiation then represents the further evolution of the plant kingdom by becoming a unicellular member of the cosmic animal kingdom. (It thus signifies the taking of an Initiation of the Monad concerned.) The human Monad has then achieved an important milestone in its own evolutionary development and can prepare its way of escape from its imprisonment from within the confines of cosmic 'dirt'. Technically, it can now generate a sideways, as well as an upward mobility. This 'sideways' movement involves the ability of the Initiate to travel to various planetary Schemes and stars in cosmos. For the cosmic first degree Initiate, such movement is limited, but becomes increasingly imperative as the higher degrees are developed. This equates with the necessity of an animal to forage for food. This 'food' represents the various forms of learning that the planetary and stellar Schools provide.

Upon taking the fourth Initiation, the Initiate can be considered to have developed into something resembling an ant upon our terrestrial sphere. They are hard working, group-conscious, totally sacrificial to their particular colony—esoterically to their specific Ray purpose. Ants can climb up tall vegetation and also quickly cover much ground in their search of fodder. One must here keep a proper perspective of the vastness of the multidimensional cosmic landscape to which such an Initiate is born. The relative scale of things must be considered, as well as the scope of the developing vision compared to others that will have passed that Initiation perhaps billions of years ago, as far as earth time is reckoned. With this in mind, the fourth degree Initiate may have a vast expansive vista of liberated awareness when compared to an intelligent person, but within the greater cosmic perspective the magnitude of what has been so far developed is small indeed—'ant-like'. This is the gist of the nature of what is revealed once the veil of *śūnyatā* is pierced.

At the attainment of the fifth Initiation the Monad has evolved to the equivalent of being a member of a beehive in the cosmic landscape, where Shambhala represents the hive to which the bees administer. They gather honey *(bodhicitta)* from the various flowers (the *chakras* conditioning our earth Scheme) in order to deposit its nectar into the various buildings (cells) of that city.

The sixth degree Initiate represents something akin to a small mammal in this cosmic landscape. A seventh degree Initiate can be considered a bird, able to fly over the systemic space and to immediately gain detailed information concerning the nature of its terrain. The Christ, therefore, has been likened to a dove of peace.

An eighth degree Initiate can be viewed in terms of being a larger mammal, or a large fish swimming in the Waters of the cosmic astral ocean. A ninth degree Initiate can be likened to a mammal the size of a horse or cow, constituting numerous groups of entities as part of its body of manifestation. Technically, they feast upon man-plants, to help free them from the limitations of the cosmic soil. A tenth degree Initiate is at a stage where Individualisation, to become a member of cosmic Humanity, is possible. Thus we get the appearance of a Logos who is able to form a planetary system as his Body of manifestation.

Having gained some idea of our path from a cosmic perspective, we are now in a position to apply this information to the cosmic laws. It is important to understand that as the Initiate gains the next Initiation level, he/she carries forward the sum of the group *maṇḍala* of which the Initiate is the central point. All are intricately united by the laws of group evolution and travel together onwards and upwards through the cosmic landscape. By the time the tenth Initiation is reached, there is a plethora of beings, *deva* and human, that have evolved and advanced with the great One. All are karmically linked and initially conditioned by the fundamental governing Rays of that One. This then sets the agenda as to the future role to be played by all in that landscape. Here the meaning of the true nature of the Bodhisattva vow is revealed: to never cease striving until all have been liberated. The Logoic One then chooses how to act, but all such choices are governed by cosmic laws and applied Love-Wisdom.

Concerning the fundamental cosmic laws, my purpose here is not to reiterate what was given in *A Treatise on Cosmic Fire* concerning these laws (part of which is provided below), but rather to put them into their proper perspective upon the cosmic mental plane, from which they emanate. To this shall be added the appropriate qualifying zodiacal sign. In doing so, information shall be provided supplementing the earlier work of D.K.'s. The signs hint as to the nature of the overall laws conditioning the Initiation path. Earnest students can then correlate and integrate the information concerning the cosmic Paths Initiates undertake, as this task would diverge too far from the main theme of this book. To provide the background, I shall provide a lengthy quote from *A Treatise on Cosmic Fire*, starting with the law of Economy.

> This law is the law governing the matter aspect of manifestation, and is the law characterizing the work of the third Logos, and of the entities who are the embodiment of His will and the agents of His purposes. Each of the great cosmic Entities who take form as the three Logoi, is distinguished by different methods of activity, which might be described thus:
>
> *The third Aspect* or Brahma aspect of the activities of those Entities who are His expression, is characterized by that method in the distribution of matter which we call the Law of Economy. It is the law governing the scattering of the atoms of matter and their dissociation from one another, wide distribution, vibratory rhythm, heterogeneity and quality and their inherent rotary action. This Law of Economy causes matter always to follow the line of least resistance, and is the basis of the separative action of atomic matter. It governs matter, the opposite pole of spirit.
>
> *The second Aspect*, the building, or Vishnu aspect, is governed by the Law of Attraction; the activities of the entities who embody this aspect are directed to the attracting of matter to Spirit, and the gradual approximation of the two poles. It results in cohesion, in the production of congeries of atoms in various formations, and this attraction is brought about by the attractive power of Spirit itself. It shows itself in:
>
> 1. Association,
> 2. Form building,
> 3. Adaptation of form to vibration,
> 4. Relative homogeneity of group unity,
> 5. Cyclic spiraling movement.
>
> The line of least resistance is not the law for this aspect. The attractive power of Spirit in form-building, and in the adaptation of the form to the need, is the secret of the pain and resistance in the world; pain is only caused by resistance, and is a necessary phase in the process of evolution. This law of attraction is the law governing the Spirit, the opposite pole of matter.

The first Aspect, or the will to exist, is governed by the Law of Synthesis, and the activities of the cosmic entities who are its embodiments are governed by the law of enforced unity, and of essential homogeneity. It is the law that eventually comes into play after spirit and matter are blending, and adapting themselves each to each; it governs the eventual synthesis of Self with Self, and finally with the All-Self, and also of essence with essence in contradistinction to the synthesis of matter and Spirit. It demonstrates as:

1. Abstraction,
2. Spiritual liberation,
3. Destruction of form through the withdrawal of Spirit (the Destroyer aspect),
4. Absolute homogeneity and absolute essential unity,
5. Progressive forward motion.

Thus can be seen the wonderful synthesis brought about by the evolutionary working of these three cosmic laws, - *each of them embodying the mode of work of certain cosmic Entities or Existences.* The final two will be taken up in their right place. Now we will touch but briefly upon the law of matter, that of Economy.

This is the law that lies back of what has been mistakenly called "The Fall" by religious writers, by which is defined in reality the involutionary process, cosmically considered. It led to a sevenfold differentiation in the matter of the system. Just as the Law of Attraction led to the sevenfold psychic differentiation of the Sons of Mind, and the Law of Synthesis results in the sevenfold perfection of the same Manasaputras, so we have an interesting connection between:

The seven planes, or the seven grades of matter.

The seven Heavenly Men, the seven Divine Manasaputras, or the seven types of wisdom-love.

The seven qualities of wisdom, which are produced by the cosmic entities, the Kumaras by the aid of knowledge through the medium of matter...

II. The Subsidiary Laws

The subsidiary laws under the Law of Economy are four in number, dealing with the lower quaternary:

1. The Law of Vibration, dealing with the key note or measure of the matter of each plane. By knowledge of this law the material of any plane in its seven divisions can be controlled.

2. *The Law of Adaptation, is* the law governing the rotary movement of any atom on every plane and sub-plane.
3. *The Law of Repulsion,* governs that relationship between atoms, which results in their non-attachment and in their complete freedom from each other; it also keeps them rotating at fixed points from the globe or sphere of opposite polarity.
4. *The Law of Friction,* governs the heat aspect of any atom, the radiation of an atom, and the effect of that radiation on any other atom.

Every atom of matter can be studied in four aspects, and is governed by one or other, or all of the four above mentioned laws.

a. An atom vibrates to a certain measure.
b. It rotates at a certain speed.
c. It acts and reacts upon its environing atoms.
d. It adds its quota to the general heat of the atomic system, whatever that may be.

These general rules relating to atomic bodies can be extended not only to the atoms of the physical plane, but to all spheroidal bodies within the system, and including the system also, regarding it as a cosmic atom.

The tiny atom of the physical plane, a plane itself, a planet, and a solar system all evolve under these rules, and all are governed by the Law of Economy in one of its four aspects.

It might be added in closing, that this law is one that initiates have to master before They can achieve liberation. They have to learn to manipulate matter, and to work with energy or force in matter under this law; they have to utilize matter and energy in order to achieve the liberation of Spirit, and to bring to fruition the purposes of the Logos in the evolutionary process.[16]

The major cosmic laws and the appearance of phenomena

There are five signs to consider here, which are the remainder of the esoteric zodiac associated with the group laws. They relate to the creative process of a cosmic Logos, thus of the path of descent into

16 A.A. Bailey, *A Treatise on Cosmic Fire,* 214-220.

incarnation of the myriad lives that come to embody the Body of Manifestation of the Logos. These five signs are Leo, Cancer, Gemini, Taurus, and Aries. They are placed in reversed order to that of the group laws because the cosmic astral plane acts as a mirror, inverting their qualities, when they impact upon the cosmic dense physical plane. The highest of the group laws manifesting on the cosmic dense physical is that of Repulse, demonstrating via the plane *ādi*. It is governed by Virgo, which precedes Leo on the rectified wheel of the zodiac.

The five signs associated with the last five stages of the Beatitudes can also be considered, but they relate to the path of ascent of the evolving lives. The two groups of signs therefore concern descent and ascent into the cosmic dense physical plane. We will also see that the two groups of five signs are similar, in that four of the five signs are the same (Pisces and Leo differ), but they are arranged differently with a different focus of interpretation. The path of descent is primarily an *iḍā* function in the Body of the Logos, and relegated to the feminine *deva* hierarchy. That of ascent is driven by the *piṇgalā* attributes of the principle of Love borne by the human kingdom. Later, *deva* and humans conjunctly progress this way in the form of the *suṣumṇā* path. There is a marriage between the fourth (human) and the fifth (*deva*) Creative Hierarchies at the sixth Initiation, therefore the concept of *deva* and human evolution here should not be viewed as it normally is. There are lines of specialisation along the *iḍā (deva)* and *piṇgalā* (human) line for high Initiates. The way of evolution of dragons could, for instance, be considered to illustrate the complexity of this interrelation.

From the point of view of the descent of the attributes of Logoic Mind, producing the phenomena of things evolving in the local cosmos, we have the following five signs.

1. *Leo the lion*—governing the domain of the Logoic Soul, the cosmic higher mental plane. From here the directives of the new Logoic impetus to 'Think' emanates, producing a new Incarnation. Leo the lion governs the attributes of the Soul form of all lives from the lowly human to the most exalted Logos. Leo literally signifies the attributes of the 'Son-Sun' in manifestation, the source of all Love and Light, the purveyor of what is known as consciousness.

2. *Cancer the crab*—the sign of incarnation, and of the mass movement of the elements of consciousness. Here upon the fourth cosmic mental sub-plane the *law of Synthesis* is utilised to gather together all aspects of cosmic Mind to build the appropriate Logoic Thought-Form of the *maṇḍala* of what is to be. The Thought construct is then projected downwards into the domains of manifestation. Cancer is part of the cardinal cross, the polar opposite of which is Capricorn. Here Capricorn represents the mountain of (cosmic) Mind, part of the substance of which is utilised in the process of the incarnation of a new solar form. The cardinal cross is that which governs the direction forward of an instigating arrow of empowering Purpose.
3. *Gemini the twins*—governing the *nāḍī* system and *chakras* through which the Logos works. Here from the fifth cosmic mental sub-plane emanates the *law of karma*. The Thought construct is sufficiently energised and clothed with the concreting energy of Mind to galvanise into activity the informing Lives, producing the action-reaction effects of the law of *karma*. It is therefore an expression of pure Mental intent (because the fifth sub-plane is that of *manas per se),* though impelled by the Love-Wisdom of the Soul. (The resident of the inner sanctum of the Temple associated with Gemini.) Here the 'immortal brother' represents the guiding Ideation from the Logoic Sambhogakāya Flower, whilst the 'mortal brother' is the Thought construct (Fohat) that is sent on its errand to produce the new universe of beings.

   Gemini is part of the mutable cross, which here signifies starting the turning of the wheel of cosmic activity. It awakens all of the greater Lives that are to inform the generated *maṇḍala* of expression. The entire zodiacal wheel is then activated, where Gemini works to integrate the polar opposites of the signs into the unity of the sanctity of the one divine Temple of Being. Their common purpose is to lead the mortal brother to that holy place wherein resides the immortal One. The *law of karma* ensures that all pathways of expression of the various lives in the solar sphere will eventually be resolved into the one path that leads to the sacred precincts of that Temple.

   The polar opposite of Gemini is *Sagittarius the archer,* who fires his arrows towards Pisces, which signifies the full turning of the wheels of Life, of the zodiac, of all that swim in the Waters of mutable experiences. The purpose for them is to eventually break the bonds of material involvement, so that they can bring the gain to Gemini where it will be appropriately processed.

4. *Taurus the bull*—that further clothes the Thought Form with the Desire of the Logos to see the Plan through to its logical conclusion. This 'Desire' integrates a Watery Element with the construct, as the communality of all Logoi with which the Logos is involved comes into view. (The equivalence here to normal human interrelationships.) Their interrelated Plans constitute the cosmic landscape through which all manifesting Lives must evolve. The qualities of the cosmic astral plane are now utilised. The constitution of this plane must be taken into account before the *maṇḍalic* expression can take up the robes of the cosmic Waters. This Thought-construct happens upon the sixth cosmic mental sub-plane, and becomes the basis to the cosmic *law of Attraction,* of which the laws of Group evolution are subsidiaries. These laws are then mirrored into the physical domain to govern the way of evolution of the streams of Lives that are the en-Souling agents of the manifesting forms.

   Taurus is part of the fixed cross, that is fixed in space and crucified to the service work of transforming the consciousness of the myriad Lives so that they can walk the path of Light and Love. Its polar opposite is Scorpio, wherein the main battles are eventuated that eventually produce the transformations, facilitated by the pull of the law of Attraction to ever higher centres of experiential Life.

5. *Aries the ram*—utilises the first ray impetus of the Will of the Logos to drive the Thought-construct that integrates the substance of primordial cosmic dust, which then becomes the concretised cosmic dense sheath. The way of organising this substance, and of the forms that evolve by means of incarnating into it are then governed by the *law of Economy,* demonstrated by means of the cyclic or ritualised impulses from the seventh cosmic mental sub-plane. The one-pointed Arian focus ensures the economy of activity of all factors constituting the evolving forms. The downturned horns of the Ram directs the 'Will of God', the Light of cosmic Mind, focussed via the Logoic Eye to whatever is perceived to come to be.

Aries is part of the cardinal cross, which facilitates its one-pointed application of the law of Economy for all manifest lives. We have economy of scale, economy of interrelated activities, economy of energy distribution, economy of time needed to accomplish certain ends, and the eventual economy of Thought sequences to produce an appropriate *maṇḍala* of ideas. *Libra the balances* is the polar opposite of Aries, and governs the cyclic impetus of all attributes of the law of Economy. It regulates the nature of the motion that integrates things into a unified organism, whilst Aries works to intensify that motion. Libra governs the ebb and flow of the tides of the *karma* delineating the movement of *saṃskāras,* and of the way the entire *maṇḍala* can spin, eventually producing the spiral-cyclic motion that reveals the higher attributes of the laws of Life. The wheels turn as Aries directs.

Upon the upward arc of the evolutionary process the returning *nirvāṇees* must come to master one after another of these cosmic laws as they undertake the higher Initiations. They do so as they begin to emulate the attributes of the Logoic Mind. Indeed they effectively become force vectors, the moving *saṃskāras* developed within that Mind and which help to produce the vibrancy and completion of the Logoic Thought-construct. The law of Economy is mastered by the fifth degree Initiate. The law of Attraction is the main law governing the approach of Initiates of the sixth and eighth degrees upon the cosmic paths. Seventh degree Initiates (that have chosen earth service as their cosmic path) wield the law of *karma* upon a planetary scale. Ninth and tenth degree Initiates demonstrate dynamic compliance to the law of Synthesis along their chosen forms of activity. Tenth degree Initiates prepare for cosmic Individualisation. They move from being a 'cosmic animal' to that of human status with the formation of a cosmic Sambhogakāya Flower for the candidates. The technical terms provided for the higher Initiations from the sixth to the ninth are: 'Decision, Resurrection, Transition, and Refusal'.[17]

---

17 A.A. Bailey, *The Rays and the Initiations,* (Lucis Press, 1970), 340, to which the reader can refer for detail concerning this subject.

The major cosmic laws

With respect to the Beatitudes, seven of the twelve signs of the zodiac have been utilised in the account of the group laws. The remaining five signs are important because they are applicable to the laws stemming from the cosmic mental plane. These signs are Scorpio, Sagittarius, Capricorn, Aquarius and Pisces. They signify the evolved qualities of the bearers of *manas*. The group laws, on the other hand, govern the evolution of the lives that are conditioned from the cosmic astral domain.

On our earth, the five signs from Scorpio to Pisces are concerned with the circulation of the five *prāṇas* within the body Logoic, and thus the interrelation with the qualities of the five kingdoms of Nature. This creates the mode of awakening consciousness within the planet. Scorpio and Sagittarius specifically relate to the testings for Initiation (Scorpio), and the path of one-pointed aspiration (Sagittarius), to reach the mountaintop where Initiation occurs. They are therefore not considered part of the major cosmic laws. The way of the Initiate consequently starts with Capricorn. Here the Initiate is symbolically represented as the transfigured, sure-footed goat. He/she has become the unicorn, possessing the horn of plenty, allowing the ceaseless fulfilling of other's needs, and the ability to fly high to the central spiritual sun. In this consideration of the Beatitudes, we therefore start with Capricorn and continue with the Initiate's further development of compassionate action through Aquarius, Pisces, Aries and Taurus.

The Initiate then stands in the guise of Jesus, who 'seeing the multitudes, he went up into a mountain: and when he was set, his disciples came unto him' (Aries), and 'he opened his mouth, and taught them' (Taurus). We have then a prime example of the life of a high Initiate following faithfully 'the Word of God' (that is, the emanation from the Logoic Mind). In this way, Jesus demonstrated his steadfast determination to follow the way of the higher cosmic laws. Thus the signs Capricorn to Taurus specifically represent characteristics possessed by the returning *jīvas (nirvāṇees),* the Dhyān Chohans (Buddhas) travelling upon cosmic paths to new destinations with the gain of their former evolutionary progress.

From a cosmic perspective, the *prāṇic* streams represent five major cosmic pathways discovered when the *nirvāṇee* exits our planet. The five cosmic paths in question are: 'The Path of Earth Service', 'The Path of Magnetic Work', 'The Path of the Planetary Logos', 'The Path to Sirius', and 'The Ray Path'. There are an added exalted two: 'The Path of the Solar Logos' and 'The Path of Absolute Sonship'.[18] The sum total of *prāṇic* circulation over the entire intricate *nāḍī* system is incorporated in the yogic teaching of the five *vayūs*. When this philosophy is extended to the Body of Manifestation of the greater Logos (of which our solar Logos is a tiny part), then the cosmic paths come into perspective. Other than linking these cosmic paths to the *vayūs* to which they relate, I shall not elaborate upon them further, as the subject is too vast to concern us here. Basic information concerning these paths can be gleaned from D.K.'s books, and then only cursorily. The *vayūs* are:

1. Apāna - the *nāḍī from the Solar Plexus to the feet.* This is related to the Element Earth, the physical plane, the Base of the Spine and the Sacral centres. The first cosmic path, Earth Service.
2. Samāna - the *nāḍī from the Heart to the Solar Plexus.* This is related to the astral plane, the Element Water and the Solar Plexus centre. The second cosmic path, Magnetic Work.
3. Udāna - the *nāḍī from the nose to the top of the head.* This is related to the Element Fire, the mental plane and the Throat centre. The third cosmic path, that of a planetary Logos.
4. Prāṇa - the *nāḍī from the nose to the Heart.* This is related to the buddhic plane, and the Heart centre. The fourth cosmic path, that to Sirius.
5. Vyāna - the *sum total of all prāṇic energies.* This is related to the *ātmic* plane and the combined Head centres. The fifth cosmic path, the Ray Path.

The instincts are also exemplified in this account as a way of comprehending somewhat the nature of cosmic evolution when the concept of transmuted correspondences is appropriately applied. Our comprehension is limited because of a lack of adequate knowledge by most people concerning the nature of manifesting divinity. Nevertheless,

18 See *A Treatise on Cosmic Fire,* 1242 *ff.*

a rough analogy can be made. The exercise of trying to conceptualise the true import of a high Initiate status should prove useful as an exercise in abstract thinking.

Little more than hints can be provided here, plus some background information that students can further develop. Full elaboration is not possible because supplementary information, such as detail of the nature of solar evolution, has not yet been provided. The laws governing the cosmic mental plane and the associated signs of the zodiac can now be analysed, starting from the lowest to the highest cosmic planes.

1 Capricorn the goat—the law of Economy

The seventh cosmic mental sub-plane. The *vayū* is Apāna, governing the manifestation of the entire Earthy Element. This *vayū* is defined as 'the *nāḍī from the Solar Plexus to the feet',* and is related to the (dense) physical plane, the Base of the Spine and the Sacral centres. It represents the nature of *prāṇic* circulation through the lower centres, the organs of generation, and governs the expression of the internal heat of the objective system, the appearance and the continuance of the dense form. The potency of *kuṇḍalinī,* the feminine force in Nature, is veiled. From our present perspective, these qualities must be viewed in terms of the body of manifestation of a Logos, and from the assumption that all phenomena by extension is an expression of the Mind. This then becomes the foundation for the eventuation of Amoghasiddhi's All-accomplishing Wisdom. This Wisdom thereby conditions the major attainment of human and *deva* Lives within the cosmic dense physical plane.

A keyword for Capricorn is patience, which refers to the quality developed by the Lords of Life to see the long evolutionary process of each kingdom to completion. It starts with the initial rotary motion of each atomic unity around its centre (the 'self' concept), causing friction, heat, and pain in its relation to other such self-involved unities. Each step of this path, of birth and death of such atomic lives, must be mastered until we eventually have the production of that fourth dimensional motion that spells the liberation for each unit. This story has been well explained in the previous volumes of this treatise, but here we are concerned with the activity of Initiates that must guide the entire process through for entire groups of such unities.

Capricorn governs the nature of manifestation of the mount of Fiery substance and associated *karma* of the cosmic lower mental sub-planes, focused via the seventh sub-plane. By extension, the conditioning Thought patterns of the Logoic Mind sweep all substance into activity, which is then externalised in the form of whatever the Logoic Ideation had conceived. Cosmos is ordained according to patterns found in the domain of such a Mind.

We saw that the alternative sign governing this seventh cosmic mental plane is Aries. Aries and Capricorn are linked in that they are both arms of the cardinal cross. (Being located upon the eastern and northern arms.) The difference being that Aries impels the process whereby substance becomes incorporated into a Logoic Thought Form, whilst Capricorn represents the sum of the gain of the concretion process as that Thought evolves.

The seventh degree Initiate enters the path of aspiration to this domain by comprehending the detailed *karma* of the sum of the cosmic dense physical plane. Such a one can then direct the evolution of the mineral Monads therein, and work to preserve the stability of all factors of the Logoic form so that the purpose for that form can be achieved. Preparatory to this, a fifth degree Initiate gains full comprehension of the qualities of this seventh cosmic mental sub-plane, and of the way that the law of Economy governs all forms of Logoic activity.

A cosmic version of the instinct of self preservation governs this level of development upon the path of return. This instinct is basic to the mineral kingdom, and is the result of the various laws of the conservation of energy. They are the laws which hold the nucleus of an atom together, and produce the rotation of the electrons around the central nucleus, thus providing the various atoms their coherent integrity. The strength of this instinct is such that only under extreme conditions can the nucleus of most atoms be destroyed or changed. It allows the concretion of substance into a dense planetary or solar sphere and the consequent aeonic evolution of such a sphere. The law of Economy thus conditions all aspects of the physical form from a universal to a minuscule scale. In our humanity it produces an innate fear of death of any aspect of the nucleus of intelligent expression constituting the personality. This translates as the law utilised by a Logos or high Initiate to build a *maṇḍala* of expression and to sustain its activity under this law for the sum of its intended duration. No energy or factor expressed within the *maṇḍala* is squandered or inefficiently expressed when using the Will to sustain and cohere all into an integral Unity. All factors are carefully chosen to produce the maximum benefit with the least energy expenditure for the sum of its components parts.

Within this *maṇḍala,* the plant and animal kingdoms adapt to its environing conditions, producing the balanced form of competitiveness for resources and energies needed for integral survival, wherein the most adaptive species will evolve the needed characteristics that indicate a gain towards perfection. We see economy of scale, economy of energy consumption, economy of ritualised activity of the petals of the great flowers of Life unfolding; all conditioning the way the developing forms manifest. All are an expression of the seventh Ray quality of the most concretised level of cosmic Mind. Cycles upon cycles come and go in economised, mathematically ordered patterns of expression before the Plan is seen to completion. That Plan is well understood in terms of the evolution of Monadic Life within the seven systemic sub-planes of the cosmic dense physical, wherein we reside.

Two of the signs, Taurus and Capricorn, embody the qualities of the Earthy Element. Here one should observe the fact that this Element is seen cosmically in terms of the cosmic dense physical plane, which reflects the qualities of the cosmic mental plane. The kingdom of Souls resides on the abstract realms of the Mind, whilst the animal kingdom aspires to the concrete realms. From this we see that the Taurean expression of this Element can be seen to represent the development of the abstract attributes of Mind, whereas the Capricornian expression relates to the empirical attributes of mind. The other Earth sign (Virgo) represents the plains of the earth. Here the downward thrust of Logoic Desire (Taurus) for Earthy experience, causes the impregnation of the fertile ground (Virgo) with the seeds of Life. Virgo thus represents substance (matter) in all of its attributes. This impregnation produces the aeonical sacrifice of the Lord of Life to see the fruits of His labour satisfy the travail of His Soul. Capricorn represents the mount of ascent of the gain of the Lord as He awaits on High for the return of the Spark of descent.

2 Aquarius the water bearer–the law of Attraction

The sixth cosmic mental sub-plane. The *vayū* is Samāna, defined as 'the *nāḍī from the Heart to the Solar Plexus'*. It is related to the astral plane, the Element Water and the Solar Plexus centre, which governs the distribution of the Watery Element. These attributes produce the eventuation of the Equalising Wisdom of Ratnasambhava. The eighth degree Initiate enters the path of cosmic discipleship under the auspices of this law. The focus is on the direction of the cosmic plant kingdom (human Monads) and the sum of their evolutionary attainment. He/she learns to control the Waters of the cosmic astral ocean to vitalise these man-plants. Cosmically, the sexual instinct governs such development via the expression of this law. Reflecting this ability, sixth degree Initiates enter into an accord with the substance of this sixth cosmic mental sub-plane. They comprehend fully the nature of the Watery disposition that facilitates the upward mobility of the evolving Lives, and which sustains their evolutionary growth.

The sixth Ray of Devotion and of high Aspiration primarily governs the manifestation of the law of Attraction via the expression of the group laws. This attraction is because of the Desire or Devotion of a Logos to see the process of manifestation evolving through to His/Her Seat of Power. The group Lives constituting that Body of Manifestation then respond to the Magnetic Impulse of the Devotion in the form of the energy of Divine Love. They therefore travel the way that this cosmic law pulls to the source of the Love upon the sixth cosmic mental sub-plane.

Aquarius is the dispenser of the Waters of this Love, the magnetic energy that draws all the Lives to the primary source of Life. This dispensation of the Logos causes the entire evolutionary pull away from form life, which is the basis to the law of Repulse. Aquarius channels the streams of energy from the Logoic Soul via the law of Magnetic Impulse, and attracts to it the Watery forms of Manasic expression developed by the Lives evolving via dense forms. The Life within the form is freed from its confining prison by means of the attractive potency of the liberating cosmic Soul. This 'attractive potency' between the Soul and the Lives constituting the form is then seen as the 'Polar Union' (the alternative name to this law of Magnetic Impulse) that is the basis to the manifestation of the sexual instinct. Sexual attraction therefore concerns this pull of Life to these Lives to unite the various separations between them. (The gain is Ratnasambhava's Wisdom of Equality.) Essentially, these Lives are floral and therefore are members of the cosmic plant kingdom. They are consequently the main focus of the effects of this great law of Attraction.

The sexual instinct developed governs the mode of interrelating *deva* and human units in such a way that the dual Ray of Love-Wisdom comes into expression. This law of Attraction, stemming from the domain of the Logoic Soul, attracts into that Soul the refined *saṃskāras* that are the gain for the Logoic *manvantaric* expression.

It is important here to try to envisage the huge variety and types of floral displays within the cosmic landscape that are attracted to each other. In the first place, this happens through affinity of colour (the Rays), similar species, and emanatory perfume. (The transmuted form of the energy of goodwill of the northwest arm of the eight-armed cross.) One should therefore note the abundant use of colour, perfume, of myriad hues, tonalities, floral shapes, and specialisation of petals as an attribute of this instinct. Its principal objective is to attract the insect world (fourth and fifth degree Initiates), offering them nectar and pollen as a reward for the act of cross pollination (the integration of diverse forms of esoteric information, as an aspect of the law of Expansive Response) that fertilises them, ensuring genetic diversity. It also produces a pleasing and healing environment for all kingdoms (an expression of the law of Service).

As these Lives merge into unitary purpose, their essences then come to be attracted to the pull of the Logoic Soul upon the cosmic higher mental plane. The fact that the plant kingdom constitutes the foundation of the food chain or Life energy that sustains the animal kingdom should also be emphasised (an expression of the law of Sacrifice), for the sexual instinct essentially allows the Life of the form nature to be adequately sustained and brought to an integral perfection. The well being of our material selves is aptly likened to a blossoming or flowering of vitality, joy, and beauty. Such well being is generally obtained by eating that which grew from or enclosed the sexual parts of plants, such as fruit, beans, grains and nuts. (An expression of the law of the Lower Four, or of 'Etheric Union'.) By desire for such foodstuffs we manifest the actions that help propagate the plant species in a progressive manner. (The law of Group Progress.) From the higher perspective, the ingestion of such 'fruits' concerns the absorption of the *saṃskāras* of all forms of loving interrelationships that develop *bodhicitta.*

The plant Life planted in the cosmic soil, therefore, is a focus of this activity and must be appropriately Watered, so that it can grow tall, and project itself towards the Light that shines forth from the second last cosmic mental sub-plane. The eventual conversion of the plants to the animal forms allows the final stages of the attraction to be completed. The animal form represents a transference of conscious focus towards cosmic Manasic development. We thus have the production of forms of *kāma-manas* cosmically considered, which is needed for absorption into the domain of cosmic Mind. From the above, we can see why this sexual instinct is so strong within the human kingdom, as it represents the strongest pull from cosmic sources upon our Monadic Life. This then effects the domain of the Sambhogakāya Flower, and thence the life of the personal-I. The Shambhalic gardeners also make sure that the 'man-plant' is well Watered and nourished from the cosmic astral domain.

In the mineral kingdom, we find that the sexual instinct expresses itself as the various laws of valency, the union of positive and negative ions that produce the many molecules and compounds constituting our dense sphere.

In the animal kingdom this instinct finds its expression in the many courtship rituals and mating displays geared towards the propagation of the most adroit and viable members of the genetic pool of any species. This hints at the forms of interrelationship upon cosmic mental levels, wherein certain Thought-forms are produced related to forms of energisation of new cycles of activity. The Thought-forms must meet the cyclic challenges of the oncoming events to fulfil Logoic purpose in centres populated by many Beings that will come from various planetary or solar Schools. All must be interrelated into one grand harmony of expression.

In humanity, this instinct is closely allied with that of self-preservation, and stems from an innate fear of isolation. At present it is one of the strongest forces motivating us, especially when reinforced by imagination.

We saw that the alternative sign to the sixth cosmic mental sub-plane is Taurus the bull. Taurus and Aquarius are the eastern and northern arms of the fixed cross. They are attributes of the cosmic Christ that is crucified upon this cross so that all lesser Lives can gain from the shedding of the Blood that nourishes their lives, and which draws them to the Heart of Life.

3 Pisces the fishes—the law of Karma

The fifth cosmic mental sub-plane. The *vayū* is Udāna, 'the *nāḍī from the nose to the top of the head'*. It is related to the mental plane and the Throat centre governing the distribution of the Fiery Element, from which is derived the Discriminating Inner Wisdom of Amitābha.

This law is the general law governing all of the domains of mind/ Mind because all mentalistic volitions affect substance of one type or another. All phenomena is an attribute of mind, and within the mind the effect of sense-contacts with phenomena produces the development of the awareness of things. Thoughts are created to interact with these things, producing volitions that change substance *(svabhāva),* and this then produces karmic repercussions *(māyā).* Inevitably, the effect of that volition must come to be equilibrated to produce a zero net effect of the energy balance. In this way the sum of the energy expended will equal the input of any *maṇḍala* of expression. Energy then is neither created nor destroyed, no thing is miraculously made to appear from nothing. Eternal equilibrated harmony is the result, which is the effect of this law of *karma.* Amitābha's Wisdom is perpetually conscious of the way such equilibrium manifests as a consequence of every *manasic* action.

Pisces is the sign of completion, of termination, hence the resolution of the *karma* of material involvement. It is also that which produces bondage to all forms of material things. Hence the Thinker (the fish swimming in the waters of sensation) attaches a thought to (elements of) *saṃsāra* and bonds with it, producing the bonded fishes. Here we have the establishment of *karma.* Such *karma* remains until the bond can be broken through producing an equal but opposite energy of the action that produced the bond. The appearance of phenomena starts the projection of the bond to its target *(manvantara),* and the ending of such phenomena (the expression of thought form construction) is the severance of the bond. This severance creates the onset of *pralaya.*

The appearance and the dissolution of things (the generation of *karma* and then its termination) are consequently happening all the time, be that upon a minute or a universal scale. Inevitably, however, it is all the function of the mind/Mind, and when such activity ceases then we have *śūnyatā,* which can be conceived of as a state wherein the coming and going of *karma* does not exist. Consequently, the keyword of Pisces is abstraction, which is the recall and conversion of all karmic threads so that they can be absorbed into the Heart of Life.

The fact that Pisces is a Water sign helps it to assimilate and process the final expression of the *karma* of the transmuted correspondences of *kāma-manasic* impulses developed by the approaching *nirvāṇees.* This Watery attribute is *bodhicitta,* viewed from the perspective of those upon the earth, but is seen as the developing animal sentience from the view of the Logoi existing upon cosmic mental domains. The *karma* must be resolved, and a method for resolution, for instance, is the appearance of World Saviours, governed by the attributes of Pisces, at the end of every major epoch upon the earth. The process of assimilating this Watery disposition (e.g., the way of evolution of the group laws) into the constructs of cosmic Mind (Mahat) is a major part of the work of the Lords upon Sirius. These Logoi are the wielding arbiters of Love-Wisdom for the stars of the local part of the galaxy,[19] of which our solar Logos is one. Sirius is therefore the cosmic destination for all 'Animal' life, from where they receive instructions of the process that makes them 'Human', cosmically speaking. From this perspective the law of *karma* is wielded from Sirius, the blue star of cosmic Love, because it directs the karmic weave of all such Lives.

In Pisces, the cosmic animal kingdom undergoes the final stages of its development and prepares for cosmic Individualisation. The ninth degree Initiate is Initiated into a detailed comprehension of the way of evolution of the members of the cosmic human kingdom. All forms of bond building within the cosmic domains come to be refused, so that abstract domains of cosmic Mind can be discovered. The Initiate learns to master the laws of projection of *antaḥkaraṇas* to the cosmic

---

19 This refers to the Body of 'the One about Whom Naught may be Said', who embodies the stars in the night sky that are generally visible to the naked eye. This One is but a 'Human' unit of a large number of similar Brethren constituting our galaxy.

Mind and of the subtleties of the expression of the *karma* of any Logoic Thought. This concerns the way that it reticulates throughout the aeons, producing many determinate and maybe some indeterminate effects. On a lower level, the seventh degree Initiate begins to gain a comprehensive view of the cosmic implications of this law as it is directed to govern the sum of the manifestation of the cosmic dense physical activities of the Logos. This necessitates understanding the subtleties of the way that *karma* originates and how it can be used to resurrect all of the lives that are bonded to the forms existing in the seven systemic planes.

The *karma* is instigated that conditions the lives in the entire Life of the Logoic Personality, of His/Her incarnation into the higher sub-planes of the cosmic dense physical. We thus have the genesis of the instinct of the self-assertion of the personality. This becomes the basis to the expression of individual *karma*.

It should be noted here that Virgo, in whose Womb this *karma* is expressed, is the polar opposite of Pisces. She governs the manifestation of the crystallised Fire that represents the cosmic mineral kingdom, and eventually the way of the resolution of the *karma* via the birth of the Initiation process.

In the mineral kingdom, this instinct is reflected in the tendency of atoms and molecules to attain the reactions and forms that produce the greatest stability. In the vegetable kingdom it is seen in the poisonous and spiky plants, in those with defence mechanisms against hostile entities. Here we have an indication of the various experiments undertaken within a human evolution that produce the various forms of division and strife via the separative impetus of the fifth Ray of Scientific Reason. Such activity develops the potency of the liberating factor of the will, and also inevitably the wisdom of knowing what not to do as a consequence of how to best deal with such protectiveness.

The carnivores develop the instinct of self-assertion amongst the animal kingdom. We also see it in the often violent courtship clashes between the male members of many animal species. Here, therefore, we have the nascent appearance of individual *karma* within the context of a purely instinctual activity. Individual masculine prowess also lays the backdrop to the process of eventual Individualisation of the animal kingdom, where each animal unit comes to be differentiated from the herd or group so that the Sambhogakāya Flower can be wrought.

From a higher cosmic perspective, the concept of carnivores concerns the development of *iḍā nāḍī* characteristics. It represents a type of comparatively forceful (wilful) development of the characteristics of Mind amongst the Love-Wisdom oriented 'herd'. Certain entities are sought out and 'devoured', so that the elements of cosmic Mind and Will can be incorporated into a *maṇḍala.* The nature of the digestive process of a Logos can be here meditated upon—what *saṃskāras* (streams of Lives) are 'digested', which ones are converted, and how a transference of properties happens as a consequence. The digested one benefits by being brought into contact with elements of cosmic Mind, which they can then develop.

Self-assertion of the individual comes to be exemplified in the human kingdom, with obvious effects, seen in the many examples of 'man's inhumanity to man'. It also produces the various personality traits and characteristics, the self-willed, self-determined attributes that are so important in the expression of karmic consequences. The latter stages of our evolution necessitate overcoming this tendency of self-will, by replacing it with goodwill, which precedes undertaking the Initiation process.

For a Logos, such self-assertion at first relates to the Thought-Form building of a construct, such as a world-sphere, whereby dark matter must be claimed and incorporated into a ring-pass-not. Then that entire construct must be seen through to its conclusion. Unique characteristics not yet found in other such spheres must be developed, and the tendencies towards the attributes of the dark brotherhood eliminated at the appropriate time. Not all Logoic Thought constructs are successful. Myriad factors are to be taken into account, and the elements of risk can produce serious karmic consequences.

For humanity, this instinct produces the fear that we may fail to be recognised by our group, and thus be left out of the group activity, or that we may lose that which seems (to us) to be necessary for our survival as individual entities.

The two signs associated with this fifth cosmic mental plane are Gemini and Pisces, which are the eastern and northern arms of the mutable cross. Such activity is the cause of the emanation of *karma.*

The bonded fishes in Pisces become the two brothers in Gemini, where the immortal brother must teach the mortal sibling how to break the bonds to the attributes of mortality, so that the inner sanctum of the Heart of Life can be found.

4 Aries the ram—the law of Synthesis

The fourth cosmic mental sub-plane. The *vayū* is Prāṇa, the *'nāḍī from the nose to the Heart'*. This is related to the buddhic plane (the fourth cosmic ether), and the Heart centre, the cosmic demonstration of which becomes the foundation for the expression of the Mirror-like Wisdom of Akṣobhya.

Tenth degree Initiates now appear by having undertaken cosmic Individualisation. They thus become a member of cosmic Humanity (a Logos) upon a transmuted level of what our present humanity represents. All cosmic animal-like energies become synthesised into one blended expression, and focused upwards (with the help of the Will-attribute of Aries the ram) to the higher mental domain, to attract to it the Solar Devas that will build the whorls of energy constituting the Soul-Form. A cosmic Sambhogakāya Flower thus comes into existence. Such a One is able to become the Logos of a planetary Scheme. Akṣobhya's Wisdom then comes into play by reflecting into manifestation the directive purpose of that Flower. The governing Ray is that of the fourth of Beautifying Harmony overcoming Strife. It is thus the fundamental Ray conditioning all levels of humanity. A keyword is sacrifice, the ending of all cyclic impulse by absorbing the All back into the One. Later we have the outpouring of a new cyclic Impulse, of giving freely the Heart's Blood.

Understanding the concept of synthesis and sacrifice requires a deep introspection of all forces pertaining to existence, of the final rectification of the *karma* of incarnation, and by drawing to the higher domain of Mind the gains expressed by utilising the laws of Economy and of Attraction. It concerns becoming the point within the sphere (of Logoic Activity). It necessitates a dynamic one-pointed application of the Commands and adjuncts from the exalted strata of Revelation. *Manasic* expression must become refined and liberated from concepts of the form by manifesting appropriate Ideas as needed. Logoic desire is transformed into the Will-to-Abstract. This abstraction process necessitates drawing to it all former *saṃskāras* of expression (lesser streams of Lives incorporated by the Initiate) and converting them to respond to energy waves of an order they are not accustomed to handling, to Mahatic Impulses from Thought strata that are the synthesis of the foundational group laws previously explained. Symbolically, the Ram charges headlong towards the goal of the new pathways to be constructed in cosmic Mental space. *Antaḥkaraṇas* must be projected to exalted Lives previously veiled via a barrier of conceptual form. Fiery substance consequently becomes ablaze with Light in the form of the new Logoic Sambhogakāya Flower that appears.

Working with this law on a lower scale, the eighth degree Initiate gains a form of second Initiation into the Mysteries of the cosmic astral Waters, wherein attractiveness originating from the Love-Wisdom petals of the Logoic Mind comes to be fully integrated into the Initiate's ken. This allows Him/Her to transmute and transfer certain cosmic *saṃskāras* to that Logoic form. A Buddha discovers a universe of 'thus gone' ones with which to interrelate, and new group interrelationships come to the fore as the higher attributes of the group laws are unfolded.

The group or herd instinct now comes into predominance. In the mineral kingdom, this is seen as the union of the various classes of atoms into molecules, and in turn, the amalgamation of these molecules into the myriad groups of solid and liquid shapes (crystals, rocks, etc.) that form the dense world that is our environment. The cosmic correspondence with respect to the law of Synthesis is that those aspiring to attain their tenth Initiation are to become Logoi, and come to build a sphere of attainment (a Logoic personality) whereby atomic unities are brought together to form a solar or planetary form.

The herd instinct is brought to perfection in the animal kingdom, and is seen in their banding together in flocks, schools, and herds composed entirely of the one type of animal. The cosmic analogy is to those preparing to undertake Individualisation, who are grouped according to Ray lines and various active methods of approach. A large number of Logoi come to Individualise within a certain limited cosmic time period. Myriads are those that work with the group laws that are the basics to developing the high Initiations that will eventually produce the tests for mastering the law of Synthesis.

In the vegetable kingdom, the tendency is for a flower to disperse its seeds (progeny) as far away from the parent or group as possible (preventing over-competition for limited resources). The ideal in that kingdom is then to have as much diversity of different species as possible in any locality. Where this instinct is seen manifesting, for instance in a field of flowers of predominantly the same type, it is essentially integrated with the sexual instinct. From this perspective then, the human Monads will come to be dispersed throughout the newly forming globes that will accommodate their forms of activity as they travel upon their cosmic paths under the fundamental law of Attraction. They then learn to abstract their awareness towards cosmic Mind, to which they become more receptive. Inevitably, this process leads to the threshold of cosmic Individualisation via the law of Synthesis.

In humanity this instinct fosters our fear of loneliness, causing us to seek friendship or comfort in the form of social, political, aesthetic, national, religious, or racial groups. This inevitably creates the appearance of human civilisations, national states, and the like. The higher correspondence of this behaviour is demonstrated via the effect of the law of Synthesis forming a new cosmic Humanity upon the cosmic higher mental plane. This population then unfolds its own version of 'civilisation' upon the landscape they reside in.

The two signs associated with this law are the southern (Cancer) and eastern (Aries) arms of the cardinal cross. What is implied here is the entire journey from mass incarnation (Cancer) to the one-pointed focus towards the (cosmic) mental plane (Aries) by those that have travelled through countless cycles of zodiacal activity (impelled esoterically by the force of the butting Ram) to do so.

5 *Taurus the bull—the law of cosmic Identity*

The third cosmic mental sub-plane, and establishing the Sambhogakāya Flower thereon. This law concerns the taking of the higher cosmic Initiations, as a planetary system embodied by a presiding Logos unfolds. We also have the appearance of an entire new cosmic Humanity (as the Individualisation process causes a new humanity to come into being), and the myriad planets and stars that they incarnate into as their Bodies of Manifestation.

There is also the full integration of the laws of Mind into the entire Logoic evolutionary path via the establishment of a planetary Head centre. This law determines the distinguishing characteristics between one Logoic sphere (Body of Manifestation) and another. It implicates the emanatory note, musical score, colour, and mathematical formula that causes one Logoic sphere to manifest a destiny that differs from another. We thus have great diversity within a unified body of expression.

The *vayū* concerned is Vyāna, the '*sum total of all prāṇic energies'*. It is related to the *ātmic* plane and the combined Head centres. The Dharmadhātu Wisdom of Vairocana comes to seed the new Logoic venture. The instinct involved is that of Knowledge, as promulgated via the activity of the cosmic mental sub-planes. The keyword is the Wisdom that must be expressed to see the new venture through, and the fruit of the Love that clothes the field of Desire to sustain its evolutionary Impetus. The Taurean Eye sees and directs the All.

With respect to the manifestation of a new Logoic Incarnation, we have the appearance of the first Creative Hierarchy, 'the Burning Sons of Desire', that build the Logoic Head centre (Shambhala) that governs the sum of manifestation. D.K. states:

> This first (sixth) Hierarchy has for its type of energy the first aspect of the sixth type of cosmic electricity, and wields special power, therefore, in conjunction with the lowest fire, or "fire by friction," as it makes itself felt on the sixth plane. These lives are called "the burning Sons of Desire" and were the Sons of Necessity. It is said of them in the Old Commentary: "They burned to know. They rushed into the spheres. They are the longing of the Father for the Mother. Hence do they suffer, burn, and long through the sixth sphere of sense".[20]

'The Mother' here represents the material form, which must come to be resurrected, turned into 'man-plants'. Thus the evolutionary story we know so well proceeds. The 'sixth sphere of sense' refers to the Sacral centre and the activation of the cycles of the generation of the species of Life and their sacral interplay. It awakens the world of the senses wherein mind evolves. They are 'burning Sons' because they carry the Fires of cosmic Mind to assist in the causation and the direction of all the appearing phenomena associated with the 'sphere of sense'. They 'suffer' in the sense of being crucified Christs, Logoi that must see the *manvantara*, the planetary existence, through from beginning to end.

---

20 A.A. Bailey, *Esoteric Astrology*, 39.

The 'longing of the Father for the Mother' also refers to the eventual awakening of *kuṇḍalinī* by the evolving lives.

We can see, therefore, that the entire process of the evolutionary paean comes under the general auspices of the sign Taurus the bull, which clothes the form impelled via Logoic Desire. It builds the *maṇḍalas* of whatever is to be. It is literally the great cosmic Mother of space and time, and the symbolism is well veiled by the functions of all cow-goddesses of antiquity.

The two signs associated with this law are the southern and eastern arms of the fixed cross (Leo and Taurus). At first Leo (governing the first Creative Hierarchy) works to produce the development of self-consciousness in Nature, to en-flame the lives with Mind so that they can eventually learn to discriminate right from wrong. Eventually, the path to Initiation is sought through travelling to the Heart and the development of wisdom (Taurus), which inevitably produces the attainment of the highest of the cosmic laws.

In the mineral kingdom, the instinct towards knowledge is seen in the form of radioactivity and the disintegration of matter into the rays that pierce or travel through space and solid matter. The transmutation of substance and the theme of the search for the Philosopher's Stone thereby must beset humanity in the earth sphere if the mineral kingdom is to be mastered. Both alchemical and scientific lore must be developed upon this path.

In the plant world, this instinct is seen in their aspiration towards light and their empathy with the animal kingdom (e.g., the insect world). In a similar manner the way of Monadic evolution proceeds.

The instinct towards knowledge is seen in the animal kingdom as their increased mobility (the use of feet and wings), and in devotion or aspiration to the human kingdom (by our domesticated animals). The way of travelling upon the higher cosmic Initiations, as already described, stands as the higher correspondence to this development.

In the human world, we see this instinct prompting our fear of the unknown, and in turn a determination to learn about it. From this instinct arises scientific investigation, and the desire to conquer unexplored territory. We also have the generation of that goodwill where we like to share our experiences with others. Inevitably, the mysteries of what constitutes conscious space, and then that of the multidimensional universe become the field of enquiry, which leads to travelling the Initiation path. This path eventually produces the attainment of the tenth Initiation by the members of the cosmic fraternity.

Of the various kingdoms in Nature, however, the way of knowledge is most developed by the kingdom of the Sambhogakāya Flower. It is a major property of their expression. This kingdom is urged towards the gathering of knowledge, first on the corporeal planes of perception (by the process of repeated incarnation into it), then on its own realm, and finally in the realm of enlightened being *(buddhi)*. Similarly for the newly Individualised Logoi, thus 'They burned to know'—what the process of manifesting a sphere of sensation will produce in terms of evolutionary gain for all.

Conclusion

The five pairs of signs regarding the laws stemming from the cosmic mental plane therefore stand in the order of a fixed, cardinal, mutable, fixed and cardinal crosses. They are associated with the expression of the five Elements: Aether (Identity), Air (Synthesis), Fire (Karma), Water (Attraction), and Earth (Economy). Once the doctrine of the Elements is utilised, then the associated sense-consciousnesses come into view. They concern the development of consciousness as derived from the use of the sense of smell, taste, sight, touch and hearing. The revelation of the ontological suppositions associated with the elaboration of this concept is possible via transmuted correspondences. It is, however, a vast area of unverifiable complexity (in terms of present scientific opinion) and explanation is fraught with difficulty due to the inefficiency of language. The lack of expanded vision of the reader produces other obstacles, much would have to be posited that readers will simply have to accept as true. This opens up sources for abuse of the doctrines, and gullibility is not what we wish to feed. Nevertheless, more information of a cosmological nature can be wisely revealed later, once the foundation for comprehension has been adequately laid.

Initiates come to Know, as it is a major part of the Mysteries of the higher grades to which they are Initiated. For them, Revelations proceed apace with their increasing development of the higher correspondences (higher *siddhis)* of the sense-perceptors commonly utilised. The sense of hearing, for instance, expands into comprehension of the mantric Sounds emitted by diverse categories of lives; and sight into multidimensional visioning. Revelations obtained from 'brief moments' of such vision could then fill the pages of a large book. For this the path of meditation prepares one, and the Initiation process makes possible. The reader is thus urged to follow that way to open the doors to revelation of what is presently unknown.

Figure 5 illustrates these five pairs of signs as a mutable cross, governing the expression of the law of *karma,* and works to integrate the higher pair with the lower, and vice versa. All activities turn this mutable wheel from right to left and from left to right, depending upon the nature of the ascent or descent of energies. It links the laws of cosmic Identity to Attraction, and Economy to Synthesis by means of the nature of the associated crosses, demonstrating ease of movement of the flowing *saṃskāras.* The law of Attraction is directly impressed by the agency of the Identity of the Logoic Sambhogakāya Flower, as both are upon the Love-Wisdom Ray line, and demonstrate the attributes of the fixed cross. Similarly, the *saṃskāras* generated by the law of Economy are transformed by the Will-to-Liberate from material activity by the Law of Synthesis, as both are upon the cardinal cross.

As energy flows from one arm of the governing mutable cross to the other, so *karma* is adjudicated to accommodate the 'burning desire' for expression, or for the drive to liberation. One way or other, this cross of karmic resolution spins from Incarnation to Incarnation of each Logoic Life. As it does so, the multitudinous lesser Lives thrill into activity to play their appointed roles in planetary and solar evolution. First the *iḍā* path, the way of Economy, rules to produce the evolution of *manas* in the scheme of things. Later the law of Attraction, the *piṇgalā* path, plays its role to integrate separative units of mind into a coherent Oneness. The generated *saṃskāras* from earlier cycles must be refined, converted and transmuted. Volume 5 provides detail of this process, where the Peaceful and Wrathful Deities can be interpreted in terms of the Lives governing a planetary system. The serene Love-Wisdom of the enlightened Ones, and the dynamic, intelligent Love of the greater *devas,* embody the attributes of the Peaceful Deities. Wrath can be seen played out in terms of climatic changes, earthquakes, famines, drought, pestilence, extinction of species and through the massed karmic effects that plague humanity. Incessantly does the wheel move from right to left and from left to right, bringing with it many changes in orientation in the evolving Lives. At each turn, *karma* is appropriately adjudicated.

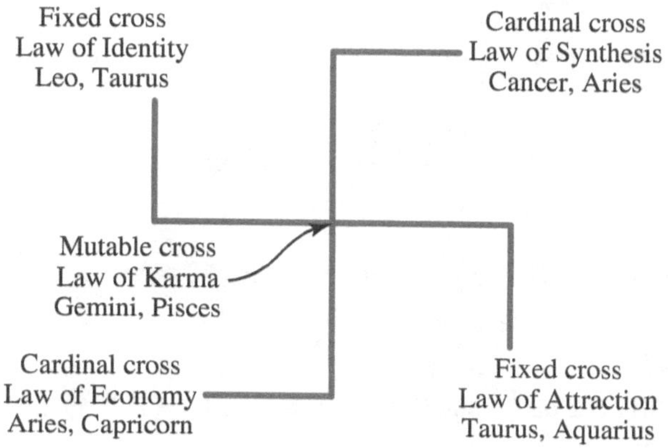

Figure 5. The cosmic mental plane laws

Inevitably, the law of Synthesis plays in the spheres of economy to produce the flowering of the Initiation path. Inevitably, the fundamental magnetic attractiveness of the Heart of Life pulls all integrated groups of Lives to the hidden Source of Life, the cosmic Identity of the Logoic Soul. Inevitably, these streams of Logoic *saṃskāras* are absorbed into the petals of that Flower with the gain for that Logoic Life. All have moved forward, and thus obscuration *(pralaya)* ensues. Inevitably, a new Logoic Personality is Breathed out in a new *manvantaric* flurry of activity, to produce streams of evolving Lives. Each will in time become Sambhogakāya Flowers and manifest Son-Suns that become 'Buddha-fields' of luminous stars in the night sky; an entire galaxy of cosmic opulence of possibilities. So will it be.

Oṁ Oṁ Oṁ

Hri

Hūṁ!

Bibliography

Avalon, Arthur. *The Serpent Power.* Madras: Ganesh & Co., 2004.

Bailey, Alice A. *Esoteric Healing.* New York: Lucis Publishing Company, 1973.

——. *A Treatise on Cosmic Fire.* New York: Lucis Publishing Company, 1977.

——. *Discipleship in the New Age, Vol. 1.* New York: Lucis Publishing Company, 1976.

——. *Initiation, Human and Solar.* New York: Lucis Publishing Company, 1970.

——. *The Externalisation of the Hierarchy.* New York: Lucis Publishing Company, 1982.

——. *Esoteric Astrology.* New York: Lucis Publishing Company, 1968.

——. *Esoteric Psychology, Vol II.* New York: Lucis Publishing Company, 1981.

——. *The Rays and Initiations.* New York: Lucis Publishing Company, 1970.

——. *A Treatise on White Magic.* New York: Lucis Publishing Company, 1974.

Balsys, Bodo. *I-Concept.* Kathmandu: Vajra Publishing, 2009.

——. *Karma and the Rebirth of Consciousness.* Delhi: Munshiram Manoharlal, 2006.

——. *Maṇḍalas - Their Nature and Development. Volume 4 of A Treatise on Mind.* Sydney: Universal Dharma Publishing, 2013.

——. *The Revelation, Volume 1.* Sydney: Ibez Press, 1989.

Blavatsky, H.P. *The Voice of the Silence.* Illinois: Theosophical Publishing House, 1998.

——. *The Secret Doctrine. Vol. 1.* Adyar: Theosophical Publishing House, 1971.

Dudjom Rinpoche, *The Nyingma School of Tibetan Buddhism.* Translated by Gyurme Dorje and Matthew Kapstein. Boston: Wisdom, 1991.

Edman, Irwin (ed). *The Works of Plato.* New York: Random House, 1956.

Evans-Wentz, W.Y. *The Tibetan Book of the Dead.* Delhi: Munshiram Manoharlal, 2000.

——. *Tibet's Great Yogī Milarepa.* London: Oxford University Press, 1951.

Gampopa. *The Jewel Ornament of Liberation.* Translated by Khenpo Konchog Gyaltsen Rinpoche. Ithaca: Snow Lion, 1998.

Garfield, Jay L. *The Fundamental Wisdom of the Middle Way: Nāgārjuna's Mūlamadhyamakakārikā.* New York: Oxford University Press, 1995.

Sopa, Geshe Lhundup, Roger Jackson, and John Newman. *The Wheel of Time. The Kalachakra in Context.* Ithaca: Snow Lion, 1991.

Govinda, Lama Anagarika. *Foundations of Tibetan Mysticism.* London: Century Paperbacks, 1987.

Guénon, René. *Man and His Becoming According to the Vedānta.* New York: The Noonday Press, 1958.

Hall, Manly Palmer, and Paul Brunton. *A Search In Secret Egypt.* Rider, 1969.

Hodson, Geoffrey. *The Kingdom of the Gods.* Adyar: Theosophical Publishing House, 1987.

Leadbeater, C.W. *The Chakras.* Madras: Theosophical Publishing House, 1987.

Maheshwari, Anil. *The Buddha Cries! Karmapa Conundrum.* Delhi: UBS Publishers' Distributors Ltd, 2000.

Matics, Marion L. *Entering the Path of Enlightenment.* New York: Macmillan, 1970.

Roerich, Helena. *Heart.* Agni Yoga Society, 1982.

——. *Infinity.* Agni Yoga Society, 1980.

Smith, LL.D., William. *Smith's Bible Dictionary.* New Jersey: Fleming H.Revell Company, 1970.

Snodgrass, Adrian. *The Symbolism of the Stupa.* Delhi: Motilal Banarsidass, 1992.

Steiner, Rudolf. *The Gospel of St. John.* U.S.A: Anthroposophical Press, 1962.

Suzuki, Daisetz Teitaro. *Essays in Zen Buddhism. Vol. 1.* Delhi: Munshiram Manoharlal, 2000.

The King James Version Bible. London: Oxford University Press, 1922.

Tiamni, I.K. *The Science of Yoga.* Wheaton: The Theosophical Publishing House, 2001.

Trungpa, Chögyam. *Born in Tibet.* Boston: Shambhala, 1995.

Weeks, Nora. *The Medical Discoveries of Edward Bach, Physician.* Essex: C.W. Daniel Company, 1973.

Index

A

Ādi. *See* Perception
Ādi Buddha, 33, 72
Akṣobhya. *See* Dhyāni Buddhas
Ālayavijñāna, 13
enlightenment, 234
initiation, 144
Alexandria, 37
Alice A. Bailey, 38–39
Amitābha. *See* Dhyāni Buddhas
Amoghasiddhi. *See* Dhyāni Buddhas
Angels. *See* Devas
Antaḥkaraṇa, 172, 272
building of, 18–19, 69, 84, 259, 267, 331, 362, 366
definition of, 18
Anupādaka. *See* Perception
Arhat
path of the, 289
Aspirant, 187–188, 350–351
Astral body, 42–43
Astral plane, 43, 206–207, 283–284
in relation to time, 42
Atlantean civilisation, 24, 111
Ātma. *See* Perception
Attachment
overcoming, 80
Aura, 115
Avatar
definition of, 30

B

Baptism
as second Initiation, 213–215, 221
Bardo experiences, 42
Beatitudes, the
in relation to cosmic laws, 378–379
in relation to group laws, 345, 349, 350, 353, 359, 363, 366
in relation to initiation process, 314–336
Bhūmis
in relation to Initiation process, 142, 143–144, 259, 331
Bible
esotericism in, 28–36
in relation to initiation, 189–194, 197–203, 206–210, 213–215, 217–229, 235–237, 242–256, 260–267, 284–300
the beatitudes, 314–316
Bījas, 145–146
Bodhi
definition of, 268
Bodhicitta, 263

as Christ-consciousness, 203–205, 320
function of, 268, 345
gaining of, 3, 81, 121–122, 184, 341, 360
in relation to Heart Centre, 20–21, 28, 319
Bodhisattva, 3, 109
cosmic Christ as, 30
Jesus as, 29–30
vow, 74, 205, 271, 312–313, 342
Bodhisattva path, 28, 111, 142–144, 240
Bodhisattvas
incarnation cycles of, 154–156, 156–158, 238, 310–311
service work of, 160–161
Breathing exercises, 110
Buddhadharma, 2, 29
evolution of, 157, 163–168
projection of, 155–156
Buddha-Mind
expression of, 12–13, 32–33, 148–150
Buddhi. *See* Perception

C

Causative Agents
definition of, 307–308
evolution of prime, 307–313, 313, 324–325
Cellular evolution, 258
Chakras
and plant analogy, 368
as expression of energies, 16–23, 324
as gates or doors, 16–17, 26, 79–80, 112, 116
Base of Spine Centre (mūlādhāra), 23
development of, 115–118
above the diaphragm, 45–46, 316–317
Head Centre (sahasrāra padma), 17–19, 248, 366–367
Heart Centre (anāhata), 20, 82, 327–328
awakening of, 28, 117–118, 314–336
function of, 345–346
higher three
definition of, 53
in planes of perception, 280–281
in relation to cosmic laws, 380–381, 383, 386, 390, 393
lower-four
definition of, 53
minor centres, 23, 27, 44
misuse of, 25
Sacral Centre (svādiṣṭhāna), 22–23
Solar Plexus Centre (maṇipūra), 21–22, 27, 82
as weak point, 44–45
the inner round, 158
Third Eye (ājñā), 19–20, 81, 108, 172
in relation to Sambhogakāya Flower, 19
Throat Centre (viśuddha), 20, 136, 331
warnings on awakening, 38–39, 113, 117
Christ-consciousness
as bodhicitta, 203–205
Christ-Jesus
role of, 201–206
Citta-vṛtti, 9
transformation of, 10
Collossians 3:12-17
in relation to group evolution, 91–96
Compassionate-understanding
development of, 252
elements for, 241
Consciousness
awakening of Initiate, 78–79, 202–206
reincarnation of, 42

seven attributes of, 10–13
Cosmic astral plane, 276
Cosmic dense physical plane
seven sub-planes, 276–284
Cosmic Laws
in relation to zodiac, 373–377, 378–395, 395–397
of Attraction, 371, 376, 383–386
of cosmic Identity, 392–394
of Economy, 371, 376–377, 380–383
of Karma, 375, 386–390, 396–397
of Synthesis, 372–373, 375, 390–393
subsidiary, 372–373
Cosmic mental plane, 276
laws of, 367–374
sub-planes in relation to cosmic laws, 380–395
Cosmos, 136–137
Council of Bodhisattvas, 121, 122, 202
communication with, 44
teaching methods of, 3–4, 143, 155
teachings of, 29–37
Creative Hierarchies, 278, 341, 355, 361–362, 365, 393–394
Creative imagination, 140
building antaḥkaraṇas, 18–19
in visualisation process, 131–132
Cross
symbolism of, 269–273, 298
Cycles of activity, 85

D

Ḍākinīs, 13
definition of, 60
Dark Brotherhood, 41, 196
battle against, 97–102, 121–122, 216, 334
black magician, 24, 39, 113, 181–182
karma with, 122
Left hand path, 23, 39, 41, 79, 251
recognising, 46–47
Death
as form of healing, 55
esoteric view of, 58, 87, 297
of the personality, 234–236, 270
premature, 117
Dependent Origination
Buddhist concept of, 65–66
Desire, 11
realm of, 145
Deva Kingdom, 88, 121, 355
Devas, 13, 44, 249, 345, 348, 361–362, 365
in relation to healing, 54, 59–61
'of the shadow', 60–61
Devil, the, 250, 252
Dhāraṇī/s
definition of, 22
Dharmakāya, 13, 18, 118, 144, 275, 321
as cosmos, 2, 69, 261
as universal Mind, 12–13, 259
definition of, 2
in relation to Monad, 258
Dharmakāya Way, 239–241
Dhyāni Buddhas, 18
Akṣobhya, 21, 276, 390–391
Amitābha, 20, 386–387
Amoghasiddhi, 22, 380
as angels, 59
in relation to initiations, 190
Ratnasambhava, 22, 383, 384
Vairocana, 20, 393
Divine Embodiment, 30–32
Divine Incarnation. *See* Divine embodiment
Divine Reason, 37
Divine Will, 48, 262–267, 309, 311–312, 315, 330, 343, 354
Divinity
question of, 246
Dreams, 228–229

Drugs
use of, 211–213

E

Eighth sphere, 41
Elect, the, 89
attainment of, 77–78
deception of, 79
definition of, 73
Element aether
in relation to Head centre, 17–18
Emotional body
definition of, 8
Emotions
control of the, 6, 8–9, 106–107, 214–216
forms of, 27
intensification of, 28–29
Energy
release of Shambhalic, 83
use in healing, 55
Enlightenment
attainment of, 114–115
levels of, 13–15
process of, 106, 240–241
Esoteric schools, 37–39
Etheric body
definition of, 7
Evil
overcoming, 96–102, 250
Evocation, 90
Evolution
cosmic analogy of, 368–370
in relation to Collossians 3:12-17, 91–96
in relation to Jesus, 265
in relation to Meditation, 72–74, 126–127
via causative agents, 308–313
via planes of perception, 276–284

F

Feelings, 11
Five alchemical Elements, 277
Form
realm of, 145–148
Formless realm/s, 148–150
Free will
manipulation of, 97
Future visioning
via meditation, 73–74

G

Glamor
overcoming, 318
pride, 319
susceptability to, 213, 249–250
God
as ontological concept, 258–259, 309
as Planetary Logos, 32, 116, 309–311
as (universal) Mind, 32
Son of, 244
Word of, 245, 246–247
Great Invocation, the, 103, 127
Group Evolution, 265–267
Group Law/s, 72, 91, 205
in relation to zodiac, 337–341
of Expansive Response, 361–365
of Group Progress, 356–360
of Magnetic Impulse, 345–349
of Repulse, 352–356
of Sacrifice, 340–345
of Service, 350–353
of the Lower Four, 364–366
Guruparamparā, 192
and meditation instructors, 156–168
definition of, 157
Hindu system, 183

H

Hatha yoga, 109
Healer
discerning a true, 47–48, 66
orthodox, 56, 58

Healing
behaviour assisting, 61–64
concept of true, 57
in relation to meditation, 52–58, 61–66
western methodology, 56–58, 59
Helena Roerich, 38
Hell
realms of, 51
Hierarchy
externalisation of, 212, 265–266
maṇḍala of, 24–25, 81
service work of, 73, 97–102, 120, 202
Hindu Guru
as a teacher, 181–185
H.P. Blavatsky, 38
Humanity
as a 'man-plant', 368–369
Humbleness
quality of, 351–352

I

Imagination, 11
Imperil. *See* irritability
Initiate
1st degree, 329–331
3rd degree, 363
7th degree, 328–329, 381
8th degree, 383–384, 391–392
9th degree, 387
10th degree, 390–391
realms of development, 44–45
Initiation, 137–138
1st, 197–201, 206–213, 224–228, 242–247, 316–317, 356–358
2nd, 213–223, 228, 247–250, 318, 345–346, 349
3rd, 41, 233–241, 250–257, 319, 361
4th, 257–261, 267–268, 320, 329, 341–343
5th, 275–279, 284–287, 364
defined, 194–197
general considerations, 223–231
group, 204–205, 338
Initiation process, 19, 45–46, 72, 119–120, 279, 288–292, 355–356
awakening of consciousness, 78–79, 224–230
cosmic parallels, 369–370
in relation to bhūmis, 142, 143–144
in relation to Bible, 189–194, 197–203, 206–210, 213–215, 217–229, 235–237, 242–256, 260–267, 284–300
in relation to the Beatitudes, 314–336
lead up to the, 187–188
testings, 82, 233, 234, 254–255
via causative agents, 308–313
Inner realms
perception of, 84, 121
Instincts, 10–11
cosmic level, 381, 383–386, 388–390, 391–392, 394
Intuition, 20
as clear light of Mind, 11
awakening of, 70–71
Invocation, 90
Irritability, 133

J

Jesus
as a Bodhisattva, 29–30, 310
as healer, 57–58
as Tulku, 305–306
revealing initiation process, 190, 197–203, 206–210, 242–256, 284–286, 290–292, 296–300, 313
symbolism of crucifixion, 270–274
Jinas. *See* Dhyāni Buddhas
Jīva/s, 172
definition of, 154
Joyfulness, 139–140

K

Karma
as sins, 34
in relation to evolution, 14–15, 73, 121, 123, 163, 169–178, 254, 326
law of, 53–54, 63–64, 88, 152–156, 156–158, 285, 354
Logoic, 277
of killing, 174–175
right education, 98–102
Kleśas, 9, 12
Kuṇḍalinī, 23, 85
raising of, 113–115, 210, 233, 252–253, 255–256

L

Lazarus
as an initiate, 293–296
Light
channelling of, 109, 170
in relation to Initiation, 202
Logoic Mind, 74, 116
Logoic saṃskāras
transforming of, 88
Lokas, 276
in relation to the stūpa, 144–150
Love-Wisdom principle, 192, 202, 336

M

Mahāmudrā
definition of, 273
Maṇḍala, 116
construction of, 11
of Initiates, 2, 91, 204–205
of Tulkus, 177–178
visualisation of, 6, 18
Mantra, 90, 107, 245
in the Bible, 214, 237
suggested, 125–127
use of, 110–113, 138, 366
Mantric Sound, 110–111
Marpa, 40
Master/s of Wisdom, 17, 121, 142, 276, 284–288
service arenas of, 14–15, 40–41, 302–306
Meditation
in relation to evolution, 72–74, 357–358
in relation to Sambhogakāya Flower, 66–74
instructors, 150–183
Hindu guru, 181–185
Rinpoches, 152, 153, 157–160, 176
system of guruparamparā, 156–168
Tulkus, 168–179
lifestyle, 64, 105–109, 122–123
practice/s, 1, 5–6, 31, 52–53
silence, 132–135
visualisation techique, 120
way of, 3–4, 43–44
Meditation-Mind
awakening of the, 86, 88, 97
developing the, 105–106
Meditation process, 120–124
major objective of, 100–102, 106–107, 230–231, 238
power of visualisation, 130–132
suggested technique, 125–129
symbolism from the Bible, 77–85
Merciful
esoteric view of, 325–327
Milarepa, 40
Mind
abstract, 149–150
as transformative agent, 75–76
clear light of, 19, 53, 119
concrete (intellect), 11
definition of, 9
realm of, 145–148
seven attributes of, 9–10
controlling attributes of, 5–6, 105–106, 119–120
converting attributes of, 10, 240

domain of, 83–84, 146
four sub-planes of, 147–148
healthy, 64–65
understanding the, 5
Mindfulness
generation of, 105
Modern Society
problems with, 246–247
Mokṣa
definition of, 2
Monad, 208, 278, 311
and plant analogy, 368–369
in relation to dharmakāya, 258–259, 366–367
in relation to fourth initiaion, 257–259, 341–342
Mudrā
definition of, 274

N

Nāḍī
definition of, 7
iḍā, 82–83
evocation of the, 20
piṇgalā, 82–83
definition of, 19
in relation to Heart centre, 21
line of development, 183, 322
Nāḍī system, 248, 253
in relation to five vayūs, 379–380
Nexus
saṃsāra-śūnyatā (śūnyatā-saṃsāra), 9, 19, 53, 118, 149, 156, 267–268, 320, 329, 365
Nirmāṇakāya
definition of, 33

O

Obsession, 31
Overshadowing, 178

P

Parables
use of, 34–36, 238, 288
Past lives
relevance of, 88–89
Peace, 292
Perception
ādi plane of, 277, 278, 281–282, 353
anupādaka plane of, 277, 278, 282
astral plane of, 283–284
ātma plane of, 17, 277, 282, 364
awakening of spiritual, 79
buddhi plane of, 250–251, 277, 283, 343
development of high, 44
development of psychic, 49–51
mental plane of, 283
of inner realms, 84
physical plane of, 284
systemic planes of, 276–284
Personality
death of, 234, 270
developing attributes of, 241–242
nature of the, 243
Personality vehicle
sheaths of the, 6–10, 364–365
Physical domain (dense), 284
definition of, 6–7
Pineal gland, 130–131, 234, 248
Power
illusion of, 251–255
Prajñāpāramitā, 264, 322
Prāṇa
conversion of, 243
correct use of, 246–247, 323
definition of, 7
in relation to cosmos, 378–380
Psychic powers, 23–29. *See also* siddhis
and creation of karma, 181
entities linked to, 26

in Hindu tradition, 181–184
premature awakening of, 31, 80–81, 193
Psychism
distortions of, 45–47

Q

Quiescence, 31, 52–53, 76

R

Ratnasambhava. *See* Dhyāni Buddhas
Ray/s, the, 89–91, 327
1st, 90, 126, 262, 264, 330, 352, 354–355
2nd, 90, 125, 328, 345
3rd, 90, 125, 325, 361, 363
4th, 90, 321, 329, 344
5th, 91, 319–320, 364, 366
6th, 91, 318, 321, 350
7th, 91, 317, 356, 360
conveying Love energy, 299
in relation to compassion, 241
in relation to cosmic laws, 382–383, 383, 388, 390
in relation to the Bible, 90–91
student disposition, 151
Realm
formless, 148–150
of abstraction, 149–150
of Desire, 145
of Form, 145–148
Rebirth
main reason for, 243
process of, 14–15, 153–155, 175–176, 318
Right Speech, 112–113, 132–133, 135–136, 137–141
Ring-pass-not, 131, 140
Rinpoche/s, 152, 153, 157–159, 355–357
in relation to Guruparamparā, 157–160, 160–161, 176

S

Sacrifice
concept of, 342
Sambhogakāya Flower, 12, 13, 149, 179, 209, 315
as consciousness stream, 278
as group consciousness, 93
definition of, 67
dissolution of, 257–260
formation of cosmic, 390
in relation to dreams, 229–230
in relation to Head and Heart centres, 18, 120
in relation to karma, 169–171, 172
in relation to meditation, 66–74, 118
in relation to Third Eye (ājñā chakra), 19
in relation to third initiation, 234
Saṃsāra
definition of, 5
in relation to mind, 5, 268
involvement in, 80
three main levels (lokas), 145–146, 276–277
Saṃskāra/s, 18, 78, 80
cleansing of, 39, 52–53
vast streams, 155–156
constituting mind, 6–10, 40–41
definition of, 7
energisation of, 83
expansion of, 86–87
fiery, 41
transforming of, 119, 121–122, 134, 171, 223–224, 318, 352
Sanat Kumāra, 48, 191, 200, 278, 311
Satan
in relation to karma, 256
Serenity, 134–135
Service work, 107, 205–206, 217
of enlightened beings, 178

Shambhala, 41, 115, 275, 343–344
in relation to head centre, 248, 361
Siddhis. *See also* psychic powers
development of, 43–45, 181–182
Silence
importance of, 132–141
Sins
as karma, 34
forgiveness of, 33
Soul/s, 172
dissolution of the, 262
Spiral-cyclic motion, 87–88
Spiritual
concept of, 193
Stūpa, 143
in relation to lokas, 144–150
symbolism of the, 144–150
Śūnyatā, 2, 13, 21, 69. *See also* Void
doctrine of, 15
experience of, 84, 263–264, 274
initiation, 144
Śūnyatā Eye, 259
Suṣumṇā
awakening energies of, 82–83
definition of, 20
Sūtrātmā, 271–272
Svabhāva, 386
Swastika
representing four winds, 87

T

Tantrism
Buddhist, 25
Hindu (Śaktism), 25–26
Tathāgatagarbha, 13
Teacher
finding the right, 124, 151–152, 162–163, 182–185
karmic responsibilities, 35–36, 39, 167
right education, 54–58
tradition vs wisdom, 161–168, 179–180
Telepathy, 75
Temple
symbol of the body, 248–250
Time
concepts of, 78
Time-space continuum, 85–87
Truth
distortions of, 50–51
Tulku/s
and the law of karma, 169–178
definition of, 30, 168–169
erroneous beliefs about, 169–178
Jesus as, 305–306
Tum-mo
definition of, 115

U

Universal Mind, 12–13, 268. *See also* Dharmakāya

V

Vairocana. *See* Dhyāni Buddhas
Vajra, 86
Vayūs, 333, 334
definition of, 323
five, 324–327, 327
in relation to cosmic laws, 379–380, 383, 386, 390, 393
Vegetarian diet, 63
Voice of Silence, 70
Void, 2, 28, 53. *See also* śūnyatā
experience of the, 84, 260, 267–268

W

White Brotherhood. *See also* Hierarchy
emissaries of, 38–39
Will-of-Love, 346
Wrathful Deities, 46
transformative nature of, 10, 39, 118–119, 121–122, 134

Y

Yab-yum, 274–275
Yoga, 317
  dangers of, 183

Z

Zodiac, signs of
  Aquarius the water bearer, 95–96, 334–335, 351–352, 383–386
  Aries the ram, 91, 315, 376–377, 381, 390–393
  Cancer the crab, 93, 318, 349, 375
  Capricorn the goat, 95, 333, 364, 366, 375, 380–383
  Gemini the twins, 92–93, 316–317, 359, 375
  in relation to cosmic laws, 373–377, 380–395, 395–397
  in relation to group evolution, 89, 91–96
  in relation to group laws, 337–341
  Leo the lion, 93, 319–320, 363, 374
  Libra the balances, 94, 325, 327, 348, 366, 377
  Pisces the fishes, 96, 335–336, 360, 375, 386–390
  Sagittarius the archer, 95, 332–333, 343–344
  Scorpio the scorpion, 94–95, 328–329, 362, 376
  Taurus the bull, 92, 315–316, 376–377, 392–394
  Virgo the virgin, 93–94, 320–321, 345, 355–356

About the Author

BODO BALSYS is the founder of The School of Esoteric Sciences. He is an author of many books on subjects centred on Buddhism and the Esoteric Sciences, a meditation teacher, poet, artist, spiritual scientist and healer. He has studied extensively across multiple traditions including Esoteric Science, Buddhism, Christianity, Esoteric Healing, Western Science, Art, Politics and History. His advanced esoteric insights, gained through decades of meditative contemplation, enable him to provide a rich understanding of the spiritual pathway toward enlightenment, healing and service.

Bodo's teachings can be accessed via the School of Esoteric Science's website: http://universaldharma.com

For any other enquiries, please email sangha@universaldharma.com

About Universal Dharma Publishing

Universal Dharma Publishing is a not for profit publisher. Our aim is make innovative, original and esoteric spiritual teachings accessible to all who genuinely aspire to awaken and serve humanity. The books published aim in part to provide an esoteric interpretation of the meaning of Buddhist *dharma* with view of reformation of the way people perceive the meaning of the related teachings. Hopefully then Buddhism can more effectively serve its principal function as a vehicle for enlightenment, and further prosper into the future.

A further aim is to provide the next level of exposition of the esoteric doctrines to be revealed to humanity following on the wisdom tradition pioneered by H.P. Blavatsky and A.A. Bailey.

Cover Design by
Angie O'Sullivan & Kylie Smith

www.ingramcontent.com/pod-product-compliance
Lightning Source LLC
Chambersburg PA
CBHW031958220426
43664CB00005B/66
9780992356859